# The Economic Section 1939–1961

Alec Cairncross and Nita Watts

# THE ECONOMIC SECTION 1939–1961

A study in economic advising

**R**

ROUTLEDGE
London & New York

First published 1989
by Routledge
11 New Fetter Lane, London EC4P 4EE
29 West 35th Street, New York, NY 10001

Typeset by Columns of Reading
Printed in Great Britain by
T.J. Press (Padstow) Ltd, Cornwall

British Library Cataloguing in Publication Data

Cairncross, Sir Alec, 1911–
   The Economic Section, a study in economic advising 1939–61.
   1.Great Britain. Economic Section, 1939–1961
   I. Title II. Watts, Nita
   354.41093

Library of Congress Cataloging in Publication Data

Cairncross, Alec, Sir, 1911–
   The Economic Section : a study in economic advising / Alec
Cairncross and Nita G.M. Watts.
      p.   cm.
   Includes index.
   ISBN 0-415-03173-7
   1. Great Britain. Economic Section—History.   2. Great Britain—
Economic policy—1918-1945.   3. Great Britain—Economic
policy—1945–   I. Watts, Nita G. M.   II. Title.
HC256.4.C27 1989
338.941—dc19      88–25965

ISBN 0-415-03173-7

# CONTENTS

# LIST OF TABLES

# PREFACE

This is a study in the practice of offering economic advice to governments. It tells the story of the Economic Section, the first group of professional economists to operate full-time as government economic advisers in this country – perhaps in any country. They started at the end of 1939 as the staff of the Stamp Survey, appointed in the previous July – rather late in the day – to review the government's economic and financial plans for the contingency of war. A year later, when the Stamp Survey was wound up, the staff was split into the Central Statistical Office and the Economic Section, both located in the War Cabinet Offices. There the Section remained until it was transferred to the Treasury in 1953.

The interest of the study lies in the light it throws on the policy-making process as seen from the inside. In order to understand why particular policies were adopted we usually need to know how the issues involved were put to ministers and what advice they were offered. This is particularly true of economic policy, where a good deal of preliminary sifting of the issues is likely to be undertaken by officials before they are submitted to ministers for decision. The Economic Section had no monopoly of advice but it did occupy a central role and its views on major issues of policy carried great weight.

In this volume the reader is taken behind the scenes and shown what advice the Economic Section offered, how far their advice differed from that of other advisers, what controversies followed, and what action was taken. It is possible to do this circumstantially on the basis of the minutes and memoranda now available for consultation in the Public Record Office under the thirty years rule. This makes it possible to carry the story in some detail up to about 1958. The next few years can be dealt with only in very general terms and no attempt is made to go beyond 1961 when the senior author took over the directorship.

The Section occupied a particularly influential position in its early days in wartime when it formed the staff of the Lord President, who co-ordinated economic policy on the home front, and when, with Lord Keynes, it joined in planning new international institutions for the peace. It continued to be influential after the war in relating policy advice to a view of the economy as a whole and as the only remaining group of trained economists in Whitehall dealing with matters of high policy.

For the first twenty years or more, the Economic Section was limited to some ten to fifteen members, with a considerable turnover. A high proportion of the leading academic economists of the last generation served at one time or another on its staff. They included, for example, two Nobel prize-winners (Meade and Stone), a President of the British Academy (Robbins), a Deputy Governor of the Bank of England (McMahon), and two Assistant Secretary-Generals of the OECD: Dow, who was later an Executive Director of the Bank of England; and Dow's predecessor in the OECD post, Jack Downie, who, but for his tragically early death, would probably have attained a reputation as a practical economist and administrator unsurpassed by any of his contemporaries.

In all, by 1960, nearly eighty economists had served at one time or another as members of the Economic Section or its earlier incarnation, the Central Economic Information Service, often for brief periods only. They are listed at the end of this volume with an indication of their later careers.

It is difficult to do justice to this galaxy of talent in a history covering the first twenty years of the Section's life. There may have been only a dozen or so in post at any one time but they were immensely productive in the subjects they covered, the ubiquity of their advisory activities, and the amount they committed to paper. There are, for example, well over 400 Section files already deposited in the Public Record Office for the years up to 1959. But much of the work of the Section, even when in written form, does not appear in these files and is to be found in the records of, for example, the Budget Committee, the National Income Forecasting Working Party, and the Central Economic Planning Staff. The written material, moreover, is often devoted to clearing the ground by working out general principles or reviewing the evidence while concrete policy proposals were often made verbally and may be recorded, if at all, in the records of departmental and interdepartmental committees. Inevitably, an account of the Section's doings, however lengthy, is bound to be incomplete and highly selective.

The Section did not decide economic policy and the policy adopted might or might not reflect their advice. The Economic Section's advice has to be seen in the context of competing advice from other parts of government and the decisions finally taken. A history of the Section, given their central role as advisers on key elements in economic policy, becomes almost inseparable from a history of the formulation of policy itself. But this in turn is only intelligible alongside some picture of the events giving rise to policy decisions and the impact of policy decisions on events. Thus a complete account would encompass the Economic Section's policy advice, their success or otherwise in securing the adoption of their advice, the development of policy, and all the complex interactions between policy and events that we call economic history.

There, is, however, a limit to what one book can do and a limit also to the reader's patience. The first requirement is a clear picture of what the Section did and how it was done, with only so much detail on the setting of policy as is indispensable, leaving the reader to draw his own morals and seek amplification elsewhere if so moved. The picture must also seek to bring out something of the personalities of those who did the job. Inevitably, attention is focused on the more dramatic episodes, when major issues of policy were in dispute or important new issues were posed, rather than on the day-to-day assembly of economic intelligence, the preparation of briefs and comments, and attendance at this committee or that. Separate chapters are devoted to the Section's role in four main areas of policy – fiscal policy, monetary policy, incomes policy, and external policy – but each of these interacts with the others so that there is necessarily some duplication and overlapping in this treatment. Other aspects of policy enter only incidentally, chiefly in the early chapters which aim to give a broader picture of the work of the Section. While some matters in which the Section's influence was plain are dealt with at length, other matters are given little attention.

The Section's influence extended far beyond the Cabinet Office and the Treasury. The first three directors all played an important role in the preparation of the White Paper on *Employment Policy* in 1944. They had the ear of Anderson and Attlee who had charge in wartime of the home front. The Section developed and drafted the *Economic Survey*. They made the running over changes in taxation and in the exchange rate and were an important counterpoise to the Bank of England in monetary policy. In many issues of economic policy theirs was frequently the decisive influence. No one seeking to understand the evolution of economic policy during and after the war can afford to neglect the contribution of the Economic Section.

Both authors of this volume are former members of the Economic Section. Sir Alec Cairncross was one of the first to join its antecedent, the Central Economic Information Service, at the beginning of January 1940, leaving to go to the Board of Trade in June 1941. In May 1961 he returned as Director, having spent the previous ten years as Professor of Applied Economics at the University of Glasgow. Nita Watts joined the Section from the Bank of England in November 1941 and served under three of its first four directors: Lionel Robbins (1941–5), James Meade (1946–7), and Robert Hall (1947–61). She left in 1956 to go to the Economic Commission for Europe in Geneva and, at a later date, St Hilda's College and the Institute of Economics and Statistics, Oxford.

In writing this account of the Economic Section we have relied primarily on the files in the Public Record Office and (to a much lesser extent) the Bank of England's archives. We are grateful to the Controller of Her Majesty's Stationery Office for permission to cite documents in the PRO, to Miss Woodbridge (Treasury Department Records Officer) for help in making documents available there, and to Mr J. S. Fforde of the Bank of England for permission to draw on material in the Bank's archives. We have also to thank Professor James Meade and Lord Roberthall for allowing us to quote from their diaries, and Dr Alan Holmans for allowing us to consult his unpublished study of demand management 1952–8.

Many former members of the Economic Section have offered us assistance in various ways: Sir Fred Atkinson, David Bensusan-Butt, the late Sir Norman Chester, Sir Bryan Hopkin, Professor John Jewkes, Dr Ian Little, Professor James Meade, Roger Opie, Professor Sir Austin Robinson, Maurice Scott, and Dr R. C. Tress have allowed us to consult their papers, commented on parts of this volume, or helped to elucidate particular points. We have particular cause to be grateful to Lord Roberthall, Dr George Peden, Professor L. S. Pressnell, Mrs K. Jones, and Christopher Dow, who have read extensive sections of the manuscript and made many helpful suggestions. Russell Jones provided us with material for chapter 19. To all of these we offer our thanks.

The senior author gladly acknowledges the financial assistance of the Leverhulme Trust in the early stages of work on the book, when he was an Emeritus Fellow. He is also deeply indebted to Mrs Anne Robinson for her careful typing and re-typing of the manuscript.

A.K.C.
N.G.M.W

# Chapter one

# STIRRINGS: THE ECONOMIC ADVISORY COUNCIL

British governments have long made use of economic advisers but have only recently come to employ them on a full-time basis. Formerly they were content to rely on staff recruited to the public service with no professional training in economics, supplementing the advice they received by consultation from time to time on specific issues with outside experts. Such experts might themselves have little or no theoretical training and be consulted for their experience of affairs (for example, as bankers or business men) rather than as economists. The Bank of England, which acted as the government's financial adviser, was equally lacking in professionally trained economists.

When economists were called in, it was rarely for consultation directly and more likely to be at arm's length as members of a Royal Commission or as witnesses giving evidence to a government committee. The main exception before 1930 had been in the First World War, when economists and statisticians were recruited on a temporary footing. Keynes, for example, served throughout in the Treasury, becoming head of the division dealing with external finance and moving at the end of the war to Paris as chief Treasury adviser at the Peace Conference in 1919. Beveridge at the Ministry of Food, Walter Layton at the Ministry of Munitions, Hubert Henderson at the Cotton Control Board, and Arthur Salter at the Ministry of Shipping are other examples.

The duties of the permanent staff were largely administrative and executive but their role as policy advisers expanded with the range of government activities and the beginnings of economic management. Learning on the job, they often developed an expertise of their own.

Many achieved distinction in the Treasury and Board of Trade in the first half of this century as economic and financial experts. The one well-known economic theorist among them, Sir Ralph Hawtrey, like Keynes, had never sat a university examination in economics when he entered the Treasury in 1905. But his writings on monetary theory were at one time ranked with Keynes's and have lately gained a renewed popularity with the rise of monetarism. For the last twenty-six of his forty years in the Treasury he was a kind of one-man Economic Section, briefing ministers and Treasury colleagues on economic issues and providing them with rejoinders to the theoretical arguments on which Keynes's policy prescriptions rested.

Hawtrey, however, was never called Economic Adviser or Chief Economic Adviser. The latter title was conferred on Sir Hubert Llewellyn Smith in 1919 when he retired as Permanent Secretary to the Board of Trade. The post was created 'in anticipation of the burden of international economic discussions which was expected to follow the establishment of the League of Nations'; and the main duties of the holder were to represent the government at international meetings on economic issues and to undertake on its behalf commercial and financial negotiations with other countries.[1] Llewellyn Smith was succeeded in 1927 by Sir Sydney Chapman, who had taken over from him earlier as Permanent Secretary of the Board of Trade. Chapman in turn was followed in 1932 by Sir Frederick Leith-Ross, a Treasury official, who was Chief Economic Adviser until his retiral in 1946 to become Governor of the National Bank of Egypt. At that point the title lapsed. It was revived again in 1953, when Sir Robert Hall was made Economic Adviser to HMG, and in 1964 it again disappeared.

Of the three pre-war chief economic advisers, only Sir Sydney Chapman had any claim to be an academic economist. He had been Professor at Owens College, Manchester, from 1901 to 1917 and had written a textbook on economics as well as two books on the cotton industry. His duties as Chief Economic Adviser were to the Board of Trade, not HMG, and were largely imperial and international. He represented the British government at international conferences on import and export restrictions, tariffs, communications, copyright, statistics, etc. These were nearly all Board of Trade rather than Treasury matters. It would seem that he was rarely consulted on domestic issues of financial or macroeconomic policy.

1 'The role of the economist in the machinery of government', report by the Official Committee on the Machinery of Government, MGO(43)32, 15 November 1943, in PRO CAB 87/72.

This is less true of Leith-Ross. He had after all been Deputy Controller of Finance in the Treasury for seven years before his appointment as Chief Economic Adviser, and it was as an expert on finance rather than trade that he was usually employed. For example, he was much involved in negotiations on inter-governmental duties, both before and after 1932, and in preparations for the World Economic Conference of 1933, which he attended as a British delegate. Like Chapman he served on the Economic Committee of the League of Nations and represented the British government at various international conferences. In the Second World War he was Director-General of the Ministry of Economic Warfare and latterly Deputy Director-General of UNRAA. Thus he had little to do with domestic economic policy, on which he was happy not to be consulted, and not a great deal more with the formative stages of international economic policy. As he himself confessed, his title did not convey his true role.[2]

The main contrast between the duties of the chief economic advisers of the inter-war period and those of economists in government service since the Second World War lies in the absence until 1940 of a full-time staff at the centre of the government machine. Chief economic advisers were experienced civil servants acting largely on their own on an international stage. They lacked the support of a group of trained economists concerned exclusively with the framing of economic advice. No such group existed within the government to advise the Chancellor or any other minister charged with responsibility for economic policy (with the possible exception of the Minister of Agriculture).

The nearest approach to such a group before 1939 came with the setting up in 1930 of the Economic Advisory Council. This had its origin in the greater realization during the First World War of the importance of organized economic intelligence. One of the first moves was Llewellyn Smith's establishment in the Board of Trade in 1917 of a General Economic Department to

> anticipate, watch and suggest means of dealing with, important questions and movements likely to arise in commerce and industry, and which, from their generality or novelty did not fall within the scope of any specialized Department.[3]

2 Leith-Ross, Sir F. W. (1968) *Money Talks*, London: Hutchinson, pp. 145–7. He did, however, take part in the work of the Committee on Economic Information (see pp. 8–9).

3 Quoted by Howson, Susan and Winch, Donald (1977) *The Economic Advisory Council*, London: Allen & Unwin, p. 7.

The Haldane Committee on the machinery of government, reporting in 1918, commented favourably on this experiment and laid stress on 'the duty of investigation and thought as a preliminary to action'. It recommended the creation of research sections in every department of government, with the possible addition of a separate Department of Intelligence and Research to supplement their work.

In the post-war economy drive these views fell on stony ground. Nothing much came of the Haldane Committee's recommendations; and Llewellyn Smith, far from recruiting additional staff either on secondment or through temporary appointments of students with degrees in economics, found himself isolated in the residual post of Chief Economic Adviser while the General Economic Department vanished.[4] Efforts to improve government economic statistics proved fruitless. A petition was presented from the Royal Statistical Society in 1919, backed by a list of distinguished economists and statisticians, urging the need for a central statistical office, and for a Royal Commission to review the defects in official statistics. It took two years for a committee under Sir Alfred Watson, the Government Actuary, to report and when it did so it rejected the proposals. When retrenchment was the watchword, it saw little value in collecting data, for example on national income and wealth, of no apparent relevance to current administrative needs.[5]

By the time the first Labour government had taken office towards the end of 1923 the pressure for better economic information and more specialized staff had begun to revive. Sir William Beveridge was urging the creation of an economic general staff to advise the Cabinet in parallel with, and on the model of, the Committee of Imperial Defence. 'Modern governments', he argued, 'are faced with problems in the field of economic science as technical as those raised by war in the field of military and naval science.'[6] These problems needed handling by a staff trained in economics that would stand above existing departments and would be headed by 'a person of high authority in the science of economics' and enjoying corresponding authority in the public service.

These were not ideas congenial to departments, which saw an economic general staff as a threat to their responsibilities. Compromise proposals were worked out, and approved by the Cabinet, for a Committee of Economic Inquiry, with Tom Jones, Deputy Secretary

4 ibid.
5 ibid., p. 8.
6 ibid., p. 10.

to the Cabinet, as Secretary of the Committee. These proposals, as Howson and Winch comment, laid 'an almost compulsive emphasis on statistical information' as the crux of the Committee's work.[7] But nothing came of it all: before action could be taken, the Labour government fell.

The Treasury memorandum setting out the compromise proposals was considered afresh by the incoming Conservative government under Stanley Baldwin.[8] Urged on by Lord Balfour, Lord President of the Council, the Cabinet agreed to set up a Committee of Civil Research, 'analogous in principle to the Committee of Imperial Defence'. This was to report to the Cabinet and be presided over by the Prime Minister (who did it once only) or by another minister nominated by him. There was to be no fixed membership. Both officials and outside experts were to attend. It was the purpose of the Committee, as seen in the Treasury memorandum, to give

> connected forethought from a central standpoint to the development of economic and statistical research in relation, more especially, to problems of an interdepartmental character or in pursuit of knowledge in spheres not within the orbit of any single Minister.[9]

The language of the memorandum, however, was altered to include scientific as well as economic and statistical research and the scope of the Committee's work was expanded to cover the Empire as a whole and the Dominions as well if they would allow it.[10] As a result the Committee acquired a strong scientific and imperial bias and did very little to promote economic and statistical research. The research it did sponsor tended to be highly technical, with a low political content and well clear of the domains of established departments. On the relatively few occasions on which its subcommittees investigated issues of economic policy, such as control over new issues on the London capital market on behalf of foreign and imperial borrowers, or unemployment in the coal industry, the Committee served largely as a convenient vehicle for resolving a disagreement between ministers with a minimum of publicity or else allowed the government to defer an awkward decision. In some cases it ended up after years of enquiry with no or only minor recommendations.

7 ibid., p. 12.
8 'Foresight and co-ordination in economic enquiry', CP(24)366, June 1924, in PRO CAB 24/172. It was reissued as CP(25)195.
9 ibid.
10 'Outline history of central organization for economic policy, 1919–1947', PRO CAB 21/2217.

The Committee had a limited and undistinguished lifespan. It continued for a short time under the second Labour government in 1929 but was wound up in January 1930 on the creation of the Economic Advisory Council. This followed a series of discussions at the end of 1929 between the Prime Minister and prominent business men, trade-unionists and economists, in which they were asked for their views on the industrial situation and the action the government might take to improve the information and advice on economic policy available to it. The government was pledged to deal with the unemployment problem but had made little headway. It was also pledged to establish a 'National Economic Committee' and 'create permanent machinery through which scientific knowledge and technical skill may be mobilized for . . . raising the standard of life throughout the whole community'.[11] Apart from putting J. H. Thomas, the Lord Privy Seal, in charge of unemployment policy, however, the Prime Minister had done little to implement these pledges before the end of 1929.

The economists consulted included Walter Layton and Keynes, who had already, in the Liberal Yellow Book,[12] revived the idea of an economic general staff under a head with the power and importance accorded to the CIGS in time of war. All questions of economic policy would be first considered in an economic policy committee of the Cabinet to which the chief of the economic general staff would act as secretary. He would have a very small staff but it should include the best experts available. There would be a council of industry, representative of employers and employed, which would keep wage and industrial relations questions under review and advise on industrial and labour legislation.

Of the other economists consulted, Clay, Cole, Hobson, and Stamp, the first two submitted memoranda favourable to an economic general staff, Clay laying stress on the drawbacks of relying instead on committees of enquiry which lacked continuity and were not integrated with the structure of administration, while Cole visualized a staff, including 'field investigators', that could take the initiative in gathering material, publish its findings on appropriate occasions, and supply practical plans for industrial reorganization.[13]

While all the economists were united in support of an economic

11 Howson and Winch, op. cit., p. 18.
12 *Liberal Industrial Inquiry, 'Yellow Book'. Britain's Industrial Future* (London, 1978).
13 Howson and Winch, op. cit., pp. 20–1.

general staff, it was not favoured by the leading administrators. Hankey, the Cabinet Secretary, attacked even the idea of attaching a few economists to the Prime Minister's office as 'feckless duplication' and would contemplate no economic general staff except one composed of the permanent heads of all the departments with economic responsibilities. Warren Fisher, Permanent Secretary of the Treasury, scoffed at 'the mere addition of half a dozen more "bureaucrats"' and seems to have assumed that they would engage in 'fundamental economic research' better conducted elsewhere.[14]

On the idea of a council of industry the economists were not agreed. Hobson, Layton, and Citrine supported it in one form or another but Keynes gave it no support and Cole was actively opposed to it. It was the politicians who were most strongly in favour of a body which they saw as likely to help in uniting opinion behind necessary change. What MacDonald ultimately plumped for went beyond an economic general staff and had a second component in addition to what he regarded as 'the thinking part' of his scheme: this took the form of an advisory committee with the task of 'moving people into the field of action'. This committee, the Economic Advisory Council, when appointed in January 1930, included twenty members, apart from any additional ministers who might be asked to attend. Five of the twenty were ministers and, of the other fifteen, seven were industrialists or bankers, two trade union officials, three economists, two scientists, and one an economic historian (Tawney). The 'economic general staff' attached to the Council consisted of Hubert Henderson (after much persuasion), Colin Clark, H. V. Hodson, and Piers Debenham (in an unpaid capacity). The total cost, including clerical staff, was £6,500 per annum and did not stretch to the purchase of an adding machine for Colin Clark.[15]

The creation of the Economic Advisory Council followed close on the setting up of the Macmillan Committee on Finance and Industry in November 1929; Keynes and Bevin were members of both. The Macmillan Committee concluded its work at the end of June 1931 and the Economic Advisory Council as such ceased to meet after April 1931, although its members continued to be consulted individually and to submit memoranda until the exchange crisis in August.[16] Broadly speaking, therefore, the activities of both the Committee and the

14 ibid., p.22.
15 ibid., p. 25.
16 There was one largely formal meeting in January 1932 but the Council was already defunct, even if not officially buried until 1938.

Council coincided with the period between the onset of the slump in 1929 and the sterling crisis in the autumn of 1931. The disclosures in the Committee's report helped to bring on the crisis, while the Council did nothing to delay it.

Not surprisingly, given the complexity and importance of the issues of policy involved, there had been little agreement between the economists and the business men, who took a resolutely non-interventionist line. The economists themselves were also divided, in matters both of theory and of policy, and the story of their debates is full of echoes of later doctrinal differences.

Although the Council did not survive, two of its committees did, notably the Committee on Economic Information, which was established in July 1931 and met regularly from March 1932 until the outbreak of war in 1939.[17] As Howson and Winch point out, 'the Economic Advisory Council's claim as an influence on economic policy and as the forerunner of future development rests on the work of the Committee on Economic Information'.[18]

The membership of the Committee included Stamp as chairman, Keynes, G. D. H. Cole, and H. D. Henderson. The early reports were written by Henderson, who acted as secretary until 1934, when Francis Hemming and Piers Debenham took over the secretarial duties. Two Treasury officials, Leith-Ross as Chief Economic Adviser and Sir Frederick Phillips (from 1935), attended the meetings and took an active part.[19] In this way the thinking of the economists on the Committee percolated to the Treasury, which studied the Committee's reports with great attention.

The work of the Committee is admirably discussed in the well-known study of the Economic Advisory Council by Howson and Winch, and there is no need to recapitulate it here.[20] The Committee's method of work, however, is of some interest in relation to later developments. This consisted in the preparation of a series of 'Surveys

17 Members of the Council were also included in the Advisory Committee on Financial Questions, appointed by the Prime Minister after devaluation in September 1931. They gave valuable advice on exchange rate policy in the ensuing six months, after which the Treasury took matters into its own hands, no longer feeling in need of advice on management of the rate. Keynes, who was a member of the Committee, and Henderson, who was its secretary, took an active part in the discussions (Howson and Winch (1977), op. cit., p. 100).

18 ibid., p. 107.

19 Citrine also attended some meetings in 1932–3. Dennis Robertson joined the Committee in 1936.

20 Howson and Winch (1977), op. cit., chapter 5.

of the economic situation', which drew attention to 'salient features of the period under review and to the tendencies of the immediate future' before putting forward a set of policy proposals. The Committee itself decided on the topics to be covered in the next report except when, as sometimes happened, the government sought its advice, for example on the problems posed by rearmament. The draft was considered by the Committee and redrafted in the light of comments, before submission 'on the basis that each member acquiesced in what was written rather than necessarily approved of the exact wording adopted'.[21] The reports of the Committee can be seen as forerunners of the economic surveys of the early post-war years, although in their published form the economic surveys recorded decisions rather than policy recommendations.

21 ibid., p. 108. The same method was used later by the London and Cambridge Economic Service and, still later, by the Clare Group.

# Chapter two

# BEGINNINGS: THE STAMP SURVEY AND THE CENTRAL ECONOMIC INFORMATION SERVICE

As war approached, the government came under increasing pressure to review its arrangements for economic co-ordination. The familiar war-cry of an 'economic general staff' had been raised again in a memorandum to the Lord Privy Seal (Sir Samuel Hoare) from Sir Arthur Salter, Sir George Schuster, and others. The same group suggested an 'association' representative of outside interests to work in co-operation with the proposed staff, thus combining the two kinds of approach – the technocratic and the representative – that kept recurring in the 1930s, as they did again in post-war years. Others, including the Prime Minister's Panel of Industrialists, wanted a department of economic planning.[1]

None of these proposals appealed to the Lord Privy Seal. The Chancellor of the Exchequer also rejected the idea of an economic general staff.[2] He wanted neither a staff nor a committee. Instead, he intended to ask one individual, Lord Stamp, to review departmental plans and proposals to keep the country going during war and advise whether they were mutually consistent and covered the ground adequately. The review would 'no doubt result in recommendations in general terms as to the lines on which . . . defects and gaps may be dealt with'.[3] This proposal was accepted by the Cabinet on 5 July 1939

---

1 'Survey of war plans in the economic and financial spheres', Memorandum by the Chancellor of the Exchequer, 30 June 1939, CP(39)146 in PRO CAB 24/287.
2 ibid.
3 ibid.

but was not publicly announced until 9 October.[4]

Stamp was to be assisted by 'one or two economists and perhaps a prominent industrialist, who should all be familiar with . . . the machinery of government', and he would have the services of 'a suitable civil servant' and 'probably . . . the Cabinet secretariat'. The 'one or two economists' turned out to be Henry Clay and Hubert Henderson and the 'suitable' civil servant was Francis Hemming, who with Piers Debenham, moved over from the now defunct Committee on Economic Information to be Secretary and Assistant Secretary of the Stamp Survey.

This approach to economic co-ordination was a curious one, given the imminence of war. It followed previous experiments in its emphasis on inconsistencies and gaps between the plans of different departments and in avoiding any direct challenge to the responsibility of individual departments. In more peaceful and leisurely circumstances it would have been entirely reasonable to invite three economists, experienced in the ways of governments and likely to be able to reach agreement with one another, to look through war contingency plans and submit general recommendations for ministers to consider. But in the summer of 1939 the Survey seemed less than adequate for the cataract of matters needing urgent decision that would pour in on the government as soon as war broke out.

When war did break out on 3 September the Survey was asked to continue its work. A few weeks later, the government decided to create a ministerial committee under the Chancellor, with responsibility for economic policy. At the official level there was also to be an interdepartmental committee of permanent secretaries of the main economic departments 'to perceive and close gaps . . . and reconcile inconsistency'. Sir Horace Wilson (head of the Treasury) was to be Chairman and Stamp was to be President and Adviser on Economic Co-ordination.[5]

Soon after these arrangements were announced, they were vigorously attacked in the House of Commons on 18 October. How could it be right to rely for economic co-ordination on the part-time efforts of one of the busiest men in London (Stamp was Chairman of the London, Midland, & Scottish Railway, a Director of the Bank of England, and

4 CM(39)35, 5 July 1939, in PRO CAB 23/106 and H. of C. Debates, new series, vol. 352, cols 28–31, 9 October 1939.
5 WP(G)(39)26, 29 September 1939, in PRO CAB 67/1. See also H. of C. Debates, new series, vol. 352, cols 28–31, 9 October 1939, and vol. 352, cols 932–46, 18 October 1939.

occupied in many other directions)? Was the Chancellor of the Exchequer, with all his other duties, the right man to co-ordinate economic policy in wartime? Did the government not realize that the whole British economy, as Beveridge had argued in *The Times*, must now become a planned economy? Why had no employment been found for the economists who had gained so much experience in the First World War – for example, Beveridge, Keynes, Layton, and Salter?

These were valid criticisms. The Stamp Survey, although it did a remarkable job, was no substitute for an effective Minister of Economic Co-ordination, nor was the Chancellor likely to prove one. The Survey could only develop lines of argument, make general recommendations, give policy a push in the right direction. Had Stamp been appointed Minister and been assigned an adequate staff, things might have been different. But until Anderson became Lord President in November 1940 and acquired the necessary authority to co-ordinate economic policy, with the Economic Section formally assigned to him as his professional staff, there was a lack of urgency and grip.

The one criticism that was less than fair was of the part-time nature of Stamp's appointment. If one may judge from the amount of paper it generated, the Survey spared no effort to do a thorough job. In the five weeks after its appointment, it held twenty-four meetings, interviewed the heads of the various government departments, examined their contingency plans, and prepared a short interim report for ministers indicating the questions which it thought needed further attention. By the end of the year it had held forty-six further meetings and circulated no less than 150 papers, followed in the first four months of 1940 by a further eighty-five most of them written by members of the Survey.[6] The flow continued in May and June but from July onwards began to dry up, only six more papers being circulated before the Survey was wound up at the end of the year. A lengthy study of the pre-war position of agriculture, prepared in response to a request from the Food Policy Committee in October and issued posthumously at the end of March 1941, was its last contribution.[7] The collection of documents prepared over the eighteen months of the Survey's

6 The papers of the Stamp Survey are in PRO CAB 89/1–9.
7 'Agriculture: pre-war position of' P(E and F)(41)1, 31 March 1941, in PRO CAB 89/9. Many of the papers in May and June by members of the Survey appear in the series of staff papers headed P(E and F)(S), to which they had very rarely contributed hitherto.

existence add up to a manual for democratic governments on the problems of converting a peacetime to a wartime economy after the outbreak of hostilities.

## Membership of the Survey

The three economists on the Survey were a distinguished and well-balanced group. Stamp, the Chairman, had begun as a boy clerk in the civil service and risen to be Director of Economic Intelligence in the Inland Revenue and a leading expert on national income statistics before embarking on a successful business career. He was now a kind of economic Pooh-Bah, sought after by business men, civil servants, and politicians, acceptable to all. In 1940 he was offered the chancellorship after the fall of the Chamberlain government but refused it. A year later he was dead, killed in an air raid in the Spring of 1941.

Stamp was unfailingly kind to his staff, however junior. In the chair he seems to have let others make the running but was never at a loss to express his own view.[8] His close contacts with ministers meant that he was the main channel through which the ideas and rcommendations of his colleagues found their way to market.

Hubert Henderson was both an extremely clear-headed economist and an experienced journalist. He was known to all young economists as the author of *Supply and Demand*, one of the most successful textbooks in economics ever written. In the 1920s he had edited *The Nation*, a weekly newspaper that economists felt compelled to read, and had been for many years a close associate of Keynes. Henderson had a typically Scottish turn of mind, with a love of argument, a stern determination to look uncomfortable facts in the face, and an aversion from compromise at the expense of logic. He carried realism to the point of contra-suggestibility, reacting critically to proposals rather than devising ways of making the best of what was to hand.

Henry Clay, the other economist on the Survey, was a Yorkshireman who had written one of the few elementary textbooks then available. He had held an Economics Chair at Manchester University and was widely respected as an authority on industrial and manpower questions. Clay was less interested than his colleagues in macro-

---

8 Sir Denis Rickett recalls meetings of the Economic Advisory Council at which Stamp, who was Chairman, arrived without having read his papers and tried to conceal his predicament by reading out one paragraph at a time before asking for comment.

economic issues although, as the first British economist to be designated economic adviser to the Bank of England, his interests had come to include monetary and financial policy. Clay had a rather quieter personality than his colleagues, and spoke with more caution and deliberation, but had wide experience and great common sense. In 1944 he went to Oxford as Warden of Nuffield College.

The Secretary, Francis Hemming, was one of the most exuberant characters in the civil service. In private life he was a distinguished entomologist and an authority on butterflies, holding simultaneously the posts of Secretary of the London Zoo and Deputy Secretary of the Cabinet (under Sir Edward Bridges).

The Assistant Secretary, Piers Debenham, was in some ways just as unusual a civil servant as Hemming. He was passionately interested in economics and had done a good deal of dabbling in quantitative economic history on his own account after coming down from Cambridge, where he studied under Dennis Robertson. He had been Assistant Secretary of the Economic Advisory Council more or less from its inception, just as Hemming had been Secretary, and was probably as well-equipped intellectually to cope with government economic problems as the average professional economist in Whitehall.

## The origins of the Economic Section

The Survey, in spite of its heavy responsibilities, had no staff except Hemming and Debenham, no executive authority, and no integral connection with any powerful administrative department. On the other hand, it enjoyed access to confidential data and departmental experience, was relieved of administrative responsibilities, and was free to take a central and comprehensive view of the proposals it considered, undeterred by the administrative or political difficulties they might present. Stamp, although not a minister, was a regular member of the Ministerial Committee on Economic Policy and had the ear of the Prime Minister. The work of the Survey, therefore, commanded attention and influence. But it is hardly surprising that Stamp and his colleagues felt increasingly the need for assistance, particularly in the assembly of statistical and other information. It was this need that led to the creation of what proved to be the forerunner of the Economic Section and it was under the banner of 'economic information' that it took the field.

It was a banner, as we have seen, that was frequently waved whenever governments contemplated the recruitment of economists. The Committee on Economic Information survived the decline of the

Economic Advisory Council, and the government retained the services of economists after 1931, even when it remained wary of accepting their advice, because of its need for more adequate data and for a more professional analysis of the economic situation.

A similar need now struck home to the wartime government: the lack of economic information was even more acute. The need for secrecy meant the suspension of publication of virtually all economic statistics. At the same time far more information was required for the conduct of the war. The government was forced to assume a vastly greater role in guiding economic activity and for that purpose needed information on a host of things of little interest to it in peacetime. Sooner or later arrangements would have to be made for its collection, presentation, and analysis.

## The Central Economic Information Service (CEIS)

Before the end of October 1939 the new Ministerial Committee on Economic Policy asked Lord Stamp and Sir Horace Wilson to make proposals for a central economic information service.[9] They suggested that the new service should be attached to the Stamp Survey and should consist of a few economists or statisticians – 'say two or three at the outset' – who would have to be recruited from 'the Universities or elsewhere' because no civil servants 'possessing the necessary qualifications' could be spared by their departments.[10] The staff would maintain close contact, through a liason officer appointed by the Minister, with each of the departments concerned with 'priority and allied economic questions'; and this officer, or a subordinate, would arrange for the supply of information and offer any necessary assistance to the new service. Administrative responsibility for the staff would rest with Francis Hemming, and their work would be directed jointly by Henry Clay and Hubert Henderson.

The immediate tasks suggested for the information service related almost entirely to exports and imports and showed concern for the danger to exchange stability if there were insufficient pressure to increase exports or reluctance to ration imports. The information service would have to accumulate data to guide policy in applying pressure or in taking priority decisions and might be asked to analyse

9 EP(M)(39) 5th Conclusions, Minute 3, 27 October 1939, in PRO CAB 72/1.
10 'Machinery for the establishment of a central information service in connection with exchange stability and priority policy', Report by Lord Stamp and Sir Horace Wilson, EP(M)(39)31, 6 November 1939, in PRO CAB 72/2.

the import content of particular items of consumption or the reaction of raw material allocations on exports.

Ministers approved these recommendations and the first appointments to what was now called the 'Central Economic Information Service' were made in December. John Jewkes, later to be the first Director of the Economic Section, came from Manchester, where he was head of one of the very few economic research departments attached to a university in the United Kingdom. He was joined by Austin Robinson, then helping Keynes to edit the *Economic Journal* and a Fellow of Sidney Sussex College, Cambridge. The third senior appointment was Harry Campion, also from Manchester and soon to be Director of the Central Statistical Office. Of these three, Jewkes and Robinson were expected to help on labour and industrial problems and Campion on the statistics needed by the Stamp Survey.

Before these appointments took effect, the Ministerial Committee became increasingly uneasy about the load that existing programmes would impose on the economy and the adequacy of available resources to meet it. The need for a survey of national resources in relation to the scale of the war effort had been seen as one of the main reasons for reinforcing the Survey with additional staff.[11] Early in December the Chancellor (Simon) pressed for a preliminary report, evidently assuming that the CEIS was already at work, and Stamp volunteered to do what he could with the material already available. Simon's anxieties continued to centre on the export trade, which he saw as threatened by a shortage of raw materials if imports were severely limited by lack of foreign exchange and shipping, and by a shortage of manpower as a result of competing military requirements.[12]

Stamp's main conclusion, when he submitted a memorandum, was that reserves of foreign exchange were likely to be run down by an extra £150–250 million in the first year of war beyond what was justifiable if exchange resources had to cover a three-year war – a view supported by the Treasury, which foresaw an increasing strain on reserves. The Ministry of Shipping pointed out that imports of dry cargo (i.e., excluding petroleum) were running at only 36 million tons a year compared with a programme of 47 million tons and pre-war imports of nearly 60 million tons. At Simon's suggestion, the Survey was invited to submit 'a preliminary, documented account of the adequacy' of each of the items that might limit the achievement of

11  See EP(M)(39)23, 11 October 1939, in PRO CAB 72/2 and EP(M)(39)8M, 9 November 1939, in PRO CAB 72/1.
12  EP(M)(39)11M, 7 December 1939, in PRO CAB 72/1.

existing plans for the war effort: foreign exchange, shipping, manpower, and raw materials.[13]

The preparation of papers in response to this remit was the staple, but by no means the sole, activity of the CEIS in the first quarter of 1940. At the end of January Stamp submitted to the Ministerial Committee a memorandum covering two staff papers, one by Austin Robinson making a forecast of the British balance of payments in the first year of war and one by Jewkes on labour requirements in the engineering and metal trades and the rate of absorption of labour into those trades.[14] In the first of these, Robinson put the deficit on current account at £369 million (or, more generally, at £312–471 million) and Stamp reiterated his earlier conclusion that it would not be safe in the first year of war to make use of more than £150 million from holdings of gold and foreign assets of all kinds. In the second, Jewkes cited figures from a report by a committee under Humbert Wolfe at the Ministry of Labour showing that, if the expressed requirements of the fighting services were to be met, it would be necessary to expand employment in the metal and engineering industries in the first year of war by 72 per cent and in the second year by a further 25 per cent.[15] The most that had proved possible in the First World War was a 54 per cent increase over four years. In 1939 only a trickle of labour had moved into these industries in the first three months of the war and very little dilution had taken place. Yet without a redistribution of labour on an unprecedented scale the services could not be supplied with the equipment they asked for. Some scaling down of the programmes or spreading them over a longer period was therefore recommended in Stamp's covering note.

The conclusions in these two papers were challenged as too pessimistic, if not defeatist, in a note by the Admiralty (presumably by Churchill's 'Statistical Section', which later played an important role in the war as part of the Prime Minister's staff).[16] A rejoinder was

---

13 EP(M)(39)12M, 15 December 1939, in PRO CAB 72/1. At this stage Stamp's tentative estimate of the deficit on current account in the first year of war was £100–200 million.

14 'Survey of national resources in relation to our war effort', memorandum by Lord Stamp, EP(M)(40)8, 29 January 1940, in PRO CAB 72/4 (also WP(40)45).

15 'Supply and manpower', note by the Chancellor of the Exchequer, covering memorandum submitted by the interdepartmental conference on the labour requirements of the proposed war programme, WP(G)(40)9 in PRO CAB 67/4.

16 'Notes compiled in the Admiralty on Lord Stamp's paper', WP(40)39, February 1940, in PRO CAB 66/5. The author was presumably Roy Harrod.

prepared and circulated at the beginning of April.[17]

Austin Robinson's forecast of a deficit of £369 million had been attacked as too high by about £150 million. In reply, the Survey pointed out that experience over the first six months of war hardly suggested so favourable an outcome: even on rather optimistic assumptions it pointed to a figure of £358 million. Moreover, in the first year of war the military programmes were far from reaching their peak and the external deficit was therefore likely to grow. Later estimates in 1940 by the CEIS yielded totals as high as or higher than Robinson's, the last, in November, amounting to £438 million. Subsequent official estimates by the CSO, in the light of fuller knowledge, indicate a figure of about £700 million.

The Admiralty also attacked the contention that £150 million was as much as it was safe to draw on foreign assets in the first year of war. If three-quarters of British imports were paid for in sterling, any deficiency would merely add to the sterling balances of the supplying countries; countries like the Argentine should be induced to accept sterling in payment for their exports; and, when quoted foreign investments alone amounted to over £3,200 million, there should be no great difficulty in making sales of over £150 million, which was only 3 per cent of annual turnover on the New York Stock Exchange.

The Survey was unconvinced. Of the £3,200 million, they pointed out, £2,000 million represented sterling loans, not readily disposed of in countries which regarded the future of sterling as precarious. The scope for making sales on the New York market had been carefully investigated by two Bank of England representatives on the spot. And while empire countries, apart from Canada, were willing to accept payment in sterling there was a limit to their willingness to supply without being sent countervailing exports. They might draw on their sterling balances in order to procure from 'hard currency countries' (*sic*) what the United Kingdom was unable to sell them, thus intensifying the overriding shortage of hard currency.

The balance of payments controversy soon died. It was only too evident by the middle of the year that a desperate shortage of foreign exchange lay ahead. The controversy on manpower was more prolonged. The Admiralty paper tended to make light of labour immobility and the problems of dilution without actually denying that there was an acute shortage of skilled labour in engineering which was

17 'Our national resources in relation to our war effort', comments prepared by the Survey of Economic and Financial Plans on certain criticisms advanced by the Admiralty.

sure to get worse when the new factories under construction were ready for operation. As the Survey pointed out, the current rate of intake into the engineering trades was far below that required to meet the service programmes in the period specified. Moreoever, all past experience suggested that constant research would throw up new weapons of war, making additional demands on the engineering trades.

Equally to the point was Jewkes's reply – for the paper was largely the work of Robinson and Jewkes – to the Admiralty's comparison with French manpower policy. If France with a hundred divisions needed only 44 per cent of Britain's engineering resources, how, they had asked, could the United Kingdom's programme of fifty-five divisions put an excessive burden on a much larger industry? Perhaps, Jewkes suggested, France might yet prove to have mobilized to excess and denuded French industry of the manpower needed to make equipment for the armed forces on the scale considered by the French military authorities to be a safe minimum or which others might consider desirable.[18]

The balance of payments and manpower remained continuing interests of the Economic Section in later years. A revised forecast of the balance of payments for 1939–40 was circulated in May 1940 and a third estimate was made in November.[19] From then on, balance of payments forecasting became a regular activity of the Economic Section. By the end of 1941 Austin Robinson was already making tentative forecasts of the balance of payments after the war. Later forecasts by the Economic Section formed the background to the loan negotiations in 1945.[20]

The manpower situation was also the subject of continuing study. At the beginning of May 1940 Hemming returned to the figures in the Humbert Wolfe Report in order to compare them with the increase in engineering employment over the first ten months of war as

18 ibid.
19 'Revised forecast of the United Kingdom balance of payments during the first year of the war', memorandum by Lord Stamp, P(E and F)(4)89, 8 May 1940, covering a memorandum by E. A. G. Robinson and A. K. Cairncross; also EP(M)(40)36; 'The United Kingdom's international balance of payments', memorandum by P. K. Debenham and A. K. Cairncross, P(E and F)(S)(40)78 Revise, 27 November 1940.
20 For a full account of wartime forecasts of the balance of payments, see Pressnell, L. S. (1986) *External Economic Policy since the War*, vol. 1, London: HMSO, appendix 27.

established by a Ministry of Labour enquiry.[21] Instead of the 72 per cent per annum required in order to meet the military programme, the actual increase was at a rate of about 14 per cent, much the same as in 1935–6 and 1936–7. This slow rate of expansion in manpower was undoubtedly a contributing factor to the disappointing growth in the output of munitions. Perhaps, therefore, the schedule of reserved occupations should be extended to cover unskilled and partly skilled men in the engineering group of industries instead of only the skilled men. But the main need was for the systematic training of skilled men and this could best be done by reserving the Government Training Centres for converting semi-skilled men into men with a higher grade of skill and abandoning the use of the Centres for the reconditioning of the unemployed.

A third subject which the Survey had been asked to investigate with the help of the CEIS was the supply position on raw materials. No comprehensive report was prepared: the Survey confined itself to steel, timber, and wool.[22] The first of these was dealt with by Henderson, the second by Austin Robinson, and the third by Jewkes. The three reports, taken together, brought out some fundamental issues. First there was the interdependence of raw materials: the danger that economy in one might be sought through intensification of the demand for another which in turn would become scarce; the waste that might arise if scarce materials were allocated to uses for which complementary materials were not available. Then there was the problem how far to encroach on stocks in a war of unknown duration and often in the absence of reliable information as to the level of stocks and the changes in progress. Economic policy, moreover, had to be related to military strategy: the timing of the main military effort, and the eventual rate of absorption of resources by the military. With limited resources, investment in all forms of new capacity – factories, ships, transport facilities, equipment for new weapons and for new military formations – had to be balanced against urgent immediate requirements, and its justification was in proportion to the length of the armed struggle that was contemplated.

---

21 'The brake on our war effort due to the shortage of manpower in the war industries', memorandum by Mr Francis Hemming, P(E and F)(S)(40)19, 2 May 1940, in PRO CAB 89/9.

22 'The supply position in regard to steel, timber and wool with reference to the survey of the national resources in relation to our war effort', memorandum by Lord Stamp, P(E and F)(40)76, 5 April 1940, in PRO CAB 89/8 (also EP(M)(40)26).

A fourth consideration was the heavy demand all three materials made on shipping and on foreign exchange. The first of these could be economized by shorter voyages but usually this involved paying higher prices; and since it often meant buying in North America it also clashed with the need to economize hard currencies. The Survey – in fact Piers Debenham – had worked out a formula for resolving the conflict between the saving in shipping and the extra cost in foreign exchange. But the formula did not provide for differences in the hardness of currencies and was of questionable value. Moreover, as the reserves oozed away in 1940 it was increasingly obvious that the war could not be carried on as planned without extensive financial help from America. That being so, economy in shipping was paramount.

But what of export requirements, from which the whole exercise took its origin? At that stage in the war, with Lend–Lease still undreamt of, the Survey continued to insist on the need for an export drive and procuring the foreign exchange needed for essential imports. It would be self-defeating to rank exports below war production and civilian consumption in the allocation of raw materials and labour. If the supply was insufficient, it was civilian consumption that would have to give way for if exports suffered this would react on the imports that could be purchased and consumers would still go short.

Thus in the first quarter of 1940, at the height of the phoney war, the Survey had provided ministers with an extensive review of the economic outlook for men and materials, shipping, and foreign exchange.[23] The picture they drew was a disquieting one. Time seemed to be slipping away and the country was only too obviously not fully mobilized. In whatever direction one looked, the war effort was endangered by growing shortages while civilian consumption had hardly been touched. Unemployment was still relatively high – it was nearly one million when the Battle of Britain was at its height in the autumn – but this left a relatively small margin in relation to the rapidly growing manpower requirements of the armed forces. There was also a major balance of payments constraint and very little foreign exchange. The import programme would have to be cut for lack of

---

23 On shipping the Survey submitted no detailed report, partly because the Ministry of Shipping was doing a first-class job while the Lord Privy Seal had reported to the War Cabinet on the need to cut the import programme because of the shipping situation ('The extent to which shipping considerations call for a review of our import programme', WP(40)64, 23 February 1940, in PRO CAB 66/5). This, too, attracted criticism from Churchill in a 'Note by the First Lord of the Admiralty on the Lord Privy Seal's memorandum' (WP(40)81).

shipping, stocks were being run down, manpower was moving too slowly into the metal and engineering trades, and all this was in the first year of war before the armed forces were actively engaged on the Continent. In the background, too, was the ever-present danger of inflation if the claims over resources continued to be excessive or if efforts were made to speed up labour transfer by the offer of higher wages.

After the first quarter, the Survey continued its work and kept up a running correspondence with departments on miscellaneous questions. But fewer papers of the kind just described were submitted to ministers. One exception was a survey of the economic consequences of the loss of Norway and Denmark in April: this was almost entirely the work of the CEIS. Later papers on the economic consequences of the loss of the Low Countries and then of France went to ministers directly, without the intervention of the Survey.[24]

The papers that have been discussed so far, although they constituted the main documents transmitted to ministers by the Survey, were only part of their output. In a review of their work over the first year of war, circulated in October 1940, they listed fifty subjects, affecting many different departments, with which they had dealt between September and December 1939 and twenty-nine more in the first three months of 1940.[25] The flow continued in the second quarter, with another twenty-four topics covered, but died away in the third quarter, when the list shows only nine.

Some of all this work was largely factual and statistical: for example, papers on earnings and employment. But nearly all of it had a substantial policy content and included proposals by the Survey or comments on proposals made by others, such as Keynes's *How to Pay for the War* or John and Ursula Hicks's suggestion for stabilizing the price of an 'iron ration' of goods entering into everyone's budget. A large number of the topics dealt with related to the operation of the various wartime controls. Other papers bore on some aspect of inflation: taxes, subsidies, the budget, wages, and prices, but not –

---

24 'The economic consequences to the Allies and to Germany respectively of the seizure by Germany of Denmark and Norway', note by the Chancellor of the Exchequer, WP(G)(40)103, 13 April 1940, in PRO CAB 67/6; 'The economic consequences of a complete or partial collapse of French resistance', memorandum by the Minister without Portfolio, WP(G)(40)155, 17 June 1940, in PRO CAB 67/7.

25 'The work of the Survey in the first year of war', memorandum by the Survey, P(E and F)(40)116, 15 October 1940, in PRO CAB 89/9.

apart from a note by Debenham in June on 3 per cent interest rates – monetary policy. These, and the subjects discussed earlier, were, so to speak, the staples. But the Survey ranged far and wide. To take half a dozen topics at random, they discussed 'film production and the exchange problem', 'the position of small shopkeepers', 'standard clothing', 'design and location of new factories', 'duplication of Iraq pipe line', and 'paper production – concentration on efficient mills'.

After the change of government in May, the Survey was asked to continue its work. But the official committee under Sir Horace Wilson was abolished and the Ministerial Committee, on which Lord Stamp continued to serve, met only twice in the third quarter. The new Chairman of the Committee, Arthur Greenwood, was put in charge of economic policy and took over as his staff for purposes of economic co-ordination, the Central Economic Information Service, rapidly augmented in May and June. These changes tended to restrict the activities of the Stamp Survey, which also felt that a stage had been reached in which the issues of policy requiring decision were fairly clearly defined. Arrangements for economic organization had taken shape and the scope for their services was narrowing correspondingly. From May onwards, therefore, the Survey was beginning to fade out while the Central Economic Information Service, now christening itself exuberantly the Economic General Staff, had emerged as a key group of policy advisers.

There can be little doubt that the Survey played an important role in clarifying the issues of adaptation to a war economy and that it gave much wise advice to ministers. If the action taken was slow and irresolute, the fault did not lie with them but with ministers. No real effort was made to bring home to the public, before the change of government, the sacrifices in which they would be involved under existing military plans or the still larger effort that would be required for victory. No minister with the necessary drive and vision was entrusted with powers to take the measures required for a comprehensive and consistent plan. The air was full of make-believe and apathy, and much of what the Survey was saying went unheard.

# Chapter three

# EMERGENCE: THE TRANSITION TO THE ECONOMIC SECTION

With the end of the 'phoney war' in May 1940 and the change of government that coincided with it, new arrangements were made for the formulation of economic policy. On 4 June Attlee, acting as Deputy Prime Minister, announced in the House of Commons that economic and home affairs would be dealt with in future by five new ministerial committees, whose work would be 'concerted and directed' by a small group of ministers (the Chancellor of the Exchequer, Sir Kingsley Wood; the Lord Privy Seal, Clement Attlee; and the Minister without Portfolio, Arthur Greenwood) under the chairmanship of the Lord President of the Council, Neville Chamberlain.[1] Two of the five committees had particular responsibility for economic policy and were both to be chaired by Arthur Greenwood: the new Economic Policy Committee and the Production Council. A third committee, the Food Policy Committee, would also be in need of economic advice. The work of the Stamp Survey was to continue but the committee of permanent secretaries over which Stamp presided was to be discontinued.

These new arrangements imposed fresh duties on the CEIS, which was now attached to Greenwood. They were given a threefold remit:

1  To advise the ministerial committees dealing with economic policy.
2  To 'provide digests of statistics bearing on the development of our war effort'.

1 H. of C. Debates, vol. 361, col. 770, 4 June 1970. Chamberlain died on 9 November 1940 and was succeeded by Sir John Anderson.

3   To 'prepare reports on the progress achieved by Departments in giving effect to decisions on economic questions reached by the Ministerial Committees'.

One consequence of these arrangements was that they put beyond dispute the need for additional staff. Hemming had been ready at the end of April to recruit Lionel Robbins and Ronald Fowler. Now, armed with Greenwood's authority, he persuaded the Treasury to let him go ahead. Still protesting that he would keep the staff as small as possible, he had added before the end of June James Meade, Norman Chester, and Peggy Joseph, and was about to recruit Evan Durbin from the Ministry of Supply, Richard Stone and Sally Chilver from the Ministry of Economic Warfare, and Stanley Dennison and Harold Wilson from the Anglo-French Organization, making a total staff in July 1940 of seventeen (excluding the members of the Stamp Survey itself). The annual wage-bill for the seventeen (including two future Nobel Laureates) came to just over £10,000.[2]

Bridges, the Cabinet Secretary, clearly felt that it was time to review the employment of economists and asked Hemming in mid-June for a statement of Greenwood's views as to the future staffing of his organization. Hemming responded with a minute tracing the development of the CEIS over its first six months and summarizing his minimum staff requirements.[3] He had talked to Attlee and Greenwood before Attlee's statement in the House and to Greenwood on several occasions after it. The organization, he told Bridges, was run on a very loose and informal basis. More specialization might well be necessary as the staff grew in size but the best results were not obtained by making economists work 'on strict civil service lines', and a high degree of flexibility was indispensable. With 'big rush jobs' like 'Urgent economic problems' (a kind of economists' manifesto circulated by Greenwood to the Economic Policy Committee), it was a case of 'all hands to the pump' since the draft had to be ready in 48 hours and was the composite product of seven members of staff.[4] Until there had been time to gain experience of the new duties, it was impossible to judge the eventual size of the staff required.

Shortly afterwards Bridges minuted Sir Horace Wilson, Permanent Secretary of the Treasury, indicating that there must be some doubt

2 Hemming to Bridges, 26 June 1940, PRO CAB 21/940.
3 ibid. He provided for an additional senior member of staff so that the total came to eighteen.
4 'Urgent economic problems' was circulated to the (ministerial) Economic Policy Committee on 3 June 1940 as EP(M)(40)40. It is in PRO CAB 72/4.

about the future of the Stamp Survey. 'My impression', he told him, 'is that the new régime has really put the Stamp Survey in the shade, and that probably the right thing would be for the Stamp Survey in its present form to be wound up'.[5] If the Stamp Survey were wound up, what would happen to the staff? The economists regarded themselves as members of the Cabinet Secretariat. As Horace Wilson subsequently made clear, however, it was only a matter of convenience that the Survey was attached to the Cabinet Office. The basis on which it was to work was settled, not with Bridges, but with Horace Wilson acting for the Chancellor of the Exchequer.[6] As Chairman of the official Economic Policy Committee, he had also been Stamp's official channel for matters not coming directly within the province of a single department, although Stamp as a member of the Ministerial Committee on Economic Policy could also raise matters directly with the Chancellor.

Horace Wilson, like Bridges, wished to consider more closely the scope and functions appropriate to a staff of economists in the Cabinet Office. He felt it necessary to clarify the principles that should govern their relations with the Cabinet ministers under whom they worked and with the departments that had executive responsibility for different aspects of economic policy. Complaints must have reached him from some of these departments of insufficient consultation over the preparation of Cabinet papers or over requests for confidential information without proper authority. He called a meeting of heads of departments to discuss the question and, like Bridges before him, asked Hemming for a brief. This elaborated the threefold duties of the staff and gave a rather more circumstantial account of their recent work, emphasizing that it was indispensable that there should be the fullest co-operation between the staff and the departments collaborating with them.[7]

As a result of the meeting, Bridges set out in a circular letter to permanent secretaries the procedure to be followed by the staff when preparing papers for the Minister without Portfolio and the Lord President. Where a minister wanted a paper for circulation, not to the Cabinet but to the committee of which he was chairman, departments were to be informed and their co-operation invited, both in preparing the document and in assembling the necessary data.

This brought comments from several departments. Sir Henry French, Permanent Secretary of the Ministry of Food, thought the new

5 Bridges to Wilson, 10 July 1940, in PRO CAB 21/940.
6 Wilson to Padmore, 2 February 1943, in PRO CAB 87/72.
7 Hemming to Wilson, 11 July 1940, PRO CAB 21/940.

procedure 'a happy reversion to the pre-war principle of co-ordination between Departments at least as to facts'. Sir Frederick Leith-Ross, who still retained the title of 'Chief Economic Adviser to HM Government' and was currently Director-General of the Ministry of Economic Warfare, complained that his department had not been consulted over information: for example, on the economic consequences of German conquests. But, although there were grumbles natural to departments observing the rise of an influential group at the centre that might influence the minds of ministers, they were comparatively mild and rare. Whatever the suspicions of permanent secretaries, relations further down were usually friendly and indeed cordial.

The reaction of the economists to these events may be gauged from Norman Chester's comment that Horace Wilson's 'attempt on the life of our organisation has not succeeded but we will have to go more slowly'. 'It is difficult', he added, 'to see quite where we are going.'[8] This latter phrase gave expression to a growing feeling from July onward of frustration, depression, and underemployment. Papers written for circulation were held up, committees did not meet, or, when they did, discussed matters of no concern to the economic staff. Part of the trouble was the incompetence of the Minister: Greenwood was too often drunk and too rarely in touch. As *The Economist* complained, there was too much wood in the Cabinet: Kingsley, Green, and Dead.

Hemming was also to blame. He had no gift for delegation and a great weakness for long documents. He took up endless time drafting and redrafting, busying himself in the autumn months with two reports, one running to 102 printed pages and offering replies to seventeen questions posed by Stettinius, Chairman of the US War Resources Board, and the second, extending to 238 printed pages, on the problem of the export surpluses that were accumulating in the producing countries for lack of a market.[9] No doubt this was work of some importance. The Stettinius document, summarizing replies from departments to questions on Britain's wartime economic organization and prefaced by a lengthy introduction drafted by Austin Robinson, was one of the earliest and most elaborate secret documents made available to the Americans before their entry into the war. The export surpluses document, in which Austin Robinson also took the leading

8 Letter to Mrs Chester, 21 July 1940, in Nuffield College Library.
9 'Britain's war-time economic organization', EGS(40)12, 7 October 1940, in PRO CAB 72/24; and 'Export surpluses and their importance to the producing countries', ES(0)(40)73, 14 November 1940, in PRO CAB 72/15.

part, was largely a factual survey of the supply and stock position in the main international commodities after the fall of France and was designed to guide ministers in taking action to prevent primary producers from falling under Nazi influence.[10] But the effort of preparing these documents brought Austin Robinson to the verge of a nervous breakdown, and diverted the Section from more urgent work. Calling on Keynes when he was resting, Meade found him reading the document on export surpluses, which he threw on the ground, exclaiming 'Not a single idea anywhere in it'.

By mid-September the Section was becoming increasingly fed up and hoping for some change that would make fuller use of their services. It was at this stage that the idea of working on problems of reconstruction first took hold.[11] Early in October Chamberlain's illness suggested a new possibility: Sir John Anderson might take over the chairmanship of the Lord President's Committee. The idea that the Section might serve as Anderson's staff in that capacity opened up new prospects and every effort was made to push it forward. In the meantime an approach was made to the Treasury to allow the Section to be brought in on financial research. At first this brought only an outraged refusal from Kingsley Wood, who told Greenwood, much to his indignation, that he wanted no interference in the affairs of the Treasury. The matter was resolved, however, by means of a tactful letter from Greenwood and Attlee, drafted by Robbins and Hemming, and Robbins was invited to call on Keynes and Hopkins with a view to arranging collaboration between the Treasury and the Section on research that the Treasury would be unable to undertake on its own.

Another development in the autumn, discussed later, was the beginning of weekly staff meetings. These were born of the frustrations of those months and were first suggested by Jewkes at the beginning of October. They were put on a more formal basis after Hemming was brought in and asked to summon a meeting, which he did for 1 November 1940.[12] Thereafter meetings were held weekly

10 Discussion of export surpluses had begun in July and continued into the spring of 1941. See, for example, 'The blockade of Europe and the problem of surpluses', memorandum by the Minister of Economic Warfare, EP(M)(40)69, 11 July 1940, and papers by Henderson and Debenham, P(E and F)(S)(40)74 and 75, 22 and 24 July 1940.

11 Chester hoped that he might 'be able to transfer my energies in that direction' (letter to Mrs Chester, 17 September 1940). Durbin called for work on social and economic reconstruction some weeks later (see p. 37).

12 ES(40)1 Conclusions, 'Meeting of the staff held in room 412 on 1st November 1940', note by Mr Francis Hemming, 1 November 1940, in PRO T 230/12.

(and sometimes oftener) with a formal agenda and discussion papers on the items listed.

Fresh issues of organization now arose. Churchill had been increasingly annoyed by the confusion created through the use of different measures of shipping tonnage: gross, net, and dead-weight. On 8 November he sent a minute to Bridges on the need to ensure that only agreed figures were circulated to ministers. His way of accomplishing this was startling:

> I wish all statistics to be concentrated in my own branch as Prime Minister and Minister of Defence, from which alone the final authoritative working statistics will issue. The various departmental statistical branches will, of course, continue as at present, but agreement must be reached between them and the Central Statistical Office [sic].[13]

Although Hemming was aware almost immediately of the proposal, he did not convey it to the Section until 3 December when he summoned an urgent staff meeting. The news that they were to be deprived of one of their principal functions came to members as a thunder-clap. Some of them wondered whether this was the thin edge of the wedge. Lionel Robbins contemplated resignation.[14]

That afternoon Jewkes, Robbins, and Meade called on Greenwood to warn him of the weakening of his own position and that of his staff. Greenwood, however, misinterpreted their intentions, thinking that they had come to ask for help in saving their jobs.[15] A few days later it was rumoured that (as was eventually decided) Hemming would be given charge of the CSO and Jewkes of the Economic Section. Later, Keynes was suggested as the first head of the CSO but declined.[16]

Negotiations for the creation of a central statistical office proceeded for some time and it was not until the end of the year that arrangements were made to give effect to the Prime Minister's wishes. These arrangements were ultimately set out in a Cabinet paper circulated on 30 December 1940 and announced by Bevin in the House of Commons on 21 January 1941.[17]

---

13 Prime Minister to Sir E. Bridges, 8 November 1940 (Churchill (1949) appendix A, p. 608).
14 Chester, letter to Mrs Chester, 3 December 1940.
15 ibid., 5 December 1940.
16 ibid., 12 December 1940.
17 H. of C. Debates, vol. 368, col. 82, 21 January 1941. For the Cabinet paper, see WP(G)(40)338, 30 December 1940, in PRO CAB 67/8.

One possible outcome had been a merger of the Economic Section with the economists in the Prime Minister's Statistical Branch under Professor Lindemann. This suggestion had been considered earlier and rejected. Hemming had talked things over with Lindemann on 14 May and come to an agreement on the respective duties of the two groups. The main duties of the Prime Minister's Statistical Branch (which had been formed while Churchill was still at the Admiralty) was to supply him, often at very short notice, with comments and statistics relating to documents submitted by ministers, whether to the Cabinet or to the Prime Minister himself. The whole of the Branch had to be available for this purpose and under the direction of Professor Lindemann. The Economic Section had quite different duties, since it served the Stamp Survey and the Economic Policy Committee. In these circumstances, informal collaboration so as to avoid duplication of effort was the proper course.[18] A meeting between Hemming and Lindemann on 12 December reiterated this conclusion.[19]

On receipt of the Prime Minister's minute, Bridges had asked Hemming for yet another brief on the functions of the Economic Section. Hemming in reply did his best to bring out the role of the Section in improving government statistics and the difficulty of separating its economic and statistical functions. The duality of function, he said, was inevitable.

> On the one hand researches in applied economics such as those undertaken by our Section must necessarily have a quantitative basis and on the other our quantitative investigations would themselves be sterile unless informed by general economic knowledge. Our aim, therefore, has been to build up a body of statistics agreed with the Departments suitable to form a basis for discussion of the various problems of policy which arise in the business of economic co-ordination. . . . The Economic Section . . . would be quite incapable of performing any useful service to the . . . Ministerial Committees dealing with economic subjects if it were to be divorced from its statistical organization which is an integral part of its being.[20]

This was pitching things rather strong and it certainly did not convince Bridges, who took his time in reaching a conclusion. The Prime Minister had asked for a central statistical office and there was a strong case for establishing such a body to co-ordinate the statistics

18 Hemming to Bridges, 11 November 1940, PRO CAB 21/1365.
19 Chester, letter to Mrs Chester, 13 December 1940.
20 Hemming to Bridges, 11 November 1940, PRO CAB 21/1365.

collected in different departments as well as the increasing flow of statistics available to newly created departments and controls. There was a need also to collect additional material (e.g. on consumer spending, stocks, etc.) that might extend beyond the limits of any one department's responsibilities; and to prepare the aggregates appropriate to national income analysis. These were duties that might conceivably have been carried on within the Economic Section, as indeed some of them had been. But there was bound to be more difficulty in persuading departments to part promptly with information to a body that might use it to attack their policies than if the information went to an independent body with no axe to grind. Moreover, it was not just economic statistics that needed to be co-ordinated. The main economic committees were already fairly well served by two secret statistical digests labelled Series A and Series B, issued by the Section. There was no similar digest of non-economic information – particularly on munitions production and the armed forces – for circulation to Defence and other committees. A CSO would have a wider scope and could do systematically for military statistics what was in process of being done for civil.

The proposed division between the economists and the statisticians was not a physical separation since both continued to work alongside one another in the War Cabinet Office and both the CSO and the Economic Section were staffed by temporary civil servants on secondment from their universities. There was no assurance that either would continue after the war, so that the post-war relationship between the two had still to be settled.

Looking back, it is by no means self-evident that the administrative division into two separate groups was inevitable or without disadvantages. It would have been quite possible for the Economic Section to have issued Series A to F and to have handled military statistics, as the economists in the Prime Minister's Statistical Section or in the Ministry of Aircraft Production did quite regularly. So long as the members of the CSO were ex-members of the Economic Section and themselves economists, it hardly mattered. But there is always a danger to the fruitful use of statistics if they come to be handled with the emphasis exclusively on their production rather than as the best available tools for tackling new problems. A division charged solely with producing agreed statistics may be neutral but is in danger of being neutered at the same time.

The split removed eight members of the Section to the CSO (Hemming, Campion, Devons, Stone, Fowler, Peggy Joseph, Joan Marley, and Mrs Chilver), and left nine, apart from Debenham, who continued to work alongside the Section until he went off to join the Army. Meade moved to the CSO in order to continue his work with Stone on national income but it was clearly understood that he would return to the Economic Section when the work was completed.

The Lord President was to take over the Economic Section, as it was now called, and so have 'the services of a body of economists of high standing, who are free from Departmental ties'.[21] Thus began an association that was not only of high importance for the conduct of the war but had a lasting influence on the role of economists in the government machine. Once Sir John Anderson, who had succeeded Neville Chamberlain as Lord President on 2 November 1940, was put in charge of economic affairs, the machinery was able to work at full power.[22] A technical staff of high calibre, seasoned by long frustration, could operate in conjunction with a supremely competent administrator, armed with all necessary authority.

Yet this was not how it looked at the beginning of January 1941. Early in the month Chester thought that 'our organization [was] never at such a low ebb', with practically every member (including Jewkes and Robbins) contemplating a move to some other job. It was not until the middle of the month that Anderson's intention to make use of the staff was established and Jewkes was able to obtain adequate assurances from Sir Horace Wilson. He would have direct access to the Lord President, members of the Section would be given proper status, and they would either be appointed to act as secretaries of the various new committees or represent the Section on them as members. Bridges himself would act as secretary of the Lord President's Committee and the Section would feed in papers and briefs. Lionel Robbins, at Attlee's request, was to have a conference with him before each weekly meeting of the Food Policy Committee. By mid-February everybody was 'on top of the world', with more than enough jobs to do though, not surprisingly, occasional friction developed within the Section, and there were grumbles as late as May that Anderson rarely if ever saw the authors of the briefs he received.[23]

The establishment of the Central Statistical Office was only one of

---

21 H. of C. Debates, vol. 368, col. 82, 21 January 1941.

22 The Section had already done some work for Anderson before his appointment.

23 Chester, letters to Mrs Chester, 13, 15, and 18 January, 6 February, and 12 May 1941. Two years later, according to Chester, even Robbins complained that he had not seen Anderson for 6–8 weeks (letter to his wife, 14 January 1943).

the changes made at the end of 1940. The Stamp Survey had been less active since the change of government in May: now it was abolished. The Ministerial Committee on Economic Policy also disappeared. Economic policy in future was to be tackled by two new bodies: the Production Executive, made up of the four ministers responsible for production activities and the Minister of Labour; and the Import Executive made up of the five ministers responsible for imports of various kinds, together with the ministers dealing with shipping, shipbuilding, and transport. Economic co-ordination was entrusted to the Lord President's Committee under Sir John Anderson, who had been assuming an increasingly important role in relieving the Prime Minister and the War Cabinet of much of the detail of economic policy. He would now have on his committee all the key figures on the home front: the chairmen of the two new 'Executives', the Chancellor of the Exchequer, and the Minister without Portfolio.

## The work of the CEIS

So much for the formal arrangements. But what did the CEIS actually do?

We have seen that in the first quarter of 1940 it took part in the preparation of a number of papers for ministers on men and materials, shipping, and foreign exchange. In the second quarter, further papers were prepared for ministers on the economic consequences of the occupation by Germany of various European countries. The most important single document in this period was 'Urgent economic problems'.[24] This was prepared at great speed at the beginning of June, when France was falling but had not completely fallen, and it had a considerable impact on ministers.

'Urgent economic problems' was a kind of manifesto, setting out the contributions of each member of the CEIS to a comprehensive revision of economic policy. First place was given to the importance of a more realistic import programme and the suggestion that the existing programme should be cut by about 25 per cent to 35 million tons.[25] Once heavy air attacks began, the limiting factor would cease to be shipping or foreign exchange and change to unloading facilities at the

24 'Urgent economic problems', memorandum by the Minister without Portfolio, EP(M)(40)40, 5 June 1940.
25 These totals are for dry cargo and exclude petroleum, whale oil, and molasses. The original programme of 46.4 million tons had been cut in March by 5 per cent to 44.25 million tons.

ports and onward transport inland, especially if east coast ports could no longer be used and the burden on west coast ports was correspondingly increased. The strain would vary from one cargo to another. Meat imports, for example, had to be discharged ex-ship into either cold storage or refrigerated vessels; 70 per cent normally came through London, which was likely to be out of action, and most of the ammonia needed for refrigeration came from a single plant. Other cargoes, such as grain, needed deep-water berths and special equipment, while other bulk cargoes, such as iron ore, made heavy demands on rail transport.

Next, there should be a stocks policy that made provision for a reserve of essential commodities and for the positioning of stocks so as to limit the burden on transport and the consequences of seizure or destruction by the enemy of key areas. Guidance was urgently required on immediate priorities in the loading of imports; at the other end, levels of consumption would have to be adjusted to a realistic view of prospective supplies.

Such a view made it necessary to decide where to make economies in imports. The answer was clear. Nearly half the weight of imports of materials consisted of timber and iron ore, while about 7 million tons out of a total of 20 million tons of food imports consisted of one item, animal feedstuffs (including wheat offals). All three would have to be cut drastically, for example through the substitution of home-grown timber, imports of finished steel, an agricultural expansion programme, and a reduction in the pig and poultry population, followed later by one in fat cattle and sheep. Lionel Robbins was particularly vehement on the need for a livestock slaughter policy and frequently cited the example of Germany in the First World War, when cattle were kept alive with feedstuffs at the expense of human food that would have relieved a starving country.

Whatever substitution might do, economy in imports was bound to react on the standard of living. If this was to be reduced equitably and without generating inflation, it would be necessary to use rationing and price control, at least for the essential commodities regarded as an iron ration, and special provision would have to be made for groups with special physiological or other needs. Under heavy enemy attack, there might have to be free issues of food and communal feeding, and a beginning should be made at once to develop the use of canteens and review the dispersion of reserve stocks of non-perishable foods.

Then followed a section on wage policy and taxation along lines already covered by the Survey: the need to hold wages steady and to this end to prevent prices from rising; the consequent need to mop up surplus purchasing power in taxation; the use of standardization (utility schemes) to keep down costs.

Further sections dealt with manpower, export policy, and the use of foreign assets. These also were largely recapitulations of earlier papers. Finally a section was devoted to French requirements, on the hypothesis that the Germans would somehow be held on a line north of Paris. A six-page summary concluded the document.

Afterwards, the CEIS looked back on 'Urgent economic problems' as the high-water mark of 1940; it may well have had an important influence on the decision to expand the staff in June and give it a central position under the Lord President at the end of the year. From time to time, suggestions were made that a new edition should be prepared; as late as August 1942 Lionel Robbins recirculated an excerpt as part of a discussion paper to show the kind of thing the Section should take as a model.[26]

Even more important than ministerial documents were the statistical digests that Campion had been preparing since early in the year. The work was accelerated by the arrival of Ely Devons from Manchester in March, and the digests began to appear from June onwards. As explained in the next chapter, the issue of the digests, with their orderly marshalling of secret statistics, revolutionized not only the supply of information readily available to ministers but also the layout and presentation of official statistical data. The *Monthly Digest*, *Economic Trends*, and other publications of the Central Statistical Office still bear witness to that revolution.

Campion had also made some progress with national income data, starting from work financed by the National Institute of Economic and Social Research. Bowley had prepared estimates for pre-war years as part of this work and included estimates for 1938 in his Presidential Address to the Royal Statistical Society in 1940. His figures were revised and improved in the Treasury (they contained some arithmetical errors) and the material was supplemented by a paper, prepared largely by the Manchester Economic Research Unit, which was published by the National Institute in the March 1940 issue of *Economic Journal*.[27] In May Austin Robinson, increasingly conscious of the urgent need for trustworthy national income statistics in the light of Keynes's *How to Pay for the War*, persuaded first Hemming, and, with Hemming, Edward Bridges, to agree to the recruitment of two economists to

26 'Future economic policy', note by Professor Robbins, EC(S)(42)22, 13 August 1942, in PRO T 230/14.
27 Campion (1984).

prepare official estimates. He then wrote to Meade in Geneva, where he was writing the *World Economic Survey* for the League of Nations, and to Stone, a recent Cambridge graduate in economics then in the Ministry of Economic Warfare, and persuaded them to join the CEIS and undertake the work. From this pair, with strong support from Keynes, sprang the famous White Paper of April 1941, with official estimates of national income in 1938 and, quarter by quarter, in 1940.[28]

Papers for ministers were a limited part of the work of the CEIS. Indeed, relatively few papers of any kind survive from the second half of 1940. Each member of the CEIS assumed increasingly specialized duties, concentrating on selected topics, attending particular committees, and keeping in touch with the departments falling within his 'parish'. But, because of the infrequency of meetings of the Economic Policy Committee and the failings of its Chairman, Arthur Greenwood, members lacked a ministerial outlet and had to fall back on official contacts in the departments.[29] Nevertheless the CEIS was far from idle and some of the activities of its members in this period are outlined in the next chapter.

Up to about the end of May 1940 one can find traces of the work done by the CEIS for the Survey in their staff papers (of which forty-three had appeared) but from then on the series is almost entirely taken over by members of the Survey. Between June and December a few papers were issued in the short-lived EGS (Economic General Staff) series.[30] It was not until the initiation of regular staff meetings in October 1940 and the circulation of discussion papers in the ES(S) series – before the Economic Section existed – that a regular flow was resumed.[31]

At the beginning of October Jewkes asked members to submit a list of the most urgent topics for discussion. Five at least did so in advance of a meeting on 16 October. Jewkes and Meade both drew attention to the impending decision by the Board of Trade to issue orders limiting the supply of goods for domestic consumption over the next nine months and the need to co-ordinate this with labour requirements for

28  Quarterly data were included so as to impress on the Americans the deterioration in progress in the economic and financial position when a case had to be submitted for Lend–Lease assistance (Campion 1984).

29  On 3 May 1940 the Economic Policy Committee held its last meeting under Simon's chairmanship. Only five meetings were held under Greenwood and few papers were submitted by him to the War Cabinet. Two of those dealt with aid from North America.

30  These are in PRO CAB 72/24.

31  Some of these are in PRO T 230/12.

the service programmes and military recruitment. Jewkes also directed attention to newsprint imports and steel exports and suggested a study of the problems of evacuating population from London. Stanley Dennison was also interested in the question of provisioning London under aerial bombardment, especially since it had already been stated that it would be impossible to keep London supplied with coal during the winter. Peggy Joseph raised the issue of compensation for war damage to property.[32] Dick Stone proposed drastic restrictions on consumption: production of consumer goods should be limited to those in a subsistence budget and a few 'simple luxuries, e.g. beer, cosmetics and books, which are necessary for the public morale'. Goods should be standardized and produced as cheaply as possible. Evan Durbin wanted a study of the Budget, exchange control, industrial controls, and 'the main problems of economic and social reconstruction'. He was in favour of fixing a maximum spendable income, paying family allowances, reducing tax exemption limits, and giving government departments a ration of foreign exchange. On this last proposal he was in doubt: it might be better to force the hand of the USA by exhausting the reserves. Since no minutes were kept, the discussion which followed these suggestions must be left to the imagination.

From November onwards meetings were frequent and habitual. The activities of the staff were beginning to follow a more definite routine. Efforts were made to assign more specific duties to members and to provide for representation of the CEIS at all the more important committees. The position at the beginning of 1941, after the CSO had been split off, was roughly as shown in table 3.1.

In 1941 fifty papers were prepared for discussion at staff meetings. Robbins was author or part-author of ten, Jewkes and Robinson of seven each, and Cairncross, Durbin, Meade, and Tress of five each. There was a wide scatter of subjects, the most popular being post-war reconstruction (four papers in February alone), manpower, employment, and wages policy (eleven papers in all, excluding two in April on the prevention of general unemployment), import policy (four in the first half-year), and government controls (three papers in December). There are also some papers in January on food rationing, and one in December on steel.

The papers, however interesting in themselves, tell us very little of the day-to-day work of the Section in dealing with wartime problems.

32 Meade's paper was recirculated on 5 November 1940 as ES(S)(40)5 and Peggy Joseph's on 10 December 1940 as ES(S)(40)13.

Table 3.1  Staff of the Economic Section at 1 January 1941[a]

| Economic Section | Duties assigned on 14 January 1941 | Committees to be attended |
|---|---|---|
| John Jewkes | General direction of Section; labour | Lord President's Committee; manpower |
| E. A. G. Robinson | Production and supply questions and associated questions of raw materials | Production Executive; industrial capacity; Export Council; export surpluses (ministerial) |
| L. C. Robbins | Food, agriculture, consumption, and associated questions of prices and wages | Food policy; scientific subcommittee on food policy; food prices; exchange requirements |
| A. K. Cairncross | Imports, shipping, transport, raw materials, and priority machinery | Import Executive; transport priority; coal supply; materials; works and buildings |
| D. N. Chester | Administration of Section; labour | |
| S. R. Dennison | Manpower and labour | Manpower |
| J. H. Wilson | Regional organization and industrial capacity | Manpower |
| E. F. M. Durbin | | |
| Mary Soutar | Assistant to the Director | |

Source: LP(41)14, 4 February 1941.

a   The duties shown were suggested at a time when James Meade and Peggy Joseph were still working intensively with Dick Stone on national income. It was hoped that the members assigned to official committees would become members of these committees and that Robinson and Cairncross would eventually assume secretarial positions on the Production and Import Executives respectively.

There is little or nothing in them about the affairs of major departments such as the Board of Trade, the Ministries of Supply, Fuel and Power, Shipping, and Transport, with all of which the Section was deeply involved. Problems affecting those departments were regularly reported and discussed at the weekly Section meetings but only occasionally gave rise to staff papers.

By the middle of 1941 the transformation of the economy to a war footing had been virtually completed. Some members of the Section concluded that it was time to move on from the Section to more positive activities and concentrate on improving the use of the resources allocated to war production. Of the five who held senior appointments in the spring of 1940 only Campion remained in the Cabinet Offices two years later. Jewkes, Devons, and Cairncross were in the Ministry of Aircraft Production and Austin Robinson in the Ministry of Production. Another to leave was Harold Wilson, who moved to the Ministry of Fuel and Power to take charge of their statistics. Mary Soutar and Joan Marley continued throughout the war as assistants, one in the Economic Section, the other in the CSO. Five further appointments were made to the Economic Section in 1941: R. C. Tress, Philip Chantler, and Nita Watts, all of whom stayed until after the war, and Paul Wilson and A. S. J. Baster, who stayed only briefly. Only two others were appointed before the end of the war: Marcus Fleming and John Wood. From the time it was formed at the beginning of 1941 until the end of the war, the Economic Section proper never had a staff of more than a dozen. The normal complement was ten.

# Chapter four

# PERPETUATION: WARTIME VIEWS ON ECONOMIC ADVISING

After the turmoil of the first eighteen months of its existence, the later history of the Economic Section as a government think-tank is relatively calm and sedate. As time went on, planning for the transition to a peacetime economy became an important part of its work, although most members of the Section remained involved also in the operations of the war economy itself. This inevitably raised the question of the Section's own future after the war and this was considered at length by the Machinery of Government Committee in 1943. The conclusions of that Committee found expression in the white paper on *Employment Policy* the following year and in the arrangements made in 1945 to continue the Economic Section as part of the Cabinet Secretariat. The only major change in these arrangements before 1964 was the decision in 1953 to move the Section from the Cabinet Office to the Treasury. In this chapter we review the discussions that took place during the war on the place of the Section in the government machine.

In 1943, for the first and only time in British history, an official committee prepared a report on 'The role of the economist in the machinery of government'.[1] It addressed itself particularly to the need under post-war conditions for a central organization on the lines of the Economic Section.

Written evidence was submitted by Keynes, Robbins, and Henderson as well as by the permanent secretaries of the Treasury, Board of Trade, Colonial Office (but not the Foreign Office), and Ministry of

---

1 Report of the Official Committee on the Machinery of Government, MGO 32, 15 November 1943, in PRO CAB 87/72.

Agriculture. Oral evidence was also taken from a number of officials and others including Beveridge, Laski, Geoffrey Crowther, Lord Hankey, Sir Edward Bridges, Norman Brook, and Sir Frederick Leith-Ross, the Government's Chief Economic Adviser. James Meade prepared written evidence but it does not appear to have been presented.[2] No member of the Economic Section other than Robbins (who no doubt consulted his colleagues in the Section) was asked to give evidence; nor were Jewkes and Robinson, by this time ex-members.

Robbins's evidence, which was much the longest, opened with a repudiation of the idea of a general economic staff drawing up plans and issuing orders, with Cabinet authority, to the various departments: 'The initiation and framing of policy should come, at least in part, from the departments which have to carry it out.' In Robbins's view, the majority of government economists should be 'diffused throughout the departments'.

Robbins went on to describe the work of the Section, which at that time consisted of himself, eight economic assistants of various grades, and a very small clerical staff. Each member of the Section had his own allotted sphere of work, such as manpower, shipping, consumption, etc., and was expected to keep in touch with developments in it as well as with whatever his colleagues were doing. The Section's routine duties were to brief the Lord President from week to week on the items appearing on the agenda of his Committee. The members also advised the Lord President on matters of economic interest that might require policy decisions. These duties involved attendance at meetings of the relevant official committees and frequent personal contact with the department officials dealing with economic affairs. The Section also supplied secretaries for some committees with a high economic content in their agenda, the most notable example being Norman Chester's secretaryship of the Beveridge Committee in 1941–2.

In carrying out those duties the Section issued few papers for general circulation apart from the occasional quarterly surveys referred to on pp. 162–5, preferring to express their views in briefs and reports to the Lord President or allowing their opinions to emerge in the give and take of committee discussion and in informal conversation with departments. Taking to heart the experience of 1940, the Section followed a settled policy of seeking 'as far as possible to work *with* the departments rather than apart from them'. This meant trying to persuade departments, where some innovation in policy seemed

2 It is to be found in PRO T 230/283.

desirable, to put it forward themselves. It meant also that, when a department was submitting a memorandum to the Lord President's Committee, any points that the Section wished to raise should be taken up in advance and that the Section should avoid acting as critic except where there was a clear inconsistency with general policy requirements. In this way, particularly where a common intellectual interest could be established with a departmental economist, a happy informal collaboration could be established and the information wanted by the Section would be supplied spontaneously rather than become the subject of continual enquiries.

The success of the Section in wartime, Robbins went on, owed much to pure good fortune.

> Had we not enjoyed the strong support of the Lord President, and the friendly and wise counsel of Sir Edward Bridges and Mr Norman Brook, had we at some time fallen out violently with the main departments, we might easily have found ourselves . . . with little or nothing to do but to write essays in a vacuum.

As any ex-member of the wartime Section will testify, this tribute to the good offices of Anderson, Bridges, and Brook was completely justified. But the good fortune extended far beyond this help to factors emphasized later by Henderson: the suspension of political controversy in wartime and the greater scope for the 'systematic technique of analysis' which the change to a war economy afforded.

Looking ahead, Robbins thought that there could be no doubt as to the need for some central machinery of co-ordination. 'The economic problems of war are child's play compared with the problems which will emerge as soon as the single objective of war disappears.' Equally, there could be no doubt as to the need for 'a preparatory sifting of issues' and 'some apparatus specifically designed to survey the problem as a whole' if the Cabinet was to discharge its reponsibility for planning and co-ordination. In such an apparatus, the professional economist had a useful part to play. Robbins then laid down four general rules governing the form of organization required.

First of all, economic advisers should be members of the civil service, bound to secrecy, and in continuous contact with the daily working of the machine. Second, some, at least, of the members of the organization must be fully trained in economics if 'the incredible muddles which continually emerge from lay discussion' of such matters as points rationing were to be avoided. Next, something more than an interdepartmental committee of high officials, or even departmental economists, was required. High officials were burdened with other duties and were bound to see things from a departmental angle. What was needed was continuous study of problems of economic policy as a whole from a more synthetic and comprehensive point of view. Finally, there was a fundamental need to attach the organization to a minister or group of ministers directly responsible for policy: without the drive of a powerful minister behind it, the organization would be little better than a research group. It must concern itself, at least in part, with the day-to-day solution of practical questions; academic economists would not give up their freedom readily without the assurance that their labours would have some immediate practical relevance.

All this pointed to an official organization at the centre of government, responsible to a minister or group of ministers, and made up in part of professional economists who would sift the implications of departmental plans for the evolution of policy as a whole. If policy continued to be shaped by a committee of the Cabinet, the organization, like the Economic Section, should work under the direction of its chairman.

How were economists for such an organization to be recruited? Robbins saw little likelihood that senior economists would be attracted for a sufficient period of service; those who were would not be the sort of person required. On the other hand, he saw no great difficulty about recruiting able young teachers of economics from the universities for a spell in government. There should also, in due course, be a steady inflow into the civil service of graduates in economics, some of whom could be seconded to the organization to provide a stiffening of administrative experience; it would be a healthy development if there were some circulation between posts in the departments and in the Economic Section. The head of the Section should have had some academic experience. This was not inconsistent, if promising young academics could be persuaded to remain in the Section, with Robbins's view that the post should normally be filled by promotion within the Section; or with the alternative which he envisaged of selecting the director from among 'the permanent civil servants with the requisite scientific qualifications for the post' who would, in course of time, be available.

There was much good sense, brilliantly propounded, in Robbins's memorandum. On three points, however, he was open to criticism. First of all, he said very little – no doubt deliberately – about what the precise duties of the Section would be after the war. There was no mention of full employment, or the budget, or control of investment, or the things that were in practice to keep the Section busy. This was coupled, secondly, with a complete silence about the Section's future relationship with the Treasury. In addition, Robbins, like nearly everybody else, was highly optimistic about the supply of economists for service in government and in particular about the role they were to play in other departments.

The first two of these criticisms were made by several others who gave evidence. Geoffrey Crowther, for example, started from 'the crucial issue of full employment'. Since all the instruments for securing full employment were matters of Treasury policy, what was needed was a strengthening of the economic staff of the Treasury, a view shared by Sir Horace Wilson and Sir Donald Fergusson, Permanent Secretaries of the Treasury and Ministry of Agriculture respectively. The latter was strongly against the attachment of the Economic Section to the Cabinet Office or to a ministerial economic committee on the grounds that this would give an undue influence in the framing and execution of policy to a centrally placed body of officials – and to economists at that! – at the expense of the responsible minister and his department. A section of specialist advisers unattached to a departmental minister would be bound to cause serious friction sooner or later. This view was shared by Sir Horace Wilson, who suggested that there would be less friction if the Section were in the Treasury, where it might still retain a distinctive title to indicate that its members should not be regarded as Treasury representatives and that it was a separate body available to all departments.

The most extreme view was that of the government's Chief Economic Adviser, who was opposed to the retention of the Economic Section except for a short time after the war. The role of the economist was simply to explain the economic consequences of the government's policy; and this did not require a separate central unit which would be likely to overemphasize the academic aspects of policy-making and create friction with the heads of departments. For the co-ordination of advice on economic matters it would be better to rely on the economic advisers at the Treasury and Board of Trade, who could take the lead in any interdepartmental enquiry.

A different note of caution was sounded by Sir Hubert Henderson. The 'impressive wartime harmony of economists' was unlikely to endure in peacetime when the issues on which economists differed might be leading issues of party controversy. Under such conditions ministers would not welcome expert advice that might show them to be in the wrong but rather arguments on their side as 'munitions in debate' and advice on the best course to pursue in carrying out a predetermined line of policy. A resumption of the party dogfight might lead to changes *en bloc* in the personnel of the Economic Section with each change of ministry and this of itself would make it difficult to maintain those harmonious relations with departments on which Robbins laid such stress. On those grounds, Henderson suggested continuing the Section on an experimental basis for a few years and delaying building it into the established machinery until there was more experience of political relationships. He also saw no serious difficulty in employing economists in particular departments.

Keynes, joining in the controversy after most of the others, started very sensibly from the problem of recruitment. He wanted an interchange between Whitehall and the universities that would not only include younger economists but also men in sight of a professorship. Appointments should be for three or five years and rarely for longer. (The resulting turnover would afford governments an opportunity of changing the complexion of their expert advice fairly rapidly if they wanted to do so.) There should be no disturbance to pension arrangements, and levels of salary would have to be attractive, especially as academic economists had considerable opportunities of adding to their stipends. It would be particularly difficult to get or keep the right men immediately after the war. Then and later, economists in government service should be allowed to retain some freedom of expression: for example, to take part in outside discussions, to write books, and to contribute to learned journals. Service in Whitehall should not be 'too much like a visit to the tomb'. Those recruited would 'only be useful if they had in fact developed dangerous powers of self-expression'.

Keynes accepted the general view that by far the greater number of professional economists in government should be attached to particular departments. There should in addition be a small group at the centre, including more senior and weighty members. This might be attached either to the Cabinet Office or to the Treasury, according as its dominant function was to serve a minister or committee of economic co-ordination or to advise on what we should now call macroeconomic policy. Since economic co-ordination embraces macroeconomic policy, the claims of the Cabinet Office should perhaps prevail but in that event the Treasury would still need some expert advice. Keynes doubted whether more than two economists would be needed and he would expect them to work in close co-operation with the larger group in the Cabinet Office.

He ended his note by considering the place of the CSO, which he assumed would remain in being. It, too, might be either in the Cabinet Office or in the Treasury. If he (Keynes) were head of the CSO he would prefer to be attached to the Treasury. If, on the other hand, the CSO and the Economic Section were both in the Cabinet Office, the CSO should be 'closely associated with the Economic Section and possibly subordinated to the head of the Economic Section, if that appointment is made a highly important one with a maximum level of salary'.

The Committee, after reviewing the evidence and noting the limitations of economics as a science, recommended the retention of the Economic Section. It recognized the danger emphasized by Henderson that a change of government might be accompanied by a change of government economists, deplored 'anything smacking of the "spoils system"', called on economists to behave like other civil servants, and left it at that. It also put forward, as the first step in ensuring proper economic advice, the employment of full-time economists within departments. Departmental economists should be kept in close touch with policy-making and be in a position to suggest lines of action to secure economic objectives.

Many of the recommendations were on recruitment. These in general followed the suggestions of Keynes and Robbins. It was proposed to recruit a few academic economists aged between 30 and 35 for a term of three to five years, supplemented by economics graduates recruited through the usual civil service examination. In addition, more senior appointments would be made for perhaps five years. The recommendations, however, are not easy to interpret, since they do not distinguish the immediate post-war situation from that achievable in the longer run. One paragraph speaks of filling 'the bulk of the places available for expert economists' by permanent civil servants with a degree in economics who have continued their studies – a very long-run prospect. The next talks of recruitment on a temporary basis of university economists, junior and senior, and dwells on the difficulties of retaining or attracting them in the post-war period. Two paragraphs later comes the proposal to recruit 30–35 year-old academic economists without any provision for more senior men except 'occasional recruitment of an economist of the highest standing'. Such economists, however, are best employed on 'specific enquiries without relinquishing their university posts'. In between, the possible employment on a temporary footing of economists in 'big business' or the banks is rejected on the grounds that people would suspect their disinterestedness. Significantly, the report concludes by stressing the need for a regular interchange of departmental staffs with that of the Economic Section. Such an interchange hardly ever occurred for the simple reason that there were hardly any professional economists left in government service a year after VE day.[3]

What kind of Economic Section did the Committee envisage? It was, as Henderson suggested, to be experimental, pending evidence of 'progress towards uniform economic opinion and the ability of the economic advisers in the Central Section to appreciate the political background'. The staff was to be no bigger; to serve under a director with postgraduate training and, preferably, some previous experience of work in the Section; and to be graded as Economic Assistants or Chief Economic Assistants so as to make it easier 'to establish contacts without standing overmuch on hierarchical ceremony'. The location of the Section was not of the first importance but, to begin with, it should be in the Cabinet Office rather than the Treasury or the Board of Trade.

The functions of the Section would be to receive, supplement, and appraise economic intelligence; to make or arrange for studies on subjects not covered by any one department; and to present 'co-ordinated and objective pictures of the economic situation as a whole, and the economic aspects of projected Government policies'. It should be able to commission special studies by universities or other institutions. It should stand ready to supply economic advice on request to departments and work closely with them, sharing frequently in the formulation of departmental policy in advance of submission to the departmental minister. Constant informal exchanges of view among all economists in the government service would be encouraged by the existence of the Section, which should maintain particularly close contacts with economists employed in departments.

The Committee concluded:

> In brief, we regard the Central Economic Section as an expert body equipped with comprehensive and up-to-date economic knowledge and trained in its appraisal, whose services would be at the disposal of the Government as a whole, both at the centre and at the circumference, and would be brought to bear both in the general and in the particular.

Thus, broadly speaking, the Committee came down in favour of the

3 The only examples that come to mind in the early post-war years are the movement to the Economic Section of Robert Hall from the Ministry of Supply/Board of Trade and Russell Bretherton from the Board of Trade. Philip Chantler left the Economic Section for the Ministry of Fuel and Power in 1947. There were also a few young administrators with a training in economics who were released by their parent department in the years after the war to serve for short periods in the Economic Section.

status quo and looked forward, rather hesitantly, to a prolongation into the peace of the kind of arrangements that had been built up in the first four years of war. Their fears of friction with departments and of faction and schism among professional advisers proved to have little substance in the immediate post-war years. At the same time the wide scope which they foresaw for economists in Whitehall outran in those years the capabilities of the small staff that elected to remain in government service or could be attracted from academic work.

The Committee's report was considered by ministers in December 1943.[4] They showed much less hesitation than officials in accepting the Economic Section as a permanent institution. Its duties should go beyond the assembly of economic intelligence and extend to 'a judgement from a central and non-departmental standpoint on the economic aspects of policy'. Whatever the practical difficulties they should 'on no account stand in the way of what promised to become an essential mechanism in the central executive Government'.

These views found expression five months later in the White Paper on *Employment Policy*.[5] There the government announced its intention 'to establish on a permanent basis a small central staff qualified to measure and analyse economic trends and submit appreciations of them to the Ministers concerned'. The emphasis, however, was on analysis and diagnosis of the economic situation rather than on policy prescription. In carrying out their 'very heavy' responsibilities in the crucial early post-war years, the central economic staff would need 'exact quantitative information about current economic movements'. This would be used in preparing a 'central analysis of our financial position . . . subject to continuous review and adjustment throughout the year'; and, alongside a budget of the nation's income and expenditure, the Ministry of Labour would prepare a parallel manpower budget. But, of how the work of budget-making and diagnosis of trends was to be divided between the central economic staff, the Central Statistical Office, the Ministry of Labour, and other departments, or what other work the staff would be asked to undertake, or what sort of staff it was to be, there was not a word.

There was, for example, the question where the economic staff advising on problems of employment policy should be located. Should they be in the Treasury or form part of the Economic Section? The Treasury would have the final reponsibility for advising ministers on the timing of action to expand or contract demand and would need to set up a new division collecting information on capital projects and

4 MG(43)6M in PRO CAB 87/73.
5 Cmd 6527, May 1944.

arranging for their acceleration or retardation. But was it wise to have rival groups of economists specializing in the economics of employment policy? A meeting in September 1944 between Bridges, Norman Brook, Robbins, and Jewkes agreed that it would be best to rely on the Economic Section so long as the Director or Deputy Director specialized on employment policy and had the assistance of a statistician from the CSO who would arrange to bring in the resources of the CSO to provide 'estimates and guesswork' lacking the usual CSO hallmark.[6]

A month later James Meade, looking to his future duties as Director of the Economic Section, began to raise similar questions about future working arrangements. In a letter to Bridges he pointed out that, as controls gave way to financial inducements once the war was over, 'financial policy is bound finally to become the central instrument of economic policy and the Treasury, accordingly, the central economic department'. Advising on the decisive aspects of economic policy would be advising on the economic aspects of Treasury policy. What role would there be for the Economic Section in these circumstances? Would the Treasury retain its own economic advisers, who at that time included Keynes, Henderson, Catto (the Governor of the Bank of England), and Leith-Ross? Would the Director of the Economic Section be admitted to budgetary discussions and share in the discussion of external economic policy?

To these questions, after consulting Sir Richard Hopkins, the Permanent Secretary of the Treasury, Bridges gave categorical replies. The Treasury would rely on the Economic Section alone for technical advice and would wish the Director to share in discussion of the budget and external economic policy. If it was to play its full part after the war, the Section would need to have 'an increasingly close and intimate connection with the Treasury'.

These arrangements held, in a formal sense, throughout the years until 1953, when the Economic Section moved from the Cabinet Office to the Treasury. But in practice the role of the Economic Section was by no means unchanged throughout that time: the Whitehall administrative machine, the conceptions governing economic policy, relations between the Economic Section and the Treasury, and consequently the ways in which the Section was able to influence policy, all underwent substantial and unforeseen changes.[7]

---

6 'Note for the record', Norman Brook, 7 September 1944, in PRO T 273/318.
7 David Butt, 'Notes on the history of the Economic Section', in PRO T 230/283.

# Chapter five

# THE ECONOMIC SECTION IN WARTIME: A PERSONAL MEMOIR

The surviving records of the Economic Section convey little of the atmosphere in which it worked in its first few years or of the personalities of its members.[1] The picture which follows is based on the personal recollections of the authors supplemented by those of former colleagues. The use of the first person singular indicates the senior author.[2]

## Early years: 1940–1

The first home of the Section when it was attached to the Stamp Survey was at 8 Richmond Terrace, an old rabbit-warren of a building shared with the military side of the War Cabinet Offices. Until the outbreak of war it had been a private house, with an imposing exterior, a spacious entrance hall leading to a broad, marble staircase, and beautiful dark red mahogany doors throughout. Converted into a suite of offices, rambling and chilly, it was far from ideal. I was

---

1 The records for 1939–41 include:
  (a) the papers of the Stamp Survey (P(E and F)) in PRO CAB 89/8 and 9 (1939–40);
  (b) the staff papers (P(E and F)(S)) in PRO CAB 89/9 (1940);
  (c) the staff papers headed Economic General Staff in PRO CAB 72/24 (1940);
  (d) the discussion papers on the Economic Section beginning in November 1940 and contained in PRO T 230/12 and 13 (1940–1);
  (e) the papers on the Economic Policy Committee in PRO CAB 72/1–5 (1939–40);
2 For a more extended account, see Cairncross, Sir Alec (1984) 'An early think-tank: the origins of the Economic Section', *Three Banks Review* December.

assigned a small ex-bedroom upstairs with an empty fireplace and, from March onwards, shared it with Ely Devons. Austin Robinson remembers sharing with John Jewkes a desk that was not much larger than a tea-table so that they could not escape discussing everything together.

Some of the deficiencies of Richmond Terrace are illustrated by Harry Campion's account of his first day in the office. When asked about figures of employment in the engineering industry

> I told them the figures they wanted were already there in the *Ministry of Labour Gazette*. There was no copy available in the Cabinet Office but it would be ordered. So I went out myself at lunch-time and bought a copy at the Stationery Office in Kingsway. The copy the Office ordered arrived a week later.[3]

Early in August we moved to the New Police Building, a large, purpose-built steel-framed building, just completed, at the far end of the Terrace, now part of the Ministry of Defence and at that time shared (not altogether happily) with Scotland Yard. At the end of March 1941 we moved once again, this time to Great George Street at the St James's Park end, into rooms formerly occupied by the Board of Trade. Since the Treasury was just along the corridor, this brought us nearer (physically at least) to the centre of things. But the association with senior military officers, such as 'Pug' Ismay and Ian Jacob, in Richmond Terrace had had its advantages too. In the spring and summer of 1940 Jewkes and Robinson were able to profit from the propinquity of military staff to keep in touch with the views of the Chiefs of Staff and the outlook on the western front.

In the middle of 1940 many of us lived, or at least slept, in Bedford College, in Regent's Park, while the undergraduates remained in Cambridge. We used to walk every morning through the three parks to Whitehall and return in time for dinner. There were other civil servants in the college besides ourselves, and for a time the entire Dutch Cabinet in exile. Our residence there gave it the atmosphere of an economists' club where banter and gossip could be mixed with shop and argument.

*Personalities*

The personalities of the three senior economists contributed greatly to the favourable atmosphere. They were all around 40 years of age and

3 'The origins of the CSO' talk by Sir Harry Campion at the CSO on 29 October 1984.

at the height of their powers. Jewkes, who usually took the lead, had built up in Manchester a highly successful economic research department. From 1934 onwards a number of young economists and statisticians had worked in Manchester, many of them later joining the Economic Section or the CSO: for example, Norman Chester, Philip Chantler, Ely Devons, Christopher Saunders, and Ronald Tress.

Jewkes was at his best with younger people, encouraging them with suggestions and amusing them with his pungent turn of phrase and love of paradox. He revelled in exaggerated accounts of the latest administrative muddle, in puncturing optimistic claims, and in prophesying fresh disasters. Himself a capable administrator and soon to be the head, in the Ministry of Aircraft Production, of a large planning department whose creation he had recommended, he had a hatred of bureaucracy and a contempt for central economic planning. His creed was that of William James in his 'small is beautiful' mood: government operations, being inherently on a large scale, could never match such a mood. So long as governments sustained demand and kept the economy in balance, they should beware of intervening in the economy and imposing controls that restricted individual initiative. Jewkes might not be an outstanding theorist: but in dealing with immediate problems he had a shrewdness, resilience, and lucidity that made him a natural choice as first Director of the Economic Section in January 1941. This was a post he held for only a few months. By September 1941 he had left the Section for the Ministry of Aircraft Production, where for over two years he led a team of academic economists in planning the activities of some two million workers in the aircraft and allied industries.

Austin Robinson had an entirely different temperament. Where Jewkes loved company and gossip, Austin liked to apply himself alone to the composition of long documents analysing some major problems of policy in quantitative terms against a longish time horizon. What he wrote was more in the tradition of state papers, intended to be read and reread. At an early age in the First World War he had been a test pilot and, later, a tutor in India to a maharajah. Although equable and helpful, he seemed rather highly strung and was both less forceful and less fanciful than Jewkes. Where Jewkes's interests tended to centre on manpower problems, Robinson's were more in industrial structure and international trade. He, too, left the Economic Section at an early stage, joining the Ministry of Production at its formation in February 1942.

Harry Campion, the third of the trio, was Reader in Statistics at the University of Manchester. He had spent several years in the cotton industry and had taken part in the preparation of a regular digest of statistics for the industry. What he learned then went to shape the succession of statistical digests that were issued to ministers in 1940–1 and prepared him for his duties in laying the foundations of the Central Statistical Office. Harry in those days was a somewhat inarticulate colleague, usually gruff or silent, but with an observant eye and a disposition to get on unobtrusively with the job in hand. He was the first of the three to leave the Economic Section, but in the Central Statistical Office he continued to keep in close touch with it until his retirement in 1967.

Among later arrivals in 1940, the most weighty figure was that of Lionel Robbins, who joined in May and succeeded to the directorship of the Economic Section after Jewkes's departure. On his first day in the Office, when shown a particularly dispiriting report by the Chiefs of Staff, he was so agitated that he had to be taken home in a taxi. Robbins had spent much of the 1930s in disagreement with Keynes, and leaned strongly towards *laissez-faire* and against reliance on government action. All this made Bridges view him as a potentially disruptive influence and hesitate to agree to his recruitment. But Robbins, like Jewkes, found no difficulty in accepting the pivotal position of government in a war economy or in devising forms of intervention calculated to permit the more effective use of resources.

Robbins played an important part in the introduction of points rationing and, as the son of a former President of the National Farmers' Union, took a keen interest in food policy and the programme for agriculture. He was particularly insistent on the need for a livestock slaughter policy to accompany a cut in imports of animal feedstuffs. Another of his enthusiasms in June 1940 was for the transformation of India into an arsenal of democracy: he visualized the mobilization of the Indian masses for the manufacture of armaments alongside that other arsenal across the Atlantic without which victory was impossible.

Robbins had a great command of language and an ample vocabulary, of which he made full use. He had a measured, eighteenth-century style that matched his Johnsonian figure and, if at times a little ponderous, he also achieved elegance and wit. He conveyed a sense of balance and wisdom that made him a trusted adviser. Whatever his earlier disagreements with Keynes, he came to feel that Keynes had been in the right in his belief that unemployment could be made to yield to state action, and throughout the war the two of them worked in great harmony. Robbins did much to raise the standing of the Section in Whitehall and maintained particularly close relations with the Treasury and the Foreign Office. Above all, Robbins hit it off with Anderson and enjoyed his complete trust. It was this more than anything that allowed the Section to play an important and useful part as economic advisers.

Of the other members who joined in mid-1940, the two most important were James Meade and Norman Chester. Meade had arrived from Geneva at the beginning of June, after a nightmare car journey across France with his wife and young family. His route intersected the successive columns of refugees streaming south before the advancing German armies. Although he had come to join the CEIS, he was directed into the Ministry of Economic Warfare and had to be dug out again. When bombed out in September 1940, he moved into the office and remained there for the next two years.

Deceptively mild in manner, with an integrity of which one was immediately conscious, Meade had an acute and lucid mind and strong convictions. He was both a scholar and a prophet, with a vision of how the economy should work and a clear understanding of what made it work as it did. His interest lay in issues of principle; and, if ministerial decisions seemed to him mistaken in principle, he thought it his duty to contest them, not to implement them without question. Much of his work was directed towards post-war reconstruction, particularly commercial and employment policy. But it was the preparation with Dick Stone of better estimates of national income that occupied him for much of his first year.

Norman Chester was the one member of the Economic Section who was not a professional economist. His training was in public administration but he was accustomed to working with economists and brought to their discussions a wide acquaintance with the functioning of institutions and a broad common sense that made him an invaluable member of the team. Lionel Robbins christened him the 'Friend of Man'; and he did in fact take a keen interest in what we were all doing and make helpful suggestions to improve our effectiveness. He had been recruited by Jewkes to monitor the implementation of ministerial decisions, in keeping with the remit to the CEIS at the beginning of June. But the decisions of ministers on economic affairs were rarely so specific, or so unaffected by later events and decisions, as to make them easy to monitor, or indeed worth monitoring, in the summer of 1940, and Chester's duties soon changed. One of his most important later assignments was that of Secretary to the Beveridge Committee in 1941–2.

To complete the picture, Stanley Dennison was a young economist from Newcastle who had been appointed to the Chair in Economics at

Swansea while still in his twenties. He had been working for some time for Monnet in the Anglo-French Co-ordinating Committee and carried out his duties quietly and efficiently. His main responsibility was for manpower, especially after Jewkes left, but he also relieved the Director from 1941 onwards of some of his administrative duties. Evan Durbin, a friend of Hugh Gaitskell's, adopted a role more like that of a junior minister than a civil servant. He liked discussion but tended to avoid other necessary preliminaries to the business of advising: drafting, for example, he usually left to others. Durbin looked at the war economy through the eyes of an aspiring politician, was in touch with Labour ministers, and concentrated on large, general issues, particularly those involving social reform. He was an interesting and attractive colleague and honest in his assessments (I remember my surprise when he defended Munich as giving us another, indispensable year to prepare for war); but he was not very industrious.

Harold Wilson, who was then in his early twenties, at no time confessed to any political ambitions. He was a little shy of us, but was obviously very clever and witty. Most of his time was spent assisting Beveridge in his manpower enquiries, so we did not see a great deal of him in the office. John Jewkes used to explain that he and Harold Wilson tried to handle Beveridge in the way a wild elephant is tamed by being led between two tame elephants: the wild elephant pushes in one direction and gets pushed back, then pushes in the other direction and the second tame elephant pushes back. In this way the wild elephant gradually learns to keep to the road set for it.

*Morals*

One lesson we learned was the importance of access to ministers. There is no point in offering advice if there is nobody to listen to it. Even if you are nominally advising the entire Cabinet, that gets you nowhere unless somebody in the Cabinet has a special reason for listening to you. Each member of the Cabinet has his or her own advisers in the department for which he or she is responsible and is not likely to welcome a second set of advisers with a very different brief. Things are different if the head of the think-tank has the ear of the Prime Minister or is allowed to attend Cabinet meetings or if he is of a standing to command the attention of other ministers. But in most circumstances a think-tank without a minister to speak for it is in danger of being consistently bypassed and closing down for lack of a market.

Another lesson, rubbed in by Lionel Robbins, was the importance of carrying departments with us. We should refrain from making implementation reports on ministerial decisions: to do so would make the departments concerned regard us 'as a sort of upstart inspectorate'. Let the departments themselves make progress reports to the Lord President's Committee: when asked by the Lord President for a brief we could then draw attention to inadequacies and (more particularly) inconsistencies revealed by and between the reports. We should also refrain from pronouncing at length on issues at the risk of raising departmental hackles when a few leading questions would be more productive of 'lively discussion' at ministerial level. Robbins's doctrine was that we should state the facts and leave it to departments to interpret them and make suggestions for improvement.[4]

What was also increasingly apparent was the great advantage to a staff exercising co-ordinating functions not only of membership of the key economic committees but of membership in a secretarial capacity. Representation on virtually all official committees concerned with any aspect of economic policy gave the Section a continuing opportunity for unobtrusive influence and made it easier to keep in touch with current issues of policy. Equally important, it meant that the Section was normally well informed when these issues were put to ministers for decision. From 1941 onwards members of the Economic Section were appointed as secretaries to a growing number of interdepartmental committees and profited greatly from these duties in their role as policy advisers.

For much of the time we acted as brokers in ideas and information: assembling and clarifying them and then making them circulate where they were in demand. Of course, the trade was not all in one direction, and we had to acquire an intimate knowledge of the market. We kept in touch with the departments that had come to form our parish, learning from our contacts there what was going on, what issues of policy were hot, who was ranged on one side or the other. In return we could sometimes offer a broader view of those issues or fresh information on the state of play at the centre. Most important of all, we could hold out the prospect of weighing in with a paper in support or a ministerial brief that steered the debate in what we took to be the right direction.

Our advantage as economists was twofold: the perspective which a

---

4 ES(S)(40)1, 'Proposal for a new edition of urgent economic problems', note by Mr Lionel Robbins, 4 November 1940; and ES(S)(40)4, 'Implementation reports', note by Mr L. Robbins, 5 November 1940.

training in economics gave to our ideas and the superior information, especially statistical information, which we assembled. Our training gave us a bird's-eye view of the economy, with all the actions and reactions between its component parts. We were, in a sense, at home in a war economy while others were not, and we could judge where it was most essential to engage in a concentrated effort of planning and co-ordination. The wider background of ideas that economists possessed gave them an important advantage over administrators unfamiliar with those ideas. They were more alive to the fundamental choices that had to be made and to the merits of the various options available.

They were also more alive to the significance of economic information. In wartime most economic statistics were secret and scattered, badly presented, and badly organized. We made it our business almost from the start to approach the various new government agencies controlling different elements of the economy for the secret data which they collected in the course of their operations. Without such information it was impossible to tell what was happening to industrial production, or the consumption of food, or the level of employment, and a host of other economic aggregates. It may be difficult to imagine it now but up to 1940 the government felt no particular need for such macroeconomic data. There were no official estimates of GNP or consumer spending, only the sketchiest of estimates of the balance of payments, nothing at all on stocks, profits, and capital formation. Economic statistics were relegated to unreadable monthly journals and annual abstracts. If they were used at all, it was usually in the most unsophisticated way with no attempt to produce a time series or adjust for seasonal and other special factors. Fragments of statistical information went on the file like other fragments of information.

All that changed in 1940. Right from the start, Harry Campion set about organizing a flow of confidential statistics from the various departments and controls to the Cabinet Office.[5] This took time, especially as the statistical branches of most of the big departments had been dispersed all over the country: for example, Food was in Colwyn Bay, Labour in Southport, Customs in Buxton, the Steel Control near Warwick, and so on.

The process was speeded up when Ely Devons was released in March by the Cotton Board and joined Campion in preparing a

5 A full account was given by Sir Harry Campion in a talk at the CSO on 29 October 1984.

monthly digest of the latest economic statistics for use by the main economic committees of the Cabinet. They took as their model the regular digest of statistics which Campion had helped to inaugurate at the Joint Committee of Cotton Trade Organizations before the war, using a generous layout to make for easy reading. At the suggestion of Ely Devons, it was agreed to introduce the Gill Sans type, then almost unknown, which is now used in official publications all over the world.[6]

The first of what became a whole family of statistical digests was labelled Series A and issued on 21 June 1940. This was a conspectus of the more important statistics, including highly secret data, and was given a very limited circulation. Indeed, when the Lord President's Committee was given new powers at the end of 1940, the circulation was limited to those who attended meetings of the Committee (i.e. to fourteen) and it was only after strong protests that this condition was relaxed to match the circulation of the papers of the Committee (i.e. to over forty). Even so, all copies had to be returned when a fresh number was issued.

Of more long-run importance was Series B, which included a more comprehensive but less secret collection of data. It was first circulated on 26 August 1940, given a fairly wide circulation and very soon recognized by ministers and officials as of particular value in the framing of policy. Series B lived on after the war when it was issued to the public as the *Monthly Digest of Statistics*.

These and other series provided, for the first time in this country, a comprehensive and up-to-date picture in quantitative form of economic trends. They also transformed the presentation of official statistics. Few people now remember how unattractive nearly all publications of government statistics looked before the war. One change in layout, however, did not persist. The practice of putting totals on the left-hand side of the page and at the top of the columns, where they were more likely to hit the eye, was abruptly stopped by an outraged Prime Minister.

Responsibility for the issue of the new digests passed to the Central Statistical Office when it was hived off at the end of 1940. But their origin in the Economic Section bears witness to the inseparability of economic statistics and economic advice.

---

6 As Austin Robinson, who was strongly in favour of the Gill Sans type, has reminded me, it is the perfect type for statistical tables because, having no ascenders and descenders, you can pack it more closely while leaving a visual gap and you can get more months or years in a table of given length.

It might also be claimed that national income accounting had its origin in the work of Meade and Stone. This would be to do less than justice to their predecessors, including Bowley, Stamp, and Colin Clark. It was in the CSO, not the Economic Section, that the system of national accounts was more fully developed. But the Economic Section remained an important contributor to their development, both as a pressure group for more adequate statistical data and as the most important consumer of statistical aggregates, seeking to ensure that in form and frequency they were such as to meet its requirements in analysing the changes in progress in the economy.

## The range of activities

Different members of the Section pursued different problems. Some concerned themselves with food, some with fuel, some with transport, some with manpower, some with financial and budgetary problems. There were also differences of approach to the work of the Section. Some liked to work out general principles of policy and then try to get them agreed; others preferred to look for specific constraints and bottle-necks, actual and potential, and seek to get something done about them. The first approach was congenial to those who were attracted to the big issues such as employment policy or the future organization of international trade: very often this meant viewing things from the side of demand or looking well ahead to post-war arrangements. The second approach was more to the liking of those who wanted to be up and doing, removing current obstacles without delay, with an eye on the immediate future and the tangles of supply. Meade preferred the first and John Jewkes the second of these two approaches. Austin Robinson, although he liked to start from what he saw as major problems calling for action, shared the inclination of those who favoured the first approach to look well ahead and was at his best when left to prepare a document on long-term plans of a quantitative character.

The problems were many and we were few so that each of us ranged freely over a wide field. The range can be illustrated most readily from my own experience in 1940–1.

## The import programme

At first my work was largely on the balance of payments constraint. This meant concentration on the import programme, assembling information on stocks, shipping and shipbuilding, and port capacity, estimating the current account of the balance of payments, and making contact with the key figures in the Ministries of Transport and Shipping. My contacts there were with the officials who planned the allocation of tonnage to different cargoes and its assignment on arrival to berths in British ports. In the Ministry of Shipping this meant talking to two elderly actuaries, Sir William Elderton and Mr P. N. Harvey, who had done exactly the same job in the First World War and invariably greeted their young visitor with the offer of snuff before we got down to business. In the Ministry of Transport it meant watching the operations of the Shipping Diversion Room, which allocated incoming tonnage to ports, and trying to explain to a mystified but sympathetic Sir John Reith (who was then Minister of Transport) what I was up to. In spite of his majestic bearing I found Reith very human: encouraging, intrigued, but (I suspect) baffled.

In my efforts to assess importing capacity I also spent some time with Leak, the head of the Statistics Division of the Board of Trade. He was a tall, thin man, not altogether unlike Dr Schacht in appearance, with a small head, metal-rimmed spectacles, a high, stiff wing collar, and a large Adam's apple. He was an administrator turned statistician, and I sometimes wondered if he had been chosen to succeed Flux, Fountain, and Plummer, his three distinguished prede-cessors, because his name carried the promise of some continuity. Leak was meticulous to the point of pedantry, mild in manner, and so formally dressed that one almost expected to see a quill in his hand. He could be mulish but I always found him very helpful if allowed to have his say.[7]

From the beginning our line was that we would need all the ships we could get, that we should set out to build up stocks of imported goods, and that we should be ready with plans to make as much use as possible of whatever ports remained open. In the spring we had worked on a proposal for a 35 million-ton import programme at a time when that seemed very pessimistic. After the fall of France we busied ourselves with one for 8 million tons, consulting experts on nutrition with a view to minimizing imports of food and pushing for the replacement of bulky materials by finished manufactures. This programme was never adopted, but it convinced us that we could if necessary ride out a submarine campaign with far fewer imports than

---

7 According to Austin Robinson, an ordinary enquiry would never extract any information from him. But 'if one sent him a draft containing uncertain information . . . he would be prepared to give many hours of work to proving that one was wrong so that in the end one got the information one wanted'.

had previously been thought indispensable. One aspect of the economies we contemplated was a big reduction in imports of feedstuffs and a corresponding slaughter of pigs and poultry. We drew on advice from a Cambridge physiologist, Professor R. A. McCance, who had been living in the Lake District on home-grown food, with a high milk and vegetables component. We also took account of experiments at Rothamsted under Dr Yeats that showed how much the potato crop might respond to far larger applications of phosphate.

But of course we were aware that a switch of the kind proposed would cost dollars that we did not possess. Papers were written on the comparative value of shipping and foreign exchange so as to let us judge how far to push economy in the one at the expense of the other. In the end what settled the matter was the need to cut the import programme with each fresh crisis and we simply ran out of dollars and turned to the US to see us through.

For most of us, and indeed for most ministers as well, the import programme was our first experience of the technique of economic planning in quantitative terms. Programmes, in a planned economy, are the meeting-place of supply and demand and are instructions from the policy-making centre to the executive periphery. But the instructions are liable to be misunderstood. Programmes cannot be taken literally as promises of supply; nor are they to be regarded as an upper limit to demand. They are simply an effort to resolve the uncertainties on both sides in the light of the information currently available and so are in constant need of updating. When ministers debated our 35 million-ton import programme they tended to ask why imports should be limited to so low a figure if more could be loaded and brought in. But what had to be decided was, first, at what rate consumption of imports should be planned to match the likely arrivals from abroad; and, second, what should be loaded from month to month to offer the best chance of achieving a distribution of imports in keeping with requirements.

What ministers agreed in the end was to allocate 15 million tons of imports to food and feedstuffs, 19 million tons to raw materials and 1 million tons to manufactured goods.[8] But, by the autumn, sinkings were at such an alarming rate that even 35 million tons looked too high and planning was conducted on the assumption that the rate of importation would lie between 25 and 31 million tons. In such a

8 For the paper submitted by the CEIS, see EP(M)(40)40, 'Urgent economic problems', 5 June 1940; and for the ministerial discussion of the import programme, EP(M)(40)14 Conclusions, 5 June 1940, in PRO CAB 72/3.

rapidly changing situation there was a great danger of planning on an out-of-date basis and it was highly important to keep track of the rate at which imports were actually arriving. At first this had meant waiting for the monthly trade returns. But by about October we had moved over to figures of shipping arrivals with cargo as an index. Returns at ten-day intervals gave us a much earlier and fairly reliable picture of the rate of importation.

## Internal transport

Another interest of mine was rail transport. There was little information about the limits to rail capacity and the collection of railway statistics had been suspended. But it seemed possible that internal transport might prove just as much of a bottle-neck as port capacity and there was already evidence of hold-ups in coal transport. The main bottle-necks were at the exchange points between what had once been independent railway systems and still to some extent functioned as such. The four main-line systems, which had not yet been nationalized, had their own specialized rolling-stock and insisted on a change of locomotive at the exchange points, although this produced queuing, delay, and obvious targets for air attack. Ministers seemed to be unaware of the situation but I succeeded in interesting H. W. W Fisher, an Under-Secretary in the Ministry of Transport, who went to see for himself and was much concerned by what he saw. I was less successful in interesting the railways in the need for statistics (which they had ceased to collect at the outbreak of war).

## Contacts and visits

We conducted a lot of our business, as is customary in Whitehall, over lunch or on the telephone. We were not much occupied in entering minutes on files – in fact for most of 1940 we got along without files except what we kept for our own use. We spent a good deal of time in committees or visiting other departments, usually for a brief talk but very occasionally (in my case) working in the department for some days. For example, I spent a week or so in the Treasury looking after Dennis Robertson's papers and another week in the Shipping Diversion Room in the Ministry of Transport under the supervision of Stephen Wilson. Sometimes we pursued our enquiries in other parts of the country. Thus I visited Liverpool in November 1940 as a member (and, I think, secretary) of a committee of inquiry under Sir Cecil Weir into shipping congestion in the port. The committee was appointed by

Greenwood to examine impediments to the flow of exports through insufficiency of shipping and transport facilities, but the more serious issue seemed to us to be how to clear imports more expeditiously, especially as Liverpool, which handled a high proportion of total imports, was such an obvious target for air attacks.

We reported within a week of our appointment, making twenty-five recommendations, all of which were given careful and immediate consideration by the Economic Policy Committee.[9]

Another inquiry that took us out of London was one conducted by Jewkes in May 1941, with help from Norman Chester and myself, in response to a request from Sir Archibald Rowlands, Permanent Secretary of the Ministry of Aircraft Production, shortly after the departure of Beaverbrook from that ministry. Rowlands wanted our advice on the scope for planning in the department; and, after taking soundings that gave us little inkling of the muddle we later discovered, we reported rather diffidently that there did seem to be a case for more planning. Jewkes was promptly asked to undertake the job and by the end of the year had recruited nearly as many economists to plan aircraft production (including Ely Devons, Frank Paish, and myself) as were currently doing the work of the Economic Section.

A third inquiry, in which again I served as secretary under Sir Cecil Weir, was into the availability of factory and storage space. In drafting the report for submission to the Lord President's Committee in December 1940 I remember being so carried away by the case for control that I nearly included office space as well.[10] At any rate a control was established – in the Board of Trade – with Sir Cecil Weir as Controller. I was persuaded to join it in June 1941 although I remained there only a few months before rejoining Jewkes in November in the Ministry of Aircraft Production.

Other members of the CEIS could tell a similar story. Austin Robinson, for example, in addition to his work on the balance of payments and export surpluses, was deeply involved at various times in 1940–1 in studying the raw material controls. He kept an eye on non-ferrous metals at the beginning of 1940, prepared a report on timber in February 1940 for the Survey, and did further work on the controls in June–July 1940, March–May 1941, and at the end of 1941,

---

9 The report is in EP(M)(40)93, 14 November 1940; and the discussion of it in EP(M)(40)20M, 21 November 1940, in PRO CAB 72/5 and CAB 72/3 respectively.

10 LPC(40)55, Report of the Committee on Warehousing, 5 December 1940, in PRO CAB 71/1.

when he prepared lengthy reports on the purposes of the controls and the problems that would arise over decontrol.[11] In the middle of 1940 he was involved, with Norman Chester, in work for Attlee, then Lord Privy Seal, on family allowances and the feeding of schoolchildren.[12] Then came export surpluses and the document for Stettinius. In the second half of 1940 he was also joint secretary of the Economic Policy Committee.

He, too, made visits to other parts of the country, sometimes to visit the controls, and sometimes on a special assignment. For example, in May 1941 he went to the Isle of Wight to investigate what could be done to reduce the dependence of local factories (Saunders-Roe, White of Cowes, and others) on a single source of electric power that was vulnerable to air attack. A month or so later he was in South Wales trying to assess the contribution to munitions production that might be expected from concentration of the tin-plate industry and the release of skilled manpower with metallurgical experience. Later that year he was on a committee on methods of ordering and another on the protection of buildings and plant from air attack. He was also involved in discussions on fuel rationing in the summer of 1941 and, at an earlier stage, made a study of electricity requirements and the danger of a shortage of electric power, particularly in regions where munitions production was growing fast. The heavy forgings required for new power-stations were needed also for munitions production and the dilemma this created needed careful consideration.[13] This list of the topics he covered is far from complete and omits a wide range of short notes on manpower, wages, and other subjects, but conveys an accurate impression of the multiplicity of his interests and activities.

## Later years: 1942–5

What has been described so far relates almost entirely to the years 1940–1. In the later years of the war under Lionel Robbins, the Section

11 EC(S)(41)48, 'Pre-war and wartime government controls over the economic system', 13 December 1941, revised later, on 29 April 1942, and circulated as EC(S)(42)15; EC(S)(42)13, 'The problem of controls over the economic system during the post-war transition', 21 April 1942.

12 EGS(40)8, 'Family allowances', brief prepared for Lord Snell, 3 September 1940; EGS(40)2, 'Feeding of schoolchildren in wartime', minute to the Lord Privy Seal (C. Attlee) by F. Hemming, 18 June 1940. Both of these are in PRO CAB 72/24.

13 He also drew the conclusion that it would be unwise to bomb German power-stations for fear of provoking retaliation in kind.

functioned much as before. Its membership changed and its work changed too as the war progressed. But its role in Whitehall and its method of work were well established by the time Robbins took over from Jewkes in September 1941.

This roughly coincided with a major change in atmosphere and prospects. When the Section began it had been in the middle of the 'phoney war', when there was cause enough for anxiety since mobilization for war was painfully slow. There had followed a series of disasters in a matter of months, leaving Britain alone to face the blitz and possible invasion. For a year there seemed little prospect of gaining the upper hand. As the armed forces expanded, the shortage of dollars and shipping space became more acute and the need to curtail civilian consumption more urgent. Then in 1941, although military disasters were far from over, a series of events – the introduction of Lend–Lease and the entry of the Soviet Union into the war in June and the United States in December – transformed the outlook and made it possible to look forward with confidence to eventual victory.

With these events, one might have expected economic policy-making to become somewhat more relaxed and base itself on a longer and more considered view. There is not much evidence of this. It is true that the Section devoted a good deal of time and effort to post-war problems. But this had already been true in 1941. Durbin wanted papers on economic and social reconstruction as early as October 1940.[14] By February 1941 Jewkes, Robbins, Durbin, Meade, and Austin Robinson were all circulating papers on the subject; and a month or so later Durbin and Meade were each preparing drafts on 'The prevention of general unemployment'.[15] Keynes had already circulated a draft on war aims and by the end of 1941 he and others were actively engaged in discussions on the post-war treatment of Germany, a subject to which the Economic Section gave much thought from 1942 onwards.[16] By the middle of 1941 the Board of Trade, too, had prepared a paper on economic reconstruction, which was discussed in the Economic Section in July. In the second half of the year Chester was at work on the Beveridge Report and Austin Robinson on a long survey of wartime controls and their future in the transition to a peacetime economy.

14 His 'Note on the work of the division' is dated 14 October and was in substance repeated in ES(S)(40)2, 'Subjects for urgent enquiry', on 4 November 1940 (PRO T 230/12).
15 The papers are all in PRO T 230/13.
16 See Cairncross, Sir Alec (1986) *The Price of War*, Oxford: Basil Blackwell, chapter 2.

Although interest in post-war problems was not new, in the later years of the war, a far higher proportion of the discussion papers produced by the Section focused on the post-war world. The proportion grew from less than a quarter in 1941 to over a half in 1942 and 1943 (nearly all in the latter year on full employment). In 1944 nearly all the papers were on post-war problems. We need not suppose that this accurately reflects how the Section spent its time. They had plenty of urgent wartime business to attend to. But the problems of the post-war world received a great deal of attention; and, since they have more interest for those who live in the post-war world than the problems that disappeared with the war, we discuss the Section's contribution at some length. We do so first in relation to employment and social policy in chapter 6 and then in chapter 7 in relation to the proposals for new international institutions that led to the setting up of the IMF and IBRD after the war and the negotiation of the General Agreement on Tariffs and Trade. Later, in chapter 19, we return briefly to wartime discussions of a third group of problems associated with wages, prices, and the danger of inflation.

If, for the time being, we set aside post-war problems, what chiefly occupied the Section in wartime from 1941 onwards? The short answer is: briefs for the Lord President. One important task was the preparation of the 'quarterly' surveys discussed in chapter 11. The Section also maintained its interest in the use of scarce resources: manpower, raw materials, shipping, and foreign exchange.

Of these, particular regard was paid to manpower, which had become in effect the currency of wartime planning. When the Manpower Committee was set up in November 1943 to deal with the allocation of civilian manpower, with Anderson (now Chancellor of the Exchequer) in the chair, the Economic Section was very much involved, Tress acting as joint secretary along with Norman Brook and Dennison doing much of the briefing both of the chairman and of Brook.[17] Interest in manpower also extended from employment to wages and from wages to prices and national income. It goes without saying that the interest in all of these was quantitative since in nearly every direction the issues presented themselves in quantitative form and could be handled sensibly only with up-to-date statistics.

As Director, Robbins was consulted on a wide variety of problems. He enjoyed the confidence of Sir John Anderson and this helped to consolidate the Section's position as the Lord President's professional

17 See, for example, 'Allocation of civilian manpower for industry and armed forces, groups II and III', in PRO T 230/91.

advisers. He was also on good terms with Richard Law, Minister of State in the Foreign Office, and kept in touch with the Foreign Office, which turned to him on occasion for advice. Robbins took a prominent part in the Hot Springs Conference in 1943, the Washington talks later in the year and the Bretton Woods Conference in 1944. After handing over to Meade, he joined Keynes for the Loan Negotiations in 1945.

As the son of a former President of the National Farmers' Union, he took a particular interest in the problems of agriculture and food throughout the war but often found himself in opposition to the Minister, Hudson, and the Permanent Secretary, Fergusson, who were both farmers and distrusted advice on their cherished industry from economists. 'Agriculture', Fergusson kept insisting, 'is a way of life, not an industry.' His ideal was 'a healthy and well-balanced agriculture', protected by import levies and restrictions and supported by subsidies – not a view likely to find favour with Robbins.

In dealing with food policy Robbins was assisted by Tress, while Mary Soutar acted as his personal assistant. One of Robbins's major achievements was to secure the introduction of points rationing for foodstuffs against strong opposition by the Ministry of Food. The officials responsible for food distribution were unable to grasp the case for points rationing or regarded the administrative difficulties as insuperable. Robbins, however, found allies within the department, including Ted Lloyd and above all John Wall, who was able in the end to persuade his colleagues to accept the scheme.[18]

So far as anyone took on the duties of administration of the Section, they were taken in hand by Stanley Dennison. But, then and later, members of the Section usually went their own way without much formal co-ordination. Dennison combined work on manpower problems with work on labour mobility, location of industry, and industrial problems generally, including monopoly policy and cartels. Latterly he had the assistance of John Wood, who joined the Section in 1944.

The Section retained its interest also in social policy. This covered food rationing, restaurant meals, housing, family allowances, and above all the social services. From the middle of 1941 until well into 1943 Chester was deeply involved in preparing, expounding, and defending the Beveridge Report. When Greenwood appointed Beveridge in May 1941 Jewkes suggested Chester as Secretary. It was a job to

18 For a full account, see Booth, Alan (1985) 'Economists and points rationing in the Second World War', *Journal of European Economic History* 14(2).

which he was ideally suited and his influence extended far beyond the Report itself. He played a major role behind the scenes in securing the acceptance of the main Beveridge proposals, in overcoming the Treasury's objections to their cost, and in briefing Morrison for the government statement of February 1943. The White Paper, when it appeared in September 1944, was '80 per cent pure Beveridge' and its proposals more, not less, costly than Beveridge's.[19]

Chester by no means confined himself to the social services. He was interested in many other subjects, including price control, compensation for war damage, and coal transport, and represented the Section on committees dealing with raw materials and building.

The Beveridge Report brought renewed interest in national accounting since it raised the question of how much the country would be able to afford in social welfare after the war. This in turn drew attention to the importance for policy of economic forecasting. The Economic Section took a continuing interest in the subject from 1942 onwards as it did in the post-war balance of payments. In July 1943 Tress circulated estimates and later helped Meade to draft one of the first papers to deal with the general problem of forecasting in employment policy.[20] We deal with the development of the technique of economic forecasting in chapter 13.

Philip Chantler covered much the same group of problems as I had worked on earlier: the import programme, transport, fuel and power, raw materials. On these problems he had assistance from Tress.

The other members of the Section, Meade, Fleming, and Nita Watts, were largely engaged on external economic policy. Meade took a comprehensive view of policy, domestic and external, and was deeply involved in the White Paper on *Employment Policy*. But he was also the leading advocate of an international trade organization and, at the invitation of Percivale Liesching, spent some time in the Board of Trade in 1943 working on commercial policy proposals. He was also the Section's expert in advising on the commercial policy undertakings given by or sought from the United Kingdom in negotiations with the United States. He and his colleagues did not share the ministerial attachment to imperial preference and felt that it was a wasting asset likely to be of limited value after the war.

19 Chester, letter to Mrs Chester, 26 September 1944. For further discussion of the Beveridge Report, see chapter 6.
20 'Estimate of post-war national income', note by Mr Tress, EC(S)(43)13, 15 July 1943, in PRO T 230/15; 'Economic forecasting and employment policy', EC(S)(45)5, 2nd Revise, 21 April 1945, in PRO T 230/17.

Marcus Fleming had started out by working on shipping turn-round times and Nita Watts on balance of payments forecasts. Nita as a junior member of the Section, like Tress, Mary Soutar, and John Wood, worked for several of her colleagues: Austin Robinson, Norman Chester, and later Marcus Fleming. Both she and Fleming came to specialize on external economic policy and continued to do so after the war.

But, as we shall see, members of the Section saw no reason to stay for ever within their chosen parish. As Norman Chester once pointed out, to be successful in the Section you needed to show versatility and flexibility. You had also in his view to have the ability to absorb a mass of information and find a use for it, to have the gift of getting on with other people, and – so he claimed – to be a bit of a buccaneer.

# Chapter six

# THE ECONOMIC SECTION IN WARTIME: POST-WAR POLICY (1) INTERNAL

A very young recruit to the Economic Section in November 1941 was somewhat surprised that her first assignment was to assist two of her senior colleagues[1] in their attempt to estimate the post-war balance of payments – assuming that the war could end, satisfactorily, on 31 December 1943! In fact, a considerable amount of work on post-war problems, opportunities, and policies had got under way in the Section during 1941. In February, at the suggestion of Jewkes, Meade produced a paper for discussion within the Section outlining:

> four fundamental groups of problems needing urgent attention after the war:
>
> (A) the problem of unemployment;
> (B) the problem of assuring a reasonable national minimum standard of living to each citizen and of achieving an equitable distribution of the national income;
> (C) the problem of determining the forms of post-war industrial structure – free competition, self-government of industry and public control of industry; and
> (D) the problem of re-establishing trading and financial relations with the rest of the world.[2]

Although the main decisions under (C) were not taken until after the war – and in some cases on the basis of quite remarkably inadequate prior consideration – work under headings (A), (B), and (D)[3] was to

1 James Meade and Austin Robinson.
2 EC(S)(41)17, 'Economic reconstruction', 26 February 1941, in PRO T 230/13.
3 Point (D) is discussed in chapter 7.

occupy a significant share of the energies of the Economic Section, of some colleagues in other departments, and, eventually, of ministers during the following war years.[4]

## The problem of unemployment

James Meade soon followed his outline of post-war problems which would need 'urgent attention' with a paper on the prevention of unemployment;[5] and this, after discussion and minor revision within the Section, was submitted in November to the Committee on Post-war Internal Economic Problems (IEP).[6] The paper focused mainly on the contracyclical management of aggregate demand but it recognized the frictional and structural elements in total unemployment and briefly advocated measures to improve labour mobility, to encourage appropriate industrial location, and to discourage restrictive practices by both industrial managements and unions. A reconstruction boom was seen as the most likely condition immediately after the end of the war with the danger of depression following, particularly if the need to keep troops in Europe for some time would mean that demobilization and decline in munitions production coincided with the weakening of reconstruction demands. The paper then developed general principles of, and suggestions for, demand management; it noted the actions likely to be needed in the immediate post-war years but did not attempt any very detailed examination of problems specific to this period.

This does not mean, however, that such problems were of no interest to the Section. Work on a number of issues was going on and

---

4 A ministerial Committee on the Economic Aspects of Reconstruction was set up in October 1941 and replaced, with no change in its terms of reference, by the Committee on Reconstruction Priorities in February 1942. It was charged with arranging for the preparation of 'practical schemes of reconstruction' which would produce 'a social and economic structure designed to secure equality of opportunity and service, among all classes of the community'. It was also charged to prepare 'a scheme for a post-war European and World system, with a particular regard to the economic needs of the various nations and to the problems of adjusting the free life of small countries in a durable international order'. An official interdepartmental Committee on Post-war Internal Economic Problems was also set up in October 1941, with the Economic Section represented.

5 EC(S)(41)22, 'The prevention of general unemployment', in PRO T 230/13.

6 'Internal measures for the prevention of general unemployment', IEP(41)3, in PRO CAB 87/54.

Stanley Dennison was already a member of an informal interdepartmental 'Resettlement Group' working on such questions as the size of
the post-war labour force, speed of demobilization, reconversions and
reopening of factories for civilian production, etc. Other papers put to
the IEP Committee by the Section also dealt with action in the
immediate post-war years, e.g. suggestions that sales of government
surplus stock be timed so as to dampen any boom or be held off the
market if a slump threatened.[7]

The list of useful long-term policy measures in IEP(41)3 included
monetary policy, though with an expression of scepticism – which
remained a characteristic of the Section throughout most of its history
– about its effectiveness 'if unaccompanied by other measures'.[8]
Contracyclical phasing of public investment, based on advance
planning of a stock of potential capital works and financial and
administrative arrangements permitting flexible implementation, was
advocated together with consideration of additional means for
influencing private investment at home and, possibly, works overseas.
Consumer expenditure could be influenced by hire-purchase controls,
by variations in income tax and indirect taxes, or through the variation
of 'direct money allowances by the State to consumers'; it was
suggested that the system of deferred income tax credits (in the latest
budget proposals) might be extended into peacetime, taxpayers
accumulating tax credits in good years which could be repaid in a
depression.

The implications for budgetary policy were clear: 'debt must be
incurred in years of depression; whereas in periods of active trade,
when revenue is increased and state expenditure is contracted, debt
may be repaid'. However, the paper expressed concern that the greatly
increased national debt to be expected as a consequence of the war
might involve, even with low interest rates, an interest burden that
would require tax rates that might themselves depress business
enterprise and employment. However, needs to reduce the burden of
debt but also to stimulate activity by reducing taxation might be
reconciled, first, by 'a moderately rising trend of prices and money
incomes', which would reduce the real burden of debt and, second, by
a once-for-all capital levy or some new form of tax 'imposed on and
paid out of individuals' capital assets' rather than out of income. A

7 IEP(41)11 in PRO CAB 87/54.
8 Though at a later stage the Section view appeared to be that interest rates might
  well play a useful part in checking an investment boom, however ineffective as
  a sole stimulus to recovery from recession (see p. 78).

somewhat naïve belief was expressed that such a tax would 'not reduce the demand for consumption goods'.

While the Section did 'not advocate attempts to reduce general unemployment by variations in the general level of wages', it did recognize that wage flexibility might help particularly depressed industries or areas and also warned against the danger of wage inflation as a threat to attempts to increase demand and employment: 'A wage policy which refrains from insisting upon rapidly rising wages, except in so far as increases in productivity permit, is . . . a necessary condition for a successful effort to prevent [general] unemployment.'

Finally, the paper noted the difficulty the UK would encounter if it were alone in attempting to expand internal demand when other countries were wallowing in economic depression. To counter the threat to the balance of payments, the UK might be obliged to restrict imports or to depreciate the exchange value of sterling. It was 'of the utmost importance to achieve international co-operation in the planning and timing of national monetary, budgetary and investment policies for the control of trade fluctuations'.

The IEP Committee 'generally approved' this paper but there is little indication in its minutes of any deep discussion. A suggestion from Sir Frank Tribe (Ministry of Labour) that the Committee should try to discover what public works 'could be brought into operation at a few weeks notice should there be a bad unemployment slump, when the war ends' might be seen as reinforcement. However, his further request does not suggest a deep understanding:

> Could some economist or body of economists advise us whether our post-war policy should be in the direction of reducing the number of persons available for employment to the minimum in order to avoid unemployment . . or should we aim at maximum employment in order to secure maximum production and particularly maximum exports?[9]

Papers circulated within the Section during the three to four months between the drafting of James Meade's paper and submission to the IEP Committee reveal differences of emphasis rather than any serious disagreement. Evan Durbin advocated influencing consumer demand directly by variations in taxation rather than relying on the indirect stimulus of public works. James Meade suggested that, provided that family allowances became general, labour mobility might be encouraged by differential rates of unemployment benefit – the higher rate

9 IEP(41)6, letter to Secretary of Committee, in PRO CAB 87/54.

conditional on the acceptance of any vacancy or training offered, the state bearing any removal costs, and subject to the offered wage being above some stated minimum. This clearly did not command sufficient acceptance by his colleagues for it to go any further.

It is interesting to note that the Section did not at this stage put forward any quantitative estimate – in the context of discussion of employment policy – of the level to which unemployment might be restricted. However, in another context – estimating the likely post-war national income and levels of trade – Section members were taking 5 per cent unemployment as their assumption (see p. 88), though in illustrating the balancing over time of a social security scheme with contracyclical variations in contribution rates they took 5 per cent as the minimum level and 8 per cent as the average at which the scheme would balance – an illustration which persisted right into the eventual *Employment Policy* White Paper.

Within the Treasury, most senior officials, including among them Sir Hubert Henderson, seem to have been concentrating their attention on the immediate post-war years and to have been taking a generally pessimistic view of employment prospects.[10] By May 1942, Sir Richard Hopkins had clearly not been persuaded of the practicability or effectiveness of contracyclical investment or taxation policies and did not envisage that a budget deficit would ever be incurred deliberately. This he made plain in reacting to a suggestion from Henry Clay (in the Board of Trade) that too much emphasis was being placed on public works rather than cutting taxation while maintaining government expenditures and covering the deficit by borrowing 'from the public if possible but if necessary . . . from the banks'. However, S. D. Waley took a far more sympathetic view:

> I hope that the war which kills so much will kill the superstition that there is any object in balanced budgets. Our object is that there should be enough purchasing power to secure full employment, but that beyond this point purchasing power should not be increased, so as to avoid inflation . . . when we . . . are running into the danger of deflation it will be desirable to reduce taxation and to speed up works of all kinds.[11]

Maynard Keynes was in touch with the Section's thinking on

10 IEP(42)21 'Purchasing power and consumer goods', in PRO CAB 87/56, and Keynes, J. M. (1980) *Collected Writings*, vol. 27, Cambridge: Cambridge University Press, p. 299.
11 PRO T 160/1407/F18876.

employment policy, as on other matters (he asked in May 1942 to be put on the circulation list for all EC(S) papers).[12] He was generally in sympathy with the Section approach but he was also rather doubtful about the usefulness of measures to influence consumer expenditure[13] and thus rather averse to using changes in normal taxation and deficits on the current budget; public capital expenditure was his preferred tool.[14]

Although the Section persisted for some time in advocating contracyclical taxation and budgetary policies, James Meade was also devising in the early months of 1942 a scheme for variations in social security contributions, intended to be presented to the Beveridge Committee on Social Insurance (see pp. 87ff.).[15] This was seen as having advantages over variations in tax rates in that, once the scheme was approved in principle, weekly rates of contributions could be varied almost overnight by simple ministerial decision or – in the scheme as eventually developed – automatically in relation to the unemployment percentage. Meade was thinking of quarterly changes, if necessary, and this contrasted with the delays inevitable if, as was then assumed, tax rates could be changed only in an annual Finance Act, with some further delay before they took effect.

Keynes was initially somewhat sceptical about this idea also;[16] but he was very soon converted and remained a convinced, and for some time lone, supporter within the Treasury. Largely because of Treasury worries about the financial implications of Beveridge's proposals as a whole, it was eventually agreed that the Section's scheme should not be included in the Beveridge Report but should be put forward in the continuing discussions on employment policy. At this stage, as later, the scheme envisaged variations in both employers' and employees' contributions, though both the Section and Keynes thought the former likely to be less useful than the latter; but the Section appears to have thought that variations affecting both parties would be politically more acceptable than one concentrated on employees's contributions alone.[17] Both at this time and later, some members of the Section were slightly

12 Keynes, op. cit., p. 207.
13 ibid., 'One can prevent perhaps an aggravation of the falling off in effective demand following a fall in investment by stabilizing consumption but that is the best one can hope for.'
14 ibid., pp. 278ff.
15 EC(S)(42)14 in PRO T 230/14, and later EC(S) papers.
16 Keynes, op. cit., p. 207.
17 ibid., pp. 208–19 and 308–13.

uneasy about advocating the use of what was, effectively, a poll-tax on all the employed. Inevitably this would vary the incomes of the poorest employees more than those of the richer; on the other hand this, in itself, tended to make the impact on consumers' expenditure all the greater.

By late 1942, the Section was urging the importance of further action on post-war employment policy, not least because of the interest generated by the Beveridge *Report on Social Insurance*, and the ministerial Committee on Reconstruction Priorities (PR) at its fourth meeting in 1943 requested from the Section a study of measures that might be taken with a view to realizing Assumption C in the Beveridge Report (i.e. full employment). A draft was sent to Keynes in March with a note from Lionel Robbins indicating that it was

> written specifically for Ministers, not for Civil Servants or Economists. . . . We have been told to assume that the subject is of such intense political interest that Ministers will be prepared to read right through a document that is rather longer than usual.[18]

Keynes's reply made two, linked, points of substance: put more emphasis on the 'multiplier' and stress the need for early action if a slump threatens, 'much less effort is required to prevent the ball rolling than would be required to stop it rolling once it has started'. He also found the draft 'terribly indigestible . . . I should like to offer a prize for any minister who reads it through without his attention wandering. Possibly John Anderson would win it but there would be no *proxime accessit*'.[19]

A further point raised in discussion with James Meade was the possible desirability of dividing the budget into separate current and capital budgets – to which Meade's attitude depended entirely on whether this would make easier or more difficult the unbalancing of the current budget if this was necessary to stimulate consumers' expenditure. Keynes, however, again reiterated his doubts about whether an intentionally temporary cut in taxation could effectively stimulate consumers' expenditure and, if it did, whether it would be politically practicable to raise taxes again as employment rose. However, he still supported variations in social security contributions, partly because a more automatic scheme would face fewer political difficulties and partly because it would not involve the 'huge time lag' before income tax changes could become effective. But now and later he also stressed that 'it is better for all of us that periods of deficiency

18 Robbins to Keynes, 11 March 1943, in PRO T 230/66.
19 Keynes, op. cit., p. 316.

expenditure should be made the occasion of capital development until our economy is much more saturated with capital goods than it is at present'.[20]

Within the Section, some differences of view appeared as Meade's paper went through successive drafts. Ronald Tress thought that there was a tendency to exaggerate the possibility of varying public investment expenditures and saw objections to deferring socially desirable public sector projects to make room for a private investment boom; he suggested more emphasis on stabilization of private sector expenditure by tax variation and special credits to stimulate investment by small firms in time of depression, a speeding up of investment in colonial development in such times, and the possible use of internal buffer stock schemes and encouragement of long-term labour contracts. Norman Chester suggested that the stabilization (rather than variation) of public expenditure might be considered if this – as he expected – was to be a large proportion of post-war national expenditure. Variation might be 'like wagging the dog to keep its tail straight'.[21]

The Section's paper as submitted to the PR Committee[22] introduced at an early stage, and elaborated later, two 'assumptions' and one desideratum essential to a national full employment policy relying mainly on the regulation of aggregate demand. The former were 'a reasonable degree of mobility' of labour and 'the absence of monopolistic price raising and the prevalence of reasonable stability in the general wage level', and the desideratum was international arrangements helping to stabilize world demand and to ensure that a country was not prevented by balance of payments problems from pursuing a full employment policy. It is interesting that the explanation of the second 'assumption', which virtually reappears in the 1944 White Paper, is that 'If an increase in aggregate money demand is taken out either in increased prices or in higher wages, then clearly the increase of employment may be frustrated.' There is a warning of the danger of a 'vicious spiral' if this assumption is not realized and of the necessity to 'impose some limitation upon the rate at which wage rates might be raised' if voluntary restraint should be inadequate to permit full employment without serious inflation. But nowhere in either paper is the danger of wage-cost inflation specifically linked with the balance of payments, though future competitiveness was already a concern (see also chapter 19).

20 Keynes, op. cit., pp. 317–20.
21 Notes, 17 and 18 March 1943, in PRO T 230/66.
22 PR(43)26, 'The maintenance of employment', 18 May 1943, in PRO CAB 87/13.

The possible need is mentioned 'either to lower money costs or the value of sterling' if falling demand for UK exports should threaten unemployment; but the main emphasis in the section on 'International demand' is on the need for any post-war international commercial or financial agreements to 'provide some latitude for adjustments of the rate of exchange and, as a temporary expedient, for the restriction of imports, when these are required to defend the balance of payments', together with advocacy of international buffer stock schemes for primary products and rather faint hopes of international arrangements which might at least prevent international flows of long-term capital from varying so as to intensify recession and which might also co-ordinate national demand management policies.

Turning to internal policies, 'if private investment requires to be controlled in a restrictive sense monetary policy can be fully effective' but to encourage a revival from deep depression an expansionist monetary policy is 'an indispensable condition' but not likely to be sufficient; possible tax incentives for investment and new public finance corporations to ease access to credit are briefly mentioned. But manipulation of public sector investment – requiring an extension of government influence over local authorities, public utilities, etc. – is seen as the more powerful weapon, though difficulties in timing activities solely in the interest of employment policy are recognized. Although the word is nowhere used, an assumption of a 'multiplier' of 2 (somewhat below Keynes's own estimate)[23] is obvious from the examples given of the effect of a change in investment expenditure.

The major difference from the Section's earlier (IEP) paper is in the section on 'The Control of Consumption'. The only reference to 'direct attempts to influence consumption via taxes and subsidies of the ordinary type' is that they 'take time to work out and may well involve political difficulty and friction'. The stress is now all on employers' and employees' social security contributions varying automatically with changes in the unemployment percentage. A suggested alternative or complement is the continuation of deferred income tax credits as a normal post-war measure, and control of hire-purchase terms is also suggested as a minor supplement.

Consistently with this change, the earlier acceptance of budget deficits now becomes far more tentative: 'All that is suggested at this stage is that . . . there are grounds for regarding the appropriate period for budgetary balancing as being longer than the traditional year.' The possibility of separate current and capital budgets is advanced

23 Keynes, op. cit., pp. 312 and 392.

very tentatively and that of a capital levy, if there should be undue growth of the national debt, so tentatively as to make it virtually unrecognizable.

While the Section was genuinely conscious of the problem of timing tax changes so as to produce the desired effects, there is no doubt that this change of emphasis was largely attributable to its belief that advocacy of contracyclical changes in tax rates and of any major change in traditional budget-balancing principles would be strongly opposed by senior Treasury officials (and some ministers) and would get only lukewarm support – if any – from Keynes. But they could rely on Keynes's energetic support for the social security scheme, even though he clearly felt that the most important policy measures should be directed to reversing or, better, forestalling any threatening decline in investment.

As earlier, the Section devoted some attention to measures to deal specifically with structural unemployment – removal of restrictive practices on both sides of industry, better training and other aids to labour mobility, consideration of some control over industrial location (the last also a very tentative suggestion). Finally a short section on the immediate post-war problems made it plain that this period would have to be one of restraint of home demand, even in the face of rising unemployment consequent upon rapid demobilization and decline of munitions production.

The circulation of this paper touched off some violent reactions within the Treasury. Sir Richard Hopkins minuted the Chancellor: 'The Economic Section's paper, unlike all their other products, is a bad paper, academic, misleading and dangerous.' Other Treasury knights also raised objections: to the social security scheme, in that forecasting difficulties might mean that the fund would run unmanageable deficits; to the idea that the unemployment problem could be anything other than structural.[24] But the major explosion came from Sir Hubert Henderson. He argued against any attempt to maintain demand for capital goods at what was likely to be an abnormally high immediate post-war level (which neither the Section nor Keynes had in fact proposed), and spelt out the difficulty of bringing about a major change in the pattern of final demand towards a larger share for consumption without heavy unemployment in the transition. He saw 'public works' as a useful but minor palliative. He objected to tax cuts and a consequent budget deficit, or to unbalancing a social security

24 26 May 1943, PRO T 161/1168/S 52098, which also includes notes by Eady and Gilbert.

fund, on the grounds that definition of years when surpluses were appropriate would be difficult, both in terms of economic analysis and politically, and also that increasing consumers' spendable incomes could not be guaranteed to increase consumer spending significantly. A better means of increasing demand for consumer goods could be state operation of buffer stock schemes for such goods, not only increasing orders to manufacturers as depression threatened but also selling on to the public at specially low prices to encourage consumer spending.[25]

Keynes and James Meade both attempted to remove the misunderstanding about the need for a switch towards consumer goods production in the transition to normal post-war activity. The latter also stressed the importance of the lowest practicable level of interest rates both to encourage an extended period of, *inter alia*, housing demand and also to ease the interest burden on the budget, which could also be reduced by 'a really serious capital levy' after the end of the war, and he urged the practicability and likely efficiency of variations in taxation and social security contributions.[26] Keynes, rather curiously, doubted whether 'much is to be hoped from proposals to offset unforeseen short-period fluctuations in investment by stimulating short-period changes in consumption' but nevertheless saw 'very great attraction and practical advantage' in the social security scheme.[27]

The circulation within the Treasury of Henderson's and Keynes's memoranda produced a note from Sir Wilfrid Eady which illustrates one of the problems confronting both the Section and Keynes – the inability or unwillingness of some senior officials to understand the issues under discussion. Eady described Keynes's note as 'a voyage in the stratosphere for most of us'. He added that the Treasury would be asking ministers first to consider policies for the post-war transition in detail before starting to look at 'the next phase. You will find your official colleagues obtuse, bat-eyed and obstinate on much of this.'[28]

Henderson's idea for a domestic buffer stock scheme seems not to have received any further attention, though, within the Section, Marcus Fleming and Norman Chester thought that it had great attractions – quick effect and the advantage, in a short-lived recession, of keeping people employed in their accustomed trades; and, unlike the

25 PRO T 230/66, 21 May 1943, published with little change in Clay, H. (ed.) (1955) *The Inter-war Years and Other Papers*, Oxford: Clarendon Press.
26 Meade to Henderson, 25 May 1943, PRO T 230/66.
27 Keynes, op. cit., p. 323.
28 Keynes, op. cit., p. 325.

social security scheme, it would not involve variations in the incomes of those still in employment.[29]

When the Section's paper came to the PR Committee, Eady's earlier promise of the Treasury attitude was fulfilled. The Chancellor (Kingsley Wood) argued that it 'went too far in the direction of treating unemployment as a single problem for which one solution could be found' and added that he 'did not wish to be understood as accepting the assumptions or conclusions of the memorandum'. He also submitted a paper which attempted to postpone discussion:

> we have little hope of establishing conditions in which any long-term policy for the maintenance of employment can hope to be successful if we do not get the position of the first three years [after the end of the war] quite sound.

The Home Secretary (Morrison) and President of the Board of Trade (Dalton) expressed general support for the Section's approach and the former pressed for immediate consideration of it, the Committee having had the problems of the transition under consideration for the past twelve months and being generally agreed on the economic policies necessary for that period.[30]

The disagreement among ministers was resolved, temporarily, by setting up a steering committee of officials under Sir Richard Hopkins, with Lionel Robbins as a member and Norman Chester as one of its secretaries, to pursue further the issues so far raised and to produce a new report. They were given certain specific questions to be covered: location of industry; mobility of labour and structural unemployment; control and timing of public and private investment; regulation of consumption; restrictive practices by employers. It was stated that the Economic Section was to be associated with all the work and the committee was to concentrate on 'normal' post-war conditions, though it could note transition problems also.[31]

In the interval before the committee started work, Keynes continued to try to argue Eady, in particular, into a more reasonable attitude; and either his influence or the remitting of the issues to the Steering Committee succeeded in preventing the Chancellor's sending a negative and muddle-headed additional paper to the PR Committee.[32]

29 Note by J. M. Fleming, 4 June 1943, in PRO T 230/66.
30 PR(43), minutes of 11th meeting, and PR(43)28 and 30, in PRO CAB 87/13.
31 PR(43)37, 13 July 1943, in PRO CAB 87/13.
32 'Maintenance of employment', draft memorandum by the Chancellor of the Exchequer (undated but probably early July 1943), in PRO T 230/66, and Keynes, op. cit., pp. 352–61.

Keynes was concerned mainly to prevent the Treasury's revealing a total misunderstanding of the issues and of the Section's arguments, and to prevent their dismissing all ideas of overall demand management on the grounds that all unemployment would be 'structural',[33] to insist that they must be willing to stimulate either investment or consumption (or both) when depression threatened, and to defend the main policy measures advocated by the Section. He argued for a separate capital budget as the basis for management of investment but, for the first time, added:

> about other forms of deficit financing [than the social security scheme] I am inclined to lie low because I am sure that, if serious unemployment does develop, deficit financing is absolutely certain to happen, and I should like to keep free to object hereafter to the more objectionable forms of it.[34]

In general, he urged that the Treasury should not give the impression that it 'would much rather be found drowned than learn to swim'.

The Steering Committee agreed at once not to fix a target figure for unemployment but agreed that the 8½ per cent used by Beveridge as the basis for his proposed social insurance fund should be regarded 'as a maximum figure non-attainment of which would be regarded in any normal conditions as very unsatisfactory'.[35] Their subsequent proceedings show the Board of Trade (where Hugh Gaitskell was interested) coming strongly to the Section's support on the general principle of managing aggregate demand and insisting that, if this is effective, the structural unemployment problem will be minimized; and they went further than the Section had recently done (in writing) in demolishing the Treasury's arguments against deficit financing, though the Section now again strengthened its arguments.[36] Lionel Robbins also had again to counter the Treasury's misunderstanding, or deliberate misrepresentation, of the Section's arguments about 'stabilization' of investment demand, as well as trying to explain to Sir Wilfrid Eady that encouragement of company saving (which the latter appeared willing to encourage by tax incentives) was not identical with encouragement of company spending on investment.

33 Eady had argued that this had been the case even in the inter-war years except in 1931–3.
34 Keynes to Eady, in Keynes, op. cit., p. 353.
35 EC(43), 2nd meeting, in PRO T 230/71.
36 See particularly EC(43)9, 10, 12 and 14, in PRO T 230/72, and EC minutes in PRO T 230/71.

But the Treasury's determination to hold interest rates down during the post-war transition was accepted by the Section, with warnings that this would mean that physical controls, and possibly direct control of bank finance, would be required to restrain investment demand in that period. For longer-term control of investment demand, the Section elaborated more detailed proposals – to build up a stock of public sector projects, releasing grants for local authority projects according to the state of demand and conditional on an appropriate starting date; monetary and fiscal incentives for private investment as necessary – and again had support from the Board of Trade for fiscal measures to stimulate re-equipment and modernization.

However, the Section's and Board of Trade's views clashed on other aspects of industrial policy. The Board advocated various bodies – an industrial commission and boards for individual industries – to promote industrial efficiency through research and training and to promote industrial concentration. These suggestions obviously aroused all Lionel Robbins's fears of industrial restrictive practices – shared indeed by his colleagues in the Section – and he was also careful to insist that measures to control location and assist depressed areas should, so far as possible, be such as to make obvious the costs of the sacrifice of efficiency.

Earlier discussions within the Section had shown Robbins particularly averse to any measures tending to distort – rather than simply stabilize – demand. A suggestion from Ronald Tress for temporary subsidies for industries suffering a sudden fall in export demand was dismissed on the grounds that it would be politically impossible to make such help genuinely temporary, and that it would provoke retaliation; and Marcus Fleming's suggestion of domestic buffer stocks for cotton piece-goods and coal seems to have received no support. Fleming also suggested lower social security contributions by employers in the depressed area industries; but this too seems to have been dismissed.[37]

The Steering Committee's report to ministers[38] laid main emphasis on the 'management of aggregate demand' approach to employment policy – though with some qualifications, recognizing structural problems and the special position of exporting industries. There was some emphasis on the need for early action to check any tendency for decline, and reference to international conditions reflected the state of thinking on policy in that field (see chapter 7). In discussing investment, a 3 per cent interest rate was not seen as an irreducible

37 PRO T 230/67.
38 R(44)6, 11 January 1944, PRO CAB 87/70.

(post-transition) minimum, and subsidies to private investment in housing and industrial re-equipment were rather tentatively suggested; on public investment, the Section's suggestions for rolling five-year programmes and varying grants were endorsed, and illustrative figures again implied a 'multiplier' of 2. To influence consumption, the only measure given any prominence was now the social security scheme, operating automatically in relation to the unemployment percentage. But there were also warnings of its dangers if structural unemployment should be the main cause of a rise in total unemployment; it should not be introduced in 'the confused conditions likely to obtain in the immediate post-war years' and the majority of the Committee recommended endorsement in principle but no legislation until the appropriate time for its introduction. On budgetary considerations the report trod a tightrope: the problem was not likely to be serious, with rising national income, but a rising interest burden could mean undesirably high tax rates; ultimately

> we desire to emphasise our view that the maintenance of Budget equilibrium must be regarded as one of the principal objectives of policy. This does not mean a rigid policy of balancing the Budget each year regardless of the state of trade. . . . if policies recommended in this report are acted upon, a year to year balance is not to be looked for.

The report emphasized the need for reasonable wage and price stability, and envisaged the possibility of centralized wage fixing, though only if all other methods of assuring wage rises not greatly exceeding the growth of productivity broke down. It also saw control of monopoly as essential and gently encouraged ministers also to express some disapproval of trade unions' restrictive practices. But Lionel Robbins parted company with the rest of the Committee on the former topic and produced a note of dissent which is a trumpet call for free competition.

The majority of the Committee recommended registration of restrictive agreements, with the Board of Trade enpowered to impose penalties if, after examination by an independent body, an agreement was found to be contrary to the public interest. Combines and very large firms might be similarly examined and the Board of Trade given power to fix prices of monopolized products. Robbins thought the first proposal both impracticable, given the hundreds of such agreements, and dangerous in that any agreement not specifically condemned would be given respectability. He recommended the definite banning of 'the more obnoxious restrictive practices' (boycotts, predatory price discrimination, etc.), establishing a set of principles to govern the licensing of others, and a reform of those laws which tended to foster monopolistic practices. Powers to control monopolies, including price control, were necessary, and 'where competition is unthinkable' public ownership might be appropriate. But the public sector should be no more free than the private sector to indulge in restriction of output or investment.

Subsidiary points in the report – on immediate post-war problems, on labour mobility and industrial location policy – raised no new issues. It recommended two new institutions to help finance small businesses and industrial re-equipment, and it also recommended the collection and analysis of statistics needed for employment policy.

Keynes welcomed the report with what, in the light of his detailed comments, seems somewhat excessive enthusiasm, as 'an outstanding state paper'. But he thought that it somewhat understated the possibilities and importance of varying investment outlays; he also regretted that it recommended delaying legislation on the social insurance scheme and that it did not advocate prescribing, and varying, minimum down payments and maximum repayment periods for hire-purchase. He thought that the report offered a rich feast of 'budget humbug' and he also strongly supported Lionel Robbins's note of dissent on restrictive practices.[39]

Sir Hubert Henderson was not impressed. He suggested a shorter version of the report:

> Mix one teaspoonful of financial profligacy with three tablespoons of economic *laissez-faire*. Dilute liberally with verbal water, and add wishful thinking according to individual taste.
>
> *Note* This prescription is to be taken in the long run. The long run must not be confused with any period, however long, that is likely to occur.[40]

Ministerial reactions to the report included more enthusiastic support for some proposals than had been evinced by the official committee. They agreed that a White Paper must be prepared and that 'maintaining aggregate demand at a high level' must be 'in the forefront'. There was general support for the social insurance scheme and several ministers also supported variations in taxation to influence both consumption and private investment. There was some support for a continuation of deferred tax credits and 'a majority' of the

39 Keynes, op. cit., pp. 364–72.
40 Henderson to Eady, 13 December 1943, PRO T 161/1168/S 52098.

Reconstruction Committee agreed that budgets need not be balanced every year. Several ministers stressed the need for quick action if unemployment threatened to rise. They agreed that legislation on restrictive practices should be prepared (the President of the Board of Trade, Dalton, supporting Lionel Robbins's views on this) though disagreement later appeared to be reconciled by a decision to include only 'a brief and general reference' in the White Paper.[41]

Pressure to produce the White Paper soon intensified, as the government wished to publish before Sir William Beveridge reported on the same subject. Several members of the Section, and of the Treasury and Ministry of Reconstruction, were involved, while Norman Brook undertook the final editing.[42]

Within the Treasury, a fairly acrimonious argument continued between Keynes and Henderson, while other senior officials tried to whittle away any positive proposals which seemed likely to appear in the white paper. This was partly, though certainly not only, because they were still obsessed with the problems of the transition; as late as the end of March, Sir Richard Hopkins was urging the Chancellor that, 'The transitional period is what matters to people' and only brief remarks were appropriate on the 'golden age' that might follow.[43] Henderson had argued also that the proposed White Paper would shake confidence in sterling in the difficult conditions to be expected in the transition – an argument that was taken up enthusiastically by Eady, who wavered between protesting that we would soon be unable to buy imports for sterling, 'i.e. for a promissory note', if the White Paper shook overseas confidence, and objecting that the draft had nothing new on policy apart from the social security scheme.

Up to nearly the last minute it was uncertain how far the White Paper would go in contemplating unbalanced budgets or a continuation of tax credit arrangements. Pressed by Lord Cherwell, the Chancellor agreed on 10 May that both tax credits and hire-purchase regulation should be included among the policy measures that might be used. But Sir Cornelius Gregg (Inland Revenue) argued that deferred tax credits could be applied only to individuals, not to companies, and suggested instead a simple variation in current tax rates in the light of the employment situation. Sir Richard Hopkins's reply

41 R(44), 8th and later meetings, in PRO CAB 87/5.
42 It had just been arranged that the Section was to have direct access to the Minister of Reconstruction (Woolton) via Brook, EC(S)(44)6, in PRO T 230/16.
43 Notes, 28 March, 3 April, 2 May, in PRO T 161/1168/S 52099.

was that it would be 'extremely dangerous to hold out any idea of the acceptance of a principle that unemployment should be a ground for a Budget deficit and high employment a ground for a Budget surplus'. In the event, a very tentative mention of the possibility of deferred tax credits went into the White Paper (para. 72).[44]

The Section was not overtly involved in these final arguments, though trying to keep the drafts for the white paper as positive as possible. Once it was published, work continued, with Richard Stone, on the development of the necessary statistical basis for planning aggregate demand, on measures for influencing capital expenditure, etc.

A brief campaign became necessary in 1945–6 to ensure that the government took powers in the National Insurance Bill to vary social security contributions in the light of employment conditions and, despite Treasury opposition, enough ministers were in favour for this to be fairly readily agreed.

In the following years, 'full employment policy' became in practice indistinguishable from budgetary and monetary policies designed to reconcile full employment with control of inflation (see chapters 14–16); and, with experience, the concept of 'full employment' or a 'high and stable level of employment' itself changed. Whereas the Section in its wartime forecasts of post-war conditions had never assumed less than 5 per cent unemployment, the government's reply in 1951 to the UN Economic and Social Council's enquiry about the UK's 'full employment standard' stated 3 per cent as the endurable maximum, implying that expansionary action would be taken before that level was reached – a statement with which the Section had no quarrel. However, experience had also reinforced the Economic Section's concern with the problem of control of wage inflation in such conditions, a concern very widely shared by the time work began on a proposed (but never published) 'White Paper on full employment' in 1950. This issue is discussed further in chapter 19.

## The Beveridge Report on Social Insurance and Allied Services (Cmd 6404)

The Beveridge Committee, set up in June 1941 after considerable pressure on the government from the TUC and from individual MPs and others, became the focus for most of the Section's work on point

44 Cmd 6527, May 1944.

(B) of James Meade's 'four fundamental groups of problems' of the post-war future (see p. 70). The Committee, with Norman Chester as one of its secretaries, had originally been intended (by the government) to do no more than survey the existing social security schemes and to suggest ways of improving their administration, removing anomalies and possibly making other very minor improvements. However, it soon became clear that Sir William Beveridge intended to consider quite fundamental reforms of the whole social security system, which official members of his Committee could hardly either oppose or endorse without committing their ministers on questions of policy, rather than mere administration. In consequence, the civil service members now became officially technical advisers to the Chairman, who would be solely responsible for the eventual report.

The Committee involved a vast amount of work for Norman Chester – assisted at times by other members of the Section, particularly Mary Soutar – from the normal arranging for the hearing of evidence and preparation of necessary memoranda and statistics to protecting the Chairman from the attentions of fanatics who proposed to cure all the ills of society by some such device as obliging everybody to drink distilled water.

By December 1941 Beveridge had produced an outline of his proposals and the Section had been formally invited to 'express their views on the economic aspects [of these proposals] and, in particular, on the basis of the employers' contribution to schemes of social insurance'.[45] The written response (16 June 1942) concentrated on three main issues: (i) whether the proposals would 'involve a heavy or insupportable burden on the country's resources'; (ii) social security and mobility of labour; and (iii) social security and the volume of employment. The basis for the discussion under (i) was an estimate of the likely post-war national income and related taxable income, undertaken in collaboration particularly with Richard Stone in the CSO and with Maynard Keynes also taking an active interest; and this started an argument with the Treasury which continued intermittently for about two years (see pp. 91–4).

Several themes that were to reappear later in the discussions on employment policy and other issues appear in the Section's evidence to Beveridge. The importance of a high level of employment, defined as maximum unemployment of 5 per cent, is stressed and this is also a basic assumption underlying the Section's estimates of post-war national income. Consistently with this, alternatives are suggested to

45 PRO T 230/101 for this and subsequent papers.

the employers' social security contribution as a flat rate per person employed, i.e. a tax on employment. It is suggested that the adverse effects on demand for labour might be mitigated by making the contribution vary with the contract of service (lower for a monthly contract than for casual labour), by raising part of the contribution through a levy on profits rather than on employment and, possibly, by raising part of the necessary money by a dismissals charge on the employer (one of Beveridge's suggestions). In internal discussion within the Section several members had favoured the financing of social security entirely from general taxation, rather than by an inequitable poll-tax on individuals in employment combined with a tax on employment itself, while others had attached importance to maintaining the 'insurance principle'. In the formal submission to Beveridge both views are mentioned, with the case for some form of contributions reinforced by the reflection that in the early post-war transition years it might be easier to raise funds in this way than by general taxation.[46]

In the interests of increasing labour productivity and the size of the national income available to bear the social security 'burden' the Section hoped that precautions would be taken against malingering and abuse and that nothing would be done to 'enforce or encourage the retirement of old age pensioners from work', and noted that a 'better fed, better housed, better clothed and better educated population' would also be a more productive population. Universal family allowances were commended as tending to promote mobility of labour and the general incentive to work by widening the gap between wage income and unemployment benefit. Better training facilities, lodging allowances, and payment of removal costs were also advocated, as well as transferability of rights in occupational pension schemes.

Finally, as already mentioned (p. 75), the Section advocated a scheme for varying social security contributions by employers and employees, from the standard rate (as then proposed) when un-employment was 5 per cent or less to 'merely nominal rates' when

46 In a letter to James Meade (8 May 1942) Keynes had agreed that he too would prefer to finance social security out of general taxation but that it would be necessary to keep a contribution system 'at any rate in the first stages of the new scheme in order that the additional charges on the Budget may not look altogether too formidable'. But he also liked the idea of the dismissals charge. He expressed some scepticism about the Section's scheme for varying contributions though, as noted above, he later became an enthusiastic advocate of it (Keynes, op. cit., p. 206).

unemployment was 10 per cent or more, in the interests of contra-cyclical stabilization of demand and employment. The detailed proposals appeared eventually in the White Paper on *Employment Policy*; but the principle of the scheme, outlined only in general terms, was commended by Beveridge in his report (para. 442).

On the basis of its projections of post-war national income and of then current estimates of the various likely increases in public expenditure, including social security, the Section suggested that 'total public expenditure in the early post-war years is likely to be some 32 per cent of total taxable incomes . . . about midway between the pre-war ratio of 25 per cent and the 1941 percentage of 40 per cent'. They neither endorsed this figure as easily bearable nor condemned it, but a capital levy was fairly clearly advocated as a way of reducing the budgetary burden of national debt interest and thus reducing any dangers of levels of taxation which would have adverse incentive effects.

The Treasury started to express doubts about the possibility of financing Beveridge's proposals almost as soon as these began to appear in their preliminary form, though they offered no paper (now or later) relating the estimated costs to taxable capacity or national income. Nevertheless some discussions between various Treasury knights, Keynes, and members of the Section took place, partly directed to reducing confusions in the minds of the former on, for example, the difference between the gross budgetary burdens and the net burdens after tax paid on benefits, national debt interest, etc. Rather surprisingly Sir Richard Hopkins appears momentarily to have seen the proposed social insurance contributions scheme as a fiction disguising what were in fact taxes; but a quick reaction by Keynes suggesting alternatives to these 'very bad' taxes immediately brought a reply from Hopkins saying that the scheme had better be considered on the basis of the traditional contributions system.[47]

In August 1942 an informal committee of Keynes, Lionel Robbins, and Sir George Epps (the Government Actuary) was set up to advise Beveridge on the financial implications of his proposals,[48] its main purpose being to see how far cost could be pruned by modifications that Beveridge could accept, *inter alia* by bringing the scheme into operation by stages. Although Beveridge had from the beginning worked on the basis that no more than 'subsistence level' benefits

47 Keynes, op. cit., pp. 223–8.
48 Keynes recorded the discussions of this group (see Keynes, op. cit., pp. 229–53).

would be provided, he did incorporate various savings into his scheme as published.

Between publication of the Beveridge report in December 1942 and the government's White Paper on *Social Insurance* (Cmd 6550) in 1944, the Section – and particularly Norman Chester – remained involved in interdepartmental discussions on the extent to which the proposals should be accepted, as well as keeping up a steady flow of briefs to the Lord President as the discussion moved on to ministerial level. So far as the balance of the scheme as a whole was concerned, the Section's view throughout was that, in terms of benefit to the economy, any conflict between provision for pensioners and provision for the young should be settled in favour of the latter. They were concerned that pension provisions which raised the living standards of pensioners inevitably meant that means had to be found to transfer real income earned by the working population on a scale increasing with the progressive ageing of the population; and they also pointed out, as often as the question arose, that family allowances could increase incentives to work and, together with health and education provision, would tend to raise the productivity of future working generations. Consistently with this attitude, they also advocated incentives to delay retirement. They also defended, against the majority of the official committee set up to advise ministers on the Beveridge Report, Beveridge's 'subsistence' basis for benefits, arguing that departure from this principle, given the political pressures to be expected, was more likely to increase than to reduce the costs to the budget.[49]

However, a major part of the Section's activity during the approximately two years of official and ministerial discussion was directed towards estimates of the post-war national income, and related taxable income, and the question whether Beveridge's proposals could be accommodated, together with other expected public sector demands, without an intolerable burden either on real resources or on the budget. In February 1943 the (ministerial) Reconstruction Priorities Committee formally asked the Treasury, Economic Section, and Central Statistical Office to agree estimates of the post-war national income as the basis for decisions on the social security proposals. The animated argument that followed – with Meade, Fleming, Chester, and Tress from the Section all involved together with Keynes, Henderson, and assorted Treasury officials, as well as Richard Stone in the CSO – produced abundant confusion and misunderstandings as well as genuine differences of view about the likely growth of national income

49 Various notes in PRO T 230/102 and CAB 123/45.

up to the first 'normal' post-war year, now taken to be 1948.

The basic estimates eventually put forward[50] were based on the following suggestions:

1   7½ per cent unemployment with unchanged average hours of work (a concession to official Treasury views by Keynes and the Section from their original assumption of 5 per cent unemployment).

2   A 35 per cent increase in prices above the 1938 level.

3   A 1½ per cent annual increase in output per worker from the 1938 level.

4   Post-war net income from overseas investments half that of 1938, and the terms of trade unchanged from the 1938 level.

The outcome is shown in table 6.1

*Table 6.1* Estimates of post-war national income

|  | 1938 | 1948 | 1950 | 1952 |
| --- | --- | --- | --- | --- |
| Real national income at factor cost (1938 = 100) | 100 | 117 | 121 | 124 |
| National income at current prices (£million) | 4,490 | 6,890 | 7,090 | 7,300 |
| Taxable income at current prices (£million) | 4,920 | 7,710 | 7,910 | 8,120 |

However, the majority of the Committee then added that they thought it reasonable to allow for a somewhat higher level of unemployment in 1948, due to immediate post-war dislocations, some slight increase in holidays, and also a slight worsening of the terms of trade, and they thus settled for a figure for the 1948 national income of £6,800 million. Henderson, who had earlier wanted to assume 12½ per cent unemployment and had objected that the assumed increases in productivity were too large, added a note of dissent saying that a lower figure should be assumed (he had in fact advocated a figure of £6,300 million). Keynes considered that anything less than £7,000 million for the national income in 1948 'makes no sense at all' and that the figure could well be £7,400 million or even higher (this was in line with the range of values earlier agreed by Keynes, Stone, and the Section, assuming only 5 per cent unemployment and a 2 per cent annual increase in productivity).[51] The Chancellor endorsed an estimate of

50  'Estimate of the national income', PR(43)35, 25 June 1943, in PRO CAB 87/13.

51  The increase in real GDP from 1938 to 1948 is now estimated at around 12 per cent; but the immediate 'strain' of the social security commitments was less than expected because of, *inter alia*, less than the assumed unemployment and a higher price level.

£7,000 million for the 1948 national income, with an equivalent taxable income of £7,825 million, and on this basis he saw difficulties in both reducing taxation after the end of the war and accepting the Beveridge commitments, though still offering no supporting figures.[52]

In a long minute (11 July 1943) to the Lord President on PR(43)35 and 36, signed by Chester, Fleming, and Tress, the various estimates of national income were again reviewed.[53] They pointed out that those in PR(43)35 assumed that 'depression unemployment is negligible . . . but structural unemployment has not yet been reduced below its pre-war level' and suggested that Keynes's estimate would imply a pressure of demand 'which we would regard as safe only if a substantial measure of wartime controls were retained by 1948', while Henderson's figure was plausible only if monetary demand were kept 'unnecessarily low'. They also sounded a warning, without relating it to the question whether the country could 'afford' the Beveridge proposals, that current very tentative estimates of post-war investment expenditures, related to a large building programme, raised the question whether they could be accommodated within a national income of £6,890 millions (at the price level assumed) 'without special measures to restrict consumption, such as rationing or high taxation'. The alternative, 'to stretch the national income' to £7,000 million or more, might be difficult without controls over workers and employers. They suggested that some scaling down of investment plans might be preferable to 'over-heroic measures of regimentation'.

On the basis of the Chancellor's own estimate of national income and related taxable capacity, they concluded that, as compared with the current situation, acceptance of Beveridge's proposals in full, together with all other new services then contemplated, would still leave room for large tax reductions (from wartime levels) if there were to be need for no more that £100 million of budget surplus (the Chancellor's provision), though they suggested that in fact there might well be need for a larger surplus to restrain total demand in the early post-war years.

However, a more direct examination of the 1948 budgetary position by Norman Chester followed a fortnight later.[54] Starting from ministers' agreed assumptions about levels of national income and taxable income and from estimates, put forward by the Chancellor and

52 PR(43)35 and PR(43)36, 'Post-war national income and taxation', in PRO CAB 87/13.
53 PRO T 230/97.
54 PRO T 230/98.

other ministers, of commitments already foreseen and accepted (national debt interest, armed services, agriculture, education, etc.), he showed that the budgetary costs of Beveridge's proposals could be accommodated with a standard rate of income tax reduced to 7s. 6d. in the £ (from 10s. at the date of writing) and a corresponding reduction in indirect taxation. His calculation indeed left a margin of £50 million for repayment of government debt, though he took the opportunity to reiterate the Section's plea that the size of budget surplus or deficit should in future be 'a function of the economic and financial conditions prevailing at the time'. It is not clear whether this note went directly as a brief to the Lord President, though it clearly played a part in the continuing arguments by the Section supporting the Beveridge proposals.

As, during 1943 and 1944, ministers continued their detailed discussions of the proposals, leading eventually to the white paper incorporating the government's plans (Cmd 6550 of September 1944), their amendments to Beveridge's scheme ran counter to much of the Section's advice in detail – a rejection of the 'subsistence principle', less for children's allowances, more for immediate pension rates (including more for those who had not made full contributions). As Norman Chester sadly pointed out, these changes – involving, *inter alia*, more reliance on national assistance – had the effect of somewhat increasing budgetary expenditures while reducing contribution income. Thus they added to the net budgetary burden as compared with Beveridge's proposals, which the Treasury had initially said were more than the State could afford.[55]

55 PRO T 230/103.

# Chapter seven

# THE ECONOMIC SECTION IN WARTIME: POST-WAR POLICY (2) EXTERNAL

The Section's work during the war on external economic policy for the post-war future divided, though with some overlap, into consideration of the problems of the immediate post-war years and of those of the longer-term trading and financial relations with the rest of the world – Jame Meade's fourth 'fundamental problem' of post-war policy outlined in February 1941 (see p. 70).

An essential background to all consideration of the immediate post-war problem and appropriate policies was the estimate of the UK's balance of payments, on which work began in the Section in 1941 and continued, as relevant issues arose, up to the eventual negotiations for the US loan of 1945. The work initially occupied James Meade and Austin Robinson, in particular, and later involved Nita Watts and Marcus Fleming, with other members of the Section being concerned from time to time. The estimates produced and the progress of the work over the war period, in co-operation with Maynard Keynes and increasingly, as time went on, with the Central Statistical Office and the Treasury, has been described elsewhere.[1] All that need be noted here is that all the forecasts started from estimates of the need for imports (assuming 5 per cent unemployment) in the first 'normal' post-war year and arrived, via estimates or guesses at invisible imports and exports and changes in the terms of trade, at a 'required' increase in exports. This usually implied a growth of exports to some 50 per cent above the pre-war volume and larger than the authors thought could be relied upon, given the problems of reconversion from war

1 Pressnell, L. S. (1986) *External Economic Policy since the War*, vol. 1, London: HMSO, appendix 27.

production and of regaining lost markets. Thus it was seen as inevitable that, for some two or three years at least after the end of the war, the UK would face an intractable balance of payments problem involving a need for tight control of capital exports, and for net borrowing abroad to finance an unavoidable current account deficit. Controls over domestic consumption and other expenditures would be needed, as a consequence of import restriction and priority for export production in conditions of still incomplete reconversion of industry to peacetime operation.

On this assessment of the immediate post-war conditions and necessities there was little disagreement between the Section and the other departments most directly interested – Treasury, Board of Trade, Bank of England – though views often differed on particular forecasts and also on the best means of dealing with the domestic policy problems that would arise. But on longer-term issues of external policy views diverged more widely.

Consideration of both longer-term post-war commercial policy and the desirable post-war international financial system developed during 1941. The Board of Trade had gained some indication of developing views within the US administration on desirable international trading arrangements during early, and abortive, discussions on renewal or supplementation of the 1938 Anglo-American Trade Agreement,[2] and in June 1941 a memorandum by R. J. Shackle on economic reconstruction argued for efforts to re-establish multilateral international trade after the war on the basis of convertibility of currencies and 'some degree' of exchange rate flexibility. If the USA was to be persuaded to co-operate, both with financial assistance and by freeing its own trade and abandoning any idea of 'hemisphere self-sufficiency', the UK would be obliged to 'modify' the imperial preference system and might be wise to offer to do so as part of an invitation to the USA to co-operate in establishing freer world trade.[3]

This paper touched off a stream of minutes from James Meade and Lionel Robbins, to the Lord President and/or Sir Richard Hopkins, building up a case for approaching the US administration on the lines suggested,[4] in opposition to the views of most senior Treasury officials

---

2 For a comprehensive account of the Anglo-American negotiations on post-war international trade and financial agreements from 1941 to 1947, see Pressnell, op. cit., which has been drawn upon for most statements in this chapter not related directly to the Economic Section.

3 PRO CAB 123/53.

4 Papers written during July–November 1941, in PRO CAB 123/53, T 272/118, and T 230/93.

who appeared wedded to a permanent regime of bilateral bargaining backed by trade and exchange controls. The main arguments of the Section were as follows.

A UK policy of permanent bilateralism, trade controls, and exchange restrictions would threaten not only UK–US co-operation but also the cohesion of the Commonwealth and would be particularly dangerous for the UK if the USA also exercised its economic strength in bilateral bargaining. But the UK would face major reconversion and balance of payments problems after the war and could not agree immediately to abandon bilateral bargaining and trade and exchange controls. However, in the longer run we should accept a regime of freely convertible currencies and an end to bilateral trade arrangements and exchange controls on current payments as soon as, and so long as, the balance of payments position allowed this to be done without the necessity for internal deflation and unemployment. In the early years we would need to be free to adjust the exchange rate; thereafter the proposed currency union (see p. 98) must provide rules for internationally controlled depreciation by a country with an unduly unfavourable balance of payments (and only by such countries) or appreciation by a country with an unduly favourable balance. Co-operation would be needed in the planning and timing of anti-depression policies, including the planning and timing of international investment in underdeveloped areas to be financed primarily by countries with favourable balances of payments. A substantial reduction in tariffs was needed but the USA should reduce its tariffs more than the UK as a contribution towards restoring balance of payments equilibrium.

Finally, there were firm warnings that the US administration was determined that imperial preference must be 'modified' though unlikely to insist on immediate abolition of the system, and the UK should try to bargain reduction of preference against cuts in the US tariff. The devotion of the dominions to imperial preference was weakening, and they were alive to the advantages for them of easier access to the US market; and a 'closed economic bloc' of the Commonwealth provided neither a desirable nor a possible alternative to the policies suggested.

By the time the negotiations over the terms of article VII of the Mutual Aid Agreement ended in March 1942 it was abundantly clear that the US administration's view of the agreed desirability of 'the elimination of all forms of discriminatory treatment in international commerce and . . . the reduction of tariffs and other trade barriers' definitely included the imperial preference system as one of the 'discriminatory treatments' to be eliminated, although some officials and ministers in London still persuaded themselves that the UK was not bound to accept this interpretation.

With the signing of the Agreement, the UK was committed to further conversions with the Americans on ways of implementing the agreed principles.

Meanwhile, Keynes had produced the first draft of his proposals for the international currency union mentioned above (and soon to be re-named International Clearing Union) in September 1941.[5] They were intended to ensure that each member of the Union would need to be concerned only with its balance of payments with other members of the Union as a group, rather than with bilateral balancing, and also to provide for automatically available multilateral credit from creditor countries in the Union to deficit countries to give both creditors and debtors time to make any necessary fundamental adjustments to their economies. A new international currency, 'Bancor', would be created by the Union and accepted as equivalent to gold, each member country would have a 'quota' in the Union – in effect an overdraft facility in Bancor – proportionate to its trade turnover; any country developing a surplus with the Union would be obliged to accept Bancor in settlement without limit; interest would be charged on both debit and credit balances with the Union; as a country moved into either heavy deficit or heavy surplus it could come under pressure to adjust its exchange rate, but in the meantime a deficit country could protect its balance of payments through import controls, barter agreements, etc. An extreme creditor country might be expected to undertake any or all of exchange appreciation, deliberate expansion of domestic demand, reduction of tariffs or other impediments to imports, and increased lending for economic development. The Union would supervise exchange rate changes and no country with a healthy balance of payments would be permitted to devalue so as to 'export unemployment'.

These proposals were welcomed in the Section unreservedly. To both Keynes and the Section the provisions putting pressure on creditors to contribute to the adjustment of balance of payments disequilibria were seen as vital elements in the scheme, giving it a significantly expansionist nature; and this was constantly stressed in arguments put to ministers (particularly Attlee and Bevin) fearful of participation in any scheme which might put the UK under pressure to

5 For the development of the proposals for a clearing union, see Keynes, J. M. (1980) *Collected Writings*, Cambridge: Cambridge University Press, vol. 25.

correct a balance of payments deficit by deflating and increasing unemployment. The importance of international supervision of exchange
rate changes to avoid 'competitive devaluations' was also stressed.

The economists brought into Whitehall by the war were virtually all
supporters of, or rapidly converted to, Keynes's scheme with only
minor reservations, the major exception being Sir Hubert Henderson;
and the senior Treasury officials were also soon converted or at least
acquiescent. Opposition came mainly from the Bank of England,
obsessed with the idea of building up a wider sterling area in the post-
war world and also reluctant to accept any international constraints on
British exchange rate policy.

There was also being developed by Keynes at this time a plan for an
international investment board which would plan projects for developing
countries and raise (untied) finance from industrialized countries with a
healthy balance of payments; and the timing of investment would be
planned so as to stimulate the world economy if recession threatened.
His third of three, partly linked, proposals was for internationally
supervised price stabilization schemes for primary commodities,
relying essentially on the operation of buffer stocks to iron out short-
term price fluctuations (see pp. 103–4).

The Section attitude to these schemes is summarized in a paper by
James Meade in April 1942 which gives his views on the 'regulation of
international economic relations':

It is clear that the main controls in this field ought to be international
or supranational. . . .
  (i) An international monetary arrangement which (a) would
      measure the lack of balance in each country's payments *vis-à-vis*
      the rest of the world and (b) would put as much of the strain of
      adjustment upon the countries with favourable, as upon those
      with unfavourable balances.
 (ii) An international arrangement for the capital development of
      undeveloped regions, directly or indirectly financed from the
      favourable balances of payments of those countries with
      favourable balances.
(iii) An international commission to co-ordinate the internal anti-
      depression policies of the various national states.
 (iv) An international system of commodity controls, acting for
      stabilization for their prices and for the gradual adjustment of
      such prices to an 'equilibrium' level rather than through the
      quantitative control of production, exports or imports.
  (v) An international commercial charter outlining which forms of

behaviour were permissible and which were not permissible in national commercial policies. (Such a charter would presumably be based upon two principles:

(i) permitting more protective devices to countries with un-favourable balances than to those with favourable balances and

(ii) complete outlawing certain of the worst forms of protective or discriminatory devices.)[6]

Just as Keynes had taken the lead in developing ideas in Whitehall on (i), (ii), and (iv) above, (iii) became one theme in the Section's work on post-war employment policy (see chapter 6) and Meade took the lead in developing discussion of (v). In August 1942, after discussion within the Section, with Keynes, and with officials in the Board of Trade, he produced his 'Proposal for an International Commercial Union'.[7] This opened with an argument that the UK 'above all other countries' would gain from general world economic and financial expansion, from a general reduction of barriers and restrictions in international markets, and from 'a removal of those discriminations and rigid bilateral bargains which remove the opportunities for multilateral trading'. But, it was urged, while the UK was committed under article VII of the Mutual Aid Agreement to action with the USA on these lines, this did not imply *laissez-faire* or the outlawing of state trading. Indeed, principles and rules must be developed that would neither automatically exclude the USSR nor prevent bulk purchase of imports or the establishment of special export sales organizations in the UK.

The suggested rules for the Commercial Union were that all members would grant 'most favoured nation' (mfn) tariff treatment to each other, subject to moderate tariff preferences (up to 10 per cent) between members of a 'recognized political or geographical group of nations'; quantitative import restrictions would be virtually outlawed except in special circumstances (but see p. 102); export subsidies and other measures resulting in export sales at prices more than 10 per cent below the price for sales to the home market would also be outlawed, though production subsidies would be permitted. However, countries in balance of payments difficulties, recognized as such by the Clearing Union, would be allowed to use quantitative restrictions (qr) temporarily and exception would be made also for 'recognized' international regulation schemes for primary commodities. State trading would be

6 EC(S)(42)12, 'Government intervention in the post-war economy', in PRO T 230/14.
7 PRO T 230/125.

subject to rules setting limits, effectively the same as those for regulating private sector trade, to its use for protective or discriminatory purposes.

The Board of Trade took up these proposals with enthusiasm, and also took over the part-time services of James Meade. On the President's suggestion an interdepartmental committee (the Overton Committee) was set up to consider proposals very nearly identical with those in Meade's paper,[8] with James Meade as one of the Board of Trade representatives and Lionel Robbins representing the Economic Section. The Overton Committee endorsed Meade's proposals in December 1942,[9] adding a precise provision for reduction in tariff rates and preference margins: members of the Union would agree to a 25 per cent *ad valorem* ceiling on mfn tariff rates and a 25 per cent cut in all existing rates, subject to a right not to go below 10 per cent, and all preference margins would be cut by 50 per cent, subject to a right not to reduce the margin below 5 per cent.

The report produced furious opposition from Sir Hubert Henderson in the Treasury and also from the Ministry of Agriculture. In the latter case, the main objection was to any restraint on the UK's ability to protect British agriculture by whatever means the government might prefer, including tariffs and quantitative import controls. Henderson's opposition went further, covering virtually every significant element in the proposals. He appeared to believe that the UK could and should evade its article VII obligations, and saw insignificant likely benefit from other countries' tariff reductions and danger for the UK and colonies (especially the sugar producers) in reduction of imperial preference. He seemed to see the possibility of great advantage for the UK from preserving freedom to use qr, ignoring the possibility that others would retaliate, as well as from the possibility of hard bargaining by state trading enterprises uninhibited even by obligations to trade on normal commercial principles. He also, rather oddly, and ignoring the proposed Clearing Union rules, seemed to see the proposals as preventing pressure on countries in balance of payments surplus to contribute to the restoration of equilibrium.[10]

Henderson's minority report was countered not only by another paper from the majority of the Committee but also by an extraordinarily

8 President of the Board of Trade to the Lord President, 5 November 1942, PRO CAB 123/221.

9 'Report of the committee on commercial policy', PRO CAB 123/221.

10 Henderson's minority report was later published in Clay, H. (ed.) (1955) *The Inter-war Years and Other Papers*, Oxford: Clarendon Press.

long minute from Lionel Robbins to the Lord President contesting Henderson's arguments point by point and, incidentally, adding a plea to help the sugar-producing colonies by reducing protection of sugar-beet farmers in the UK.[11]

Keynes had included in his Clearing Union proposals rather summary provisions for ceilings on tariff rates and preference margins, outlawing of export subsidies, import quotas, barter agreements, and exchange restrictions on current transactions, all subject to States being allowed 3–5 years after the war to give full effect to these provisions and to their being allowed 'to fall back on the forbidden protective devices' if this was justified by a deficit position in the Clearing Union. Nevertheless he declared himself 'a bit scared' of the Overton Committee's recommendations. So far as preferences were concerned, he wanted a let-out for full customs unions (a point later introduced into the British proposals); he also now objected to any ban on the use of qr, for which he considered 'we shall need quasi-permanent arrangements, not merely to rescue us from achieved disaster [i.e. balance of payments deficit] but to prevent us from reaching that stage of things', and he clearly envisaged its normal use to protect the development of new import-saving production. He wanted freedom for deficit countries to apply discriminatory qr, on the grounds that this could allow them to obtain a larger volume of imports than would be possible with no discrimination. Finally, he doubted – realistically as events proved – whether the US Congress would be induced to accept so far-reaching a multilateral scheme.[12]

Correspondence at this time between Keynes and James Meade shows Meade agreeing that qr might reasonably be used for protective purposes, provided that the effective protection given was no more than the tariff ceiling, and suggesting that the auctioning of import licences could both ensure non-discrimination and give some indication of the degree of protection.[13] He also again urged the benefit for the UK of a multilateral agreement on tariff ceilings and reductions, as against Keynes's suggestion that agreement with the USA would be more likely to be reached on the basis of bilateral negotiations under

11 Seven pages of single-space typescript which the side linings and the Lord President's later attitude suggest was read with care and carried conviction (PRO CAB 123/221).

12 Keynes, op. cit., vol 25, pp. 50–1 and 80–1, and vol. 26, pp. 251–82, covering also correspondence with James Meade.

13 Meade obviously decided later that this was too dangerous a concession to the protectionists and reverted to his initial insistence on a ban on qr except to deal with balance of payments difficulties.

the cover of some multilaterally agreed principles. If the latter were precise, they would amount in effect to the Overton Committee's scheme; if they were not, we risked having to extend mfn rights and cuts in preferences to the USA against cuts in other countries' tariffs and, overall, less pressure on the US for their tariff reductions, which were our major concern.

Although Keynes eventually acquiesced in approaches, first to the dominions and India and later, after their general agreement had been obtained, to the US administration, on the basis of both the Clearing Union and the Commercial Union proposals, he never became an enthusiastic supporter of the latter.

The Clearing Union proposals had been conveyed to Washington in August 1942 and published in April 1943[14] at the same time as Harry White's alternative plan for a Stabilization Fund was published in Washington; and Keynes and White had already discussed the alternatives several times, neither convincing the other of the superiority of his own scheme. In July 1943, the Cabinet approved an *aide-mémoire* inviting the US government to confer, under article VII of the Mutual Aid Agreement, on both these proposals and commercial policy, and also approved a brief for the UK delegation which virtually reproduced the Overton/Meade proposals, though with $x$, $y$, and $z$ per cents in place of the precise tariff ceilings and tariff and preference reductions mentioned above.[15]

But in the meantime an invitation from the President of the United States in March to a conference on food and nutrition had taken Whitehall by surprise and aroused fears that discussion might have to be confined to pious aspirations about improvements in nutrition and living standards if it was not to raise issues of British agricultural policy, commercial policy, and international regulation schemes for primary products, on which firm and logically linked decisions had not yet been reached by the Cabinet.[16]

Lionel Robbins had been involved in interdepartmental discussions on commodity policy during 1941–2, finding himself allied with Keynes, Roy Harrod, the Treasury, and the Board of Trade in opposing Sir Donald Fergusson's efforts to extend his demand for unconstrained freedom to protect British agriculture to a general support for producer operated restriction and price support schemes

14 *Proposals for an International Clearing Union*, Cmd 6437.
15 WP(43)334, 'Commercial policy', in PRO CAB 78/5.
16 Lionel Robbins to Sir Edward Bridges, 22 March 1943, and to the Lord President, 25 March 1943 in PRO CAB 123/145.

for primary commodities in general.[17] The Economic Section had generally supported Keynes's proposals for short-term price stabilization by the operation of international buffer stocks, with the price range at which the stocks management bought and sold being adjusted over time towards an equilibrium price and restrictions on output or exports being used only temporarily and in conditions of otherwise unmanageable surplus. Moreover, they and other advocates of the proposals insisted that consumers as well as producers must be represented in the authority operating any scheme. Robbins had made the additional suggestion to Keynes that any price stabilization scheme should also contain provision that, if at any time restrictions of output or exports were in force, not only should the buffer stock price range be steadily reduced but also the production or export quotas of low-cost producers should rise at the expense of those of the high-cost producers. However (and partly to deal with known US fears that world market prices might be depressed by protectionism in importing countries), the obligation to reduce the buffer stock price range when restrictions were in force might be suspended if the international authority certified that such protectionism was a major factor causing the need for restrictions.[18]

Robbins was now invited to prepare the brief for the British delegation to the Hot Springs conference. This, as approved by the Cabinet, instructed the delegation to advocate the general principles for any stabilization schemes on the lines outlined above (of course without the addition suggested by Robbins) though not to put forward specific proposals.[19] In his report to the Cabinet on the outcome of the Hot Springs conference, Richard Law[20] praised 'the remarkable skill with which Professor Robbins deployed the principles of the Commod. Plan without giving any indication that such a plan existed'.[21] The conference resolution on international commodity arrangements contained nothing contrary to the UK brief.[22]

The Hot Springs conference was soon followed by the first round of

---

17 Keynes, op. cit., vol. 27; USE(41) and (42), papers and minutes of Official Committee on Post-war External Economic Problems and Anglo-American Co-operation, in PRO CAB 87/60.

18 Robbins to Keynes, 17 June 1942, in PRO T 247/9. But he clearly felt that discussion with the Ministry of Agriculture in the Committee was already so difficult that these propositions should go no further at that stage.

19 WP(43)97 and 185 in PRO CAB 66/34 and 36.

20 Minister of State, Foreign Office, and leader of the British delegation.

21 WP(43)275 in PRO CAB 66/38.

22 Final Act of the UN Conference on Food and Agriculture, Cmd 6451, pp. 33–4.

'article VII' discussions in Washington, (September–October 1943) with both Lionel Robbins and James Meade on the UK delegation. The former was designated to take the lead in discussions of commodity policy and James Meade to operate in support of Percivale Liesching (Second Secretary, Board of Trade) on commercial policy. The rest of the agenda covered the Keynes/White Clearing Union/ Stabilization Fund and International Bank, employment policy, and cartel policy. On the last two items, the British delegation would have to be non-committal, in the absence of firm policy decisions in London.

It is clear, from the papers and minutes of meetings of the delegates in Washington[23] and from James Meade's diary, that both Robbins and Meade played major parts in the discussions, and not only on the topics on which they had been assigned particular responsibilities.

Robbins did not manage to carry commodity policy far beyond the general principles agreed at Hot Springs partly because, as he saw it, the US side seemed still to be in some confusion about their objectives. The main practical points in the British desiderata – price stabilization through establishment of international buffer stocks and avoidance so far as possible of quota restrictions – still remained for further discussion at the end of the conference, with no US enthusiasm expressed for the former.[24]

Negotiations on the proposals for a Clearing Union/Stabilization Fund, (soon to be given the agreed title of International Monetary Fund) had to deal with major differences between the Keynes and White plans on which the Cabinet had given firm instructions and/or Keynes had strong feelings:

1 White's plan provided for extreme rigidity of exchange rates, which would initially have to be approved by the Fund, whereas the British plan envisaged a deficit country's right to devalue by a small amount without the Fund's consent, and the Cabinet's latest instructions were that an attempt should be made to agree on some 'automatic test' that would justify a further exchange rate change rather than having to submit to the Fund's judgement.[25]

2 In contrast with Keynes's proposals for a new international

23 PRO CAB 78/14.
24 WP(43)559 Revise, in PRO CAB 66/44, is the report to the War Cabinet on the discussions, and is summarized – on all except the Stabilization Fund – in Pressnell, op. cit., appendix 13.
25 James Meade noted in his diary (8 September 1943) his feeling that Keynes is 'apt to underestimate the importance of exchange rate adjustment and to pay little more than lip-service to the possibility of devising an effective automatic test'.

currency, 'Bancor', White proposed that the Fund should be able to deal in a basket of currencies, in effect granting credit by increasing its holdings of the currency of a deficit member country and supplying the foreign currency the member required. This was unacceptable in London, the Bank of England apparently envisaging the fund acting so as to weaken the position of sterling, *inter alia* by being unwilling to accept it in repayment of credits granted.

3 The British wanted virtually automatic access to credit up to the limit set by a member's quota; the White plan required justification to the Fund's satisfaction for all drawings exceeding the member's initial gold subscription.

4 A major merit of Keynes's scheme, in the eyes of both officials and ministers who supported it, was the pressure on creditor countries to contribute to restoration of general balance of payments equilibrium. In place of the various pressures in the British plan, White offered the 'scarce currency clause' allowing the Fund to ration its supplies of the currency of a country in extreme surplus and allowing other members to discriminate against the exports of the surplus country concerned.

James Meade proposed (within the UK delegation) an 'objective test' under (1) which would apply both to the right to devalue and to the right to apply qr to protect the balance of payments. The right to devalue by $x$ per cent would depend on the fall over a year in the sum of a country's immediately usable reserves (in gold, convertible currency, and available right to credit from the Fund) reaching $y$ per cent of its trade turnover; qr could be imposed in the same conditions and also if net liquid assets were below an agreed proportion of trade turnover. Meade then found himself having to counter a suggestion from Keynes that the objective test might take into account the movement of prices and costs in one country relative to others; a country inflating faster than others might need to devalue to maintain full employment even if in surplus. This rather odd reversal of Keynes's earlier insistence on pressure on surplus countries to revalue was countered by Meade's pointing out that such a country could still devalue under his conditions if it was lending long term on a scale to bring about a fall in its liquid reserves.[26] This argument reflected a point also made by Meade about the proposed obligation on members of the Fund to control capital movements – that the UK should not be precluded from adjusting its exchange rate to the extent necessary to

26 James Meade's diary, entries for 9 and 15 September 1943. He later concludes that Keynes is against any kind of objective test – a suspicion that had occurred earlier (diary 8 and 22 September).

regain its capacity to export long-term capital, though 'hot money' movements should, of course, be controlled.[27] However, the idea of an 'objective test' for qr was now rejected in London and the whole idea was eventually abandoned.

Meade, Robbins, and Dennis Robertson put considerable effort into persuading Keynes that point (2) above was a non-problem, at first without success; but later Meade thought that Keynes was becoming convinced, though still persisting in his public opposition to the US proposal.[28] Point (3) caused no difference of view among the British delegation; and references to point (4) now make rather amusing reading. From the moment the scarce currency clause appeared in White's draft some in Whitehall (notably Roy Harrod) saw it as an extremely valuable addition, or even alternative, to Keynes's proposals for pressure on creditor countries, but others found it very difficult to believe that all elements in the US administration yet realized its implications or would accept it when they did. The UK delegation decided that care must be taken now not to alert the State Department! But Meade found later that a cautious mention of the implications of the scarce currency clause did not seem to cause 'alarm and despondency' among the State Department representatives.[29]

It proved impossible to reach UK–US agreement on the Fund provisions, and it was not until four months after the end of the Washington talks that the *Joint statement by Experts on the Establishment of an International Monetary Fund*[30] could be published, still with a statement that 'It in no way commits the Governments concerned.'

On the International Investment Bank, discussion did not get very far, partly because White's latest draft became available only during the talks. Robbins and Meade welcomed the general idea, and particularly the provision for untied lending; but they wanted the Bank to raise its funds mainly from countries in balance of payments surplus. They also persisted in what today, in the light of actual experience of the IBRD, looks like a rather naïve belief that an international bank could take the initiative in planning investments in developing countries and timing expenditure in the interest of, *inter alia*, general economic stabilization.

27 ibid., 20 September 1943.
28 ibid., 28 and 29 September and 2 and 6 October 1943. A note to the same effect as the arguments of Meade *et al.* went to the Lord President (probably from Marcus Fleming) on 11 October 1943 (PRO T 230/40). In April 1944 the Treasury formally agreed, with no dissent from Keynes, to accept the American variant (PRO T 160/1287).
29 James Meade's diary, entries for 1 and 4 October 1943.
30 Cmd 6519, April 1944.

The commercial policy discussions went far more smoothly than those on the Fund. The initial British statement was welcomed by the US side, and clearly the British and American delegates concerned had no difficulty in establishing friendly personal relations. There seems, indeed, to have developed a strong mutual respect and liking among Liesching, Meade, and Harry Hawkins of the State Department, in particular.[31] The briefings from their respective governments naturally differed in many respects, but the two delegations were united in trying to find compromises which would minimize the political difficulties on both sides.

The agreed Anglo-American statement on commercial policy[32] sets out both the agreements and the remaining differences between the two sides at the end of the talks. The US administration was clearly wedded to a process of tariff reduction through bilateral negotiation by each country with its main supplier of each product, the reduction then being generalized on an mfn basis, rather than the UK's preferred multilateral agreement on ceiling rates and percentage reductions; but the statement lists both systems as possibilities. On preferences, the obligations of article VII would be given final effect only by 'definite provision both for an adequate reduction of tariffs and for the ultimate substantial abolition of preferences', and, once again, it was clear (as the British officials informed London) that the US government regarded the UK as committed to abolition of imperial preference and only acceptance of this would bring about a possibility of significant cuts in the US tariff. It was agreed that, once past the immediate post-war difficulties, the use of quantitative import restrictions and exchange controls on current transactions should be virtually confined to relief of balance of payments difficulties and discrimination should be minimized (Robbins and Meade had again floated the idea of auctioning global import licences as a way of ensuring non-discriminatory qr but without finding much response).[33] Production subsidies were approved, but not export subsidies, and the US side did not, eventually, insist on a linking of allegedly damaging production subsidies with limits on the volume of subsidized production.[34] This would have raised a storm in London and a more anodyne provision for complaint and review of allegedly damaging production subsidies

31 James Meade's diary, various entries; and on Hawkins especially 21 October and 19 November 1943.
32 Pressnell, op. cit.
33 James Meade's diary, entry for 22 September 1943.
34 A proposal noted by Meade, diary, 8 and 9 October 1943.

was substituted. State trading was declared acceptable and the setting up of a commercial policy organization 'essential'.

Within little more than six months after the end of the Washington talks, the Bretton Woods conference was under way, with Lionel Robbins again a member of the British delegation, and inter-governmental agreement was reached on the setting up of the International Monetary Fund and the International Bank for Recon-struction and Development.[35] But the British government was by no means united in support of the proposed IMF, and neither was there agreement on continuing to work out detailed commercial policy arrangements on the lines of the principles agreed in the Washington talks. The main ministerial opposition came from Lord Beaverbrook, violently objecting to the proposed IMF and supported by the Bank of England, from Leo Amery objecting with Beaverbrook to any modification of imperial preference or any move towards freer trade, and from R. S. Hudson, still demanding total freedom to promote a 'healthy and well-balanced agriculture' by whatever means seemed good to him – including import regulation, tariffs, and subsidies – and objecting to the commodity policy ideas also. The Prime Minister wanted major US tariff concessions in return for any concessions on imperial preference. Ernest Bevin was still afraid the 'we shall be crucified on a cross of gold' despite the fact that the IMF agreement had achieved one of the government's major objectives – freedom to vary the exchange rates by up to 20 per cent – to correct a 'fundamental disequilibrium' and by more than 20 per cent still on a country's own initiative but subject to *ex post* approval by the Fund, which would not be permitted to object that disequilibrium should rather be corrected by changes in the country's 'social or political policies'.

In the United States also, after an initial unsuccessful effort to induce the UK to resume commercial policy discussions with little delay, attitudes changed from those of the Washington talks. There was no further progress towards US–UK agreement on commercial policy until, with the end of the war, discussion had to be resumed as a matter of urgency in connection with the American loan negotiations of 1945. Once again Lionel Robbins joined the UK delegation, and it was these discussions which were the essential prelude to the eventual negotiation of the terms of the draft charter for an International Trade

35 *United Nations Monetary and Financial Conference, Final Act*, Cmd 6546, August 1944.

Organization in 1947, which, incidently, is full of echoes of the 1943 Washington talks.[36]

Early in 1944 members of the Economic Section were active in attempting to soothe ministers' fears about the outcome of the Washington talks and also urging that the discussion with the USA should be kept going.[37] The themes are that the UK is not committing itself to a gold standard or to deliberate deflation and unemployment in any circumstances, even a US slump;[38] there is little prospect of being able to build up an 'empire bloc', and no advantage to the UK likely even if we could do so, as compared with the arrangements proposed in Washington; the sterling area will not inevitably be destroyed by adherence to the IMF; the UK has more to lose than to gain from freedom to use protective and discriminatory trade and exchange controls if other countries do the same; the obligations we propose to undertake will not prevent the promotion of a 'healthy and well-balanced agriculture'; the UK should not discriminate against imports from low-wage countries as such – if they are in extreme balance of payments surplus, pressure to correct will exist under the IMF rules and, if low wages are the result of exploitation, pressure for reform may be exerted through the ILO.

Keynes's correspondence during this time shows continuing efforts by the Economic Section to convince him – or to keep him convinced – that the commercial policy proposals gave sufficient freedom to the UK to make justifiable use of quantitative import controls, and also that a change in the exchange rate would be an effective way of improving the balance of payments in normal conditions and preferable to permanent quantitative import restriction.[39] More important was the alliance with Keynes to fend off the Bank of

36 For the complicated and confused history of 1944–5 see the admirably clear account in Pressnell, op. cit.

37 *Inter alia*, minutes to the Lord President, the Minister of Labour, the Minister of Reconstruction, and the President of the Board of Trade (PRO T 230/41 and 173 and CAB 123/96II and EC(S)(44)16 in PRO T 230/16).

38 This question arose again in November 1945, when James Meade was instrumental in ensuring that a statement to Parliament by the Chancellor stressed both the right of the UK under the Fund agreement to depreciate rather than deflate if in balance of payments difficulties and suffering from actual or threatened unemployment and the protection given against competitive depreciation by others (Presnell, op. cit., p. 183, and PRO T 230/83).

39 Keynes, op. cit., vol. 26, pp. 283–304 (paper on qr produced after consultation with James Meade, correspondence with Marcus Fleming on exchange rate changes); note by Meade, 8 June 1944, in PRO T 230/173.

England's new attempt to persuade the Cabinet to reject the IMF in favour of efforts to build up a wider sterling area on the basis of trade and payments agreements with European and Latin American countries. Such an overt discrimination against the USA would, Keynes and the Section argued, rule out the financial help from the USA which would be needed in the early post-war years; and taking responsibility for the dollar deficits of Europe and part of South America would alienate the existing sterling area countries by forcing still more limitation of their non-sterling expenditure.[40]

A major attack on the commercial policy proposals mounted by the Ministry of Agriculture in 1944 led to prolonged official discussion, involving the Economic Section in trying both to prevent the most far-reaching concessions to agricultural protectionism and also to devise some concessions from the Washington principles that would mollify the Minister of Agriculture without ruling out all prospect of agreement with the USA. These concessions were essentially based on a somewhat higher minimum incidence of protection for agriculture than the general level envisaged at the time of the Washington talks, exerted through quantitative import controls if necessary but with a proviso that protection would be diminished as the country's production of any agricultural product rose above a certain percentage either of its pre-war production or of current world production. Non-discrimination might be ensured by auctioning import licences; in the case of bulk purchase 'normal commercial considerations' would not necessarily imply always buying from the (temporarily) cheapest source.[41]

Informal discussions with US officials, including Harry Hawkins, were resumed in London in late 1944 and early 1945 on the whole range of the commercial policy proposals, and Robbins and Meade were again involved. These obviously friendly and relatively uninhibited talks further clarified the main problems, but did no more than that.[42]

In 1945 wartime planning of post-war external economic policy really ends, with final decisions on commercial policy still to be reached. But the Section's concern and activity of course continued into the post-war period. Members of the Section were involved in the

40  Robbins to Lord President, 22 February and 13 April 1944, in PRO T 236/302.
41  Pressnell, op. cit., pp. 194–200, and PRO T 236/172, especially papers by Robbins, 'Methods of securing agricultural protection and stability in the spirit of the Washington proposals', and Meade, 'Commercial policy, programming of imports'.
42  'Report on proposals put informally to US officials in conversations in London', in PRO CAB 21/1247.

setting up of the UN Economic and Social Council in 1945 and establishing its co-ordinating role in relation to the Fund, the Bank, and ultimately GATT, and in its early concern with national full employment policies, as well as in the negotiations for the draft ITO charter and GATT themselves. But these later activities hardly involved either such new ideas or such controversy as had developed during the wartime discussions, both national and international.

# Chapter eight

## THE ECONOMIC SECTION UNDER JAMES MEADE

Before the war ended it had been arranged that James Meade would take over the directorship as soon as Lionel Robbins returned to the LSE.[1] Meade continued as Director until mid-April 1947 when he entered hospital suffering from stomach ulcers and somewhat disillusioned by Dalton's treatment of him.

From 1940 onwards Meade had been a dominant figure in the Section and was much the most important contributor to its proposals for the post-war management of the economy. As we have seen, he had set going the discussions on employment policy that issued in the white paper of 1944 and was the moving spirit behind proposals for an International Trade Organization. After his work with Stone in 1940–1 on national income accounts, he gave much of his time to the economic problems of the post-war world. To those problems, as is evident from his published work, he brought a rare clarity of mind, a systematic economic philosophy, and a flair for visualizing how new economic institutions would function. He had an eye for the central issues of policy and a constructive approach to them and could exercise his expository powers without, as Frank Lee put it, being 'led astray by the gift of lucidity'.

In directing the work of the Section, Meade, like Robbins, maintained an academic and collegiate atmosphere, in which all were free to contribute their ideas and all contributions were treated on merit. He took pains to keep the Section informed, circulating to them exchanges of minutes with Bridges and Gilbert and sometimes inviting

1 Meade did not assume the Directorship until 1 January 1946 but in Robbins's absence in Washington he was in charge from the autumn of 1945 onwards.

comments on his drafts before despatch. Members briefing the Lord President sent minutes over their own name once they had the Director's approval and, however junior, they represented the Section, often alongside much more senior officials in interdepartmental committees. Richard Sayers and Marcus Fleming acted as joint deputy directors; otherwise there was an absence of hierarchy – an absence which, however, meant a corresponding lack of senior posts and a constant battle with Establishments over pay and promotion.

Of those who had joined during the war nearly all had gone by the end of 1945. The exceptions were Marcus Fleming, Nita Watts and (until 1947 only) Ronnie Tress, Philip Chantler, and John Wood.[2] Additional staff had to be found at a time when the trend was strongly outwards from the civil service. A number of recruits came from other departments, some of them for very short periods. Few of those who joined stayed beyond 1947. More and more of the older members left, so that by 1948 the Section was composed largely of young economists with little previous experience.

## The role of the Section after the war

Meade had given a good deal of thought during the war to the role of the Section under peacetime conditions and, as we have seen, raised a number of pertinent questions in 1944, particularly as to its relationship with the Treasury. He had no doubt that the Section would be fully occupied. In a long note, probably written for the Machinery of Government Committee in 1943, he foresaw that there would be a general exodus of economists from Whitehall, leaving it to the Economic Section to fill part of the vacuum that would result.[3] A resumption of party government might spell less reliance on independent experts but there would still be objectives, such as the preservation of full employment, which were not in dispute and would require general policies on which there was also a wide measure of agreement. 'No one', Meade suggested, 'now disputes that the essential thing is to maintain the general level of total demand, and to allow a large measure of freedom of consumers' choice and of workers' choice of occupation.'[4] The help and advice of the Economic Section would be indispensable for that purpose.

2 Norman Chester and Stanley Dennison stayed a little beyond the end of 1945.
3 'The post-war position of the Economic Section', undated draft, unsigned, in PRO T 230/283.
4 ibid. See also James Meade's diary, entry for 5 November 1944.

In reviewing the post-war agenda of the Section, Meade listed some of the questions that were almost certain to arise in 'the first decade of peace' although no one could say exactly when. One example was whether to adjust the exchange rate and a second was what help in maintaining the level of economic activity would come from a reduction in the long-term rate of interest. These should not be the subject of instant decision but of 'more systematic and more leisurely investigations' in a far-sighted Economic Section. Other examples of what called for long-term investigation by the Economic Section were the technique of forecasting (including forecasting the level of demand which would permit full employment without inflation) and a survey of the influence on industrial productivity of such things as restrictive practices and methods of wage payment.

The first call on the time of the Section, as Meade saw things, would continue to be the preparation of briefs for whatever minister was designated chairman of the Cabinet committee entrusted with the co-ordination of economic policy. Such a committee could inherit the work of the Lord President's Committee but cover a wider field, including industrial questions relating either to private industry (for example, monopoly policy) or to the nationalized industries (for example, on what principles should they be operated?). As in wartime, the members of the Section would be wise to equip themselves for these duties

by making contacts and friendships with officials in other Departments responsible for economic problems, and to influence the views of those officials and through them the Departments concerned, at an early stage rather than invite an intervention at a later stage at the Ministerial or high official level.

The two main things likely to occupy the Section were employment policy and external economic policy. The first had four aspects, on each of which he enlarged: the maintenance of demand at a high and stable level; the problem of adjustment to external economic conditions; labour market aspects such as ensuring mobility of labour and moderation in wage policy; and issues of economic policy in the location of industry. Since inflation of wage rates would ruin the chances of maintaining full employment, wage policy was of central importance. Equally, in dealing with structural unemployment, a high level of geographical and occupational mobility, unimpeded by restrictive practices and reinforced by wage differentials, was fundamental. As for industrial location it was only too likely that economic factors would be neglected in favour of political and social considerations.

Meade then listed in some detail the issues of external economic policy, both in the long run and in the transition that would have to be faced. From these he returned to industrial policy and the problems of particular industries, such as coal, building, steel, transport, and agriculture, and mentioned briefly some miscellaneous issues: social security, nutrition, and town and country planning. His last word, however, looking back on the rush of business in wartime, was on the need for 'time and opportunity for some quiet (even academic) contemplation and thought on economics'. It must be 'the positive duty' of members of the Section to read books as well as official papers, consider fundamental economic problems as well as current issues of policy, and even write scientific papers for publication as well as briefs for ministers. There should be a proper library, perhaps shared with the CSO, and regular staff meetings 'with a slightly academic flavour', to permit of a more leisurely exchange of ideas between members of the Section and help towards the formation of an agreed view.

What was missing from this survey of the future was any discussion of the controls employed in wartime to allocate resources of all kinds under the aegis of the Lord President. These controls called for frequent, detailed, and arbitrary decisions in the operation of a complex machinery of rationing, allocation, and licensing, and largely superseded the financial controls, relying on the price mechanism, that were the domain of the Treasury. The Economic Section had played its part in wartime in advising the Lord President on some of those controls, notably manpower, but Meade himself had had little to do with that side of its work and his inclinations were all in favour of reverting to the use of financial instruments of control such as the budget, monetary policy, and the exchange rate.

The controls remained largely in place after the war and were seen by ministers as a superior way of organizing economic activity. When they talked of planning, they meant the use of just such powers of detailed intervention whereas Meade thought in terms of planning for full employment through demand management and financial policy. Moreover, the division which had existed in wartime between responsibility for economic co-ordination, exercised by the Lord President, and responsibility for financial policy, exercised by the Chancellor of the Exchequer, was continued into the peace. The Economic Section, still under the Lord President, was correspondingly distanced from financial policy, on which it laid such stress.

In the early post-war years, therefore, things fell out rather differently from Meade's vision of the future. But in many respects his expectations were fulfilled. Whitehall was almost emptied of economists and even the Treasury, after Keynes's death in April 1946, had none. The one group remaining was in the Economic Section and their main duty was to brief the Lord President. The focus of their activities, as he foresaw, was employment policy and external economic policy. Meade was right, too, in expecting the methods of work of the Section to be unchanged from wartime. It remained a group of like-minded economists, each keeping track of what was going on in some assigned 'parish', and seeking to form a common view through internal debate.

## The economic background

The two years of Meade's directorship were full of drama and suspense. The country had emerged from the war with enormous external debts such as no other belligerent incurred and a level of exports which had been allowed to fall by two-thirds in order to release manpower for the war effort. The consequent balance of payments problem dominated the transition from war to peace: there was a constant danger that the country would be unable to obtain or afford the volume of imports required even for a wartime standard of living and to meet the needs of industry under conditions of full employment. Heavy military expenditure abroad continued to strain the country's finances and delay the mobilization of manpower needed for the rebuilding of British industry. To plan the allocation of resources under these conditions, as the Economic Section was attempting, was to struggle against uncertainties of a high order. Not altogether surprisingly, the post-war transition was punctuated by successive crises, culminating in 1947.

First came a crisis over negotiations, led by Keynes, for a grant or loan from the United States. The Economic Section's balance of payments forecasts formed the background to these negotiations and they were represented at the negotiations themselves in the person of their Director, Lionel Robbins. Until April 1946 and beyond, it was uncertain whether Congress would approve the loan and it was not until July that it was voted. Yet without it Britain's reserves would have run out in 1947 unless swingeing cuts had been made in imports already 30 per cent lower than before the war.

A second crisis followed in February 1947 when industry in large parts of the country was denied electric power as coal stocks fell below the danger level. The loss of output fell heavily on exports, which had been climbing satisfactorily. It was six months before the climb was resumed and in the interval the reserves ebbed away faster than ever.

This in turn was followed by a third crisis in July–August 1947. The obligation imposed under the American Loan Agreement to make the pound convertible into dollars within a year matured in mid-July to the accompaniment of a run on the pound and a drain from the reserves of $600 million in six weeks.

In these two years of crisis, the country moved from the jubilation of victory to the verge of bankruptcy. The year 1946, in spite of anxieties over the Loan, had seemed to go well. But the crisis of 1947 caught the government unprepared, did great damage to its standing in the country, and left it faced with some grave decisions. Although the Americans seemed about to come to the rescue with Marshall Aid, it was well into 1948 before this could be taken for granted.

The events of 1947, the turning-point in the process of post-war reconversion, led to a major shake-up in the government machine. In the course of 1947 it was transformed at both the political and the administrative level, with important consequences for the Economic Section.

The transformation began in March when, shaken by the fuel crisis, the government appointed a Chief Planning Officer in the person of Sir Edwin Plowden and attached to him a 'central economic planning staff' (CEPS) to help in introducing more coherence into economic policy. The CEPS had instructions to collaborate with the Economic Section and the Central Statistical Office, 'both of which have important contributions to make towards economic planning'.[5]

This was followed in September, after the convertibility crisis, by the appointment of Cripps as Minister of Economic Affairs, replacing Morrison who had previously been in charge of economic policy as Lord President. Six weeks later, in November 1947, Cripps took over also from Dalton at the Exchequer, bringing with him the planning staff to form part of the Treasury. Meanwhile, Robert Hall had succeeded to the direction of the Economic Section, moving from the Board of Trade on a part-time basis in June and on a full-time basis from the beginning of September.

Thus four important changes were crowded into the months between March and November. The Lord President quit the scene; economic and financial policy was united under the new Chancellor; the Treasury acquired a planning staff under Plowden; and the Economic Section, which had lacked a full-time Director from April to September, faced a new situation under a new Director.

5 Cripps, announcing the creation of the CEPS, H of C Debates, vol. 434, col. 971, 10 March 1947.

These events marked a turning-point in the affairs of the Economic Section as they did in many other directions. As Meade had foreseen, the decisive elements in economic policy were coming to be financial instruments rather than physical controls: the budget, the exchange rate, and monetary policy. Yet Dalton sought to retain exclusive control over those instruments and to preserve strict budget secrecy, even from Morrison. The Economic Section found itself advising a minister who had neither the powers necessary for co-ordination, nor the understanding of what his advisers urged, nor the time from his many other duties to take the action necessary.

If Morrison was hard to advise and ineffective, Dalton was almost equally so. He felt quite capable of deciding on economic policy without collective discussion at official level or personal advice from James Meade, whom he pooh-poohed and told not to disclose budgetary matters to Morrison. Thus access to the Budget Committee gave the Economic Section limited leverage on policy.

All of these difficulties were resolved in the aftermath of the 1947 crisis. Instead of advising a minister who was extremely busy and not very responsive, the Section were now able, in alliance with the planners, to brief a Chancellor who was, like Anderson in 1942-3, the undisputed fount of economic policy. The Section also had the ear of Plowden, who was trusted by the new Chancellor as a kindred spirit and who in turn worked closely with Robert Hall.

## Relations with the Treasury

Meade had always been anxious for a close working relationship with the Treasury. This was not because of any high opinion of senior Treasury officials, with the exception of Sir Richard Hopkins, the Permanent Secretary − the post-war Treasury without Keynes was a bleak prospect[6] − but because he recognized that the Treasury was bound to resume its traditional position as the key economic department. He was delighted, therefore, when Hopkins started in December 1944 to send budget papers to him (and to Robbins) and call him into consultation on budgetary matters. He had taken the opportunity to 'lecture' Hopkins on the importance of regular forecasts of national income and expenditure by the Treasury, CSO, and Economic Section, and on the desirability of starting to move from

6 Meade, diary, entry for 7 January 1945. He records Keynes as denouncing Treasury officials (Hopkins excepted) as 'utterly incapable and incompetent to deal with technical economic matters'.

physical controls over the economy to the use of financial instruments.[7]

It was Hopkins's intention that the Director of the Economic Section should join the Budget Committee after the war and this intention was fulfilled under his successor, Edward Bridges. Before assuming his new duties as Director, Meade arranged with Bridges that he should serve on the Budget Committee and other Treasury committees and take a full part in Treasury discussions on economic and financial policy. He was also to have free access to Bridges as head of the Treasury. So far as Bridges was concerned, this arrangement was fully observed: for example, it was chiefly on Meade that Bridges relied in deciding on the procedure to be followed in economic planning. But, so long as Meade served two masters and might use information supplied by the Treasury to brief the Lord President independently, there was bound to be some reserve in the Treasury's attitude to the Economic Section: especially when the Section differed from the Treasury over the use of instruments of policy like taxation that were under the Treasury's control. Meade – at heart a Treasury man – was a believer in these instruments when many of the senior Treasury officials were reluctant to use them with the necessary vigour. Whereas Meade wanted to check investment and sought consistently to ensure that 'the Budget should be regarded as the main instrument of carrying out the Plan', the Steering Committee of Permanent Secretaries had no use in 1946 for 'the traditional correctives' of 'a sharp rise in interest rates and substantial increases in taxation' because the one would discourage investment and the other was thought to ignore the overhang of accumulated savings.[8]

One source of friction arose from the Treasury's responsibility for estimating and forecasting the balance of payments. Meade's diary contains several references to disagreements over the way in which statements of the balance of payments were prepared. In November 1945 he is in conflict with Eady over the the import programme and denounces 'hole and corner Treasury methods' of dealing with it. In May 1946 he finds Eady unaccountable in calling on the Economic Section to help in interpreting balance of payments figures and then asking for the appointment of a special assistant for the purpose. In

7 ibid., entry for 22 December 1944. For Hopkins's account of his meeting with Robbins and Meade on 21 December, see 'Budget Committee 1945', in PRO T 273/260. According to Hopkins, Robbins did most of the talking.

8 Meade, diary, entry for 6 April 1946; draft 'Economic Survey for 1947', covering memorandum by the Chairman of the Steering Committee, MEP(46)16, paras 12–13, 21 December 1946, in PRO CAB 134/503.

September he notes a threefold disagreement with R. W. B. Clarke on the presentation of data in balance of payments estimates. There were disagreements on policy too. Meade campaigned for the auctioning of import licences without making any impression on the Treasury.[9] He looked forward to the removal of balance of payments restrictions when the Treasury wanted to see them continue indefinitely. There was also a feeling in the Section, which continued under Robert Hall, that they were not kept adequately informed or not informed until the last possible moment on key economic indicators: for example, on changes in the balance of payments and in the gold and dollar reserves.

## Economic planning

The main job of the Section was seen as planning for full employment. Since full employment was hardly a pressing matter in 1945, the emphasis shifted, first to stabilization of demand and from that to planning. Planning was then a popular but hazy idea that could be interpreted in many different ways. The Economic Section's contribution was the preparation of a series of economic surveys which served as plans. The surveys, together with briefs for the Lord President, took up most of the time of the Section in 1945–7. They are discussed in detail in chapter 11.

Nobody in Whitehall, whether officials or ministers, seemed to have much idea what was to be planned, or how, beyond what was contained in the white paper on *Employment Policy*. Meade lost no time in putting his ideas on the subject before Bridges and between them they hammered out a procedure. In the first paper submitted to the new Steering Committee of Permanent Secretaries, economic planning was represented as involving a review of the resources likely to be available, a forecast of the extent to which these resources would be employed on the basis of the current programmes and policies, and, in the light of this, suggestions for such adjustments in those programmes and policies as would 'ensure that the total claims on the community's resources are neither excessive nor deficient'.[10]

9 The proposal seems to have been revived in 1956 when the practical difficulties were forcibly stated by Douglas Allen in the Treasury (Allen to Symons and France, 25 January 1956, in PRO T 230/395).

10 ED(45)1, 'Economic planning', 7 November 1945, in PRO CAB 134/186. The paper was drafted in September, revised, and sent to the Lord President on 10 October 1945 (EC(S)(45)28, 2nd Revise, Meade to Lord President, in PRO T 230/18).

A plan had been called for by Cripps, President of the Board of Trade, who whould have liked to take over the Economic Section but was unable to persuade Morrison to let it go to the Board of Trade. He wrote to Bridges at the end of August asking that a plan for the allocation of resources between exports, investment, personal consumption, etc., should be put in hand and a large expert staff given the job. What he wanted was clearly a long-term plan. Meade's initial advice to Bridges was that planning should cover the first five years 'in broad outline' and the first year 'with more precision'.[11]

In practice, work in the Economic Section on the five-year plan proceeded slowly and led nowhere while the one-year review developed naturally out of the Section's wartime quarterly economic surveys and was for some years a valuable instrument of economic co-ordination. In practice, too, an attempt was made at first to adjudicate between the claims on resources of the ultimate buyers. The claims were shown as requirements for the year ahead as estimated by government departments after trimming them as they thought fit to match their expectations of what they might actually get. The sum total of these requirements was compared with a target level of money national income consistent with full employment and current levels of productivity. The excess of departmental demands over this target was one measure of the inflationary gap; and it was the object of planning as the Economic Section conceived it to eliminate the gap through ministerial decisions based on the Economic Survey.

The Economic Section's role in the preparation of economic surveys and plans is discussed in chapters 11 and 12. In the two years while Meade was Director three surveys were prepared in conjunction with the CSO. The last of the three was rewritten and published as the *Economic Survey for 1947*. All followed the same prescription: they were based on what would now be called national income forecasts, supplemented by a manpower budget. The analysis was framed round an estimate of an 'inflationary gap' of excess demand, both in money and in manpower, and was designed to put in front of ministers the main options in seeking to close the gap. Until the spring of 1947,

11 EC(S)(45)27, Bridges to Meade 22 August, Meade to Bridges 29 August, 30 August 1945, in PRO T 230/18. Meade's reply outlines the administrative arrangements as to committees and working parties which he thought necessary for planning purposes and which, with few changes, were put into practice by Bridges (e.g. the Steering Committee of Permanent Secretaries, the Economic Survey Working Party, the Balance of Payments Working Party, the Investment Working Party, the Statistics for Full Employment Working Party, and so on).

however, ministers and officials found the idea of shortage (of labour, dollars, fuel, and materials) more compelling that that of excess demand, and rarely connected the inflationary gap with the behaviour of prices or, for that matter, inflation. Dalton, indeed, rather liked excess demand, and the controls that went with it, since these appeared to provide a better grip on the economy and make planning easier.

There was also a more theoretical side to this work. Acceptance of full employment as an objective had to be supplemented by an understanding of how to maintain it once achieved. In reviewing the future work of the Section in November 1945 Meade put right at the top the need to undertake research into methods of controlling each of the main elements in total demand.[12] This point was elaborated a month or so later in a minute to Bridges on the need to give consideration to ways of exercising control over the economy once excess demand disappeared. Most of the existing controls were purely restrictive and would be of little use in a depression.[13]

A series of papers were prepared, beginning with one by Dow on 'Variations in income tax as a short-term instrument for national income stabilization' and another by the same author on the familiar proposal for 'Variations in national insurance contributions'.[14] These and a later paper on income tax credits were brought together in December 1946 in a study, also by Dow, of measures for the control of consumption expenditure. This was revised after discussion with Customs and Inland Revenue some months later, and in the meantime Dow circulated another paper on control of private investment.[15] These early papers suggested that, while a slight deficiency of demand might be dealt with successfully by the release of post-war credits and variations in national insurance contributions, a serious depression would require cuts in income tax. All of this was in keeping with Meade's view that physical controls would be of little help in a depression and that fiscal policy (for which the Chancellor, not the Lord President, was responsible) was much the most effective

---

12  EC(S)(45)(43), 'Future work of the Section' by J. E. Meade, 27 November 1945, in PRO T 230/19.
13  EC(S)(46)1, Meade to Bridges, 'Future work on economic planning', 2 January 1946, in PRO T 230/20.
14  EC(S)(46)12 and 21, dated 15 February and 2 May 1946, in PRO T 230/21.
15  EC(S)(46)46 Revise and EC(S)(47)29, 'The control of consumption expenditure in the interests of employment policy', 17 December 1946 and 12 August 1947, in PRO T 230/23 and PRO T 230/26; EC(S)(47)9, 'The control of private investment', 12 March 1947, in PRO T 230/24.

instrument for controlling demand. Since most of the papers dealt with fiscal policy, they trenched on the affairs of the Treasury, but Meade had no hesitation in tackling issues so central to economic policy. As a member of the Budget Committee he put forward proposals to it for disinflationary action in 1946 and again in 1947.[16]

Some of the Economic Section's papers were a response to apprehensions of a post-war slump. The Ministerial Committee on Economic Policy asked Meade in July 1946 to prepare a study of this danger and a paper was prepared on 'The possible magnitude of a future depression'.[17] At the beginning of 1947 the Economic Survey Working Party was invited to examine the effects of a depression in the United States starting towards the end of the year or early in 1948 and becoming a major slump by 1949. Earlier, the Working Party was sufficiently pessimistic to put 'normal' unemployment at 425,000 in 1946 rising to 700,000 in 1948–50 and to suggest that a depression in export markets might raise this total by 150,000.[18] Later in the year Robert Hall found it necessary to point out to the Lord President that the real danger to employment lay, not in a collapse of demand overseas, but in a shortage of fuel and materials and the dollars to pay for them.[19]

Long after the war the Section continued to be asked for papers on what to do in a depression that never occurred and had to offer reassurance on the immediate outlook.[20] Since depressions tended to be international, this meant reviewing economic prospects overseas, particularly in the United States, which British ministers (like their Soviet counterparts) regarded as a highly unstable element in the world economy. Fleming and Meade also considered what could be done to

16 See chapter 15. Dow's paper on 'Control of consumption expenditure' had also been circulated to the Budget Committee early in 1947 as BC(47)13.

17 EC(S)(46)36 Revise, 23 October 1946, in PRO T 230/22. The revised version is credited to Dow but the original draft was by Meade (ESWP(46)18 in PRO T 230/56). See also 'The balance of payments in a depression', unsigned, 27 December 1946, in PRO T 230/276.

18 ESWP(46)8 and ESWP(47)2M, 'Long-term economic survey 1948–51', 23 January 1947, in PRO T 230/61.

19 Hall to Lord President, 'Measures to be taken against a world slump', 24 September 1947, in PRO T 230/214.

20 In 1946–7 these included EC(S)(46)48, 'Control of depression' (Meade to Gilbert), 25 November 1946, and EC(S)(47)2, Meade, 'Control of the next depression', 22 January 1947, both in PRO T 230/22 and 24. A. J. Brown also contributed papers on recession in the United States (e.g. EC(S)(47)11, 21 March 1947, in PRO T 230/24).

promote an international full employment policy.[21]

Work on planning for full employment was very much under Meade's direction. In the preparation of economic surveys he acted as Chairman of the Working Party while Tress, in collaboration with Stafford of the CSO, took charge of the drafting. Dow's work on the stabilization of demand was also undertaken at Meade's instigation. Since he put his faith in financial instruments, Meade spent little time on a rationale of the controls which still existed; but in 1947 papers by other members of the Section began to appear on theoretical aspects of central planning and control. Butt, who had joined the Section in the previous year, produced two papers, one on 'The Monnet Plan' and the other on 'The theory of the integration of the investment programmes of Britain and France'.[22] Later in the year Tress circulated papers on 'The philosophy of planning' and 'Planning and cost' while Butt wrote a paper on 'Controls'.[23]

Discussion on planning continued into 1948 and beyond; but it was already evident by the end of 1947 that, as Meade had foreseen, central planning through administrative controls was gradually giving way, as inflationary pressure diminished, to demand management through financial controls. Commenting in mid-1947 on the financial implications of the draft economic plan for 1948–51, Tress suggested that the objective for 1950 (or earlier) should be 'to bring consumer demand within a range such that, apart from shortages like clothing, fiscal controls would be able to contain the pressure'.[24]

## Nationalization

Meade's work schedule in November 1945 listed three other subjects for research. Next after full employment came socialization of industry (Morrison preferred to speak of socialization rather than nationalization).

21 EC(S)(46)25, 'International full employment policy', J. M. Fleming, 20 May 1946, and EC(S)(46)26, 'International employment policy', J. E. Meade and J. M. Fleming, 21 May 1946, in PRO T 230/22. The very idea of international full employment reduced Sir James Grigg at the World Bank to near hysteria. He cabled the Treasury to say that 'full employment is not a snark but a boojum' (Meade, diary, entries for 27 July and 21 September 1946).
22 EC(S)(47)1, 'The Monnet Plan', 6 January 1947, and EC(S)(47)4, 'The theory of the integration of the investment programmes of Britain and France', 3 February 1947, in PRO T 230/24.
23 EC(S)(47)24, 8, and 18 respectively in PRO T 230/24.
24 Tress to Hall, 'Balance of payments: general policy', 17 July 1947, in PRO T 230/276.

This was followed by wage incentives and labour mobility. Finally, more research was needed on restrictive practices and obstacles to competition. Of those three, the first took up most time, the second troubled Meade most of all, and the third remained largely neglected.

Since the Lord President had charge of the programme of nationalization, this was one subject on which he felt badly in need of advice. Soon after he took office the Section submitted to him a list of eight questions on 'Problems and principles of nationalization'. These raised a wide range of issues including the principles that should govern compensation and in what form and on what scale it should be paid; the form of organization that should be adopted and the place of regions and sections of an industry in that organization; and the principles to be followed in fixing prices and wages, engaging in foreign trade, and deciding on the level and timing of investment.[25]

As will be readily appreciated, the preparation of answers by the Section gave rise to some lively controversies. This was particularly so over pricing. Meade and others in the Section were firm believers in marginal cost pricing even though it was likely to imply prices below average costs, and hence a financial loss in many, if not most, nationalized industries. Other members of the Section (for example, Tom Wilson) expressed scepticism. The Treasury remained unconvinced and a series of committee reports rejected the idea. The Lord President was baffled. When told that co-ordination (e.g. between road and rail) was a matter of price policy, best achieved by keeping prices in line with long-run marginal cost, he indignantly pointed out that this was a prescription for competition, not co-ordination.[26] He summoned the entire Economic Section to explain matters and for the first and only time Meade asserted his authority and called on his colleagues to allow him to do the talking. There is not much indication, however, that the Section was able to convey to the Lord President the full subtlety of their views, even if they succeeded in writing what would have been a first-class textbook had it been released for publication (as it now has).[27] If an enterprise was run at a loss, how, he asked, could one be sure that this did not reflect inefficiency rather than pricing at marginal cost?

25 The questions and the Economic Section's answers are in Meade, J. E. (1988) Collected Papers, vol. 2, pp. 51–78.
26 Meade, Diary, entries for 2 December 1945 and 17 April 1946.
27 Meade, J. E. (1988) Collected Papers, vol. 2, pp. 51–77.

## Prices and wages

Issues of price policy arose in other contexts: the use of food subsidies to stabilize the cost of living; the future of price control; control of monopoly and restrictive practices – the lack of which Meade thought 'the most serious deficiency in the government's domestic policy'.[28] The Board of Trade took a soft line on restrictive practices, arguing that they were not necessarily good or bad but must be looked at to see whether they were misused. Meade wanted a list of prohibited practices, with the onus on industry to show why an exception should be made.[29]

With price policy went wage policy in all its aspects: the danger that wages might rise indefinitely in conditions of continuous boom and might even continue to rise in the absence of excess demand; the problem of wage incentives and wage differentials; the difficulty of redistributing labour between places and industries without setting off a general rise in wages. The undermanning of industries like coal and agriculture was of particular concern and the subject of frequent and increasingly desperate minutes. Regional problems, on the other hand, occupied the Section comparatively little. Since they were being actively pursued in the Board of Trade, which had an entire division dealing with them, there was no great need for the Section to take part and the subject is rarely mentioned in the Section papers.[30]

## Allocation of duties

These larger issues absorbed only a limited amount of the Section's time. From day to day they were busy on the matters assigned to them, attending interdepartmental committees, preparing briefs and memoranda for the Lord President, and keeping track of current developments.[31] As we have seen, Tress was drafting economic

---

28 ibid., entry for 12 May 1946.
29 ibid., entries for 27 July and 21 September 1946.
30 There are papers by R. S. Sayers and P. Jefferies on regional differences in wage rates in 1946 and papers on 'Distribution of industry policy' and 'Reconversion in the regions' by J. B. Wood and Dennison respectively in 1945–6. All of these papers are in PRO T 230/18 and 22.
31 The Lord President's queries were not always on immediate issues. See, for example, a memorandum by Nita Watts prepared at his request on 'The economic effects of giving up the empire', 10 September 1946, in PRO T 230/276.

surveys and consulting other departments on the draft. Dow was working on economic stabilization. Work on nationalization involved Norman Chester, Marcus Fleming, Richard Sayers, and Philip Chantler. On the labour market and regional policy, Stanley Dennison and John Wood were mainly responsible with Sayers taking a hand on wage policy; industrial problems were the concern of Sayers and Chantler. Fleming, Arthur Brown, and Nita Watts concentrated on external economic policy.

Of all the industrial problems in 1945–7, those relating to coal and steel occupied the Section most. While papers were written by Chantler and Sayers on price policy, organization, and development plans in coal and steel, the critical issue in those years was how to improve supplies of coal, and to a lesser extent of steel, or at least avoid an acute shortage. Unable to make any impression on Fergusson, the Permanent Secretary of the Ministry of Fuel and Power, Meade told Morrison in July 1946 that 'he had better accept as inevitable a serious shortage next winter' and consider instead how best to allocate what coal was available.[32] When the coal crisis did arrive in February 1946, it was not for lack of advance warning. Indeed, a strong warning had already been given by the Section as far back as July 1945.[33] Fergusson was also arguing for a uniform pithead price for coal throughout the country although, as Chantler showed, this was a very inefficient method of pricing.[34] Similarly, the Ministry was obsessed by the danger of Polish competition and wanted to secure, through bilateral deals, markets for the coal it was unable to supply.[35]

Other work done in the Section, mainly at the end of 1945, was on commodity policy. Fleming and Dow both did papers for the Buffer Stocks Working Party, of which Robert Hall was a member, in January 1946; and a paper on 'Centralised importation' was circulated at the same time to a Committee on Bulk Purchase.[36] Another example of work for an interdepartmental committee is Richard Sayers's paper on 'Transport charges', which deals with the principles that the railways should follow after nationalization.[37]

32 Meade, diary, entry for 27 July 1946.
33 LP(45)127, 'Survey of the general economic position', 25 July 1945, in PRO CAB 71/21.
34 EC(S)(46)17 Revise, Chantler, 'An economic policy for the socialized coal industry', 23 May 1946, in PRO T 230/21.
35 Meade, diary, entry for 21 September 1946.
36 These papers (EC(S)(46)3, 8 and 6 respectively) are all in PRO T 230/20.
37 EC(S)(47)10, 18 March 1947, in PRO T 230/24.

## External economic policy

The Section had an expanding role in external economic policy, which is reviewed in chapters 17 and 18. Here we need note only the kind of issues that occupied them in 1945–7, leaving aside the key problem of the balance of payments.

First of all came the American Loan negotiations at the end of 1945. Lionel Robbins took an active part in these as Director and James Meade was much involved at the London end in helping to draft replies to the stream of telegrams from the delegation and in discussing the issues raised with Douglas Jay at No. 10 and James Helmore at the Board of Trade.[38]

Another matter of keen concern to the Section was the problem of the large balances of sterling that had accumulated in wartime as debts to India, Egypt, and other countries. The Section took for granted the need for extensive blocking. It did not share the optimism of the Board of Trade, which was inclined to see positive virtue in sterling balances as a store of demand for British exports that would prove very useful as international competition increased.[39] It attacked what it regarded as the Bank of England's 'super-banker's bluff' in pretending that the pound was as good as gold so that neither cancellation nor blocking was necessary and no limit need be set to withdrawals.[40]

Meade was always alive to the possibility of lowering the exchange rate, recognizing the need for a larger share of world trade and the link between this and lower British export prices. When both Sweden and Canada revalued their currencies, he turned over in his mind the possibility of following suit, but does not seem to have urged at any stage letting the pound float. Though he would have liked to aim at 'a free market for currencies in London', he was at a loss to see how this could be reconciled with control over capital movements.[41]

Meade also continued his wartime interest in commercial policy and his last duties as Director took him to Geneva in the spring of 1947 to take part in the discussions there on the proposed International Trade Organization. Other members of the Section also began in 1947 to represent the Section at meetings abroad, Fleming and Nita Watts in Geneva and Tress and Nita Watts in Paris on the Marshall Plan. From

38 Information from Mrs K. Jones.
39 Meade, diary, entry for 30 June 1946; EC(S)(46)56, Nita Watts, 'The settlement of the sterling balances', 9 December 1946, in PRO T 230/23.
40 Meade, ibid.
41 Meade, diary, entry for 27 July 1946.

then onwards it became normal practice for a member of the Section to be involved in preparing in London the briefs for UK delegations to the UN, ECOSOC, ECE, etc., on economic issues and often to provide a member of the delegation attending the meetings.

Reporting on world economic developments was undertaken single-handed by A. J. Brown, who prepared a rapid succession of papers in 1945–6 for a lengthy Overseas Economic Survey.[42] Brown also kept the Section informed on economic prospects in the United States, the outlook for world trade in manufactures, and so on, and made calculations of the fundamental elasticities in British trade, which Fleming denounced as 'poison' if applied experimentally (i.e. in deciding whether to devalue).

## Conclusion

The Economic Section in 1945–7 was in a state of transition. There was a rapid turnover of staff and a major change in the framework of policy. At the ministerial level the Section lacked the powerful support of a minister of unquestioned authority; at the official level, the Treasury was reasserting itself as the central economic department and felt free to reject Economic Section advice. Meade, as Director, had a clear and coherent view of the instruments of policy necessary for the management of the economy and of the place of the Section in relation to those instruments. But he was advising the wrong minister at the wrong time. His influence on Dalton could never have matched what it had been on Anderson and might have been on Cripps. Moreover, he was uncomfortable in a world of physical controls when his vision was of a world of financial controls. He was impatient to speed up the transition from one set to the other without making sufficient allowance for the limitations of financial controls and the positive need for physical controls in a world that was badly out of balance. Meade, more than any man – more than Keynes – was the prophet of demand management when the world was not yet ready for demand management.

42 An eighty page draft was circulated on 13 February 1946. The final, shorter, version, EC(S)(46)15, is in PRO T 230/21 and is dated 4 March 1946. A Second Overseas Economic Survey was circulated early in 1947. These papers went to the Ministerial Committee on External Economic Policy, which was wound up in 1947.

It was not his fault if the Economic Section in 1947 was at a low ebb. The channels of economic advice were blocked and it took two major crises to free them. The political atmosphere, the ministerial arrangements, and the personal links between advisers and advised had all undergone a revolution by the time Meade's successor took up his duties.

# Chapter nine

# THE ECONOMIC SECTION UNDER ROBERT HALL

Robert Hall, who took over from James Meade on a full-time basis on 1 September 1947, held office as Director of the Economic Section for fourteen years – twice as long as his three predecessors put together and much longer than any of his successors. From 1947 onwards it was through him that the views of the Section reached ministers and it was mainly through him that the Section made its influence felt on economic policy. He proved an outstanding success under both Labour and Conservative governments as adviser to a long line of Chancellors – eight in fourteen years.

Throughout his term of office it was the Economic Section's assessment of the economic situation as put forward by Robert Hall that formed the starting-point of budget discussions. He played an important part in the various crises and turning-points in economic policy from 1947 onwards. It was he more than anyone else who prepared the ground for the devaluation of 1949, rearmament in 1950–1, and the rejection of Robot in 1952.[1] He fought for and secured the introduction of the investment allowance suggested by John Jukes in 1953.[2] He had great influence on Cripps (although he exercised it mainly through Edwin Plowden), less on Gaitskell, a good deal on Butler, and varying success with Butler's successors (Macmillan, Thorneycroft, Amory, and Selwyn Lloyd).

1 For a detailed study of each of these episodes see Cairncross, Sir Alec (1985) *Years of Recovery*, London: Methuen, and the testimony of Lord Boyle, 'The economist in government', in the volume of essays in honour of A. J. Brown, Bowers, J. K. (ed.) (1979) *Inflation, Development and Integration*, Leeds: Leeds University Press.
2 Jukes to Hall, 'Economic policy', 28 November 1952, in PRO T 230/328.

An Australian Rhodes Scholar, who had started in engineering in Queensland before turning to economics in Oxford, Robert Hall had been a Fellow of Trinity College, Oxford, since 1927. He was known to his colleagues from his study of the economics of a socialist state and more particularly for his attempts to submit economic theories to empirical tests. He took a prominent part in pre-war research in Oxford into the working of the price mechanism, including surveys of business reactions to changes in interest rates that showed what was thought to be surprisingly little response.

Throughout the war Hall was on the staff of the Ministry of Supply, with a spell in Washington at the Combined Raw Materials Board. In April 1945 Meade tried to induce him to join the Section after the war, in effect as his deputy, but Hall declined.[3] In October 1945 he returned to Oxford but continued on a part-time footing in the Board of Trade (which had absorbed the Raw Materials Division of the Ministry of Supply) so as to help in the preparation of a buffer stocks scheme to stabilize international commodity prices under the proposed International Trade Organization. He was released to join the Section on a part-time basis in June 1947 and took up his duties full-time in September. His arrival coincided broadly with the manning of the Central Economic Planning Staff under Plowden, which went on over the summer months.

The Section when Hall took over was in poor shape. Morrison's illness in the first half of the year had deprived them of ministerial direction and it was still lacking in the autumn when the economy was in crisis. Meade had been either ill or absent for much of the year. Nearly half of the staff – the more experienced staff – had left or were on the point of leaving. There was an obvious contrast with the rise of the CEPS although the CEPS also played little part in the convertibility crisis when it broke in August 1947.

It was symptomatic of the low state of the Section that Hall was not at first a member of the Budget Committee. He was told by Bridges – himself a firm believer in the Treasury's need for advice from the Economic Section – that Dalton, being himself an economist, felt that he could dispense with such advice. It was just such an attitude that had disposed Meade to abandon the job. However, it was not long before the Director was once again a member of the Budget Committee. Dalton resigned as Chancellor; and each of his successors in turn found wisdom in accepting Hall's advice, most of all on their budgets.

3 Meade, diary, entries for 1 and 14 April 1945.

Hall was a very different personality from Meade. Meade liked to approach economic problems from the theoretical end, with a systematic, precise, and articulate exposition of principle. Charged with being academic, he would take pleasure in the charge, pointing out that to be academic one must have engaged in deep study of the subject. Hall, on the other hand, had always an eye on results and was sparing in his use of theory. Where James Meade was prepared to make sixteen points to a meeting that had expressed a unanimous contrary view, Hall was quick to recognize when the battle was lost and switch to a more promising issue. He had great common sense, an intuitive grasp of the practicable, and a strong natural judgement of men and affairs. He believed in getting involved in the tedious work of government and took on much of the drafting of ministerial speeches – a task for which he had a particular gift.

Hall belonged to the one-handed school of advisers. He told Jack Downie:

> In general, administrators find that a balanced view from an economist is no use at all. In particular, the Economic Section is expected to say what course they themselves would take in a given situation and to say it positively. In my experience it is not much use giving advice to Ministers unless it is very loud and clear.[4]

In his relations with staff he was always approachable, even if not always available. He encouraged debate and controversy within the Section. He did not, however, delight in communication, almost for its own sake, as James Meade did. He preferred to dictate short minutes, which he never amended, rather than draft lengthy memoranda, and, where Meade like to bring in his colleagues, he usually worked on his own, leaving other members of the Section to get on with their various jobs or discover for themselves what they could most usefully do. Members of the Section, however, would have hesitated to launch a new initiative or go out on a limb in opposition to one of the big departments without making sure in advance that the Director knew of it.

It was always true in the Economic Section that the work of the Director cut him off for much of the time from his staff and vice versa. He had frequent meetings of senior officials to attend, occasional discussions with the Chancellor and other ministers, speeches to draft, papers to prepare, and visits to make to America, France, and elsewhere, often lasting for several weeks, in addition to all the routine

4 Hall to Downie, 26 October 1949, in PRO T 230/163.

administrative duties, reading work by his professional colleagues, trying to recruit staff, and so on. Even so, the regular meetings of staff went on every week; the Director was not too busy to take an afternoon off to visit the Battersea funfair with a large contingent of his staff during the Festival of Britain; and the Section Christmas party became an annual institution under Hall.

## Staff problems

Finding staff of the right calibre continued to be a serious problem. Although there was an inflow of three or four a year from 1946 to 1949, with six (including Robert Hall himself) in 1947, it was a constant struggle to keep up the numbers in the Section: a struggle that was bound to occupy the Director personally. Academic economists were few in number and only too happy to resume their university duties. They were not attracted by civil service salaries and in many cases were hesitant to offer their services to a government that struck them as accident-prone and in the grip of an uncongenial ideology.

Meade had complained in 1944 of his 'great difficulty in persuading the Treasury to offer sufficiently attractive terms' to induce temporary economists to stay on.[5] It was a cry echoed by Hall at frequent intervals after he took over. He was constantly badgered to recruit more staff but no action was taken to make recruitment easier. There was virtually no prospect of promotion beyond the level of Economic Adviser (treated as equivalent to Principal) and in 1953 the Treasury withdrew the prospect previously held out of moving over to the administrative grade, in which officials of less ability stood far better chances of promotion.

By the end of 1947 Hall was left with a much denuded staff, of whom only three had served in the Section in wartime: Marcus Fleming, Nita Watts, and Peggy Hemming (née Joseph). Eight others had joined since the war but, of those eight, four stayed with him only for a year or two – G. L. S. Shackle, G. P. Jefferies, S. Abramson, and Jennifer Forsyth. The four who remained were Christopher Dow, David Bensusan-Butt, J. W. P. Keane, and Kit Jones (née Howell), who acted as Hall's assistant. To supplement this group Hall was able to borrow J. M. Fearn for a few months from the Scottish Office and Meade had arranged for Trevor Swan to come for a year from the

---

5 Meade, diary, entry for 19 November 1944. A month later Keynes commented that 'economics was not yet taken as a serious subject', ibid., entry for 31 December 1944.

Prime Minister's Department in Australia. This left Hall at the beginning of 1948 with a staff of twelve, one of them seconded for a year only and some less than satisfactory from Hall's point of view. The Section had plenty of able but inexperienced young recruits. What it lacked was a group of senior economists such as had established its wartime reputation.

In each of the next two years Hall recruited four more economists: first Jack Downie, Bryan Hopkin (on secondment), John Jukes, and J. W. V. Licence; then Fred Atkinson, John Grieve-Smith, Joan Kelley, and (again on secondment) Russell Bretherton. By the end of 1949 he was thus in a much stronger position, with two senior economists, Bretherton and Fleming, as Deputy Directors, and some outstanding young economists among the other thirteen members of staff.

Thereafter there was a more stable situation and recruitment of young economists by advertisement seems to have ceased for the time being. Another administrator, Peter Le Cheminant, was borrowed for two years in 1950 and two economists, D. J. C. Jones (1950) and Robert Neild (1951), were recruited. On the other hand, Bretherton and Fleming left in 1951 and for the next two years Hall was without a Deputy.

Hall continued to make use of administrative officers on secondment (Michael Franklin from 1952 to 1955 and Frank Figgures from 1955 to 1957) and borrowed Peter Lawler in 1952 from Australia. But at this point, under pressure from Norman Brook, he turned increasingly to the universities – and particularly his own University of Oxford – for recruits and began in 1952 to make arrangements for academic economists to join the Section for two years on leave of absence. This arrangement not only brought in a succession of able young economists to renew the link with academic life but allowed a sprinkling of the younger generation of economists to gain experience of policy-making in Whitehall.

From Oxford came a steady flow of young dons: Dick Ross (1952), Ian Little (1953), Maurice Scott (1953), Kit McMahon (1954), and, in later years, David Henderson (1957) and Roger Opie (1958). Wynne Godley (1955), although an Oxford graduate, was an employee of the Metal Box Company when recruited, not of the University. Only Kit McMahon and Wynne Godley stayed much beyond two years.

Other academics who joined the Section briefly in the 1950s were Miles Fleming (1952–4) from Bristol, Alan Day (1954–6) and Alec Nove (1956–8) from LSE, W. S. Scammell (1956–8), and Athole Mackintosh (1959–61). Of the half-dozen others who came and went in the 1950s only Philip Watts stayed for more than two years, leaving in 1959 for the Central Electricity Generating Board. Those who stayed into the sixties or later included Michael Kennedy (1956–65), John Brunner (1959–61), Patricia Brown (1956–85), and David Howell (later a Cabinet minister under Mrs Thatcher), who was a member for a year in 1959–60. In all, including five recruits who joined in 1960, sixty economists, or economist–administrators, served in the Economic Section under Robert Hall.

When the Section moved to the Treasury, in November 1953, it was a very different body from what it had been in wartime or under James Meade. Nita Watts and Peggy Hemming were the sole survivors from wartime and Christopher Dow, now promoted to Senior Economic Adviser after a long battle with the Establishment Division, was the only other member apart from Kit Jones who had served under Meade. Ian Little had come in as Deputy to Robert Hall; and there were six Economic Advisers (Miles Fleming, Mrs Hemming, John Jukes, J. W. P. Keane, Dick Ross, and Nita Watts), four Economic Assistants (Michael Franklin, John Grieve-Smith, Joan Kelley, and Robert Neild), and another (Peter Lawler) on loan from Australia, making fourteen in all.[6] In addition, the Section had the benefit for the time being of two former members of Lord Cherwell's staff, Jack Parkinson and Maurice Scott. Waiting in the wings, so to speak, was Kit McMahon, for whom there was no room in the Section but who had accepted a temporary post with the Treasury Information Unit in preference to competing for an All Souls Fellowship.[7] In addition to those in Whitehall, Martin Fearn, although firmly established in Edinburgh as Economic Adviser to the Scottish Office, was still regarded (by Establishment) as on the strength; Fred Atkinson was posted to Washington, Jack Downie was on loan for two years to ECE in Geneva, and John Licence was on indefinite loan to NATO, all three of them graded as Economic Advisers. There was also one Economic Assistant, D. J. C. Jones, on loan to OEEC. Thus the total number attached to the Economic Section in one way or another, including a couple of transients and Fearn in Edinburgh, but not Kit McMahon, was 21.[8]

Salaries ranged from £500–£600 for the Economic Assistants to

6 Keane left in November 1953. Until he did, the Section was one above strength.
7 Frank Blackaby and Kit Jones were also serving at that time in the Treasury Information Unit.
8 'Transfer of Economic Section to Treasury', PRO T 199/257.

£2,400 for Ian Little and £3,750 for Robert Hall (an increase of £1,000 over his salary in the Cabinet Office). While a few members of staff were established (Christopher Dow, for example), most were either on five-year contracts (renewable) or on leave of absence for two years from academic posts.

However much he might gird at the inadequacies of the staff he inherited and despair throughout his term of office of building up the strength of the Section, Hall was able to preserve a remarkably high intellectual standard and maintain the prestige of the Section. There might be no future Prime Ministers or Nobel Laureates as there had been in 1940 but the staff did include many who achieved distinction in their later careers: a Deputy Governor of the Bank of England, two Assistant Secretary-Generals of OECD, a Reith Lecturer, and two Heads of the Government Economic service. Many who served in the Section under Hall went on to fill university chairs or important appointments elsewhere.

## The economic background

Hall's fourteen years as Director of the Economic Section fell into two parts: the first consists of the six years 1947–53 when the Section was still in the Cabinet Office and Hall worked in close association with Plowden; the second consists of the ensuing eight years after the move to the Treasury and the departure of Plowden.

In the first of those periods the outstanding events were the convertibility crisis of 1947; the launching of the European Recovery Programme and the formation of the OEEC in 1947–48; the devaluation of the pound in 1949; the Korean War and rearmament, beginning in mid-1950; the change of government in October 1951; the exchange crisis of 1951–2 and the long battle with the Treasury over Robot, the secret proposal by the Bank of England for sterling convertibility combined with a floating pound; and the recovery in 1953 from the check to economic activity in 1952.

It will be observed that most of the crises of policy arose from balance of payments difficulties, the major exception being the shortages, bottle-necks, and other difficulties associated with rearmament. Throughout the first four years, from 1947 to 1951, inflationary pressure was a constant problem, easing a little in 1947–50 and becoming acute again in 1951 before subsiding in 1952. The major problem of policy more or less throughout the period was how to preserve external balance and moderate this pressure without creating too much unemployment.

The second period from 1953 onwards was one of consumer boom. The terms of trade, which had moved more and more against the United Kingdom from the end of the war until 1952, now swung the other way. Import prices, instead of making the running in pushing up the cost of living, lagged behind, damping down inflationary pressure. Exports and investment, which had absorbed the bulk of the increment in output in the early post-war years, now climbed more slowly, leaving a larger residue for consumption. Nevertheless, the pressure of demand increased from 1952 to 1955 and remained very high over the following two years until the exchange crisis in September 1957 when the bank rate was put up to 7 per cent. The measures then taken produced or aggravated a recession in 1958 from which the economy recovered in 1959–60 until a fresh exchange crisis occurred in the summer of 1961.

The economic problems of the second period were thus rather different from those of the first. The transition from war to peace was over. Nearly all the wartime controls had been abandoned by 1954, with the notable exception of exchange control. External balance had been recovered and the dollar shortage of earlier years was much less acute. The consumer was doing well and had been promised a doubling in his standard of living within twenty-five years. The pressure on the economy from excess demand was much reduced except in the middle fifties when unemployment fell as low as 0.9 per cent.

The second period also saw the emergence of economic growth as a policy objective. Not that anyone had an infallible recipe for growth such as was claimed for full employment. What was clear was that the path to economic growth lay through full employment and that, while some forms of planning might be counter-productive, planning for full employment had to continue in the interests of economic growth.

This came to be recognized by private industry just as much as by the government. By the early fifties business had sufficient confidence in continuously expanding markets and a slump-free future to plan for economic growth; this helped to produce the growth for which they planned. The change was most readily apparent in 1954 when a recession in the United States had remarkably little effect on the continuing surge in activity in Britain and other European countries. Business men complained in the later 1950s of stop–go policies that checked expansion in order to strengthen the balance of payments. But they retained their expectations of long-run growth in spite of these short-term disturbances and looked to the goverment to follow their example and plan on a long-run basis. Thus by the end of the 1950s planning, which had become a dirty word by the late 1940s, was coming back into fashion under pressure, not from the Labour Party, but from the Conservatives, who had earlier derided it. By 1961 Selwyn Lloyd had created, in the National Economic Development Council, a body committed to economic planning – or at least to agitating for it.

## The development of policy

By the autumn of 1947 ministers were in a different state of mind from that of a year before and so, too, were officials. There was a greater willingness to listen to the kind of radical advice that James Meade had offered unsuccessfully. Views that had much in common with Meade's were already being expressed by Plowden, so that when Robert Hall took over he could count on a more sympathetic hearing. The country had awakened to inflation and the dollar problem, begun to talk of Marshall Aid and European integration, and was being forced to accept that the rift with Russia had deepened into a rupture.

The political upheavals in the autumn mentioned in the last chapter had included the rise of Cripps as the most powerful Chancellor of the post-war period. The Treasury was in process of reasserting its authority over a more highly centralized economic administration than any in pre-war years and an elaborate planning machinery was taking shape. To the Steering Committee of Permanent Secretaries was added an Economic Planning Board to sound out industry – employers and trade union representatives – on the government's plans: not a very useful addition since ministers were never present and officials could not commit the government. Beneath the Steering Committee was a whole clutch of new interdepartmental committees of which the most important was the Investment Programmes Committee (to prune investment plans), the Programmes Committee (to control imports and review the balance of payments), and the Overseas Negotiations Committee (to supervise bilateral trade with other countries and look after overseas economic relations). Yet another committee (the 'London' Committee) co-ordinated policy towards the OEEC in Paris and the negotiations in progress there.

The autumn of 1947 was probably the low point in the post-war years in Whitehall morale. Ministers seemed incapable of taking painful decisions. They called for national unity while they pressed on simultaneously with divisive decisions such as nationalization of the steel industry. They seemed to have no answer to the problem of inflation and to be unwilling either to restrain demand through the budget or to interfere with collective bargaining. There were those who feared that ministers would seek an easy and convenient answer to their difficulties in renewed help from the United States. By October, however, Cripps and Dalton had pushed through the Cabinet a number of cuts in imports and investment and Cripps had embarked on a series of speeches setting export targets and calling for austerity.

Over the winter of 1947–8 things changed radically. The budget of November 1947, in which Dalton had screwed himself up to be deflationary, was judged by Hall at the time to yield too small a surplus for the purpose. But by 1948 the medicine was beginning to work: prices were more stable, the balance of payments was improving, and the pressure on the economy was easing. Cripps had restored morale, the country's self-confidence was returning, and the outlook was altogether more hopeful. Cripps became the undisputed controller of economic policy, Plowden his trusted adviser, and Hall in turn the source of the advice.

After 1948 came three crowded years, with devaluation in 1949, the Schuman Plan for a Coal and Steel Community in 1950, the Korean War and rearmament, beginning in 1950–1, and an exchange crisis early in 1952. In all of these the Section was deeply involved, with battles over devaluation in 1949 and over Robot during the exchange crisis in 1952. Things were never quite so hectic thereafter, except in 1955 and 1957 when there were fresh crises and sharp disagreements over policy.

In 1952 there had been a minor depression and recovery from it appeared to be slow. In 1953 and even 1954 it sometimes appeared to the Section that the economy had begun to run out of steam and that, with rearmament subsiding and the housing boom past its peak, there might be nothing to carry the economy up in the absence of some governmental stimulus. In fact, however, investment mounted steadily and the pressure on the economy remained intense until 1958.

It had seemed in 1952–4 as if inflationary pressure was receding: the rise in retail prices had greatly moderated. But with the development of a major boom in 1955–6 inflation accelerated again and the government found great difficulty in slowing it down. The struggle against inflation returned to the forefront of policy but without the various controls that had earlier been available and no new instruments to take their place except monetary policy.

The intense pressure of demand in the mid-1950s was combined with a continuing rise in wages. With full employment had come an annual round of wage increases that outstripped the growth in productivity and pushed up wage costs per unit of output, eating into competitive power and weakening the balance of payments. Between 1953 and 1961 money wages rose by 45 per cent compared with about 50 per cent over the previous eight years while for retail prices the comparable figures were 25 per cent and 40 per cent. Thus the slowing down in wage increases was rather slight in comparison with the slowing down in price increases; an acceleration in the rise of real wages had done little to make money wages more stable.

The long continued rise in wages and prices created increasing public concern. So far as wages were concerned the Conservative government had consistently refused to adopt any form of incomes policy as the Section kept suggesting. Until 1961 they did not go beyond a white paper in 1956 on *The Economic Implications of Full Employment* and the setting up of a Council of Prices, Productivity, and Incomes in 1957 to issue guidance to the parties engaged in collective bargaining – guidance which the trade unions undertook in advance to ignore. They could not reduce the pressure of demand, which was the more immediate danger, through the use of fiscal policy so long as they were set on reducing taxation and unable to make large reductions in public expenditure even with Chancellors publicly committed to doing so. Since they were also anxious to encourage investment, they hesitated also to raise interest rates.

The instrument to which they turned in order to moderate inflation was nevertheless monetary policy. This they regarded as a relatively anonymous way of checking demand, and they used it in 1952 in order to bring interest rates back into play, in 1955 as an alternative to higher taxation, and in 1957 to give effect to the quantity theory of money. Their efforts to revive the use of monetary policy are discussed in chapter 14. They were not, to say the least, conspicuously successful and left in doubt the much debated question of how monetary policy works – a question referred in 1957 to the Radcliffe Committee.

## The work of the Section

We shall be dealing with the work of the Section in the chapters that follow under a series of headings corresponding to the main aspects of macroeconomic policy. Inevitably, however, these will focus on the discussions at the top between the Director, senior Treasury officials, and the Chancellor, while many of the contributions made by the staff are passed over. It is not possible, and would be wearisome, to describe in detail the activities of each member of the Section, but it would give a very distorted picture if no effort was made to convey something of what went on within the Section.

First, something can be said about the allocation of duties between members of the Section, even if it was rare that there was any formal allocation of duties and members felt free or might be invited to invade the territory of their colleagues. In such a small group everybody had to turn his hand to whatever needed to be done and had to try to keep in line with Section thinking or, if in disagreement, feel at liberty to argue the matter.

Second, we can learn something of the interests and activities of individual members from the discussion papers they wrote, although they do not throw much light on what occupied them from day to day. The papers were usually written for discussion at the Section's weekly meetings and tend to deal with the less urgent matters and with issues of principle or theory or to report the results of research.

Third, there is the story revealed in the hundreds of Section files, now in the Public Records Office, of minutes and briefs and memoranda: and not only in the Section files but in the files of other Treasury divisions, the minutes of interdepartmental meetings, and other sources. It would be possible to construct from these an outline of the main preoccupations of the Section from year to year and the part played by individual members of the Section in advising on the key issues. But this would inevitably duplicate the story in later chapters or consist of the scraps left over. We have preferred, therefore, to weave into later chapters a fuller account of the role of individual members of the Section than the narrative strictly requires.

We start with a word on the duties of the Economic Section. Under James Meade the prime function of the Economic Section had been to brief the Lord President. From the autumn of 1947 this was no longer so. The Section acted now as advisers to the Chancellor. He was in receipt of advice from two other sources: the departmental Treasury and the Central Economic Planning Staff (CEPS). However, since the CEPS came to rely on the Economic Section for professional advice and the Treasury itself had no professional economic staff, the way was left clear for the Section to continue in its role as specialist advisers on economic issues. This was not quite how things worked out. It made more sense to prepare single briefs for the Chancellor than to supply him with three. But there were, of course, occasions on which Robert Hall minuted the Chancellor direct and the Chancellor was always aware of the Section's views.

There were certain specific duties which the Section discharged, such as drafting the annual *Economic Survey*, engaging in forecasting exercises, and representing the Section on the numerous economic committees with which Whitehall was honeycombed. Other duties, equally time-consuming, were more general. The business of gathering economic intelligence and interpreting it came high on the list. The Section had to keep track also of policy on the main economic issues, to compare it with actual development as recorded in current statistics, and draw attention to the way in which the balance of the economy was being affected: a change in inflationary pressure, a weakening of the current balance, and so on. 'Our most useful job,' Robert Hall told his staff in 1948, 'and one which no one else will do, is to watch those cumulative effects of separately trivial changes, and weigh in when necessary with a general comment.'[9]

The most important of the Section's duties lay in demand management. Much of their work revolved round issues of macroeconomic policy: the stabilization of economic activity, investment policy, the maintenance of internal and external balance, and so on. They contributed to an assessment of the economic outlook in various committees, notably the Economic Survey Working Party, the National Income Forecasts Working Party, and the Working Party on World Economic Problems. They also undertook pioneering work to throw light on how the economy functioned and submitted proposals for policy changes. Hall, as Director, was a member of the Budget Committee and played a main role in framing the budget judgement and drafting speeches for the Chancellor.

Public expenditure, the traditional area of Treasury control, occupied the Section very little. This was almost inevitable when the Section did not form part of the Treasury and the Planning Staff was the more natural adviser on policy. But even after 1953 the Section's interest in public expenditure derived largely from its responsibilities for demand management and was concentrated on changes in the aggregates. Members of the Section were not assigned a specific area of public expenditure on which to advise and were rarely called in by the expenditure divisions. They were, however, always interested in investment and represented on the Investment Programmes Committee and its successor, the Treasury Investment Committee. They prepared many papers on agriculture, coal, and steel which had a direct bearing on public spending. In 1950-1 they took a leading part in the planning of the rearmament programme. But the major issues of pensions (apart from the preparation of evidence to the Phillips Committee in

9 EC(S)(48)1, 'Progressing the *Economic Survey*', note by R. L. Hall, 7 January 1948, in PRO T 230/27.

1953),[10] health, education, and (except in 1950–1) defence were rarely the subject of Economic Section advice.

On the external side, the Section was constantly occupied. First, there were all the problems of the balance of payments and exchange rate management: the dollar problem; the recurrent fears of an American depression; the development of the European payments system both before and after the formation of the EPU; the struggles over sterling balances; the decline of bilateral monetary agreements; the moves towards convertibility from its suspension in 1947 to the Robot proposals of 1952, the long debate that followed, the support of the rate for transferable sterling in February 1955 and the final establishment of convertibility in December 1958; relations with the IMF, for example after Suez; the succession of balance of payments crises in 1949, 1952, 1955, and 1957. Then there was the effort to rebuild British trade and to establish a more liberal trading order: the relatively slow growth of Commonwealth markets and the loss of share in them, first to the United States, then to Japan, Germany, and other countries; the gradual liberalization of European trade and the birth of a keener interest in trade with Europe; the reduction of trade barriers and the abandonment of import quotas and of discrimination against dollar imports. Third, there was the wider issue of the links with the United States, the Commonwealth, and Western Europe – an issue that remained acute throughout Robert Hall's term of office and beyond.

Not all of these were matters primarily for the Treasury, much less the Economic Section. The Foreign Office, the Board of Trade, the Ministry of Agriculture, and other departments had a strong interest in most if not all but the Treasury was undoubtedly in the lead on the first set of problems and took a leading part in the other two. The Economic Section was also intimately involved and at times its influence was decisive. This was the more so because the Foreign Office had no economists and after 1949 there were virtually no economists elsewhere in Whitehall except in the Ministry of Agriculture and on intelligence work in the Ministry of Defence.

A tentative allocation of duties in 1948 listed groups of topics, the committees dealing with them, and the economic adviser or assistant to be assigned to each group.[11] The work was divided between ten

10 The papers are in PRO T 230/274.
11 EC(S)(48)1. There does not appear to be any later allocation of duties in the records.

economists, including two assistants still to be appointed. David Butt would be expected to cover investment programmes, and Christopher Dow and Trevor Swan a large group of subjects ranging from inflation to food consumption, national income, and the budget. The same pair were nominated to cover manpower, wages, and productivity. Other topics were the balance of payments, the terms of trade, Marshall Aid, and bilateral agreements (Marcus Fleming and Nita Watts), exports and imports (Pat Jefferies, Nita Watts, and a new assistant), and two industrial groupings, one covering fuel and power, transport, and agriculture (J. W. P. Keane) and the other, steel, raw materials, and stocks (Peggy Hemming).

Even for the year 1948 this is a very misleading summary of the allocation of work. It makes no mention of such matters as monetary policy, controls, or economic activity in other countries, in all of which the Section took an interest; it omits various members of the Section, such as Shackle and Kit Howell; and above all it gives no inkling of how the work in progress issued in action either through the Director or in some other way.

On monetary policy, for example, Robert Hall spent some time in 1948 in argument with the Bank of England over their failure to control monetary expansion when the Budget was in surplus. At the same time Shackle was asking why there should be any connection between the two things. Central banks, he pointed out, were able to regulate the supply of money when budget surpluses were unheard of. Could it be, he asked, that 'monetary means of dealing with inflation are now such a gross form of political bad manners that they must be disguised as fiscal measures?'[12] On controls, Hall had persuaded the Treasury to set up a committee to review their effect on efficiency and incentives. Dow and Polly Hill (then in the Board of Trade) were appointed joint secretaries of the Committee and submitted two papers to it to form the basis of a report.[13] As for economic activity abroad, when A. J. Brown's 'Overseas economic survey' was discontinued the Section retained an interest in economic trends in the United States and Europe.

What really matters, however, is not what appeared on the agenda for a particular year but how the work was organized. In his early years Hall made great use of Butt and Dow on domestic issues and

12 EC(S)(48)35, G. L. S. Shackle, 'Money and interest in 1948', 13 October 1948, in PRO T 230/28.
13 EC(S)(48)27, 'Policy on controls', 20 July 1948, and EC(S)(48)33 Revise, 'The alternatives to materials allocations', 3 November 1948, in PRO T 230/28.

relied also on his Deputies, Marcus Fleming and Russell Bretherton, the one for external policy and the other for domestic policy. Butt's main responsibility was as Secretary of the Economic Survey Working Party while Dow took over much of the national income forecasting work previously undertaken by Tress. They worked in conjunction with Jack Downie, a recent arrival on whom Hall came to rely heavily, and with Trevor Swan during his year in the Section in 1948.

Butt worked on long-term plans as well as annual surveys. He helped Austin Robinson on a *Long-term Economic Survey* and Douglas Jay on a long-term programme for submission to OEEC. One of his papers, written in March 1948 on the economic consequences to be expected if Britain received no Marshall Aid, was used by Hall in June to help in overcoming ministerial reluctance to accept American conditions for proceeding with the European Recovery Plan.[14] In April 1949 he handed over the drafting of the 1949 *Survey* to Downie before he left for a year in Australia in repayment for the loan of Swan. Few members of the Section wrote memoranda that were so pungent and entertaining as Butt's.

Dow, as we have seen, was already busy with issues of demand management at the end of 1947. In 1948 Hall brought him increasingly into budgetary problems. When Hall and Plowden persuaded the Budget Committee to meet throughout the year so as to take a longer-term view of budgetary problems, it was Dow who was asked to do most of the preparatory work. It was also his job to keep an eye on the general economic situation and help to prepare economic forecasts.

With Fleming, a more senior economist, Hall's relations were not altogether happy. He felt no natural rapport with him and no confidence that they saw eye to eye. But on technical issues Fleming had a free hand and there was never any doubt as to his outstanding intellectual ability. Until he left in 1951 he was assisted by Nita Watts, who then took over more responsibility for international issues, briefly by Jennifer Forsyth, who dealt with such matters as reparations policy and proposals for a customs union (either with Europe or with the Commonwealth), and in 1950–1 by Kit Howell (e.g. in a working party on Japan). Peggy Hemming, Pat Jefferies, J. W. P. Keane, and George Shackle had less specific duties, the first two working for a time on pricing policy in the coal industry. Kit Howell was given the job after the 1948 budget of preparing monthly reports on the economic situation under the supervision of Dow. The request for

14 CP(48)61, 'Economic consequences of receiving no ERP aid', memorandum by the Chancellor of the Exchequer, 23 June 1948, in PRO CAB 129/28.

these reports, which went to ministers and were abandoned only in December 1950, reflected Cripps's concern that he might have gone too far in the direction of deflation and his need for reassurance that there was no immediate danger of a slump.[15]

If we move on to a year like 1953 it is more difficult to identify the precise duties of the staff since many of them wrote on both domestic and external policy. This was true, for example, of the Deputy Director, Ian Little, who had recently joined the Section. Nita Watts now focused almost entirely on external policy and was a regular member of the Progammes Committee and other interdepartmental committees dealing with external relations. Christopher Dow organized much of the work on domestic problems and served as secretary to a Budget Committee Working Party. He, Franklin, and Neild all dealt with monetary problems. Franklin was also joint secretary of a Coal Exports Policy Committee and a working party on relations with the European Coal and Steel Community, while Neild was secretary of three committees: the National Income Forecasts Working Party, started in 1950, the Export Trends Working Party, and the Statistical Working Party on Effects of a US Recession. Dick Ross took charge of national income forecasting and was joint secretary of a Working Party on Employment Policy. John Jukes supervised a study of long-term growth in which Peter Lawler, Maurice Scott, and Miles Fleming were also engaged. John Grieve-Smith was secretary to working parties on Home Defence and National Economy in War. Peggy Hemming by this time had moved over to work on international economic trends. Joan Kelley was attached to the Phillips Committee on Economic and Financial Problems of Old Age. Downie, Atkinson, Licence, and Jones as we have seen, were all posted to jobs abroad.

## Discussion papers

Since forty to fifty discussion papers were issued every year (with some falling-off in numbers after 1952), it is not possible to give any comprehensive account of their contents. All that is possible is to indicate the range and balance of topics discussed and the more prominent of the contributors.

15 The reports were issued as discussion papers. They led Dow to review the statistical information indicative of changes in inflationary pressure and so to the first seasonally corrected figures of unemployment and vacancies. Hall was satisfied that the symptoms in 1948 were of less inflation, not actual deflation, but the Section tended to be rather more expansionary than he was.

In the early months of Hall's directorship, two subjects predominate: the balance of payments and inflation. Fleming and Nita Watts continued to report on the critical state of the balance of payments while Dow, Fleming, and Trevor Swan engaged in analysis of the process of inflation and disinflation.[16] Swan's massive study of 'The theory of suppressed inflation' was particularly influential and convinced Robert Hall that it was easy to carry disinflation too far: differences in local circumstances meant that there were bound to be variations in pressure between one industry or area and another so that a general lowering of demand would produce unemployment in some parts of the economy without removing shortages in other parts. These were 'think pieces', not policy prescriptions.

In 1948 the topic attracting most discussion was once again pricing policy in the nationalized industries. The Lord President was arranging in June for a fresh discussion and Alexander Johnston in the private office had asked for guidance from Hall, pointing out that principles enunciated as axiomatic in previous Section papers seemed to be disputed by other economists, such as Tom Wilson. There were also practical difficulties in industries where 'functional costing' was non-existent. Dow, in response, argued that the issue was one of production policy, not pricing, and that what was required was an adjustment of output to equate marginal cost with price. This did not satisfy Fleming who doubted whether the boards of the nationalized industries could be argued out of wanting to fix prices. The boards needed to think in terms of opportunity costs, which varied with the period in which output could be adjusted, and should be helped to maintain prices in line with marginal costs by subsidies and taxes.[17]

In 1949–50 wages policy also reappears as a favourite topic, with papers by Downie (four), Atkinson, Dow, Fleming, Mrs Hemming, and Miss Kelley. Of these Downie's are in some ways the most interesting. In his first paper he concluded, after talking to Butt, that, since it was impossible to reduce the power of the trade unions under full employment to bargain for higher money wages, the only thing to do was to educate them in the economic folly of bringing on inflation and find them other things to do than agitate for higher wages. A year

---

16 EC(S)(47)36, 'The theory of deflation', by J. C. R. Dow, 9 Decmber 1947; EC(S)(47)38, 'Some thoughts on inflation', by J. M. Fleming, 15 December 1947; and EC(S)(47)39, 'The theory of suppressed inflation', by T. Swan, 22 Decmeber 1947. All are in PRO T 230/26.

17 EC(S)(48)32, J. M. Fleming, 'Price and output policy in socialised industry', 29 September 1948, in PRO T 230/28. See also EC(S)(48)19, 21, 22, 24, 26, 29, and 31, papers by Dow, Fleming, Jefferies, and Mrs Hemming.

later he admitted that nobody had yet found an answer to the problem. It was no solution for the government to limit itself to computing and announcing the average increase in wages consistent with a stable price level: negotiators needed to be given information that could be used in settling a specific wage claim in a particular industry. Employers and employed also needed to be taught to take into account wider interests than their own and only the government could state what those wider interests were. By the end of 1950 he was considering, with a lively sense of the objections, the possibilty of a preview of all wage claims by the TUC or a review by a wage tribunal.[18] Atkinson in his paper suggested limiting the guarantee of full employment by creating only enough money demand to allow of full employment at constant prices (i.e. use a money GNP target increasing at the same rate as productivity) and letting the trade unions trade off higher wages against higher employment. He was even closer to some current ideas in suggesting limitation of the note issue as a way of giving effect to such a policy.[19]

Another subject of debate was the desirable level of unemployment. This began early in 1949 with a controversy between Downie and Butt on the one hand and Dow on the other as to the figure to be shown for 'target' unemployment in the *Economic Survey*. Dow thought the current level too low at 325,000 and indicative of excess demand. Not necessarily, said Downie and Butt. More deflation might help exports but this did not require higher unemployment. It was doubtful whether higher unemployment would improve productivity or allow undermanned industries to recruit more successfully; and it would need much more unemployment to damp down wage inflation. Robert Hall, joining in, was more of Dow's view. The figure of 350,000, which even Downie and Butt accepted (Dow suggested 350,000– 400,000), was at least an improvement by 25,000 on the current position and unemployment might well rise by that amount or more.[20] The debate continued, Grieve-Smith returning at the end of 1949 to the figure of 400,000 as a possible 'danger line' for unemployment.[21]

---

18 Downie's papers are in EC(S)(49)11 and EC(S)(50)14, 24, and 30 in PRO T 230/143 and 338. See also below p. 331.

19 EC(S)(50)22, F. J. Atkinson, 'The wages problem', 2 May 1950, in PRO T 230/338.

20 EC(S)(49)3, 'Unemployment figures in the *Survey*', 3 February 1949, in PRO T 230/143. In the first half of 1949 unemployment fell to 280,000.

21 EC(S)(49)41, J. Grieve-Smith, 'The problem of unemployment', 19 December 1949, in PRO T 230/143.

A further topic in those years was central planning. Early in 1949 Butt reflected on what the Economic Section believed in and what division they would favour between what the State should decide and what should be left to the market. The issue was one of long-term policy, the extent to which the State should impose its view of the future well in advance of events, and the 'fierceness' of policy instruments. Butt distrusted attempts to forecast the long-term future in statistical detail although he saw no harm in them as ways of satisfying curiosity and they might offer some help to short-term plans. What was needed, he argued, were long-term policies rather than plans. The State had some advantages over the market but the chief of these in his view was the lower rate of discount it could impose on future events.[22]

Robert Hall's views on planning were circulated later in the year in a paper written by Douglas Allen on the basis of a note by Hall.[23] Interdepartmental committees were not enough to co-ordinate economic policy, he argued, unless the task was assisted by a staff for that purpose. The key instruments of policy were three – budgetary policy, investment policy, and import policy – and each was the province of a separate committee – the Budget Committee, the Investment Programmes Committee, and the Programmes Committee.

Another subject that figures prominently in 1949–50 is the proposed European Payments Union. On this Fleming circulated five papers in 1949 and there were two more in 1950, one by James Meade. We shall return to Fleming's important contribution to the scheme in chapter 17. Fleming did not confine himself to intra-European payments arrangements but circulated six other papers in 1949 and four others in 1950 on subjects ranging from wages policy to the theory of capital exports and the principles of international commercial and financial policy.[24]

Among the papers in 1950 were one by Abramson which described the methods in use in other countries for the control of commercial bank credit; one by Nita Watts on a proposed international tin agreement, arguing in opposition to the departments concerned that in a buffer stock scheme the management should not deal at prices between the upper and lower limits; and a paper by Bretherton that

---

22 EC(S)(49)10, D. Butt, 'The Economic Section's beliefs', 27 April 1949, in PRO T 230/143.

23 EC(S)(49)33, 'Notes on central planning', 24 November 1949, in PRO T 230/143.

24 Fleming's sixteen papers are in PRO T 230/143 and 338.

formed one of a long series on British agriculture prepared in the Section.[25] There were also a number of papers on national and international measures for full employment and on the idea of a full employment target which the government was promoting at the United Nations.

In 1951 when the Chancellor had to declare a full employment target (which he announced as implying a 3 per cent level of unemployment), there was a full-scale review of the implications of full employment in ten discussion papers, three by Miss Kelley, two by Atkinson, and the others by Butt, Downie, Jones, Grieve-Smith, and Le Cheminant.[26] Butt and Atkinson were the most prolific authors, each producing at least six discussion papers during the year. With the departure of Fleming early in the year there were comparatively few papers on external economic policy. But Miss Watts had two on the EPU and one on sterling liabilities; there were two papers on the US economy and its influence on the world economy, one by Jukes and one by Le Cheminant; and Butt and Bretherton between them contributed three others. Other subjects discussed were controls (four papers) and raw materials (three papers). These reflect the upheavals of the rearmament programme in 1951 and the resulting shortages. With the change of government in October, Robert Hall circulated a paper on 'The new-old monetary policy', the only available statement of his views on monetary policy in the early post-war period.

In 1952 there is another symposium, eight members of the Section contributing to papers on economic conditions in various parts of the world.[27] Many other papers deal with international affairs. There are proposals for revising the IMF (Robert Neild) and for an international finance corporation (Neild and Dow). There are papers on commercial policy (Dow), GATT (Neild), sterling area arrangements (Neild), and international liquidity (Butt and Jones). For the first time there are discussions of the problems of the less developed countries (Downie and Butt). On the domestic side, a regular series of quarterly reports on the monetary situation by Jones begins in May. Butt and Downie each produced a paper on agricultural policy. Dow turned again to the statistics needed for employment policy – a subject on which the Section kept pressing over the next few years until Macmillan's budget

---

25 EC(S)(50)3, Abramson, 'The control of commercial bank credit', 11 January 1950; EC(S)(50)29, Watts, 'Proposed international tin agreement', 8 June 1950; EC(S)(50)9, Bretherton, 'The future of British agriculture', 8 February 1950.

26 The discussion papers for 1951 are in PRO T 230/340.

27 The discussion papers for 1952 are in PRO T 230/245 and 246.

speech of 1956 promised better things. At the end of the year, for the first time since James Meade's day, two discussion papers on tax policy, by Dow and Dick Ross, were circulated.

There is no file of discussion papers for 1953 so we cannot know all that appeared in that year. But one item was an important study by Dow of the working of monetary policy in 1952. Other papers by Dow, Jukes, Lawler, and Miles Fleming dealt with long-term economic policy, looking back to the *Long-term Economic Survey 1948–52* and forward to the potentialities of the UK economy for growth over the next four years.[28]

By 1954 the number of papers circulated had shrunk from a peak of sixty-two in 1950 and forty-two in 1952 to eighteen. Of these, one of the most interesting is Ian Little's 'Foreign economic policy', which deals with such matters as the future of convertibility and European payments arrangements. A paper by Neild on supply and demand for US dollars concludes that 'within a few years the dollar problem may have vanished'. More papers were circulated on monetary policy, including one by Scott on its influence on stock-building.[29] The 1954 papers also include a long analysis by Grieve-Smith of the record of national income forecasting in the years 1948–52, an examination by Scott of the effect of removing discrimination against exports from dollar countries, and yet another long piece, this time by Franklin, on agricultural policy.

Agriculture continued to occupy the Section: in 1955 three out of twelve discussion papers, and in 1956 three out of sixteen, deal with the subject. But by that time the think pieces of earlier years were becoming rare. More papers were summaries of reports, or backward-looking surveys of past trends or forecasts, or studies of a single industry or product, or accounts of problems and practices abroad. The Section concentrated increasingly on short-term economic forecasting, the annual budget, and immediate issues. Its horizon shrank and less and less was written on long-range, non-quantitative problems.

28  These papers are in PRO T 230/267.
29  The discussion papers for 1954 make up in bulk what they lack in number. They are in PRO T 230/341–4.

# Chapter ten

# INTEGRATION: THE MOVE TO THE TREASURY

In 1953 arrangements were made to transfer the Economic Section from the Cabinet Office to the Treasury. The precise timing of the transfer seems to have been determined by a personal factor. Throughout most of 1952 and early 1953 there had been constant friction between the Section and OF (the Overseas Finance Division of the Treasury) over the Robot proposal to make the pound convertible at a floating rate. There was a time when Hall was not on speaking terms with Rowan and Clarke. Meanwhile Plowden, who did not enjoy the close relationship with Butler that he had had with Cripps and Gaitskell, had been offered attractive posts outside the Treasury and had finally made up his mind to leave. With this example, and with friction continuing, Hall was tempted to go too. When he announced his intention of doing so, Bridges and the Chancellor were taken aback and begged him to stay. By the middle of 1953 the Chancellor had come to rely heavily on his advice and was anxious that any obstacles to his retention in the Treasury should be removed. It was this situation that precipitated the integration of the Economic Section and a 'general post' within the Treasury, one effect of which was to move Clarke out of OF to other duties.

The move to the Treasury originated in two minutes from Hall to Bridges in May and June. The first of these set out Hall's views on how the Treasury should be organized for purposes of dealing with economic policy. In his view – and it was a view which he held even more strongly in later years – Bridges tried to do too much and badly needed a deputy. As Hall put it later, when Bridges was on the point of retirement, he never had time 'to act as the real Head of the Treasury on the economic side'. He would move in when there was a crisis but 'up to that point he was always giving the impression that his mind was on his next appointment and that he was grasping at anything that seemed like a workable solution'. A deputy, Hall suggested to Bridges, could take on the responsibilities that Plowden had shouldered of co-ordinating economic policy and advising the Permanent Secretary and the Chancellor. No other Treasury official (except presumably the Permanent Secretary) should have the right of access to the Chancellor on matters of economic policy. There should also be three second secretaries for economic affairs, one dealing with home finance, one with external finance, and a third to act as staff officer to the deputy and deal with general economic policy. The deputy, the three second secretaries, and the economic adviser should form a team, consulting one another regularly and not limiting themselves to acting as heads of Treasury divisions. When there was a change of Chancellor, he should be at liberty to appoint a new deputy. Similarly, the Director of the Economic Section should serve only for a definite term and not enjoy tenure of his office until he reached the age of retirement.[1]

The Chancellor, in a minute to Bridges a few days later, asked for the creation of an economic and planning division under Robert Hall, 'whom I intend to regard as my Chief Economic Adviser'. Hall would have the assistance of Strath and Trend and would take over the Planning Staff, which would be reduced in size and amalgamated with the Economic Section to form a new Treasury division. Bridges in reply insisted that the Planning Staff could not be amalgamated with the Economic Section and must run in parallel with it. Nor could Robert Hall be in charge of an economic and planning division. He did agree, however, that after Plowden's departure someone would have to be put in charge of economic policy.[2]

The choice fell on Sir B. Gilbert, who thus became Bridges's deputy. It was an appointment that Hall was to regret bitterly. When Gilbert retired along with Bridges in the middle of 1956, Hall noted in his diary that Gilbert had 'made no efforts whatever either to co-ordinate or to take a lead'. 'A good many of our troubles and a good deal of the criticism now made of the Treasury', he thought, 'have arisen because he would not do anything at all until he was heavily pushed.' Hall blamed himself for failing to make a big enough fuss

1 Hall to Bridges, 22 May 1953, in PRO T 273/138.
2 Chancellor to Bridges, 27 May 1953, and Bridges to Padmore, 29 May 1953, in PRO T 273/138.

when he saw how much harm was being done and felt that Bridges, too, had been weak in leaving Gilbert in such a key post.

At the time Bridges had justified the appointment (which he realized was not ideal) because it got the structure right. But the structure did not survive more than a year or two. Nor did it take the shape that Hall had suggested. By 1958 the Treasury was headed by joint permanent secretaries, Brook and Makins (neither of them a Treasury man), with only one second secretary (Padmore) instead of a single permanent secretary, his deputy, and three second secretaries working as a team.

Hall's second minute to Bridges a fortnight later gave notice of his intention to leave the Treasury. He needed more pay in order to support two daughters at Oxford Univeristy ('I am a poorer man than when I came here'). Then there were the continuing bad relations for more than a year between the Economic Section and OF, which had more the character of 'a religious war' than of an effort to compose legitimate differences of opinion. When this was brought to the attention of the Chancellor he scribbled a note to Bridges:

> I saw Robert Hall – he actually mentioned *money* as a consideration . . . I feel all this is very distressing and wrong indeed. The discrepancy between the salaries of Plowden and Hall is very wrong. Could you and Norman Brook handle this at once?
>
> Robert Hall wishes to stay and I intend that he should.[3]

Hall's salary was duly increased (to £3,750 a year) and at the end of the year he was made a KCMG. On the Chancellor's insistence the Economic Section was moved to the Treasury ('already practically the *de facto* situation' according to Hall) and the Director was given the title of 'Economic Adviser to HMG' – a title that lasted only until 1964.

Hall had discussed the move to the Treasury with Norman Brook early in June and both of them put on record their reasons for approving of the change.[4] Norman Brook looked back to wartime and contrasted two ways in which the Economic Section could contribute to policy-making. Their views and advice might be presented, as in wartime, directly to a single minister responsible for economic co-ordination or alternatively at an earlier stage when policy was being formulated by officials for submission to ministers. Brook admitted that even in wartime members of the Section did play a part in

3 Chancellor to Bridges, 11 June 1953 in PRO T 273/138.
4 Brook to Bridges and Bridges to Brook, 23 September 1953, in PRO T 199/257.

discussions between officials and served on interdepartmental committees. But their influence in Whitehall rested on their closeness to the
Lord President, while at the official level their very independence
operated against a close working alliance, particularly with the
Treasury. Officials, Brook suggested, were reluctant to take into their
full confidence economists 'whose leading role was to offer directly to
Ministers at the stage of final decision advice which often included
outspoken criticism of Departmental proposals'.

Once the Treasury became the focus of economic co-ordination
under Stafford Cripps, it was inevitably only through the Chancellor
that the Economic Section could offer its advice to the government.
But the Chancellor had other advisers – the official Treasury and the
Economic Planning Staff. As Brook saw it, the natural solution was
for the Chief Planning Officer to rely for economic advice on the
Economic Section and in particular on its Director: in course of time
almost the whole of the work of the Section would be done for and in
conjunction with the Economic Planning Staff. The Director became
'almost indistinguishable' from other senior Treasury officials, while the
Section, Brook suggested, forfeited some of its earlier independence.
All this meant a switch-over to the second method of working: in
collaboration with other officials engaged in the formulation of policy.
The change was hastened by Robert Hall's own temperament and
experience. He was more ready than his predecessors to take account
of political and administrative considerations and less interested in
matters of doctrine.

Seeing things in this way, Brook might have been expected to
favour a much earlier transfer to the Treasury.[5] But, when he and
Bridges considered such a step in 1950, Brook hesitated to assume that
the full span of responsibilities exercised by Cripps and Gaitskell
would remain indefinitely under one minister and decided 'to keep the
official organization sufficiently flexible to meet a situation in which,
under some future Government, part of the tasks of economic co-
ordination were entrusted to a Minister outside the Treasury'. There
were in fact some signs when the Conservative Government took
office in 1951 that some such division might be made. But, as the
Chancellor consolidated his position and decontrol lightened his duties,
Brook concluded that there was no longer any good reason for
delaying the move.

5 When he discussed the possibility of a move with Hall in December 1948 he
  thought it best to leave the Section where it was. The Treasury, he pointed out,
  had not yet succeeded in integrating Rowan and Plowden.

Bridges in his comments on the transfer, said that it had been urged on him by Lionel Robbins and others whom he had consulted that the right place for the Section was in the Treasury in order to keep it in touch with 'the main economic thinking in Government'. He had felt, however, that there was no real risk of being out of touch with the Treasury and that if the Section stayed in the Cabinet Office it would be used by other ministers who might otherwise doubt the Section's neutrality if it went to the Treasury and might set up their own economic sections – particularly those who had no department immediately under them. He thought that events had justified these views and that the Section had enjoyed the best of both worlds. The setting up of the Planning Staff, however, had made it desirable for the Section to work closely with them and had shown that the scope of the Section's activities depended on its place in the scheme of economic planning and co-ordination. The inclusion of the Director in the Budget Committee had also strengthened links with the Treasury and conditioned the Section's responsibility for 'providing material to support the general direction of budget policy'.

A fuller picture of working arrangements in the Economic Section emerges from an exchange of minutes between Robert Hall and David Butt after the latter had submitted in August 1953 a short history of the Section.[6] This suggested that 'the proliferation of official Committees under Treasury chairmanship' after Cripps's appointment as Chancellor had virtually put an end to:

> the previous system by which the Economic Section as a whole exerted what influence it had through briefing Ministers independently. Contact with Ministers became almost entirely confined to the Director, and largely verbal. The remainder of the Section increasingly worked through official Committees.[7]

When Hall pointed out that before 1947 contact had been virtually confined to one minister, the Lord President, with access also to the Prime Minister, Butt amplified his comment. 'When I first joined the Section' (in 1946), he wrote:

> we all regarded our main duty as writing briefs for the Lord President on Cabinet papers. Broadly, a brief was written on every paper dealing with economic subjects by the member of the Section responsible for that subject, and it usually went to the Lord President

6 All of these are in PRO T 230/283.
7 David Butt, 'Notes on the history of the Economic Section', in PRO T 230/283.

under his signature. Copies were also sent . . . to various other Private Offices. . . . From the point of view of practical results, [this arrangement] was an utter flop. . . . The change that took place in 1947 . . . added to the Section's effective influence.[8]

In his comments on Butt's 'History', Hall explained how the appointment of a Planning Staff had affected the work of the Section. He had agreed with Plowden that he would be consulted 'on all matters involving economic analysis'.[9] When Austin Robinson left the Planning Staff in 1948 he was not replaced and thereafter Plowden looked exclusively to Robert Hall for technical advice. When Cripps took over responsibility for economic policy from the Lord President, Hall went on, it was no longer possible for the Economic Section to brief him in the way they had briefed Morrison. Something had to be done to prepare a single brief representing the views of the Economic Section, the Planning Staff, and the departmental Treasury. Matters were argued out at meetings between the Chancellor and senior Treasury officials and as Hall could have his say at these meetings he saw little point in briefing the Chancellor subsequently from the Cabinet Office.[10] All important issues went to the Economic Policy Committee or the Cabinet, over both of which Attlee presided. Hall was entitled to brief the Prime Minister direct, but from the time Cripps became Minister for Economic Affairs this power, in Hall's opinion, was of no real value. This was partly because it would be pointless to give the same brief to the Prime Minister and the Chancellor, but also because Attlee showed no signs of being interested in the views of the Section. Under Churchill, who gave up the chairmanship of the Economic Policy Committee, briefing the Prime Minister was of even less importance. Macmillan, however, retained a keen interest in economic affairs when he moved from 11 to 10 Downing Street and sometimes sent for Hall to discuss them.

Another remark by Butt on the 'increasing familiarity among departmental officials with the technique of considering the economic problem as a whole' drew from Hall the comment that this was mainly due to the NIF (National Income Forecasts) Working Party, which he had deliberately set up to provide just such an education. It was from similar motives that he took steps some years later to encourage competition with Treasury forecasts by inducing the National Institute

8 Butt to Hall, 13 August 1953, in PRO T 230/283.
9 Hall to Butt, 13 August 1953, in PRO T 230/283.
10 ibid.

to issue from January 1959 an *Economic Review* containing forecasts similar to those used in government.

This educational role of the Economic Section, however, went back well beyond the establishment of the NIF Working Party or even, as Butt suggested, the writing of *Economic Surveys* in co-operation with departments. From the very beginning, the presence of economists at the centre of the government machine, and their inevitable involvement in discussion with departments, raised the general level of understanding of economic issues throughout Whitehall, although there was perhaps more familiarity with economic language and conclusions than firm grasp of the complexities of economic concepts and analysis. As was to become evident also, the task of education was a great deal easier when economists were in general agreement with one another, not bitterly divided on matters of theory.

The Economic Section at first retained its independent identity within the Treasury. The Section was seen as having a special responsibility for advice on macroeconomic policy and in particular for the economic forecasts underlying the budget. The Director as Economic Adviser to Her Majesty's Government could also offer advice on all other aspects of economic policy. He continued to be available for consultation by ministers in other departments. It was rare, however, for such consultation to take place or for a request to be made by the Prime Minister or the Cabinet for the personal views of the Director. At the same time if the Director disagreed strongly with the Chancellor – as happened over Robot – the latter would report this to the Cabinet. By 1961, when a new Director was appointed, consultation by other ministers had virtually ceased and the title of Economic Adviser to HMG was already a misnomer although it was not abandoned until 1964. The Economic Section had become in practice the staff of the Chancellor in his capacity as Minister of Economic Affairs – a fact not appreciated by the incoming government in 1964.

Members of the Section continued to take part in departmental and interdepartmental committees without feeling obliged to support 'the Treasury line'. While they naturally consulted their Treasury colleagues whenever possible, they were encouraged, and indeed required, by the Director to continue to operate as independent professional economists and to express a Section view at meetings even if it differed from that of the official Treasury. Their advice had often been sought while the Section was in the Cabinet Office because of its reputation for independence, and they were also given up-to-date information, including statistical information, that departments did not make freely available. These good relations and contacts, which were highly important to the work of economic co-ordination, remained after the move to the Treasury and the Section retained its reputation for expressing an independent view.

It continued also to be a collective view. Papers were circulated and referred to as Section papers, expressing the views of the Section, not of the individual author. In committees and working parties the chairman would ask, not 'What is the view of Mr X?' but 'What does the Section think?' As a collective view it gained added force. It was the outcome of continuous debate, both at the weekly meetings of staff and in exchanges of minutes between members. It expressed a coherence of intellectual outlook that was the strength of the Section and lasted as long as it remained a small island of economists in an ocean of administrators.

There was also a Section 'memory' – a continuity of view which was not as apparent in the administrative civil service. Departmental representatives, who changed their jobs frequently, were often found to know less about the history of an item under discussion at a committee meeting than did the Section representatives, whose influence was correspondingly enhanced. According to Mrs Jones, this 'had something to do with the filing system: the Section kept subject files where committee papers, minutes, correspondence, even Cabinet papers and briefs, were all on the one file'. Even today it is easier to trace what was going on from what remains of the Section files in the Public Record Office than from those of other divisions.

The working relations between the Section and the departmental Treasury became increasingly close. By the early 1960s they were beginning to be planted out in other Treasury divisions as advisers on the economic aspects of policy. Some were on occasion lent to other departments or posted abroad (from about 1950) to serve with international organizations. Increasing use was made of academic economists released from their university duties to serve two years with the Section. There remained a chronic difficulty in attracting economists of the highest calibre to goverment service and the number of economists in Whitehall remained very small until 1964.

# Chapter eleven

# SURVEYS

Throughout its life the Economic Section devoted much of its time to two regular tasks: surveying the current economic situation and forecasting how it would develop. The two things were to some extent inseparable. On the one hand, a comprehensive survey of current economic information was indispensable to the preparation of a forecast; on the other, the information available for a survey of the current situation was inconsistent, unreliable, or out-of-date so that it was necessary, as Robert Hall put it, 'to forecast where we are now'. Indeed, the most trustworthy way of assessing current trends on the basis of available data of mixed reliability was often to effect a reconciliation between conflicting information in the form of a forecast and job backwards.

## Wartime surveys

Economic surveys were an indispensable ingredient of the Section's work: it had always to make up its mind what was happening, i.e. what were the underlying trends. Such surveys, however, tended at first to be partial and to relate to some one area of economic activity such as manpower, imports, or prices. It was not until the autumn of 1941 that a comprehensive economic survey was prepared, bringing together the perceptions of economic trends by the members of the Section and suggesting what action was required. Surveys were intended to be quarterly but in fact only seven were prepared, the first appearing in October 1941 and the last on 25 July 1945, the day when the general election results were announced.[1]

These wartime surveys differed significantly from those that began to appear annually once the war was over. They did not, for example, include systematic forecasts of the main demand components of GNP or of the balance of payments. The usual practice was to single out significant trends and suggest lines of policy.

The first survey, for example, which runs to thirty-three printed pages, opens with an analysis of the current manpower situation: the changes in progress in labour supply and employment, the distribution of labour between civil and military requirements, the entry of women into the labour market, and so on. This is followed by a discussion of future prospects, not only in relation to labour but in relation also to raw materials, shipping, and industrial capacity. A third section deals with the scope for a fuller mobilization of resources, especially labour, cites the experience of the First World War in finding employment for women, and suggests that two million more workers might be found for the armed forces and the supply services.

One interesting passage in the section on shipping shows that dry cargo imports fell heavily from 43½ million tons in the first year of war to 31½ million tons in the second while stocks nevertheless increased. The survey urges that advantage should be taken of 'our present relatively easy circumstances' to increase stocks further, not just to form a more adequate reserve but 'against the very grave pressure on exchange and shipping resources which may emerge when the war is over'. Thus even the first survey had an eye on the post-war economic situation.

The second survey, which was even longer, examined the changes that had occurred in consumption, using national income data, and was intended to balance the picture of mobilization for war in the first issue by a study of the limitation of supplies available to the civil sector.[2] By the sixth survey, which was only half as long, the emphasis was on the shortage of manpower as the dominant factor in the situation, with a review of shipping, raw materials, food, and

1 LP(41)172, 'Quarterly survey of the general economic situation', 20 October 1941, in PRO CAB 71/5 and LP(45)127, 'Survey of the general economic position', 25 July 1945 (recirculated on 16 August 1945 as LP(45)138) in PRO CAB 71/21. Other surveys were issued on 4 March 1942, 24 July 1942, 20 October 1942, 9 April 1943, and 12 December 1943.

2 For ministerial reactions, especially those of the Minister of Agriculture, see PRO CAB 123/52.

consumption levels. The economy was now (December 1943) fully mobilized.

Thereafter no surveys were circulated for eighteen months. The seventh and last in the series, another lengthy document, was no doubt meant to serve as a brief for the new government taking office at the end of July 1945. An earlier draft had been prepared in the autumn of 1944 in the expectation that the war would end within a few months and had been put aside when the Cabinet ruled that it should be assumed to continue until the middle of 1945. The main question in preparing a fresh survey was thought by Meade to be 'how far and how fast to move from manpower budgeting to an analysis in terms of national income and expenditure, typifying the freer economy in which financial inducements rather than direct controls are the order of the day'.[3]

In the revised survey the centre of interest was inevitably the post-war situation. Prospects were viewed, as in the post-war surveys, in terms of an inflationary gap. Relatively few figures were given but the approach, again as in later surveys, was to compare the rate of saving required to close the inflationary gap by withdrawing purchasing power with the rate of saving likely in the circumstances. Although the survey dealt at some length with the components of aggregate demand and with the factors that would govern the level of output and productivity, the argument was in general terms without statistical precision so that the outcome of the factors enumerated was left vague.

The most dramatic conclusions of the survey were about the danger of a coal shortage and a balance of payments crisis. 'It is no exaggeration, but a sober statement of fact', ran the penultimate paragraph, 'to assert that our external problem after this war will be at least as considerable as that of Germany after the last war.' As for coal, it was arguable that 'next to the consolidation of peace itself, an improvement in the coal position comes highest in the scale of immediate necessities'. Exports and coal supplies were singled out as the key objectives on which the government should concentrate.

These views rested on explicit forecasts. The coal situation had occupied one or more members of the Economic Section from 1940 onwards and the trends in employment and output were kept under constant review. The Section continued to warn of an impending crisis for lack of coal, the delays in European recovery that would result because no margin was left for coal exports, and the overriding need to find additional manpower for the mines. But this was one case where

3 Meade, diary, entry for 13 May 1945.

forecasting was relatively easy while action proved extremely difficult; the crisis foreseen in 1945 duly arrived in 1947 and the coal shortage lasted well into the fifties.

## Post-war surveys

A new and more macroeconomic kind of survey was put in hand once the war was over. The first two of these, in December 1945 and June 1946, remained unpublished; and for some years those that followed were completely rewritten before publication. Their primary purpose, as James Meade explained in the autumn of 1945, was to highlight the emerging problems of economic management so as to focus ministerial attention on them. They were an important part of the machinery of planning as he conceived it since they were intended to elicit decisions based on the view of the future presented in the survey. It was not intended that they should be published as submitted. But, if the government saw a need to generate public support for its plans, it clearly had to communicate those plans in some form to the public.

The mechanism did not work too well for a number of reasons. One was that the government was decidedly vague about what sort of plan it wanted. There were ministers who did not see eye to eye with the Economic Section on the extent to which use should be made of the price mechanism, or who identified planning with the use of direct controls such as import quotas and building licensing. There were some who thought of plans as extending over several years, preferably five, and would not have applied the term to sketches of the next eighteen months or so intended primarily as a background to decisions on the allocation of resources. Then there were those for whom planning meant setting fixed objectives to which all else was to be subordinated rather than a constant effort to adapt to a changing future.

On top of these difficulties was the problem of jurisdiction. The economic survey was submitted to Morrison as Lord President but the action to which it pointed tended to lie with Dalton as Chancellor of the Exchequer. This was got round by presenting the inflationary gap – the centre-piece of the survey – as either a shortfall in savings or a shortage of labour. The two things were interconvertible since additional savings whether by individuals or governments, released the labour required; but ministers felt more at home when the issues were posed in terms of a manpower budget while the Treasury was able to pretend that its budgetary freedom was not compromised.

An Economic Survey Working Party was set up in the autumn of

1945 as part of the new planning machinery instituted by Bridges.[4] Meade acted as Chairman and editor while the text and tables were prepared by Tress and Stafford (CSO) in consultation with the members of the Working Party.[5] The 'Economic survey for 1946', the first of the series, was submitted to the Steering Committee of Permanent Secretaries under Bridges in December 1945 and sent on after discussion to ministers. It was quite a short document, the main text occupying twelve pages, supplemented by four appendices, each relating to a set of forecasts.[6] The exposition was in terms of the various gaps shown in the tables, the strain on resources that this indicated, and the consequent danger of inflation. In the case of manpower, for example, there was a prospective gap of 940,000 at the end of June 1946 and 1,246,000 at the end of December. In the balance of payments there was a prospective deficit of £750 million (of which £150 million represented an addition to outstanding credit extended by exporters). The so-called inflationary gap – the excess of planned spending over probable supplies – was £470 million. If the inflationary gap had to be closed by additional private saving on the part of individuals and businesses it would have to exceed the level in 1944 when 26 per cent of net spendable receipts (net of direct taxes) was saved compared with only 8 per cent in 1938. Alternatively, and more plausibly, the government might cut its deficit in half by raising direct taxes or cutting expenditure to close the 'gap'.

The details of the situation in 1945 do not concern us here. The more relevant question is whether the procedure used was legitimate and fruitful. In appearance the tables in the survey looked like forecasts and some (e.g. the balance of payments) were intended as such. But most of the gaps *ex ante* were bound to disappear *ex post*, whether because of deliberate action such as cuts in departmental spending and higher taxes, or in default of such action, through forced saving brought about by inflation. So long as no one knew what action the government would take, any forecast involving excess demand was of a state of disequilibrium that was intrinsically evanescent.

4 PRO CAB 134/186 (first meeting of the Steering Committee on 14 November 1945).

5 This was at first an informal group consisting of Meade, Austin Robinson, and Reddaway (Board of Trade), Clarke and Proctor (Treasury), and Reeder (Ministry of Labour). The papers of the Working Party for 1946–7 are in PRO T 230/56–63 and 163; for 1948–9 in PRO CAB 134/267–8.

6 ED(45)5, 'Economic survey for 1946', memorandum by the Economic Survey Working Party, 12 December 1945 in PRO CAB 134/186.

What remained as a forecast was the persistence of certain fundamental relationships such as that between income and spending, the assumption of certain trends, e.g. in exports, and the acceptance of departments' estimates of what they would succeed in spending. The margin of error under all three of these headings was bound to be high in the transition to a new set of circumstances. No one could suppose, whatever the logic of the procedure, that any precise significance attached to the estimate of excess demand that emerged. It could even be argued, as Keynes argued, that some excess demand was in the circumstances desirable (and would not necessarily produce inflation).[7] There might also be a built-in tendency to overestimate some elements in demand such as fixed investment.[8] But what of the procedure itself? Presumably there was such a thing as excess demand. Were the survey tables the best way of measuring and presenting it?

Keynes for one thought not. He did not trust the statisticians in the CSO as he had trusted Meade and Stone when they first introduced 'the inflationary gap' into budget discussions in 1941. He was against the whole apparatus of the survey and in favour of intuitive hunch.[9] In this he was at one with Dalton.[10] But how else were ministers to be brought to take highly unpleasant decisions? The fact that some figures in the survey represented 'what simply cannot happen' did not rob them of significance if they were consistent with spending intentions. The survey might convey a phoney precision but it did make use of a highly effective technique for throwing into prominence the danger of excess demand.

The main object of the first economic survey was to focus the attention of the Cabinet on the manpower situation and in particular on the slow rate of demobilization. In this it was successful, for, although it was only one of the influences on government thinking, it was in fact the means by which a Cabinet decision was precipitated. This was largely because it offered both a diagnosis and a prescription – indeed a choice of prescriptions since the various lines of action suggested added up to a diminution in demand by £730 million compared with an estimated excess of £470 million. The Cabinet agreed to cuts in military requirements that should have been nearly

7 Cairncross, Sir Alec (1985) Years of Recovery, London: Methuen, p. 413.
8 ibid.
9 ibid.
10 Dow, J. C. R. (1964) The Management of the British Economy 1945–60, Cambridge: Cambridge University Press for National Institute of Economic and Social Research, p. 28.

enough to close the gap and in addition the working population fell by much less than the survey had forecast. But, at the end of 1946, excess demand seemed as great as ever.[11]

A second economic survey, which also remained unpublished (but unlike the first did not go to the Cabinet) was prepared in the spring of 1946 covering the financial year April 1946 to March 1947. Like the first it was drafted by Tress and Stafford and followed similar lines, but at somewhat greater length. For the first time it gave a picture of developments quarter by quarter. This showed a much smaller inflationary gap than in the previous survey at the end of 1946 but with an upward trend in the first quarter of 1947. Manpower requirements were moving up to levels above pre-war while the additions to supply were drying up as demobilization slowed down. The impending rise in the school-leaving age in April 1947 and the release of prisoners of war would also add to the labour shortage. In addition to these indications of increasing pressure in 1947, it would also have been possible to point to the danger that the big build-up of stocks forecast earlier for 1946 might be slipping back into 1947 with powerful inflationary consequences.

In analysing the danger of inflation the second survey supplemented the quarter-by-quarter forecasts of the balance between demand and supply with a review of the overhang of surplus purchasing power. Consumers had accumulated unspent balances amounting to over £6,000 million during the war and held most of these balances in highly liquid form. The goods available for purchase in wartime had been restricted to 80 to 90 per cent of the 1938 level and a backlog of demand had built up. But in 1946–7 the flow of consumer goods and services would equal, at best, only 85 per cent of the net, after tax, spendable income of consumers as a group. Businesses had accumulated over £2,700 million in undistributed profits and unspent depreciation allowances. No wonder, with such excess purchasing power, that wage rates were rising at 11 per cent per annum.

The Steering Committee of Permanent Secretaries in its comments, took the danger of inflation rather calmly but recognized that it would intensify.[12] It was much more concerned about the coal situation but devoted most attention to the balance between investment and

11 For a fuller discussion of the first economic survey, see Cairncross, op. cit., pp. 385–9, 411–14.
12 ED(46)19, 'Economic Survey for 1946/47', note by the Chairman of the Official Steering Committee on Economic Survey, 11 July 1946, in PRO CAB 134/503.

consumption, a matter on which the survey too had touched. The Committee made no specific proposals for action under any of these three headings, apart from some damping down of public investment. Indeed, it implied that inflationary pressure would ease eventually through a growth in productivity – not at all what the Economic Survey said on the subject.

## The 1947 survey

A third economic survey was prepared at the end of 1946 and submitted to the Steering Committee. The survey continued to grow in size, and so too did the comments of the Steering Committee, which ran to sixteen pages of text and were virtually a fresh version of the survey. On this occasion, with great reluctance, ministers felt obliged to publish some kind of survey – Morrison had promised one in November 1946 – and arranged for the preparation of yet a third version, which appeared on sale as the *Economic Survey for 1947* in the middle of the fuel crisis in February 1947. None of the third version was written by the Economic Section: part was the work of Stafford Cripps, then President of the Board of Trade, and part of R. W. B. Clarke, an Assistant Secretary in the Treasury.

The most interesting feature of the Steering Committee's comments and of the published survey is the almost complete suppression of any mention of an inflationary gap and of any attempt to make use of a national income framework in measuring it. The apparatus of thought consistently adopted by the Economic Section was largely ignored and only came into its own a year later in the *Economic Survey for 1948*. By that time popular discussion of inflation and a series of articles by economists in the bank reviews and elsewhere had made it impossible to go on disguising chronic excess demand as a manpower shortage.[13]

The Economic Section's draft of the 1947 survey continued to make use of the device of an inflationary gap but offered a choice between a figure of £266 million and one of £648 million according as the rate of private saving was 12 per cent of spendable income or at the 1938 level of 7.3 per cent. No such choice was offered on the manpower gap, which was put at 630,000 at the end of 1947. On either showing, the pressure on resources was expected to increase again.

The gap was arrived at as before, by comparing departmental programmes as a measure of demand with output at full employment (i.e. with 500,000 unemployed or about 2½ per cent of the working

13 Cairncross, op. cit., p. 442.

population) as a measure of supply. Meade had told Keynes at the beginning of the year that when the 'gap' became smaller he would be in favour of taking spending intentions, regardless of supply difficulties, as the measure of demand.[14] But that point had not been reached.

Curiously enough, the arithmetic pointing to increased inflationary pressure was combined with a forecast of an improving balance of payments, the deficit for 1947 being put as low as £200–250 million. Such a forecast would have been inconceivable but for the firm grip on imports exercised at that time by the government and the momentum behind the export drive at the end of 1946.

Where the Economic Section saw excess demand, senior officials and ministers saw specific shortages, the consequences of which were more readily grasped. Coal, steel, timber, and electrical power were all limiting production; there was a shortage of consumer goods; investment was on too large a scale; the manpower shortage was almost universal. There was an 'increasing gap between resources and requirements'. But this was seen in terms of manpower, not purchasing power. The stress was on inadequate supply, not excess demand. Prices and the price mechanism did not enter. In consequence, the problem was not a budgetary one and the Chancellor had no part in it except in relation to imports and the shortage of foreign exchange.

This was not how the Economic Section saw it. James Meade continued to point to the budget as the centre-piece of economic planning and to the need for a budget surplus if excess demand was to be removed. A more rapid rundown in the armed forces and supply services would certainly help; but other action, such as a cut in the food subsidies, should also be considered.

## The preparation of the survey

The drafting and editing of the survey remained an important responsibility of the Section even after the appointment of a separate planning staff under Plowden. In the preparation of the 1948 *Economic Survey* Robert Hall took a hand as James Meade had done with the draft survey for 1947. David Butt acted as secretary of the working party and prepared a first draft. This was taken over by Austin Robinson of the Planning Staff, whose draft in turn was amended by Douglas Jay, the Economic Secretary. When it appeared, Butt was so chagrined by the changes to his draft that he resigned and had to be

14 Meade to Keynes, 18 January 1946, in PRO T 236/54.

talked round by Hall. According to the latter, it was the changes in Butt's prose rather than in his economics that gave most offence.

Most of the work between 1947 and 1952 was done by David Butt, Jack Downie, and Christopher Dow. The administrative responsibility for handling the draft, however, was taken over by the CEPS.[15] Work began in September with a view to publication the following March.[16] The draft was submitted first to the Economic Survey Working Party, which now included representatives of the Economic Section, Central Statistical Office, CEPS, Treasury, Board of Trade, and Ministry of Labour. The Working Party occupied itself with two different kinds of survey, one looking a year ahead and one four years ahead. We deal with 'long-term surveys' below.

Beginning with the 1948 *Economic Survey* the procedure was to submit the first draft to the Economic Planning Board, then to the Steering Committee, then to the Ministerial Production Committee, and finally to the Cabinet. The survey would be amended in the light of the comments made at each stage and edited for publication after the Cabinet had indicated its views.

The preparation of the survey involved a number of administrative problems. First of all, the language had to be acceptable to the departments with whose affairs the survey dealt. There was usually little time to consult each department as the draft took shape, and they had to be reassured that their comments would be taken into account at a later stage. Some departments – notably the Ministry of Fuel and Power under Gaitskell – were liable to offer extensive redrafts that did not fit well with the rest of the document or raised editorial hackles for other reasons. Others also joined in the business of redrafting. The Treasury liked to wait until the last minute and then insert new balance of payments figures, redrafting the relevant passages and leaving no

15 In 1949, for example, it was William Strath of the CEPS who wrote to departments inviting their co-operation in preparing the *Economic Survey for 1950* and setting out the timetable to be followed. Similarly, Strath took over from Robert Hall the chairmanship of the Economic Survey Working Party and the secretaryship was shared between David Butt of the Economic Section and Robin Marris of the CEPS.

16 The *Survey* covered the calendar year, not the financial year. The timing of its publication had been the subject of debate from the start, Meade seeking to make it the economic counterpart of the budget while Dalton was strongly against any association between the two and wanted publication to be distanced from Budget Day. In 1947 the first published *Survey* appeared in mid-February, and the next three *Surveys* in March. Publication of the 1949 *Survey* was at one time contemplated for December 1948.

time for further revision. The Planning Staff might seek to produce a new text, as Austin Robinson did with the 1948 survey; Douglas Jay, as Economic Secretary, offered no less than thirty-five comments on the 1949 survey. On top of this was the difficulty of obtaining information in time from the Treasury and the Central Statistical Office. The white paper on *National Income and Expenditure* was published about the same time as the *Economic Survey* and was liable, as in 1948, to use figures for national income and expenditure that were markedly different from those in the survey. There were times when the CSO supplied figures for the previous year only a day or so before publication so that on one occasion the survey had to go to Cabinet with blank tables. As a consequence, any forecasts included in the survey tended to be introduced at the very last minute instead of being the centre-piece of argument as in 1946–7.

## Later surveys

The centre of interest in the 1948 *Economic Survey* moved to the balance of payments and the danger of a crippling shortage of imports. The survey was written after the disastrous experience of 1947 and before there was any certainty of Marshall Aid. The reserves of gold and dollars were falling fast and little was left of the American and Canadian loans. In those circumstances, the survey looked no further ahead than the first half of 1948, leaving open the possibility of a larger import programme in the second half if Congress voted through the European Recovery Programme: or alternatively of further drastic cuts if the Programme collapsed. Imports in 1947 had been limited to 75 per cent of the 1938 volume and only a tiny increase was provided for the first half of 1948. Both in the early and in the concluding sections the survey dwelt on the terrible consequences of letting the reserves run out or alternatively having to make further drastic cuts in gold and dollar purchases with consequences in unemployment, distress, and dislocation of production that would 'delay for years the prospect of a decent standard of living for our people'.[17] There may have been some readers, however, who found this picture of disaster hard to reconcile with a forecast for national income in 1948 that was just as much above that for 1947 as 1947 was above 1946 – and all three years not widely different from the level in 1938. Similarly, if bigger cuts had had to be made in domestic investment in 1948 than those already agreed upon, they would have been from a far higher level than in 1938.

17 *Economic Survey for 1948*, Cmd 7344, para. 245.

The 1948 *Economic Survey* is notable for its inclusion of the first published forecast of national income, the only assessment in any *Economic Survey* of success in fulfilling the objectives set in the previous year (this is an appendix), and the first statement by a Prime Minister on what we should now call 'incomes policy' (a statement already made in the House of Commons but now given wider publicity).

Of the three further surveys issued by the Labour governments, those for 1949 and 1951 are of particular interest, the first for its emphasis on productivity growth, the second for its analysis of the economic problems of rearmament. The 1950 survey was more factual since it had to be drafted in advance of a general election in February 1950.

In the 1950s the *Economic Survey* became progressively more bland and circumspect. As David Butt put it in 1954,

> all major surveys of the forward position were increasingly designed to conceal unresolved issues of policy from the Opposition, rather than to expose them to Ministers. Such documents may describe economic problems with precision, but in place of frank discussion of the alternative policies . . . they naturally tend to substitute bald assertions of virtuous intentions.[18]

As the *Economic Survey* lost its novelty it occupied ministers less and less. It ceased to be a vehicle for eliciting key planning decisions from ministers and became increasingly a public relations document, providing a factual account of developments over the previous year, an analysis of current problems, and an indication, often rather vague, of future prospects.

It was simply not possible to conduct the economic policy of the country through Cabinet decisions taken at wide intervals when a document called the *Economic Survey* was submitted. Once the co-ordination of economic policy became the clear and unchallenged responsibility of the Chancellor of the Exchequer, whether advised by the Treasury, the Central Economic Planning Staff, or the Economic Section, the key decisions rested with him either as head of the Treasury or after discussion with his colleagues on the Economic Policy Committee. Submissions were made to him or the Committee as occasion arose, usually after discussion by some official committee – the Budget Committee, the Investment Programmes Committee, the Programmes Committee, and so on – on all of which the Economic

18 'Notes on the history of the Economic Section', David Butt, 11 August 1954, in PRO T 230/283.

Section would be represented. It was through membership of these committees rather than as editors of the *Economic Survey* that the Section exerted its influence on ministers.

Under the Labour governments of 1945–51 the survey continued to reach the Cabinet, latterly after a full discussion in the Production Committee. But the Cabinet showed little interest and no disposition to reconsider policy in the light of the draft submitted to it. Ministers might argue, as in 1949, over the manpower target to be included for the coal industry but they did not argue on such an occasion over measures to increase manpower in the mining industry and by February 1949 were in two minds whether production targets should not be abandoned.[19] They usually asked for a shorter and less technical document when there would have been a good case for a longer technical one, on the lines of the Annual Report of the US Council of Economic Advisers.

When the Conservatives took office in October 1951 they seem to have been in doubt about continuing the publication of the survey. Ministers did not conceal their dissatisfaction with the inclusion of 'prophecies, forecasts and targets' although little of these remained in 1951. The manpower budget had disappeared completely: no table showing how manpower might be redistributed between industries was included. Detailed investment plans had also gone. The only output targets that remained were for coal, steel, and agriculture. Even forecasts had almost vanished.

Nevertheless, when a draft of the 1952 survey came before the Cabinet, ministers insisted on the removal of anything that smacked of planning. The Chancellor (R. A. Butler) said that he wanted 'a more factual document'. A year later he was still complaining of 'too many forecasts'. In 1952 he told the Cabinet that he would submit a revised draft to the Economic Policy Committee and discuss it with his colleagues.[20] There was therefore no discussion in Cabinet. From then on the *Economic Survey* ceased to be submitted to the Cabinet. Ten

19  For the Cabinet treatment of the survey from 1948 to 1951, see CM(48)16, 23 February 1948, CM(49)16, 28 February 1949, CM(50)11, 16 March 1950, and CM(51)22, 22 March 1951, in PRO CAB 128/12, 15, 17, and 19.

20  CM(52)31, 12 March 1952, in PRO CAB 128/24. When the Economic Policy Committee considered the revised draft, it was not the vestiges of planning that drew criticism. It was attacked for glossing over the mistakes of their predecessors by failing to demonstrate that the economic situation had been deteriorating early in 1951 and not just later in the year (EA(52)10M, meeting of the Economic Policy Committee, 2 April 1952, in PRO CAB 134/842).

years later it was discontinued and its place taken briefly by an *Economic Report*.

## Conclusion

The *Economic Survey* in the 1940s and 1950s was by far the best exposition of the economic problems facing the country and of the government's views on those problems. In the transition to a peacetime economy the problems were dramatic and challenging. They could be represented as changes that had to be accomplished and therefore planned in advance. Once the transition was over, the problems changed their character and lost some of their earlier starkness. The balance of payments ceased to dominate economic prospects and even the dollar problem lost its urgency. Inflation became endemic but there was little new to be said about it in the survey. The investment programme was no longer a device for rationing capital development. The government developed doubts as to its power to raise industrial productivity. With the passing of Marshall Aid, international economic problems, too, changed their character. The issues that remained, such as convertibilty and European integration, did not lend themselves readily to public discussion in the *Economic Survey*. The themes and topics included lacked the simplicity and urgency of the early surveys and the preparation of an annual *Economic Survey* became a routine operation even if accomplished by the Economic Section with great expertise.

# Chapter twelve

# PLANS

It had been the original intention to prepare a long-term survey or plan alongside the annual one. From time to time this idea came to life, first in 1946, then in 1948, and again in 1953; but on each occasion it soon died. All that emerged in public was a single document submitted to the OEEC in Paris in 1948 entitled *The Long-term Programme of the United Kingdom*.[1] This had to be submitted (and published) because the Americans operating the Marshall Plan wanted some reassurance that the aid they were bringing to the European economies would make them self-supporting within a reasonable time, taken to be four years. Thus Europe was urged to engage in central economic planning by a country bitterly opposed to such planning within its own borders. Meanwhile in the United Kingdom a Socialist government committed to economic planning shrank from issuing a national plan to its own people and sent a rather ersatz plan for scrutiny abroad.

This was not, however, quite so paradoxical as it may seem. It was natural that the Americans should want government pledges to take effective action in return for aid and that these pledges should bear the appearance of a plan. On the other hand, it was also natural that a government faced with one crisis after another should be chary of committing itself to firm promises four years ahead.

In January 1946 the Economic Section started work on an economic survey of 1950. Meade had minuted Bridges to suggest that such a survey would be useful 'in order to see the sort of post-transitional

1 Published (in *European Co-operation: Memoranda submitted to the OEEC relating to*) as (Official) *Economic Affairs in the period 1949 to 1953 (including the Long-term Programme*, 1948, Cmd 7572).

goal towards which the economy should now be changing'.[2] In his view more work needed to be done on techniques of government control: over imports, over exports, over investment, over consumption. There was also a further problem of attracting labour from declining to expanding industries and devising a wages policy that would contribute to such movements. A discussion between government economists followed on how a long-term plan should be prepared, and agreement seems to have been reached on the successive stages necessary for this purpose. Ministers agreed that a small group of officials should consider the preparation of a preliminary survey of the position in 1950 'when conditions would have returned more nearly to normal'.

The discussion in January 1946 had involved R. C. Tress of the Economic Section, Christopher Saunders and Jack Stafford of the CSO, and Austin Robinson, now Economic Adviser to the Board of Trade. The longest and most systematic analysis came from Austin Robinson, who argued that 'the purpose [of planning] is to *perfect* rather than to *oppose* the operations of an ideally functioning market economic system'.[3] This was consistent with his postulate that there should be 'the maximum freedom to spend, save, earn as individuals wish'; that there should be no controls over workers' freedom to work where and in what industries they like; and that equilibrium in the balance of payments is maintained 'with the minimum of restrictions on freedom of imports and free choice between home and foreign markets'.

Controls would be limited. Consumption would be controlled chiefly by fiscal measures affecting relative prices; investment could be directed into channels held to be most desirable in the interests of efficiency, employment, and social progress; control over foreign trade would be such as to be consistent with international obligations and necessary to secure a balance of payments; and monopoly pricing would also be subject to control. On this showing, the main purpose of planning was to foresee disequilibria and remedy them 'by administrative and budgetary action and by control of investment

2 EC(S)(46)1, Meade to Bridges, 'Future work on economic planning', 2 January 1946, in PRO T 230/20.

3 'Notes on long-term planning', by E. A. G. Robinson, undated, in PRO T 230/163. The papers by Tress, Saunders, and Stafford are in the same file, the first of them dated 25 January 1946, the other two undated. They were circulated to the Economic Section by Tress in EC(S)(46)9, 'Problems involved in an economic survey for 1950', 28 January 1946, in PRO T 230/20.

more quickly than would happen through the ordinary operations of the price mechanism'.

Attempts to redistribute wealth should be dealt with, ideally, outside the market system, wages being governed by net product and any supplement on the basis of need taking the form of state payment of allowances or of direct social services. It would be the relatively big and predictable changes on which planning should concentrate, where errors of 5 per cent or so would be looked after by 'the ordinary flexibilities of the economic system, by more or less intensive work, overtime and shiftworking and the like'. Plans, even in wartime were never fulfilled 100 per cent and in peacetime, too, a margin would be necessary. 'We do not want to plan all elasticity away.'

Robinson's conception of planning pictured the government outdoing the market, seeing in advance what the market would eventually impose and short-circuiting the process of getting there. It was a conception that tallied with the kind of planning required by the need to restore equilibrium in the balance of payments. The large adjustments called for might be brought about by market forces but could be accelerated by appropriate government action. Robinson's conception was more difficult to reconcile with a determined effort by the government to mould the economy in the interests of fixed objectives of its own choosing that might prove inconsistent with the free choice of consumers. The antithesis affected investment planning particularly. It was one thing to 'estimate what volume of investment would be necessary to cover expansions in demand', industry by industry, but quite another to channel investment 'in the interests of efficiency, employment and social progress'.

The essence of Robinson's prescription (from which the Economic Section did not dissent) was to make a forecast of 'the whole pattern of the economic system four years ahead and to see where the shoe will pinch and what ought to be done to remedy it'. Part of the job could be subcontracted to a Treasury working party under Otto Clarke. The Balance of Payments Working Party had suggested in November 1945 that it would be useful to prepare a balance of payments for 1950 and Clarke had written to James Meade on 19 January 1946 in pursuit of this idea.[4] His working party, on which the Economic Section was represented, did not meet until March, when he wrote to Austin Robinson to apologise for the delay in making a start because of pressure of work. At the end of April he succeeded in holding a

4 Clarke to Meade, 'Balance of payments: general policy', 19 January 1946, in PRO T 230/276.

meeting at the Treasury attended by representatives of the Economic Section (R. C. Tress and A. J. Brown), the CSO, the Board of Trade, and the Bank of England. Not much progress was made except to move on from 1950 to 1951 as a 'normal' year and, after a further note from Clark to Austin Robinson in May, the working party seems to have vanished.[5]

Progress with the Economic Section's survey was also slow. Economists had too much to do in 1946 and found it difficult to look beyond the pressing problems of the immediate future. The whole business of long-term planning must have seemed lacking in urgency.

After the appointment of Sir Edwin Plowden as Chief Planning Officer in March 1947 James Meade sent him the existing papers of the 1948–51 survey and explained that a first draft (prepared by Tress) would be ready in a month's time. This was circulated in June 1947 and discussed towards the end of the month at a meeting of the Economic Survey Working Party chaired by Robert Hall.[6] Revised drafts were circulated in August and October, Hall explaining to departmental representatives that Cripps wanted a finished text by mid-November with a view to publication in December. But as the Treasury pointed out, no firm plan could be prepared until it was known whether (and how much) Marshall Aid would be voted by Congress. The Planning Staff (Austin Robinson) was also claiming responsibility for the work on a long-term survey or plan, leaving to the Economic Section the drafting of the (annual) *Economic Survey for 1948*. In the end it was on the latter that work was concentrated over the winter months.[7]

The *Economic Survey for 1948* announced that work was proceeding on a long-term plan but that the future was 'still too uncertain for any specific decisions or forecasts to be made about future years [*sic*]'. The uncertainties the government had in mind related to the European Recovery Programme, which still had to be voted through Congress. In May the Chancellor reiterated the government's intention 'to publish the general nature of our long-term plans' but again declined to give a date. Meanwhile the Economic Section's draft was worked up into a long-term economic survey in the first half of 1948, largely by

---

5 Clarke to Robinson, 10 May 1946, in PRO T 230/276.

6 ESWP(47)1M, 'Economic survey long-term 1948–51', 25 June 1947, in PRO T 230/62.

7 ESWP(47)1 Revise, 5 August 1947; ESWP(47)2, 16 October 1947; Clarke to Hall, 17 October 1947; Butt to Hall and Hall to Butt, 22 October 1947; all in PRO T 230/63.

Austin Robinson, who had rejoined the civil service as a member of the CEPS in the autumn of 1947.

Austin Robinson and others made extensive criticisms of the Economic Section's draft. This assumed that productivity would increase by 2½ per cent per annum, that exports would rise to 175 per cent by volume of the pre-war level, and that this would permit of imports up to 90 per cent of the pre-war level. All of these assumptions, which turned out to be quite reasonable, were thought too optimistic. It was also thought to be too optimistic in ignoring the dollar problem and assuming that exports could be readily diverted from non-dollar to dollar markets. On the other hand, it assumed no Marshall Aid.

Other aspects of the survey were also called in question. It set out targets for a wide variety of industries without indicating what controls could be used to make output hit these targets. It did accept, however, that there was a problem of attracting manpower to the 'right' industries, which it took to be agriculture, mining, and textiles, and away from the steel-using industries which would still lack raw materials. But would a transfer of labour in that direction, supposing it could be arranged, still be desirable in 1951?

To a large extent, as might have been foreseen, the first issues thrown up by the long-term economic survey were identical with those already familiar from the annual surveys. Some saw the problem in manpower and physical terms, dominated by the need to redistribute labour between industries, while others started from the balance between savings and investment, exports and imports, with the main issue one of restoring internal and external balance.[8] The CEPS, no doubt in agreement with the Economic Section (and indeed borrowing from the original line of argument developed in the Section's draft of the *Economic Survey for 1947*) focused on the problem of inadequate savings and came down in favour of a higher budget surplus and a lower investment programme – as the Section had argued a year previously. By the middle of July Plowden was following in the footsteps of James Meade and pressing on the Treasury the central importance of the budget in economic planning and the need for maintaining a larger budget surplus. He asked for an assurance that the Treasury would be prepared to carry out any fiscal policy that was agreed to be desirable and necessary, and received a favourable, if qualified, response.

8 The financial implications of the survey were developed by Tress in a minute to Hall, 17 July 1947, in PRO T 230/63.

It was at this point that long-term planning was given a boost by the European Recovery Programme. The Paris Conference that framed a reply to the Marshall offer in 1947 asked member countries for information on their long-term plans. While an immediate reply could be largely based on the 1948–51 economic survey, later developments called for the submission of a more elaborate plan for the four years 1948–52 in order to establish whether the policies of the member countries were consistent with one another and with so-called 'viability' (i.e. a satisfactory balance of payments) by 1952 when aid would cease. The preparation of the long-term economic survey encouraged the British government to support this proposal.

The 1948–52 survey took a much less optimistic view of the future than the 1948–51 survey had done. Where the latter had assumed an increase in the volume of exports of 75 per cent above the pre-war level, what was now estimated (rather than simply assumed) was an increase of 45 per cent. If, as was judged, the terms of trade would be no better than in 1947 and invisibles improved somewhat, foreign exchange earnings would allow only of 75 per cent by volume of pre-war imports. (No account was taken of the capital balance.) On this showing, it would be necessary to get by in 1952 with a volume of imports no higher than in 1947, and well below the level planned for 1948–9, even after seven years of peace and four years of Marshall Aid. To mitigate the repercussions on the standard of living (which presumably would rise steadily nevertheless if productivity continued to improve) it was argued that agricultural output should be expanded by 50 per cent with an offsetting cut in food imports.

It was this document more perhaps than any other that made the case for austerity and persuaded ministers of the need to hold back from some of their cherished ambitions. The views expressed did not originate in the Economic Section but neither did they contest them. After the experience of 1947 it was difficult to sustain a more robust, expansionary view in Whitehall, especially when the future of Marshall Aid was still in doubt.

What was submitted to OEEC (and published) was not the long-term economic survey: it was a somewhat different document, *The Long-term Programme of the United Kingdom*. This was drafted by the CEPS and the Economic Section in consultation with departments and took a more optimistic view of balance of payments prospects as well as a remarkably cool view of the limitations of economic planning under British conditions. Exports in 1952–3 were put at 50 per cent above the 1938 level and imports at 15 per cent below. These estimates were said to be consistent with a surplus on current account of £100 million per annum out of which to pay off sterling balances and supply capital for Commonwealth development.[9]

Among the Economic Section's contributions to long-term planning in 1948 was a paper by Christopher Dow dealing with 'Budgetary prospects and policy 1948–1952'.[10] This projected government revenue at current rates of taxation, allowing for a 20 per cent rise in prices. Extrapolating government expenditure at current trends, it indicated a budget surplus of £1,000–1,500 million by 1952. This bold piece of forecasting was coupled with a discussion of the development of the tax system which argued strongly for a reduction in the level of government expenditure because of the ill effects of high taxation. Industrial structure and technical change were affected adversely by the difficulty small private businesses experienced in growing, the reinforcement of the grip on the market of large and monopolistic concerns, and the break-up of the capital market into small, imperfect areas. 'Instead of worthwhile schemes attracting finance to them,' it argued, 'projects go forward where the finance happens to be.' There was also a gradual effect on the attitude to work and enterprise that might be an important constituent of 'that relaxing climate which some observers of the British economy have claimed to observe'. Even if high taxation was necessary in the interests of closing the inflationary gap, the extra revenue came in part from private savings so that a cut in expenditure, and with it in taxation, would have the double advantage of strengthening incentives and adding to savings.[11]

This was good supply-side doctrine a generation before its time. Dow went on to make specific proposals, not all of them new. For example, 'a suitable budget surplus must be considered to be as essential a charge on the revenue as any other expenditure'. It might also be necessary to make fiscal adjustments between budgets and for this purpose the repayment of post-war credits would provide a flexible instrument (it was in fact being used in the 1960s); to get expenditure down the abolition of food subsidies by 1952 should be considered. Any price rise occurring might be allowed to exercise some deflationary effect on demand, and the responsiveness of revenue

9 David Butt in his 'Notes on the history of the Economic Section', 11 August 1954, in PRO T 230/283, decribes the *Long-term Programme* as 'a document tailored to fit OEEC's requirements and tremendously bedecked with caveats and qualifications . . . eventually published with minimum publicity under a deliberately rebarbative title' (of his own invention).

10 The document ran to twenty pages and an appendix. It was dated 8 June 1948 and is in 'Economic survey 1948–52', in PRO T 230/145.

11 ibid., paras 27–9.

to such a rise might be improved by moving from specific to *ad valorem* indirect taxes. Depreciation allowances should be based on current replacement costs. Finally, it would be desirable to raise tax thresholds and remove several million small taxpayers from income tax.

In 1948 planners were still wrestling with the theory of the matter. How could you plan without compulsion? How should you plan in conjunction with other governments? Was Austin Robinson right in 1947 in contending that 'the main object of planning should be to make planning unnecessary'? How could one plan four years ahead when things took an unexpected turn every year? What, above all, was a four-year plan for?

The planners themselves were diffident and reluctant; they moved steadily away from targets and programmes to policies and institutional arrangements. Exchanges took place between Austin Robinson, Otto Clarke, and Robert Hall in the latter part of 1948; but these were more about relations with Europe and the United States than about domestic economic policy.[12] It was external pressure from the balance of payments that provided the impetus to planning, not a desire to supersede the market in the allocation of resources.

The Economic Section had always shown a preference for financial instruments of economic management over physical controls. They tended to be sceptical of plans for the economy as a whole. No member of the Section was more sceptical than David Butt, who kept writing minutes asking what purpose was served by putting down on paper so many figures far in advance of events and nearly always far in advance of the time when decisions had to be taken.[13] 'Plans in the semi-socialist State', he suggested, 'seem to be much what Cathedrals are to the Church: they have an inspiring and soothing effect for the faithful in a wicked world.'

There were questions of practicability and implementation. How, with its limited powers, could the government get the distribution of manpower, or the level and pattern of investment, or the volume of exports and balance of trade it wanted? There were also questions of usefulness. Would the plan alter effective economic action from what it would otherwise be? A target for the recruitment of miners by the end

---

12 Robinson to Hall, 27 October 1948; Cohen to Hall, 6 November 1948; Robinson to Clarke, 21 November 1948; Clarke to Robinson, 26 November 1948; Robinson to Hall, 26 November 1948; Berthoud to Rowan, 7 December 1948. All of these are in 'Long-term planning', in PRO T 230/109.

13 For example, Butt to Hall, 'Numerology', 11 June 1948, and 'Questions for a numerologist or planner', undated, in 'Economic survey 1948–52', in PRO T 230/145.

of 1948 would help 'to set the tone' for current action: would it be any different if targets were set for 1949, 1950 and 1951? There were admittedly cases, involving for example 'investment in complex highly capitalised industries', in which 'what is done today depends very closely upon what is to be done in two or three years'. But such cases were comparatively rare. Similarly, there was everything to be said for undertaking research into long-term trends in demand and supply conditions as a preliminary to deciding on the scope for new investment. But this was so only as a help to the taking of current decisions. 'We want all the information we can get about 1953 for the purpose of right action in 1948: not for deciding what to do in later years.'

There was also a third question. Would the figures in the plan prove right? Britain was 'a very small island in a very large world'. It had no control over trading conditions outside its borders and any plan for the balance of payments was essentially no more than a forecast. The totals set down might be reached at the dates given but 'it is much more likely that events will scoff at the Planners'; and if one figure proved to be wrong, many of the other figures would have to be altered. A shortfall in textile exports, for example, would make it necessary to increase exports of metal goods, lower home investment, and use more manpower to replace the lost machines, changing three segments of the plan at least. The more critical the economic position, the more flexible must policy become; and since a four-year plan amounted to a set of policy pronouncements four years ahead did this not imply that the plan, too, would have to be modified more and more with the passage of time? Long-term plans, Butt concluded, were bound to be impracticable, probably of little value for policy, and almost certainly wrong as precriptions for action beyond the first year.[14]

Interest in long-term prospects revived at the beginning of 1949 with 'a first look at 1955' which concluded that 'the economy will still be under inflationary strain' even at that date (as indeed it proved to be).[15] The Economic Section was asked to update the long-term economic survey in association with the CEPS, and the Economic Survey Working Party resumed discussion of long-term planning. Material for a revised draft was circulated at the end of April and a short outline of the topics to be discussed was circulated in May.[16] These documents

14 Butt, 'Questions for a numerologist or planner', undated, in PRO T 230/145, paras 6–10.
15 'Britain's economic position post–1953', in PRO T 229/154.
16 ESWP(49)2, 'Existing material on long-term economic prospects', note by the Secretary, 29 April 1949; 'Draft outline for the economic survey 1952', note by the Secretary, 11 May 1949; both in PRO CAB 134/268.

made use of a revised balance of payments forecast for 1952–3 by the Programmes Committee. Although the terms of trade were now assumed to be 6 per cent worse than in the long-term economic survey, changes in the forecasts for exports and invisibles (chiefly in oil) improved the outlook for imports quite substantially: they indicated that a level 10 per cent below that of 1938 could be afforded in 1952–3. On the other hand, the revised balance of payments implied that the survey had been too optimistic about the dollar balance in 1952 and that a deficit, estimated at \$125 million, would still continue.

The topics proposed for treatment in the revised survey are indicative of the change that was taking place in thinking. They included, for example: a discussion of subsidy policy; the fiscal problem in relation to government expenditure and investment; the 'right' level of investment, the function of investment planning, and the problem of controlling investment; the problem of 'wage inflation' and wage policy; and a study of the normal characteristics of the British economy in the long term (i.e. after 1952).

It does not appear, however, that the Working Party got very far with this programme. The devaluation crisis of 1949 was already beginning and was followed nine months later by the Korean War and rearmament. It was 1953 before the Economic Section began to think again of long-term planning. By that time a large amount of slack had developed in the economy and it was natural to look ahead to examine the problems that might arise as the slack was absorbed.

Early in 1953 Miles Fleming and Dow prepared minutes raising questions about the future pattern of output.[17] It was accepted policy to aim at an external surplus of £350 million on current account; and Fleming drew attention to the consequences for inflationary pressure if this surplus had to be created out of an increment in total output of £1,000 million without any change in rates of tax, terms of trade, or government expenditure. Christopher Saunders of the CSO had raised a somewhat similar issue: he made the same assumptions but asked instead what increase in capacity would be needed to achieve the external surplus without inflationary pressure. Christopher Dow, on the other hand, was analysing the implications for the balance of the economy and for fiscal policy of maintaining the investment goods industries at the same size relative to the rest of the economy. All three reached the conclusion that tax rates would have to be maintained or

17 The various papers referred to are all in 'Long-term economic planning', in PRO T 230/267. J. Miles Fleming should not be confused with J. Marcus Fleming, who left the Section in 1951.

even increased in spite of the large increase in productive capacity. This seemed repugnant to common sense and was challenged by Dick Ross, who wanted to broaden the discussion so as to examine the various shortages (in coal, steel, electricity, building materials, etc.) that would emerge if output expanded by about 10 per cent between 1953 and 1955. It would also be necessary to ask what would happen if exports failed to provide the necessary momentum for expansion and investment remained flat.

After discussion at a Section meeting Dow set out the agreed programme of work.[18] First of all, the National Income Forecasts (NIF) Working Party was invited to prepare quarterly estimates of national income and expenditure. This was an important development in the evolution of short-term economic forecasting and would allow a report on current trends to be prepared six to eight weeks after the end of each quarter. There was to be a series of quarterly reports on monetary developments, separate from the NIF reports. A third quarterly report on world economic trends should be prepared, initially within the Section, with Mrs Hemming taking the lead. It was presumably this that led shortly afterwards to the setting up of the Committee on World Economic Problems (WEP)

A long-term plan was not envisaged. Instead Dow called for a tentative outline of the main long-term policies appropriate to the United Kingdom. Miles Fleming and others would continue work on projections of national production with a view to throwing light on the future size of different industries. Maurice Scott would be asked to advise on export prospects in the light of calculations by Austin Robinson, and John Jukes would prepare a general paper setting out the main issues, supervise the various studies, and circulate a preliminary paper on policy.[19]

What was discussed in 1953 were the implications of an expansion in economic activity closer to the limits of capacity. This led on to a study in 1954–5 of the problems of economic growth, exploring the limits within which action was likely to be possible or necessary over a period of continuous development for, say, five years. In 1956, and on later occasions, the Section continued to look into the more distant future in order to review such matters as the obstacles to expansion in particular industries, the scale of investment the economy could

18 'Future work', note by J. C. R. Dow, 28 April 1953, in PRO T 230/267.
19 Peter Lawler also prepared a lengthy note on 'The draft economic survey for 1948–52 in retrospect', EC(S)(53)12, 3 June 1953, in PRO T 230/267.

support without inflation, and the long-term growth of incomes and outputs.[20]

There was never any question of a national plan – at least not until 1964. It was not until the end of the 1950s that the idea of central economic planning revived under the influence of what was considered the success of indicative planning in France. By that time planning was thought of as the antithesis of stop–go, a way of injecting greater stability and less uncertainty into industrial prospects. What was not recognized was that such success as French planning enjoyed reflected the faster rate of growth common to nearly all continental countries and the assurance of government support for the kind of co-operative effort that in Britain would have fallen foul of the Monopolies Commission.

When in 1964–5 the vogue for indicative planning was at its height, all memory of earlier debates seemed to have faded. Planning was greeted with an enthusiasm it had never enjoyed in the early post-war years and credited with a power to move economic growth into a higher gear – a power which the French planners themselves were hesitant to advance. In 1964 as in 1948 the Economic Section remained sceptical of such claims. It was no surprise when the plan folded at the first whiff of deflation, for the plan assumed away such a measure, preferring to believe that the government would rather choose the devaluation it had dismissed as 'unmentionable'.

20 For the papers on growth in 1954–6, see 'Long-term survey of the income of the United Kingdom', in PRO T 230/284–5.

# Chapter thirteen

# FORECASTING

One of the most important responsibilities of the Economic Section was the preparation of economic forecasts. It goes without saying that policy advice must rest on a view of the future whether or not it is explicit and makes use of a set of consistent predictions in quantitative form. Such predictions were an integral part of the economic surveys discussed in chapter 11. Even when not made by the Section itself they were indispensable to its work.

No such predictions were made before the war in respect of the various components of GNP, if only because the estimation of economic aggregates was still in its infancy. The first official estimates began in wartime with the publication of the white paper of April 1941, prepared largely by James Meade and Dick Stone. Official estimates of the balance of payments went back further. They were rare until the 1930s when they began to be prepared on a regular footing by the Board of Trade and the Bank of England but were given little publicity. The only official economic forecasts with a lengthy history behind them were those relating to budget revenue and expenditure, prepared by the Inland Revenue. These, however, were not particularly reliable. They allowed for additional revenue from higher taxes and additional expenditure proposed in Parliamentary votes but took no account of changes to be expected in the level of economic activity and money incomes.

## Balance of payments forecasting

The first economic forecast which the Section was asked to prepare was of the balance of payments in the first year of the war.[1] This did not, like later forecasts, rest on an analysis of the likely movements in consumer demand, domestic and foreign, but was essentially an assessment of the extent to which departmental programmes would be achieved in spite of shipping difficulties and of the loss of earnings from various sources likely to be inflicted by war conditions. When Austin Robinson submitted a forecast he did not claim more for it than that many of the figures were 'reasonable guesses of the probable order of magnitude'.

He was not content, however, merely to estimate the balance of payments with the whole of the rest of the world. From the point of view of policy the crucial issue was the rate at which it was safe to use up reserves and what mattered to this rate was the adverse balance between the whole sterling area and 'hard currency' countries, then consisting of the United States, Canada, Argentina, the Netherlands, Belgium, Scandinavia, and Switzerland.[2] He went on to point out that the adverse balance in hard currencies, while highly important, was not the relevant magnitude in reviewing the disposition of available resources. It might be taken to imply that the volume of exports to sterling area countries was a matter of indifference when these countries, if not supplied from the United Kingdom, might demand hard currencies to make purchases elsewhere or might be unwilling to go on accumulating sterling balances if refused this facility. Robinson's effort to relate forecasts to policy decisions was characteristic of later Economic Section forecasts.

The first forecast of the post-war current balance of payments was undertaken by the Economic Section in 1941. In August of that year, James Meade included in his 'Programme of work on post-war reconstruction' an 'assessment of what our balance of payments will look like after the war'. This he regarded as 'of basic importance' and after talking to Jewkes he arranged that Austin Robinson and Evan Durbin should take responsibility for the work with assistance from R. C. Tress.[3]

---

1 P(E and F)(S)(40)5 Revise, 'The British balance of payments', 25 January 1940, in PRO CAB 89/9. See above, chapter 2, p. 19.
2 During 1940–1 a small group in the Bank of England were working on short-term forecasts of the balance of payments with such countries. These were sent on to Dennis Robertson in the Treasury but there is no evidence of their ever reaching the Economic Section.
3 Meade to Jewkes, 10 August 1941 (Robinson papers in Churchill College Library).

A first forecast by Austin Robinson was circulated in November 1941 and revised in January 1942.[4] This took the view that the deficit foreseen would be difficult to remove by devaluation of the pound. A later memorandum by James Meade in December 1943 was more hopeful and put the improvement to be expected from devaluation at either £131 million or £195 million according as the elasticity of demand for British exports was either two or three.[5] Other forecasts of the post-war balance of payments followed in 1945 in advance of the loan negotiations in Washington.[6] These were all based on the Economic Section's work but some were prepared in the Treasury.[7]

Balance of payments forecasts were central to post-war economic strategy. A series of deficits seemed inevitable and the problem for the government was how to keep them within the limits of what could be financed. The Treasury, the Bank of England, the Board of Trade, and other departments were all interested in the size of the prospective deficit. In 1945 many different forecasts had been prepared. It was then decided to set up a Balance of Payments Working Party to prepare forecasts three times a year, beginning in February 1946. These were submitted to ministers and superseded forecasts prepared elsewhere, including those of the Economic Section, whose responsibility for this critical element in economic forecasting then ceased.

While the Balance of Payments Working Party co-ordinated the forecasts after 1945, the primary responsibility rested with the Overseas Finance (OF) Division of the Treasury as the main department dealing with external economic policy and the Bank of England as the Treasury's agent in matters of foreign exchange. Since OF kept its cards close to its chest and did not disclose information to other officials until it was ready to advise ministers, this led to some friction with the Economic Section, which had its own reasons for keeping track of the balance of payments. With the setting up of OF Stats in 1947 after the convertibility crisis, the Treasury became better equipped to handle balance of payments forecasts and submitted them

4 'The post-war balance of payments', memorandum by the Economic Section, in PRO T 230/4.
5 EC(S)(43)14, 'The post-war settlement and the UK balance of payments', memorandum by J. E. Meade, 11 December 1943, in PRO T 230/15.
6 The Economic Section's seventh quarterly survey gave an estimate of £810 million for the current account deficit in 1946, 25 July 1945, in PRO CAB 71/21.
7 For a full account of wartime forecasts of the balance of payments, see Pressnell, L. S. (1986) *External Economic Policy since the War*, vol. 1, London: HMSO.

for consideration to the interdepartmental Programmes Committee which had taken over the duties of the Balance of Payments Working Party. This arrangement continued until well into the 1950s, when the preparation of balance of payments forecasts passed to the Balance of Payments Prospects Working Party.

Since balance of payments forecasts were not the work of the Economic Section we need not pursue them further. The Section did not, however, lose interest in the forecasts and played a prominent part in the World Economic Problems (WEP) Working Party which ultimately took over responsibility for them. This was set up in December 1953 shortly after the transfer of the Economic Section to the Treasury. The Working Party was initially under the chairmanship of Christopher Saunders of the CSO, Christopher Dow representing the Economic Section. Its terms of reference invited it to submit 'a monthly analysis of the current world economic situation' but it prudently limited itself to the more modest aim of a quarterly report and soon found even that too much.

What seems to have provided the impulse to the establishment of the Working Party was concern over signs of an economic recession in the United States that might turn into the long-awaited American slump. Most of the papers of the Working Party in its first year deal with the recession in the US and its consequences for sterling area trade. The first balance of payments forecast, which it produced within weeks of its creation, provided for both contingencies: that there would and there would not be an international recession. Thus did the Economic Section institutionalize its burden of coping with fears of an American slump that never came.[8]

## National income forecasting

Forecasts of national income in a normal post-war year originated in the context of the Beveridge Report, when some yardstick had to be found of what could be afforded for social security under post-war conditions. Estimates for the year 1948 were submitted to the Committee on Post-war Reconstruction and were brought together in a paper by Ronnie Tress and Dick Stone in July 1943.[9] This 'threw

---

8 WEP(53)7, 'Impact of the US recession on UK and sterling area balance of payments', 17 December 1953, in PRO CAB 134/1187. The margin on current account between the two forecasts was no more than £55 million in 1954 for the UK and £130 million for the rest of the sterling area.

9 EC(S)(43)13, 'Estimates of post-war national income', note by Mr Tress, 15 July 1943, in PRO T 230/15.

into the same form as the National Income White Paper the "estimates" of post-war national income, expenditure and public finance as they have been thought out so far'. The estimates were taken from earlier papers with the exception of those showing the division of aggregate income between the factors of production in accordance with a formula based on experience from 1924 to 1942. What was new was not the estimates but the presentation, with its white paper system of double-entry social accounting. It was this presentation that was later adopted in the post-war economic surveys. Meanwhile the estimates by Tress and Stone, somewhat amended, became the basis for consideration by ministers whether the country could afford the Beveridge proposals discussed in chapter 6.

A later estimate in September 1946, again involving collaboration between the Economic Section and the CSO, yielded a remarkably accurate forecast for the movement in output over the three years 1946–8.[10] This put the increase in productivity between 1939 and 1948 at 10 per cent and the increase in national income over the same period at 11 per cent, both estimates very close to what would now be accepted. While the rise in prices was accurately predicted at 5 per cent per annum, the rise in wages from mid-1945 to mid-1948 was expected to work out at 7½ per cent compared with present-day estimates of 17½ per cent.

In post-war years more elaborate forecasts were prepared, first by the Economic Survey Working Party, and from 1950 by the National Income Forecasts Working Party. Income was calculated at current (factor) prices by adding together wages and salaries at expected rates of pay and employment, the pay of the armed forces, profits at assumed profit margins and levels of turnover, and interest and rents. This was then compared with an estimate of desired expenditure based on departmental requirements and expectations, the total at market prices being converted to factor cost by subtracting indirect taxes and adding subsidies. This procedure, which was modified later, yielded a gap between supply as measured by income and demand as measured by desired expenditure. This 'inflationary' gap – since excess demand was likely to issue in inflation of prices – could be represented in various ways:[11] in terms of manpower by comparing available

10 EC(S)(45)32, 'Memorandum on net national income in 1946, 1947 and 1948' by the CSO and the Economic Section, 29 September 1945, in PRO T 230/54.
11 For an account of the procedure followed in calculating the inflationary gap and an indication of its limitations see Little, I. M. D. (1952) 'Fiscal policy', in G. D. N. Worswick and P. Ady (eds) The British Economy in the Nineteen-Fifties, Oxford: Clarendon Press, pp. 165–8.

manpower at full employment with manpower requirements; or in financial terms as a gap between the expected supply of consumer goods and desired expenditure out of disposable income, or between expected total savings and expected total investment, or between expected personal savings and the level of personal savings required to make up the difference between expected investment and other sources of finance. Whether the gap was in manpower or finance, it dramatized the danger of inflation and was intended to bring home to ministers the need to eliminate excess demand. In the absence of such action the economy would be overloaded and the gap would be closed not by deliberate government planning but by the random pruning of demand by inflation through forced saving and the revision of spending plans in response to price increases.

Curiously enough, although the danger of inflation was put in the forefront by the Economic Section, they did not include in their forecasts any explicit indication of the rise in prices to be expected. Where the gap was expressed in terms of manpower, as ministers and senior officials preferred, there was no ambiguity. But it was by no means clear to the reader whether the forecasts in terms of money were at fixed prices or not and what change in real national income was being predicted. In the first Economic Survey all we are told is that the price assumptions on the supply side are consistent with those on the demand side. It is only in the appendices that we discover that wages are assumed to rise at 4 per cent per annum over the year from September 1945 to September 1946 and that only a small allowance has been made for an improvement in productivity. We also discover – although only after a little arithmetic – that consumer prices are assumed to be 3½ per cent higher in 1946 than in 1944.

Since output was not governed by demand this might be assumed to simplify the calculation, but the forecasters still had to decide what minimum level of unemployment would be feasible. In the early post-war years there were other uncertainties: the pace of demobilization and the rate of withdrawal of women from the labour market: the availability of adequate fuel and imported raw materials; the impact of these and other factors on the growth of productivity. Later still, in the Korean War, rearmament in Britain and abroad gave rise to fresh raw material shortages. From one year to the next, the continuation of excess demand was not enough to put beyond doubt the level of output.

Nevertheless it did dispense with the need to forecast the behaviour of each of the main sub-aggregates of demand so as to arrive at an estimate of GNP at current factor cost. The estimates made were statements of requirements, given sufficient supply, or of how much demand would receive satisfaction, given that supply was insufficient. The first assumption went with the idea of an inflationary gap, the second with an effort to predict what might conceivably happen if the government failed to take the necessary action to cut down demand and close the gap. The gap procedure lent itself to the idea of a shortage of manpower since excess demand, measured in money, could easily be converted into its manpower equivalent. But, as the Economic Section saw it, it was more fundamentally a shortage of savings or an excess of investment. Expressing the gap in manpower terms was simply a way of avoiding a direct confrontation on budgetary policy and winning the support of the Chancellor for action that had immediate budgetary implications. The alternative procedure, which yielded a forecast not a gap, was free of the inconsistency of indicating one outcome while expecting another, but was bound to yield forecasts at variance with government targets. Instead of a manpower budget that did not balance, there was a prediction of a distribution of manpower between industries and sectors of the economy that did not accord with government aims.

In the first three (unpublished) economic surveys prepared by the Economic Section the forecasts are summarized in a set of social accounts showing, in comparison with previous years, income and expenditure, first for the economy as a whole and then for public authorities and for the private sector separately. In financial terms the gap emerged as a deficiency of savings in relation to the investment that had to be financed, a deficiency that could be expressed either as a failure of personal savings to reach some higher proportion of disposable income or as a failure to plan for the necessary budget surplus and close the inflationary gap in that way. The deficiency of savings was brought out in a combined capital account showing the contributions forecast from public and private sectors (including depreciation allowances) and the capital investment (also gross of depreciation) which each sector would try to carry out.

It is implicit in this way of proceeding that one can never tell afterwards whether the forecast was right or not. The gap, which is at the heart of the forecast, is automatically closed in one way or another, destroying the hypothetical separation of demand and supply. It is fairly clear, however, that some parts of the forecasts were based on false assumptions. To illustrate this we need only look at the 1947 white paper (Cmd 7099) and compare what were then regarded as 'actuals' for 1946 with the forecasts in the first survey. Personal consumption in 1946 instead of being 7 per cent below the level in

1938, was 1 per cent higher. Domestic capital formation (including stock-building) fell short of the forecast (at current prices) by nearly 40 per cent. Private savings (including undistributed profits) were nearly £1,000 million less and public savings £300 million more than forecast. The balance of payments deficit is now estimated at £230 million compared with a forecast of £750 million (less £150 million in additional outstanding export credit).[12]

The point is not that the errors were large – a substantial departure from forecast was inevitable – but that some of them were in directions opposite to what the forecasting procedure would lead one to expect. The rise in consumer spending was much greater, not less, than so-called 'requirements'; stock-building was less, not greater, than in 1945; and so on. The survey does not prepare the reader for the large departures from forecast, says nothing about the wide range of possible outcomes, and does not indicate the most likely sources of substantial error. Agreed, the outcome was dependent on government reactions to the projected gap and on how the gap was closed. Agreed, too, little was known with certainty in 1945, or even in 1946, about post-war trends and there were no quarterly data to facilitate an up-to-date assessment. From the point of view of technique, this was an important handicap. But the main problem in forecasting is to know which elements in the forecasts are most liable to error; and the errors listed in the previous paragraph afford some clues.

Long before Keynes it was recognized that the most unstable elements in demand lay in investment and exports. Keynes broadened this by formulating his theory in terms of the balance between savings and investment, with international receipts and payments acting as a second source of imbalance. It was investment (domestic capital formation), savings (both private and public), and the balance of payments that were most in error in the early surveys. The biggest single error in 1946 was in stock-building, which had been put at £550 million[13] and is now estimated to have fallen by over £100 million or at

12 These comparisons, except the last, are with the estimates for 1946 published in April 1947. These figures in turn are subject to substantial error and were changed, often substantially, in later white papers. For example, the balance of payments deficit was originally put at £400 million, or nearly twice more recent estimates.

13 This is described as the 'change in value of inventories and work in progress' and presumably included stock appreciation. As *Sources and Methods* (p. 44) explained in 1956, 'the reliability of estimates of changes in capital formation at current prices is poor; and the corresponding estimates of stocks and work in progress are very poor'.

best to have remained constant if stock appreciation is included. Much of the difference represented the difficulty under post-war conditions of procuring imports in sufficient quantity to satisfy departmental requirements. The shortfall may well account for the whole of the error in the balance of payments forecast and nearly all the error in domestic capital formation. The unexpected fall in stocks went some way to offset the much too optimistic forecast of personal savings.

Stock-building was the joker in the forecasting pack. It was not only difficult to guess it correctly in relation to the coming year but errors in assessing stock-building in the previous year torpedoed a whole succession of forecasts in the 1950s.[14] Yet the first published *Economic Surveys* omitted any discussion, record, or forecast of the physical change in stocks. It was not until 1950 that the *Economic Survey* included any estimate of stock appreciation and even then no figures were given for stock-building in the usual sense of 'value of the increase of stocks of goods and work in progress'. Until 1951, investment was discussed in terms of a single aggregate for 'gross capital formation at home', including both stock appreciation and repair expenditure on building and works. It was only then that current usage in the treatment of investment was adopted.[15] In earlier

14 See pp. 200–4.
15 In all this, the *Economic Survey* followed the white paper on *National Income and Expenditure*. This first gave figures of fixed investment, as well as figures of stock-building that included stock appreciation in 1949. In 1950 stock appreciation was shown separately for 1948 and 1949 (as in the *Economic Survey* for that year) but it was not until the following year that estimates were included for 1946 and 1947. The 1951 estimates for stock-building (net of stock appreciation) and for stock appreciation compare as follows with those in *Economic Trends Annual Supplement 1981* and the 1954 white paper on *National Income and Expenditure* respectively (figures in £million):

|  | Stock-building | | Stock appreciation | |
|---|---|---|---|---|
|  | 1951 est. | 1981 est. | 1951 est. | 1954 est. |
| 1946 | −165 | −102 | 100 | n/a |
| 1947 | 140 | 292 | 350 | n/a |
| 1948 | 200 | 175 | 250 | 325 |
| 1949 | 215 | 65 | 40 | 200 |
| 1950 | 115 | −210 | 350 | 650 |

The stock-building figures for 1948–50 have undergone no change since 1954.

years any forecast, whether of fixed investment or of stock-building, was largely a shot in the dark and nobody could measure its accuracy before the next forecast was made.

After 1947 national income forecasting continued to be linked to the *Economic Survey* issued in March or April. The difficulty of publishing the *Economic Survey* in advance of the White Paper on *National Income and Expenditure* meant that the forecasts had to be hurriedly prepared at the last minute as soon as the CSO supplied estimates for the previous year.

From 1948 to 1951 forecasts were published of GNP at current prices subdivided into three or four main components: personal consumption, gross investment (usually with details of fixed investment by sector), and government current expenditure, with balance of payments figures taken over from the separate forecast prepared by the Programmes Committee. The forecasts could not be converted into fixed price comparisons in volume terms since no price forecasts were given: the first year in which figures were given for real output and expenditure changes was 1951. In 1948–50 one had to make what one could of hints and approximations.

The published forecast for 1948, predicting a fall 'of the order of 3 to 5 per cent in gross national expenditure' (including foreign borrowing) was a good deal too pessimistic.[16] For 1949 the forecast was said not to 'give more than a broad illustration of the tendencies at work'.[17] In both years and in 1950 the estimate for personal savings was not a forecast but a requirement if the forecast level of investment was to be financed without inflation.[18] The average increase in productivity was put at 2½ per cent in 1949 and again in 1950, the figure being 'more an assumption than a forecast'.[19] This increase corresponded to one of 3½ per cent in the industries covered by the index of production.

The forecasts included in these three *Economic Surveys* were no different from those submitted to ministers in the earlier drafts intended only for their eyes. They showed little evidence of any

16 *Economic Survey for 1948*, para. 201. The actual fall would appear to have been under 1 per cent.
17 *Economic Survey for 1949*, para. 94.
18 ibid., para. 115.
19 *Economic Survey for 1950*, para. 69. The increase related to the whole economy, excluded the armed forces and government employees, and was for output per man-year. An increase of 2½ per cent was criticized by Douglas Jay (who argued for a figure of 3–4 per cent) and he insisted, with the approval of the Chancellor, on an indication (in para. 69) that 2½ per cent might prove 'conservative'.

appreciable advance in forecasting technique. What advances were made seem to have sprung from the preparation of the long-term economic survey in 1948 rather than from the annual *Economic Survey*. The advances in the 1950s rested heavily on the great improvement in national income statistics that began in 1951 with the issue of the blue books and the later preparation of quarterly data after 1955.[20] They may also have been promoted by the establishment of the National Income Forecasts Working Party to concentrate exclusively on national income forecasting. From 1950 on, this took responsibility for all forecasts of national income and expenditure. The Working Party's first chairman was Christopher Saunders of the CSO and the other members included E. F. Jackson of the CSO, Douglas Allen of the Planning Staff, and Jack Downie, Christopher Dow, and Peggy Hemming of the Economic Section.[21]

One of the main purposes of national income forecasts had been from the start to form a background to budget calculations. In the early post-war years the unpublished economic surveys were intended to fulfil this purpose. But from the end of 1947 it became the practice for the Economic Section to submit one or more economic assessments of the outlook incorporating their forecasts. Once the NIF Working Party was set up, these forecasts came to be prepared on a regular footing, a preliminary forecast for the next calender year being submitted in December and pre- and post-budget forecasts in February and May. The forecasting record for the 1950s, so far as it is publicly available (i.e. to 1958), is discussed in the next section.

## Forecasting in the 1950s

The history of the 1950s is one of expansion in final demand from 1950 onwards, checked abruptly in 1952, resumed in 1953, losing steam in 1955–6 as the limits of capacity were approached, and coming to a halt for a second time in 1958. The sudden fall in demand in 1952, the equally sudden recovery in 1953, and the petering out of the boom in 1955–6 all represent major changes of which advance warning from the

20 A review of national economic forecasting methods was prepared in 1951 for transmission to the OEEC National Accounts Unit (NIF(WP)(51) 10 Final, 23 May 1951 in PRO CAB 134/522). Apart from the treatment of profits and stock appreciation there is little in the document that could not have been written five years previously.

21 ESWP(50)2, 'Working Party on National Income Forecasts', note by Robert Hall, 23 January 1950, in PRO CAB 134/892. For the reports of the Working Party, see PRO CAB 134/1058–61.

Table 13.1  Annual changes in the main components of expenditure, 1948–60 (£m. at 1954 prices)

| | Consumers' expenditure | Public authorities' current expenditure on goods and services | Fixed investment | Value of physical increase in stocks | Exports of goods and services | Total final expenditure | Imports of goods and service |
|---|---|---|---|---|---|---|---|
| 1949 | +234 | +185 | +162 | −200 | +322 | + 703 | +221 |
| 1950 | +310 | − 4 | + 99 | −275 | +421 | + 551 | + 85 |
| 1951 | −161 | +212 | + 4 | +805 | + 49 | + 909 | +445 |
| 1952 | − 66 | +294 | + 9 | −525 | − 25 | − 313 | −366 |
| 1953 | +451 | + 95 | +230 | + 90 | − 43 | + 823 | +232 |
| 1954 | +549 | − 11 | +205 | − 80 | +250 | + 913 | +184 |
| 1955 | +420 | − 74 | +132 | +265 | +221 | + 964 | +407 |
| 1956 | +105 | − 5 | +131 | − 50 | +254 | + 435 | +125 |
| 1957 | +254 | −108 | +121 | + 35 | + 50 | + 352 | +111 |
| 1958 | +326 | − 33 | + 10 | −122 | − 89 | + 92 | + 88 |
| 1959 | +562 | + 61 | +225 | + 60 | +126 | +1,034 | +475 |
| 1960 | +513 | + 66 | +303 | +367 | +222 | +1,471 | +662 |

Sources:  National Income and Expenditure 1959 (for 1949–57) and 1961 (for 1958–60).

forecasters would have been useful. We shall see what success they had presently.

When we look to see what the volatile elements in demand were, we find fluctuations in all five components shown in table 13.1. The figures are at 1954 prices and are as seen in retrospect in 1959. While they may have been amended since then, they convey with sufficient accuracy the variability of the main components of demand and the relative importance of the fluctuations occurring in each of them.

The most volatile element was undoubtedly stock-building, which accelerated one year and slowed down the next all through the 1950s. It was by far the most important element sustaining demand in 1951 and the major factor in the decline in demand in 1952, almost to the exclusion of all other factors. If it played a less important role in the recovery in 1953, it would still appear to have made the largest single contribution to it. Similarly in 1956 it ranked alongside the check to consumers' expenditure as a principal contributor to the slowing down in final demand. In 1959–60 it again emerged as a leading factor in the upswing in those years.

Of the other elements in demand fixed investment was remarkably stable, with some reduction in the rate of growth in 1950 after the devaluation cuts in October 1949 and a more pronounced check in 1951–2 in face of the growth in defence expenditure in those years (included under public authorities' current expenditure). Exports of goods and services show a similar check, prolonged into 1953, but otherwise climb at a fairly steady rate until 1957 when they begin to droop, recovering slowly in 1959–60. The growth of the final element, consumers' expenditure, is also checked in 1951–2 by the rearmament boom. It then becomes very buoyant for the three years 1953–5, is checked again in 1956, and recovers to a higher rate than ever in 1959, helped by tax concessions.

The check to consumer spending in 1951–2 can be explained by the sharp rise in import prices, which exercised a deflationary effect accurately predicted by the Economic Section. This was reinforced in 1952 by a rise in unemployment and a halt to economic expansion. The opposite forces came into play the following year with improving terms of trade and renewed economic expansion. The later check to consumer demand in 1956–7 can be attributed to government policy.

The growth in final demand was paralleled by less dramatic changes in gross domestic output, imports acting as a rule as a stabilizer. As can be seen from table 13.2, the annual increment in GDP remained between £400 million and £600 million except in 1952 and 1958 when growth virtually ceased, in 1954 and 1960 when demand was

*Table 13.2* Annual increment in gross domestic product, 1948–60, forecast and actual (£m.)

|  | Pre-budget forecast | Post-budget forecast | Estimate in following year | Estimate in 1961 |
|------|------|------|------|------|
| 1948 | − 75 | n/a | +300 | n/a |
| 1949 | +225 | n/a | +425 | +466 |
| 1950 | +300 | +454ᵃ | +450 | +466 |
| 1951 | +325 | n/a | +250 | +464 |
| 1952 | +250 | +270 | −200 | + 53 |
| 1953 | +445 | +575 | +500 | +591 |
| 1954 | +190/+360ᵇ | +195/+370ᵇ | +560 | +729 |
| 1955 | +465 | +505 | +525 | +557 |
| 1956 | +425 | n/a | +310 | +310 |
| 1957 | +175 | n/a | +300 | +241 |
| 1958 | +115 | (small fall) | −120 | + 4 |
| 1959 | +160 | +440 | +816 | +816 |
| 1960 | +600 | +500 | +300 | +300 |

*Sources:* For 1948–51, EC(S)(54)3, 'National income forecasting in the UK 1948–52', J. Grieve-Smith, 9 March 1954, in PRO T 230/341. The figures in col. 1 are taken from the *Economic Survey* or the White Paper on *National Income and Expenditure.* For 1952–8 the forecasts are from NIF Working Party reports and are at factor cost one or sometimes two years previously. The estimates in col. 3 are on the same basis. The estimates in the final column are all at 1954 factor cost and are taken from table 13 of *National Income and Expenditure 1959* or *1961.* For 1959 and 1960 the forecasts are those of the National Institute and relate to the increase from fourth quarter to fouth quarter (*National Institute Economic Review*, May 1961). The 'actuals' are on the same basis and all figures are at 1954 factor cost.
ᵃ Assuming a 2½ per cent increase in productivity: from EPC(50)46, in PRO CAB 134/225.
ᵇ Two forecasts were prepared in 1954, one assuming an American depression, one not.

expanding strongly, and in 1956–7 when the economy was at full stretch and there was little or no slack to draw on.

Finally, a word on imports. To some extent imports fluctuated with the growth in final demand and especially stock–building; the correlation between the oscillations in stock-building and in imports is very close. To that extent the fluctuations in stock-building did not impinge on domestic activity. But the swings in stock-building tended to be wider than those in imports so that there was an overflow on to domestic production; and there were, of course, other influences on imports. In 1952, the only year in which the volume of imports fell, import restrictions accounted for some of the fall below trend, though probably for less than half.

Thus the general picture in retrospect is of a decade of relatively steady growth at or near to full employment, with a major upset in 1951–2 arising out of rearmament, a falling away in 1956–7, and a second halt to expansion in 1958. But the period was not free from anxieties: no one could be sure that the fluctuations that occurred would prove self-correcting or that when expansion was checked, as in 1952 and 1958, it would be quickly resumed with the same momentum as before.

A main source of anxiety was the balance of payments. The gold and dollar reserves had fallen to a very low level at the time of devaluation, fell back to much the same level in 1952, and remained throughout the decade well below what would have been appropriate in a country with Britain's international responsibilities, extensive trade, and heavy short-term liabilities. There was every reason to aim at a balance of payments that would allow the reserves to be built up. But over the decade 1950–9 the surplus on current account averaged less than £100 million per annum while at least as much was invested abroad (net of inward investment). In these circumstances an increase in reserves of any size was out of the question except through aid, borrowing abroad, or adding to sterling liabilities. Starting the decade at £600 million, the reserves at the end of 1959 had risen only to just under £1,000 million. Fluctuations that with larger reserves could have been shrugged off assumed an importance of a different order.

We turn next to the forecasting record, starting with GDP. A comparison between the forecasts after 1950 and the statistical record as seen at the end of the decade shows a tendency to under-predict the changes, up or down, in the level of activity.

Apart from 1952 and 1956 the forecasts uniformly fell below what was taken to have been the increase in GDP. When the economy slowed down in 1952 and to a lesser extent in 1956 the forecast registered some slowing down but not enough. When the economy speeded up in 1953 the forecast registered some acceleration but again not enough. In 1954 a slowing down was predicted when the economy was gathering speed and in 1955 the expansion again exceeded expectations, although to a much smaller extent. There is a marked contrast between the gradual dying away of the boom (viewed from the point of view of annual increments in output) between 1954 and 1958 and the much more erratic course traced by the forecasts. While the forecasts in 1957 and 1958 seem to have been close to the mark it is unlikely that this was so in 1959 and 1960.

Even when the forecasts were not far wrong in assessing the probable growth in GDP there could be large errors in the component elements making up the total. In 1951, for example, the forecast for

Table 13.3  Value of physical increase in stocks and work in progress, 1948–57 (£m. at current prices)

| Official estimate in March or April | 1948 | 1949 | 1950 | 1951 | 1952 | 1953 | 1954 | 1955 | 1956 | 1957 |
|---|---|---|---|---|---|---|---|---|---|---|
| 1950 | 75 | 150 | | | | | | | | |
| 1951 | 200 | 215 | 115 | | | | | | | |
| 1952[a] | 195 | 70 | −168 | 387 | | | | | | |
| 1953 | 145 | 35 | −225 | 465 | −100 | | | | | |
| 1954 | 153 | 35 | −210 | 610 | − | 170 | | | | |
| 1955 | 175 | 65 | −210 | 615 | 70 | 125 | 175 | | | |
| 1956 | | | −210 | 575 | 50 | 125 | 125 | 350 | | |
| 1957 | | | | 575 | 50 | 125 | 75 | 300 | 200 | |
| 1958 | | | | | 50 | 125 | 50 | 325 | 250 | 425 |
| 1981 | 175 | 65 | −210 | 575 | 50 | 125 | 56 | 300 | 259 | 238 |

Sources:  White Papers on National Income and Expenditure of the United Kingdom; Preliminary National Income and Expenditure Estimates; Economic Trends Annual Supplement (1981 edition).

[a]  The 1952 estimates are taken, exceptionally, from the Blue Book issued in August 1952, not from the White Paper issued earlier.

GDP was only a little too low but stock-building was under-predicted by about £600 million (as it was over-predicted to the same extent in 1952) and other less volatile components were also in error. Defence spending in particular lagged behind forecast sufficiently to produce a shortfall in public expenditure on goods and services of nearly £300 million at 1954 prices. Reviewing experience between 1948 and 1952, the Economic Section found there were large errors in nearly all the aggregates and that even the forecasts of government expenditure were 'remarkably inaccurate'.[22]

Throughout the 1950s, the level of stocks, the rate of stock-building, and even the direction of change in the rate were all subject to wide margins of error. The offical estimates for any given year might be changed drastically between one year and the next without any certainty that the latest figure was more accurate than the first (see table 13.3). What seemed at the time a year of stock accumulation could be transformed by revisions in the estimates into one of decumulation as in 1950, or vice versa as in 1952; and what was thought at one time to be a year of faster accumulation might later be seen as one of slower accumulation as in 1949 and 1954, or vice versa

22  EC(S)(54)3, John Grieve-Smith, 'National income forecasting in the United Kingdom, 1948–1952', 9 March 1954, in PRO T 230/341.

as in 1957. To make matters worse, the factors governing the movement of stocks were largely unknown and often unpredictable.[23]

In 1952 apart from a slight error of optimism on exports there was only one thing wrong with the forecast.[24] It seriously underestimated the fall in stock-building and was correspondingly in error on GDP. The forecasters accurately predicted the direction of change of each variable and were not far out in four out of six cases. But just as the statisticians had underestimated the level to which stocks had risen in 1951 – and indeed partly because of this error – so the forecasters underestimated the fall in stock-building in 1952.

Looking back at the end of the year, they still felt some surprise that a year in which defence expenditure was due to increase strongly should have ended with demand running flat. In the first half of the year they had apparently no inkling of change: the forecasts in early May indicated more or less the same expansion in GDP as in the previous November although unemployment had been rising since the last quarter of 1951.[25] The falling-off in demand was not so much predicted as observed when it was already in progress. It was attributed to three factors: the low level of personal consumption early in the year; a fall in exports in the spring and summer; and a reversal in the middle of the year of the upward movement in stocks.[26] The first two of these explanations are valid: consumer spending fell in 1952 when it had been expected to show a modest recovery; and exports, which were not expected to do well, did even worse than had been forecast. But the third explanation shows how much in the dark the forecasters were on the movement of stocks. Given the size of the swing between 1951 and 1952, it is most improbable that the turning-point came as late as the middle of 1952. The deceleration in stock-building must have started much earlier, probably before the end of 1951, and dwarfed all other elements in the situation.

The experience of 1952 seems to have made a deep impression on the forecasters. It was the first year after the war when GDP more or less stood still and it became obvious that the economy was running

23 NIF(WP)(53)3, 'National income in 1953', 26 January 1953, in PRO CAB 134/1059, para. 25.
24 The forecast is taken from NIF(WP)(52)3 1st Revise, 'National income and expenditure', 31 January 1952, in PRO CAB 134/1058.
25 For the NIF forecasts see NIF(WP)(51)18, NIF(WP)(52)3, and NIF(WP)(52)7, all in PRO CAB 134/1058.
26 NIF(WP)(52)14, 'Economic developments in 1952 and the prospects for 1953', 5 December 1952, in PRO CAB 134/1059.

well below capacity. This had consequences for the methodology of forecasting since one could no longer take for granted that output would be governed by changes in supply rather than demand. It became necessary to predict the level of demand instead of assuming the persistence of excess demand, satisfied only within the limits of full employment and after allowing for bottle-necks and shortages.

In February 1953 an estimate was made for the last time for six years of economic potential at full employment.[27] Over the previous two years industrial production had registered no net increase after expanding at an average rate of about 8–9 per cent in the years 1947–50, in spite of recurrent shortages of fuel and raw materials. With the slower growth in the labour force a rate of 8–9 per cent might not be attainable but there was scope for a rate of perhaps 6 per cent. This suggested that, if the upward trend in productivity had continued unaltered and the slack accumulated over the past two years were now absorbed, output might be raised by the equivalent of about £1,000 million per annum.

In 1953, the initial expectation was of a fairly modest recovery, resting heavily on stock-building. The budget was reckoned to add about £140 million to demand in that year, chiefly to consumer spending, with some slight encouragement (through the restoration of initial allowances) to fixed investment as well. The post-budget forecast turned out to be reasonably accurate in total but significantly wrong in detail. On this occasion the error arose, not from stock-building, which fell well below expectations, but from the beginnings of the consumer boom and an increase in fixed investment twice as high as had been predicted. Most of the increase in investment was in house-building: investment in manufacturing industry actually fell in spite of the rising pressure of demand. Exports also continued to fall. It was very much a consumer-led boom that had been initiated in the 1953 budget.

By the end of 1953 the American economy was in recession and studies were set on foot (as so often in the past) of the likely impact on British trade and employment. Fears that a recession might be on the way had been expressed as early as April and were reinforced by the expectation that rearmament in the United Kingdom would reach its peak and begin to decline in 1953. The official studies reported in May that an American depression on the scale of that in 1937–8 would

27 'The potential capacity of the economy in 1953', note by Mr Neild, 19 February 1953; and NIF(WP)(53)3, 'National income in 1953', 26 January 1953, in PRO CAB 134/1059, paras 34–8.

worsen the sterling area's current account for the first year by £325 million and might sweep away half the reserves and increase unemployment to a million. A recession like that of 1949 would present much less of a problem and was unlikely to cause substantial unemployment.[28]

These studies did not affect the initial national income forecast in December 1953 which assumed a world untouched by recession and arrived at a view of expansion in domestic demand far below what was currently being experienced. Indeed, the level of demand predicted for 1954 was not much higher than had already been reached at the end of 1953 since the rapid expansion in that year had brought production in December well above the average for the year.[29] This cautious assessment was partly due to inadequate information: stock-building, for example, was assumed at that stage to have amounted in 1953 to about double later estimates and the lower rate expected in 1954 was correspondingly deflationary. But there was also a failure, as in 1953 and again in 1955, to appreciate the full impetus behind the consumer boom.

The Economic Section drew pessimistic conclusions from this forecast. If so little expansion was in store even in the absence of an American recession, the economy must be running out of steam. 'Granted no outside influences,' Robert Hall told the Budget Committee on 7 December, 'we could expect the present level to be a plateau, on which, on present policies and trends, we might rest for some time'.[30] The consequences of this assessment of trends are discussed in chapter 16.

Two months later the evidence of a recession in the United States was too strong to be ignored. It was assumed that it could be comparable with that in 1949 but rather more severe, sufficient to cause a slight fall in exports in the first half of 1954 and a 4–5 per cent fall in the second half. A reduction in stock-building, particularly in the second half of 1954, was also to be expected. The result would be to arrest completely the expansion in demand by the autumn although for the year as a whole demand would be slightly higher than in 1953.

By May it was apparent that the US depression was having less effect on the world economy than had been feared. It continued to be the view of the Economic Section, however, that, even if the decline in

28 PAR(53)8, 'Effects of a United States recession', 18 May 1953, in PRO T 230/357.
29 NIF(WP)(53)16, 14 December 1953, in PRO CAB 134/1059.
30 BC(53)26, 'The budgetary problem in 1954; first assessment', 7 December 1953, in PRO T 171/437, para. 23.

the US economy ceased as was generally expected, 'activity here can be expected to hold up and probably expand somewhat. But it seems unlikely to expand very much.'[31]

Thus throughout the first half of 1954 the forecasts were such as to warrant expansionary measures in the budget. Except in relation to public expenditure, where there was a shortfall on estimates, the forecast was uniformly too bearish. Contrary to expectations exports at last resumed an upward trend instead of wilting in a world depression; fixed investment again increased twice as fast as forecast; the same is true of consumer spending; and stock-building yet again performed very differently from expectations. If no expansionary measures were taken in the budget, it was just as well. Looking at the rapid expansion in demand and the correspondingly rapid fall in unemployment, it would perhaps have been more desirable to take the first steps in 1954 to introduce some restraint on the expansion in progress.

When we come to 1955, with the boom in full swing, the forecasters stepped up their estimates but continued to under-predict the expansion in demand. Yet again, their major error was in stock-building, which proceeded at a rate not seen since 1951 instead of slowing down somewhat, as expected in February, or accelerating very little, as predicted in April. In the post-budget forecast, which took account of the fillip to consumption given in the budget, consumer demand, too, was under-predicted, as it had been in each of the two preceding years. Defence expenditure, however, was well below estimates, as in 1954, and this produced an overestimate of the growth of public expenditure that more than offset the error in personal consumption. Moreover, there was an offset to the high rate of stock-building in an unexpectedly high rate of imports, so that, in the end, the increase in GDP was not much above the April forecast.

In trying to assess the current economic situation and prepare a forecast the Section felt increasing frustration at the inadequacy of the available information. From the middle of 1953 they were pressing for quarterly national accounts in money and in real terms, such as existed in the United States.[32] They were also concerned to use seasonally

---

31 BC(54)45, 'The post-budget prospects for 1954', 19 May 1954, in PRO T 171/437. The forecast given in this paper assumes that UK exports would be unaffected by the US depression and is not strictly speaking a post-budget forecast.

32 'A quarterly review of economic developments', C. R. Ross, 24 June 1953, in PRO T 230/402.

adjusted figures and to bring together the separate forecasts for the national income and the balance of payments.[33] Some months later they were asking for surveys of investment plans, of industrial capacity, and of the spending intentions of consumers. They wanted more data on new orders and the length of order books.[34] Two years later, when there had been little response from the CSO, Macmillan was encouraged to refer in his budget speech in 1956 to the danger of relying on 'last year's Bradshaw', and an organized effort to improve the available data was put in hand.

As the data improved, so, too, did the technique of forecasting. Forecasts were no longer in terms of annual comparisons but showed expected developments quarter by quarter so that a clear picture was presented of the forecast situation at the end of the forecast period. The use of seasonally adjusted figures made possible at the same time a more accurate view of the changes in progress in the labour-market and these could be linked more firmly to the simultaneous changes in national income and expenditure to show the lag in employment behind output. Wage and price forecasts were also made separately so that the forecasts could be presented in money or in real terms. By the early 1960s these forecasts were coming to be supplemented by parallel forecasts of financial flows.

## Conclusion

Although the technique of economic forecasting improved greatly, it remained a chancy business. When the NIF Working Party was set up in 1950, Downie confessed that available information made it possible to form 'little more than a hunch about the relations between income, expenditure and supplies during the immediate past'.[35] Even with quarterly data and computers, these relationships remained uncertain and turning-points in particular continued to be largely unpredictable. As Robert Hall put it in 1952 in commenting on papers he had commissioned on the likelihood of a slump: 'We cannot *forecast* a slump at all. . . . It is mostly hunch and half one's hunches are wrong.'

33 Note by Dow, 6 October 1953, in PRO T 230/402.
34 J. Grieve-Smith, 9 March 1954, in PRO T 230/341.
35 NIF(WP)(50)34, 'Appraising the internal economic situation', note by J. Downie, 26 June 1950, in PRO CAB 134/521.

# Chapter fourteen

# DEMAND MANAGEMENT: MONETARY POLICY

The monetary policy pursued during the war owed little to the Economic Section. They were, however, interested in the role that monetary policy would play under post-war conditions and there are occasional references to this from 1941 onwards in papers by James Meade.[1] He in particular saw a need to make use of variations in interest rates as an instrument of employment policy. Its use under immediate post-war conditions to control inflation was more in doubt.

It was as a result of an initiative by Meade that an official committee was appointed in January 1945 to consider a number of related issues in post-war monetary policy and debt management – the National Debt Enquiry (NDE) Committee.[2] Meade had asked originally whether the Economic Section might usefully prepare a note on the case for a capital levy – a matter in which Attlee had expressed an interest. Later he had suggested widening the enquiry to consider ways of lightening the post-war burden of debt. The question had also arisen how a cheap money policy – however that was interpreted – could be sustained in the long term. The retiring head of the Treasury, Sir Richard Hopkins, arranged for representatives of the Treasury, the Inland Revenue, and the Economic Section to review these issues under the chairmanship of

---

1 See, for example, EC(S)(42)12, 'Government intervention in the post-war economy', 8 April 1942, in PRO T 230/14, para. 4, where he lists 'control over the total supply of money and the rate of interest' as instruments needed for employment policy.
2 The papers of the Committee are in PRO T 233/157–9 and T 273/389. See also Howson, Susan (1987) 'The origins of cheaper money, 1945–47', *Economic History Review* August.

his successor, Sir Edward Bridges, and fifteen meetings were held in the first six months of 1945.

The Committee was dominated by Keynes, who expounded in three successive meetings his views on the forces governing interest rates and his ideas as to the basis on which debt management should be conducted. It was an occasion unique in the history of the Treasury and had a profound influence on post-war policy.[3]

The report of the Committee argued in favour of the maintenance of low interest rates, long and short, 'far beyond the transitional period'. It was assumed that rates of interest would be largely insulated from financial conditions in other countries by a permanent control over capital movements and that there was no need, therefore, to raise short-term rates in order to protect the reserves. Short-term debt was firmly held; and, 'given close understandings with the banking and financial world', the interest it carried should be no more than enough (for domestic holders at least) to meet the cost of market and banking machinery. Conditions later on might call for fluctuations in short-term rates but continuity of policy should be preserved and sudden changes avoided. Longer-term issues should be made, as in wartime, through the tap with a range of maturities and terms to match the public's liquidity preference, not the Treasury's propensity to fund. In the transition the danger of inflation could not be countered adequately by higher interest rates or higher taxation and required the continued use of physical controls. On the other hand, to move to a lower long-term rate would be premature while opportunities for investment were exceptionally abundant and before normal post-war conditions had been established. If, subsequently, the long-term rate encouraged new capital formation on a scale tending to produce inflation, it should, in general, be raised.

These were views with which Robbins and Meade, the Economic Section representatives, were in general agreement. Robbins was anxious to preserve some flexibility and feared that there would be upward pressure on interest rates either because the physical controls might crumble or because of trade union pressure on wage rates under full employment conditions. Interest rates might also be pushed up in Europe and other countries where there was little danger of secular stagnation and this might put a strain on exchange controls and force

3 For Keynes's contributions, see Keynes, Lord (1980) *Collected Writings*, vol. 27, Cambridge: Cambridge University Press, pp. 388–414. The minutes of the meetings and the report of the Committee ('The question of future gilt-edged rates') should also be consulted.

an adjustment in exchange rates. On funding, however, he was very much in agreement that a rigid policy should at all costs be avoided.[4]

James Meade, at the theoretical level, was at pains to point out that interest rates were affected by the forces of productivity and thrift, as would be apparent if the money supply were held constant. Although the use of interest rates should be avoided in the transitional period, they ought to contribute, in the longer run, along with fiscal policy and physical controls, to the avoidance of inflation. Both he and Robbins repudiated the idea that small changes in long-term interest rates would have little effect on capital formation. 'We remain unconvinced', they remarked in a postscript added to one of their papers, 'that the effect of even a one per cent change would be negligible.'[5]

From these interventions the Economic Section would appear to have been less optimistic than Keynes about the power of the authorities to maintain low interest rates indefinitely and over the wisdom of attempting to do so. They were also more insistent on the need to use fiscal policy in the transition in order to discourage spending. High rates of purchase tax for a limited period might induce consumers to defer expenditure. On the other hand, tax cuts that increased the disposable income of consumers were even more likely to add to effective demand than their possession of capital funds accumulated in wartime. Proposals already current for cuts in excess profits tax, income tax, and purchase tax would release a great deal of additional purchasing power and put a heavy strain on the physical controls. Others on the Committee took a different view. Lower rates of tax would ease the negotiation of a temporary stabilization of wage rates and strengthen the incentive to work overtime in industries short of manpower. A reduction in excess profits tax from 100 per cent might also stiffen the resistance of employers to claims for higher wages.[6]

4 Minutes of fifth meeting of NDE Committee, 5 April 1945, in PRO T 233/158.
5 'The control of inflation: the three alternatives', note by the Economic Section (initialled by Robbins and Meade), 3 May 1945, in PRO T 233/158.
6 Among the papers submitted by the Economic Section were 'The fiscal problem set by the debt' (no. 4); 'The capital levy' (no. 5); 'Debt repayment and employment policy (no. 6); 'The control of inflation' (no. 10); and two unnumbered papers, 'Employment policy and economic forecasting' and 'Income tax credits'. Of these two, the former was a Section paper first circulated on 27 March 1945 and twice revised (EC(S)(45)5). All of these papers are in PRO T 233/157.

At the final meeting of the Committee on 28 June 1945, Meade raised the flag of budget deficits for what was to prove the last time for many years. He 'foresaw a period, perhaps only ten years hence, when the only fresh capital expenditure of any size open to the State' would be the equivalent of digging holes and filling them up again. 'It would be as well', he argued, 'not to formulate too rigidly a new orthodoxy which would preclude revenue budget deficits while allowing borrowing for capital purposes.' This drew from Keynes – and, rather surprisingly, Robbins – the retort that 'the new orthodoxy was more likely to take the form of the doctrine that the sole purpose of taxation is to avoid inflation'.[7]

In the preparation of the Committee's report, the Bank of England was not consulted but they would seem to have been in broad agreement. There were some elements in the monetary policy pursued by Dalton in the first two years after the war that were based on the report, had the support both of the Bank and of the Treasury, and were not inconsistent with the views expressed by the Economic Section. This was emphatically not true, however, of Dalton's efforts to force down long-term rates since the Committee had warned that such a move would be premature. The reduction in the Treasury bill rate to 2½ per cent had been one of the Committee's proposals and Keynes had urged in addition the issue through the tap of ten-year bonds with a 2 per cent coupon. Dalton also claimed in his diary that Keynes had been in favour, shortly before his death in April 1946, of a conversion of 3 per cent Local Loans into 2½ per cent Treasury stock.[8] But he added that the proposal had been opposed both by the Bank of England and by 'others' (i.e. the official Treasury). The Economic Section was not consulted but would certainly have opposed the effort to bring down long-term rates. Meade's one reference in his diary for 1946 to Dalton's cheap money policy is adverse; and his bias at that stage towards holding back investment so as to permit of a larger increase in consumption and a reduction in inflationary pressure tells in the same direction.[9] This was not the time to lower interest rates; if existing expectations were to be disturbed, there was every reason to expect later circumstances to be more propitious.

Since no use was made of monetary policy, other instruments of policy were required in order to reduce the overload on the economy, the most important being budget surpluses and administrative controls

---

7 Fifteenth meeting of NDE Committee, 28 June 1945, in PRO T 233/158.
8 Dalton, diary, entry for 12 April 1946.
9 Meade, diary, entries for 7 June 1946 and for 27 July 1946.

over investment. The Economic Section pressed consistently for a tighter budget and Meade wanted the deferment of fixed investment wherever possible and the scrutiny of all large projects in excess of £½ million. When ministers decided in the middle of the convertibility crisis in 1947 to review the investment programme and cut it, particularly where it made no contribution to an improvement in the balance of payments, it was Hall who suggested a target of £200 million for the cuts. The report of the working party undertaking the review started from this figure and reached a total of £180 million; but, as the cuts allowed other work to go ahead more quickly, the total amount of fixed investment in 1948 actually increased.[10] Hall's membership of the Investment Programmes Committee appointed in August 1947 allowed the Section to contribute to policy on investment from then on.

Under the post-war Labour government the Economic Section had at first little to do with monetary policy, so far as there was one, or with debt management. Bank rate remained at 2 per cent and long rates of interest drifted up after the failure of Dalton's effort to bring them down. The emergence of a budget surplus in 1947–8 did, however, raise the issue of how such a surplus should be used to limit the growth in the money supply or actually reduce it. The controversy that ensued focused not on interest rates but on the money supply on one side and on the creation of bank credit on the other. It was a controversy in which the Economic Section took an active part through Robert Hall's membership of a working party under Douglas Jay which included both Bank and Treasury officials.[11]

The Bank and Treasury did not see eye to eye on the contribution that monetary policy might make to keeping inflation in check. Douglas Jay and Robert Hall, both of whom felt that the Bank had surrendered control over the money supply, proposed a ceiling on bank advances. This greatly alarmed the Governor (Catto), who thought the proposal 'not practical'. Inflation was inevitable and no greater than was to be expected in the circumstances. It was 'an entire fallacy to suppose that pressure from the Bank of England on the

---

10 *Economic Survey for 1948*, Cmd 7344, para. 179; Cairncross, Sir Alec (1985) *Years of Recovery*, London: Methuen, pp. 452–3.

11 The papers of the working party are in PRO T 233/482–4. Economic Section views are in PRO T 230/469. For a full treatment of the discussions on the working party see Cairncross, Sir Alec (1987) 'Prelude to Radcliffe', *Rivista di Storia Economiche*, December, and Howson, Susan (1988) 'The problem of monetary control in Britain 1948–51'.

banks could rectify inflationary pressure which comes from over-gearing the country's economy'. Disinflationary pressure through the banking system, he went on, could only operate through pressure on the borrower. It could not work through higher interest rates without adding to the heavy burden on the exchequer; and if kept within normal limits would do little or nothing to deter industrial borrowers at current profit levels.[12]

The Bank's reaction made it clear that it did not aim to control the money supply but was content to let it respond at fixed (short-term) interest rates to the public's asset preferences. It was strongly opposed to a ceiling on advances or to a directive to the banks to limit their lending and relied heavily on a cash surplus in the budget to moderate the growth in deposits. It saw inflation as the fruit of past deficits and budget surpluses as the natural cure. So far as it had no power to operate on short-term rates and was inhibited in operating on long-term rates, monetary policy could amount to little more than moral suasion and requests to the banks on the one hand and various manoeuvres tending to shorten or extend the maturity of government debt on the other.

It was characteristic of the controversy that it was not over interest rates (nor over the need for a budget surplus) but over the money supply and bank advances, neither of which had been prominent in earlier discussion. So far as the money supply was concerned it took some time for the Treasury to appreciate that the monetary base was not a determining factor. Ratio control had gone in wartime and the clearing banks were now supplied 'week by week with the cash reserve necessary to support the amount of floating debt which they were asked to hold'.[13] As for advances, these had shrunk by 1945 to an abnormally low proportion of bank assets and it was natural that as the private sector recovered the banks should seek to accommodate its financial needs and at the same time earn a return on their assets very different from the ⅝ per cent payable on Treasury Deposit Receipts.

The working party ceased to meet early in 1950. It was to be seven years before a similar group of Bank/Treasury officials was appointed and it, too, would debate how to control the money supply and operate a ceiling on bank advances.

Robert Hall's experience on the working party did not leave him with a high opinion of the Bank of England or with much confidence

12 Governor to Chancellor, 17 December 1948, in PRO T 233/483.
13 Minute of second meeting of working party, 11 January 1949, in PRO T 233/483.

in their collaboration in giving effect to a restrictive monetary policy. He continued to think that monetary policy had a part to play in combating inflation and that it was through a limitation of bank credit that the policy could be expected to operate. The Bank, on the other hand, remained convinced of the need for fiscal measures – particularly cuts in public expenditure – as the indispensable means to fight inflation or restore confidence abroad. The Treasury for a time held views similar to Hall's. In the late forties their hopes centred on restrictions on bank advances, which the Bank of England heartily disliked, and it was only in the 1950s that they were also willing to make use of changes in interest rates. In every crisis for many years to come, whatever the cause, the Bank was almost certain to propose cuts in public expenditure while the Treasury would look first at almost any other device.

Other members of the Section joined from time to time in the discussion on monetary policy. Early in 1948 Shackle pointed out that a rise in interest rates acted as a kind of capital levy by depressing the value of bonds and could serve also to deter long-term investment without having much effect on re-equipment.[14] Dow took an early interest in the influence of exchequer financing on the money supply and challenged the view that early redemption of government short-term debt was disinflationary.[15] He and other members of the Section studied the experience of continental countries in using credit policy to keep inflation under control and noted that this approach appeared to have been more successful than reliance on budget surpluses. France, which had been 'the despair of Europe' in 1948, had succeeded in making prices fall in 1949 but had done so only after abandoning selective credit control in favour of quantitative restrictions.[16] In the devaluation crisis, Fleming pointed to the absence of monetary measures from the action proposed in contrast to their use abroad and argued that a rise in the long-term rate of interest to 4½ per cent would depress financial markets and check investment more promptly than the administrative measures on which the government was relying.[17] Atkinson and others in the Section also wanted higher

14 EC(S)(48)9, 'Money, interest and expenditure', 17 February 1948 (circulated with a covering note by the Director, 5 April 1948), in PRO T 230/469.
15 Dow to Hall, 23 December 1948, in PRO T 230/469.
16 Dow to Hall, 'Disinflationary Policies in Europe', 14 July 1949, in PRO T 230/469. Other papers on the subject by Abramson, Atkinson, Fleming, and Jones are in the same file.
17 Fleming to Hitchman, 24 August 1949; Eady to Fleming, 26 August 1949; Fleming to Eady, 29 August 1949; in PRO T 230/1400.

interest rates. Fleming seems to have been alone, however, in preferring action to limit the money supply to control over bank advances (alternative sources of finance being always available). There were also those who doubted whether the problem of inflation was one of an expanding money supply rather than high investment and government expenditure. One sceptic (Jones?) doubted whether monetary policy could ever be very effective when the banks were loaded with government debt and advances to the private sector were far below normal.[18]

In the devaluation crisis Robert Hall had suggested that the bank rate should be made effective and then raised to 3 per cent.[19] At the end of 1950, when the Governor (by this time Cobbold) proposed somewhat similar action and the Treasury opposed it, Hall found himself on the side of the Bank. Gaitskell was arguing that anything higher interest rates would do could be done by more direct methods. Hall pointed out that control of investment would be difficult by any combination of methods, that administrative control required a large staff, and that selective credit control would need nearly as many.[20]

When the bank rate was raised from 2 to 2½ per cent in November 1951, Robert Hall was consulted and raised no objection except to the size of the increase. 'Odium', he argued, 'will be incurred because of the change not because of the rate. . . . If the government acts it should act strongly.'[21] The important thing was to make the rate effective and get the market into the Bank so as to produce a sense of insecurity. Hall regretted that the Bank of England was so firmly against the idea that the banks should continue to hold government paper at ½ per cent or so.

When the 1952 budget was under discussion, Hall laid a good deal of stress on the contribution to be expected from the monetary measures proposed, including 4 per cent bank rate. The proposed increase, he thought, 'would have a severely deflationary effect'.[22] When he returned to the subject a few days later he emphasized that to the higher cost of borrowing and the greater caution business men would show in borrowing from the banks had to be added the effects of a

---

18 Manuscript draft on 'Monetary policy', unsigned, January 1951, PRO T 230/469.

19 Eady to Gilbert, 26 July 1949, in PRO T 233/1400.

20 Hall to Chancellor, 5 January 1951, in PRO T 230/469.

21 Hall to Eady, 'Credit policy', 31 October 1951, in PRO T 233/1684.

22 Meeting of Budget Committee, 29 February 1952, in PRO T 171/408.

simultaneous tightening of credit, 'which has a more direct influence than the rate itself'.[23]

The Economic Section also played a part in the first introduction of hire-purchase restrictions in February 1952. In 1950 Bretherton had put to the Board of Trade the case for varying credit terms cyclically since the goods concerned were precisely those most affected by swings in the pressure of demand. In January 1951 Dow returned to the subject, pointing out that a tightening of hire-purchase terms would help to clear the way for the expansion in defence expenditure; and it was on those grounds that the restrictions were introduced a year later by the Board of Trade.[24]

From then on, the Economic Section took an active interest in monetary policy, starting with a series of regular reports on monetary developments. The first of these appeared in May 1952. It was followed by two more later in the year, a succession of quarterly reports in 1953, and a survey of monetary development in 1953 in March 1954.[25] Some of these were sent by Compton of Home Finance (HF), almost apologetically, to the Bank of England, which itself produced no similar survey.

At the end of 1952 the Section conducted a post mortem on 'the new monetary policy'. Their analysis, which continued into 1953, led to a good deal of controversy, first with others in the Treasury and later with the Bank of England, over the part played by monetary policy in the falling-off in inflationary pressure and the recovery in the balance of payments in 1952. The ministerial view of the year's experience was expressed by the Chancellor when he told the Economic Policy Committee in November 1952 that 'the deflationary effect of monetary policy has been much stronger than had been generally expected'.[26] The Bank of England held a similar view: experience had shown

23 Hall to Armstrong, 5 March 1952, in PRO T 171/408. See also chapter 16, p. 261.
24 Bretherton to White, 22 August 1950, Dow to Hall, 26 January 1951, and 'Hire-purchase general policy', 19 March 1951, in PRO T 230/458. See also Dow, J. C. R. (1964) *The Management of the British Economy 1945–60*, Cambridge: Cambridge University Press for National Institute of Economic and Social Research.
25 The early reports were by D. J. Jones, those in 1953 first by Michael Franklin and then by Maurice Scott, and the 1954 report by Franklin and Neild. The first three (EC(S)(52)14, 31, and 35) are in PRO T 230/245–6, the 1953 reports are in PRO T 230/470, and the 1954 report is in PRO T 230/342.
26 EA(52)30M, Economic Policy Committee, 26 November 1952, in PRO CAB 134/842.

conclusively just how powerful a weapon monetary policy could be.[27] Both were encouraged in their faith in its capacity to control inflation, with unfortunate consequences three years later.

The Economic Section drew different conclusions, although they were not entirely of one mind and watered down some of their more sceptical comments. Their view of the evidence was that it suggested that the effect of monetary policy on domestic demand had been small and that it had not been a factor of any importance in the improvement in the current balance of payments. As the Bank of England and HF both pointed out, this took no account of the traditional influence of the bank rate on the capital balance. The Bank of England went so far as to argue that without the new monetary policy 'there would have been no alternative to Robot' (i.e. to letting the pound float) while HF claimed that the rise in the bank rate to 4 per cent in March had stopped the dollar drain 'almost overnight'.[28] Both claims overlook the impact of a budget which took bears of sterling by surprise by *not* including Robot.

In a detailed analysis of 'One year of the new monetary policy', the Section argued that the impact on domestic demand was likely to be principally on investment, although, as the paper admitted, there might also be a slight reduction in consumption because of a reduction in 'personal and professional' bank advances and a fall in Stock Exchange prices.

So far as fixed investment was concerned, it had increased in 1952 by the same small amount as in the previous year, a rise in housing investment more or less offsetting a fall in other fixed investment. The latter was not greater than might be expected in view of the withdrawal of initial allowances in the 1951 budget (operative from 5 April 1952) and the use of building and other controls to check civil investment at the end of 1951. The impact of monetary measures must therefore have been quite minor.

The Economic Section paper suggested that the effect on stock-building, which declined from £575 million in 1951 to £50 million in 1952, was 'general and contributory rather than direct and major'. A further study by Maurice Scott in January 1954 was equally sceptical of 'any close direct relationship between bank advances and stocks. . . .

27 For the Bank of England's view see Compton to Trend, 22 June 1953, in PRO T 233/1665.
28 For the Bank's contention see Compton to Trend, 22 June 1953, in PRO T 233/1665; for the HF view, see Goldman to Dow, 30 May 1953, in PRO T 230/470.

For the average firm, changes in bank advances from year to year do not correspond at all closely with the changes in stocks.' To restrict bank advances without restricting other forms of credit or raising interest rates would have no serious effect on decisions to hold more stocks.[29]

The movement in bank advances was no more conclusive than that in stocks. Of the fall of £200 million in the total between November 1951 and November 1952, over three-quarters (£156 million) occurred between May and August. This timing largely coincides with the change of the business outlook over the summer, when the price of imported materials fell, the upward movement of prices slowed down, and there was stagnation in the market for consumer goods. If the timing was thought to reflect the change in monetary policy, especially the rise in the bank rate in March, experience in 1955 threw doubt on so prompt and substantial an effect.

The Economic Section concluded that, while monetary policy had had some effect, it was relatively small. This conclusion applied also to the balance of payments. If the effect on home demand was small, so also must have been the effect on imports. The effect on exports, which fell in volume, could hardly have been very significant, especially as the fall was concentrated on textiles and other goods that could not find an adequate market at home. In any event, the situation at the end of 1951 had been so abnormal that subsequent events were not a reliable guide to what monetary policy might do in very different circumstances in the future. As Home Finance agreed, things might work out very differently if monetary policy were used by itself to check a boom in which demand was still expanding.[30]

There were, however, differences of view within the Economic Section. John Grieve-Smith thought that, in retrospect, the timing and direction of policy had been mistaken since it had merely aggravated a depression that was already under way. Christopher Dow, while conceding the verdict of the *Economic Survey for 1954* (para. 55) that 'monetary policy undoubtedly played its part in checking the rise in stocks and work in progress', thought it 'difficult to show that monetary policy has helped price stability very much' since the main

---

29 EC(S)(54)1, 'Bank advances, stocks and monetary policy', note by M. Scott, 18 January 1954, in PRO T 230/341.

30 Goldman to Dow, 10 May 1953, in PRO T 230/470. Dow, commenting to Robert Hall on an article in the *New Statesman* (1 November 1952) arguing that monetary policy had had little tangible effect, said the 'expert opinion is fairly well agreed that the general [monetary] policy has been useful' (PRO T 233/1397).

factor, as usual, was a fall in import prices. The influence of the policy, he argued, had been exerted mainly through requests to bank customers to reduce their overdrafts, not through higher interest rates, and changes in bank liquidity hardly entered given that the Bank automatically adjusted bank cash to the level of bank lending.[31] Robert Hall was more impressed by the correlation between monetary policy and the emergence of slack, and emphasized that 'we don't really know a great deal about how bank rate changes work'. When Compton submitted HF's assessment of the effect of monetary policy to the Budget Committee in March 1953, Hall supported Compton's more favourable view and would appear, like others in the Treasury, to have carried into 1955 a strong belief in the efficacy of tight money.

From the point of view of monetary policy the next two years were comparatively uneventful. In February 1953 Robert Hall recommended a continuation of credit restriction, particularly to wholesalers and retailers so as to moderate an upward movement in stocks, a view reflected in the Chancellor's budget speech.[32] The bank rate was reduced to 3½ per cent in September so as to keep it more closely in touch with market rates and the banks were warned that this should not be interpreted as a relaxation of policy. A second reduction of ½ per cent, for similar reasons, was made in May 1954, again on the initiative of the Bank of England. No attempt was made to use monetary policy to influence the level of demand. The only serious monetary issue in those two years related to hire-purchase restrictions.

The Board of Trade seized the opportunity offered by a reduction in the bank rate to press for the removal of controls over hire-purchase, arguing that economic conditions no longer required them, that they were difficult to enforce, and that they did nothing to affect the volume of credit since hire-purchase merely used funds that would otherwise have been employed by others. The last of these arguments could be shown to be fallacious: any financial intermediary, if free of control, can add to the level of demand without adding to the money supply. Sir Robert Hall's advice was that relaxation of the control would do no harm under existing conditions but that, rather than abandon it, the government should put the control on a permanent footing under statutory powers instead of Defence Regulations.[33] This

31 Dow to Compton, 19 June 1953; Dow to Couzens, 23 June 1953; Dow to Scott, 27 October 1953; all in PRO T 230/470.
32 BC(53)7, 'The economic and budgetary problem in 1953', 9 February 1953, in PRO T 171/413.
33 Hall to Gilbert, 'Hire-purchase general policy', 24 May 1954, in PRO T 230/458.

ministers were unwilling to do and the controls were withdrawn completely in July 1954. It soon proved that the government had misjudged the thrust behind demand for consumer durables. Before a year had passed fresh restrictions on a more enforceable basis had to be imposed.

The Economic Section watched the increase in bank advances in 1954 with some concern and asked themselves whether 'some slight tightening of credit in an unobtrusive manner' was not called for.[34] True, the increase over the winter of 1953–4 had not been exceptional by post-war standards and indeed the money supply in the four years from the end of 1949 to the end of 1953 had risen less than in any other industrial country.[35] But, as Hall noted in August, 'there is a boom atmosphere about the City which we don't want to encourage'.[36] Any restrictive measures, it was agreed, should if possible avoid injury to industrial investment, which did not look like rising and would suffer if monetary policy became more stringent. This limitation pointed to selective credit controls such as existed in the United States rather than general credit restriction.[37]

Before the 1955 budget the bank rate was raised twice but advances continued to expand. According to *The Banker* the rise in February was by far the fastest ever experienced and half the rise was financed from the sale of investments. Hall proposed that the Bank of England should take action to restrict credit. 'If a central bank hasn't got adequate powers to control the other banks,' he told Bridges, 'it undoubtedly ought to have such powers.'[38] The banks ought to be told not to find money for expanding their advances by letting their investments decline. Ian Little went further and suggested (following Hugh Dalton) that the holding of a fixed proportion of gilt-edged securities be made compulsory.

In his April budget, as explained in chapter 16, the Chancellor of the Exchequer took sixpence off the income tax when the economy was in full boom, justifying this apparently risky move by calling in aid 'the resources of a flexible monetary policy' – a phrase probably inserted into the budget speech at a late stage by Robert Hall. It is not clear

34 Minute on 'Monetary policy' by I. M. D. Little, undated but probably mid-1954, in PRO T 230/384.
35 Neild to Hall, 28 June 1954, Dow to Hall, 5 August 1954, in PRO T 230/384.
36 Hall to Compton, 6 August 1954, in PRO T 230/384, arguing that while there was no need for the Capital Issue Committee it was no time to relax.
37 Ross to Little, 23 September 1954, Little to Hall, 10 November 1954, in PRO T 230/384.
38 Hall to Bridges, 9 March 1955, in PRO T 230/384.

how the Bank of England was informed of the importance attached by the Chancellor to credit restriction but presumably it was thought that the increases in the bank rate and the budget speech were sufficient for the purpose. There is also no evidence of any prior discussion of the magnitude of any contribution that monetary policy might make to keeping demand in check.

By the beginning of May it was clear that, as Hall had warned, the clearing banks were still increasing their advances and finding the money by selling investments. Either the banks would 'have to be told quite plainly to tighten up on advances' or it would be necessary 'to force gilt-edged prices down far enough to prevent the banks from selling investments'.[39] Gilt-edged prices in the middle of May were in fact 8 per cent below their level in January and the banks, according to *The Economist*, were running out of short-dated investments. Some of the increase in advances, moreover – indeed, not far short of half – was attributable to a special factor: the Gas and Electricity Boards had had to defer the bond issues they had planned to make, and borrow from the banks instead, because the rise in bank rate, strikes, and other circumstances had depressed the stock market. At this stage Robert Hall was only mildly disquieted since he recognized that credit restriction took time to work.[40]

In the course of June, a rift began to develop between the Treasury and the Bank of England. The banks were reluctant to restrict credit to their customers in the private sector if the Gas and Electricity Boards were exempt; and, with the agreement of the Governor, they informed the two Boards that they must keep within their overdraft limits. This infuriated the Treasury, who suspected that the Governor was encouraging the banks in their insistence that the public sector should not be immune from the credit squeeze. As Robert Hall pointed out, the private sector, too, had received more credit – quite as much as the public sector, which was carrying out investment programmes officially approved.[41]

Thanks to his contacts with clearing bank chairmen, Hall had become aware that the Bank was not putting across the message that credit restriction was now the government's main anti-inflationary weapon. Until late in June the clearing bankers were under the impression that, so long as their liquidity ratio was above 30 per cent,

39  Ross to Little and Dow, 4 May 1955, in PRO T 230/384.
40  'The economic situation', note by the Director of Economic Section, 26 May 1955, in PRO T 171/456.
41  Hall to Brittain, 4 July 1955, in PRO T 233/1397.

they were following to the full the intentions of official policy.[42] The Bank of England thought that it was discharging its responsibilities if it kept the money supply from expanding. But what the Treasury wanted was to limit the flow of credit to the private sector.

For the first time, formal meetings were arranged between Treasury and clearing bank representatives at the Bank of England. Hall attended the second of these and found that no one had put it to the banks that credit restriction should be pushed to the point of causing redundancies and bankruptcies, although the banks were quite prepared to act if they could refer their customers to a statement to that effect. An appropriate statement was made by the Chancellor on 26 July and the banks subsequently agreed to his request for 'a positive and significant reduction' in total advances over the next few months.

Looking back in 1957 Hall thought that it had been a mistake in 1955–6 to delay so long letting the long-term rate of interest 'rise to an equilibrium level: that is to say, our funding policy was too passive. . . . For the years ahead I favour a high level of medium and long-term interest rates as one instrument of restraint.' What was also needed was 'a consistent and steadily applied view of the whole structure of interest rates'. These views were indicative of the long road travelled since the National Debt Enquiry in 1945.[43]

## The working of the monetary system

The failure of monetary policy to check the boom in 1955 left the Treasury uncertain as to how the monetary system actually worked under full employment. Robert Hall was as puzzled as the rest. In July 1955 he concluded a long minute to the Chancellor with the suggestion that

> We should now find out from the Bank of England exactly how they consider the system works and whether they think their powers are sufficient to enable them to control the total lending by the banks and if not what extra powers are needed. . . . We ought to make it clear that in future the Government will expect advances to be limited because the banks cannot lend any more without departing from their cash and liquidity ratios.[44]

In March 1956 he again suggested, this time to the Budget Committee,

42 *Financial Times*, 28 June 1955.
43 Hall to Makins, 22 November 1957, in PRO T 230/385.
44 Hall to Bridges and Chancellor, 28 July 1955, in PRO T 230/384.

that the Treasury and the Bank of England ought to get together and come to a clearer understanding of the mechanism involved.[45] Fred Atkinson had already prepared a paper outlining the different instruments of control that might be brought into use, including variable liquidity ratios, and Hall drew on this to interest the Chancellor.[46] This started off a correspondence between the Chancellor and the Governor on compulsory liquidity ratios with the Governor attacking the idea as neither desirable nor effective: the banks would simply fortify their liquidity by retaining the proceeds of maturing loans in cash or Treasury bills instead of converting them. The Governor, however, volunteered no alternative method of control, leaving the Economic Section to ask why, when the government leaned so heavily on monetary mechanisms, the initiative should always have to come from the Treasury. They were also conscious that in other countries, such as the United States, the powers of the central bank over the other banks in the system were more extensive and peremptory than in the United Kingdom.

Meanwhile an all-party Parliamentary and industrial group, led by Robert Boothby and Nicholas Davenport, had called for a new 'Macmillan Committee' to undertake an inquiry into the conduct of monetary policy. A deputation to the Treasury on 20 March 1956 made a strong case, supported by memoranda that were critical of both government statistics and government policy.[47] Officials advised the Chancellor against the proposal, Rowan commenting that sterling could not stand such an inquiry. Hall had more sympathy with the view that more knowledge and better statistics were needed. But he accepted the general verdict that there should be no inquiry into government policy.

After the budget, however, it was agreed that there should be a joint Bank/Treasury review of monetary control and a committee was set up at the beginning of May consisting of Leslie O'Brien and Maurice Allen from the Bank of England and Hall and Compton from the Treasury.[48]

The situation, as the Bank saw it, was dominated by the unwillingness of a bond market, weakened by fears of inflation, to absorb issues of debt by the nationalized industries. It was difficult to

45 BC(56), 4th meeting, 2 March 1956, in PRO T 171/469.
46 Hall to Chancellor, 'Liquidity ratios', 15 March 1956, in PRO T 171/469.
47 The papers are in PRO T 171/469.
48 The papers of the committee are in C40/69 in the Bank archives and in 'Development of monetary policy', in PRO T 230/472.

fund on a sufficient scale to avoid government borrowing from the banks and to keep the banks short of liquid assets. Maurice Allen listed four ways in which monetary policy affected the 'real' economy but dismissed three of them as either not of any importance currently or not very powerful. This left only the expectation that rates of interest might come down again, which could lead to a postponement of expenditure on investment. If it was thought that spending decisions were not much affected by the liquidity of the spenders, then it was to the asset side of the banks' balance-sheets that action should be directed. But how was this to be done and how big an effect would it have?

The report, signed on 25 June, rejected the use of an advances ratio: for one thing, there was no rigid rule governing what constituted an advance; for another, commercial banks differed too widely to allow of a uniform ratio. The report also came down against a prescribed liquidity ratio except in 'dire necessity'. If governments were unable to raise the money they needed by taxation or by long-term borrowing, they inevitably lost control over the money supply. There had, therefore, to be a big enough exchequer surplus to leave the government with the initiative in deciding on debt management operations. Thus the report, which the Governor thought 'a very convincing document', pointed to the government rather than to the central bank to take the necessary action.

Robert Hall, to assist in the preparation of a report, had sent a suggested outline to the Bank which O'Brien, in forwarding it to the Governor, found 'full of woolly half-truths' that 'will make you shudder'. It is not easy to see what produced this reaction. Hall admitted that the government had been slow to wake up to the boom that was already under way in mid-1954, largely because the necessary economic information was 'too much delayed'. The question raised by experience in 1955 was whether higher interest rates would have succeeded where a credit squeeze had failed. 'Those closest to the market', Hall suggested, took the view that 'an aggressive selling policy on a weak market' would not help since people would hold off buying government bonds in the expectation of a fall. The monetary authorities had had to resort to the issue of an additional £500 million in Treasury bills. All this was very much in accordance with the Bank's interpretation of events.

Hall's analysis also tallied with the Bank's in laying emphasis on business sentiment as a factor to be ranked alongside changes in interest rates and the money supply. What was new in the report was the insistence that business confidence was affected by action over which the Bank had no control, such as changes in exchequer finance. The Governor, seizing on the reference in the report to 1954, told Bridges that it was not only monetary policy but 'general and economic and financial policy which, as we can now see, should have been more restricted at an earlier date'.[49] It would have required a reversal of 'fiscal and other encouragement to expansion and investment' as well as a tighter monetary policy at the end of 1954 if inflation was to be avoided.

Cobbold went on to suggest, much to Bridge's annoyance, that a stage might be reached when a credit squeeze 'does more harm than good': this when the economy was at full stretch and the problem was to set limits to expansion. The Bank felt that the credit squeeze had had its day and on 28 June Maurice Allen minuted that a 'really serious tightening of advances' would only occur if there was an 'explicit statement by HMG that they 'understand and desire that financial pressure should make it impossible for domestic trade to continue at its present level and for an increase in costs to be financed'.[50]

Hall was at first satisfied with the report, which he felt to be the most important development of its kind since the Macmillan Committee Report of 1931. Within a year, however, he was expressing 'grave doubts about . . . our Report' and asking whether there was any control over the volume of credit.[51] By this time the Bank of England had put forward a proposal for an inquiry into the working of the monetary system and in April 1957 the Chancellor announced the appointment of a committee under Lord Radcliffe.

## The September 1957 measures and after

While the committee was sitting, a fourth attempt was made to get on top of inflation by the application of monetary policy. In 1948, 1951–2, and 1955–6 the aim had been to check the growth either of the money supply or of bank credit through the use of a budget surplus or higher interest rates or a ceiling on bank advances. Now the quantity theory of money was invoked by the Chancellor in the hope that tighter control over 'the supply of money to both the public and the private sector' would work through into more stable prices.

Although the rise in prices slowed down to just over 3 per cent in the year to June 1957, inflationary expectations were stirred in the spring by the apparent unwillingness of the government to resist

49 Governor to Bridges, 27 June 1956, in C40/69 in the Bank archives.
50 W. M. Allen, 28 June 1952, in C40/69 in the Bank archives.
51 Hall to Compton, 25 February 1957, in PRO T 230/0472.

strikes for higher wages. The British Transport Commission was allowed to pay a 5 per cent increase to railway workers, who had rejected a 3 per cent award by the Railway Staff Tribunal; and strikes by shipbuilding and engineering workers were settled at 6½ per cent soon afterwards. The impression gained ground in financial circles that, as the *Financial Times* put it in July, 'the government has . . . given up the fight against inflation'.[52] The spread of inflationary expectations was reflected in a fall in the demand for gilt-edged securities and a build-up of bank liquidity as well as in an outflow of capital through the Kuwait and Hong Kong gaps in exchange control.

The Economic Section, though sharing the concern over inflationary wage settlements, saw no immediate cause for alarm. The outlook at midsummer was for a 6 per cent expansion in industrial production over the coming year, with private investment still expanding and heavier expenditure on durable consumer goods as hire-purchase debt increased again. A record surplus of £200–250 million in the balance of payments was also expected in the first half of 1958. Nevertheless ministers were advised by the Steering Committee that the forecasts 'in no way justified any relaxation of present monetary and fiscal policies'.[53] The Economic Section was a little less negative: there would be no need to increase taxation in 1958 and tax concessions might be possible on a limited scale.[54] Neither they nor anyone else was able in July to predict the downturn in production and employment that began in the fourth quarter of 1957.

The Chancellor was much more disturbed. He was particularly alarmed by the constant pressure by departments for higher public expenditure and wrote to the Prime Minister in May to warn him that, unless their claims were resisted, cuts in taxation were out of the question, prices would go on rising, and there was 'a good chance that we may have an economic crash'. By July he was asking the Prime Minister for a directive – issued in August – calling on ministers to limit their current civil expenditure in 1958–9 to the level in 1957–8. He also drew the attention of his Cabinet colleagues to the large prospective rise in public investment, inviting them to refrain from further increases pending an autumn review.

What the Chancellor (and the Prime Minister) wanted was to put an end to wage pressure on the price level without having to face a row with the trade unions or a series of costly strikes. Their remedy was deflation designed to increase the level of unemployment to 2–3 per

52 *Financial Times*, 20 July 1957.
53 ES(57), 4th meeting, 10 July 1957, in PRO CAB 134/1835.
54 BC(57), 6th meeting, 22 July 1957, in PRO T 171/487.

cent and brought about by what they thought of as control of the money supply but what in fact consisted of setting limits to various forms of expenditure (public investment, current government expenditure, and bank-financed private sector expenditure). They took it for granted, as others have since, that, if the continual increase in wages and prices was no longer validated automatically by an expansion in the money supply, this would arrest the upward movement. This assumed that wage increases were highly sensitive to the pressure of demand – a very dubious assumption. Moreover, if what really had to be controlled was the pressure of demand, operation on the money supply was only one way, and perhaps not the most effective way, of doing this.

Although the Chancellor couched his ideas in terms of the money supply, he was obviously thinking of controlling not the money supply but the growth of money GNP. The proposals which he put to the Cabinet were that public investment should be limited to £1,500 million in 1958–9 and 1959–60 irrespective of the movement of costs and prices and that bank advances should be limited in 1958–9 to a total 5 per cent lower than in 1957–8. A standstill on current government expenditure had already been agreed. Two other measures – the reintroduction of building controls and tighter hire-purchase restrictions – were dropped after opposition by other ministers.

Meanwhile speculation against the pound had flared up after a devaluation of the franc and expectations of a possible revaluation of the mark in advance of the annual IMF meeting in September. The outflow of funds led to the inclusion at a late stage of an increase in the bank rate to 7 per cent (the highest level since 1921) in the measures announced on 19 September. The addition of this item was purely coincidental. The measures represented a clear change in the government's priorities: a readiness to sacrifice full employment in the interests of controlling inflation. If protecting sterling was a second objective, it was an afterthought, and the prime consideration was the domestic one.

The Economic Section took little part in all this. Robert Hall did not dissent from an effort to run the economy under rather less pressure provided a change was made over time in the whole emphasis of policy. The use of deflationary measures to deal with wage pressures which the government felt unable to resist because of the high cost of strikes would be unlikely to have an immediate effect on wages over the winter. Hall doubted whether the government had considered the political consequences of higher unemployment and was sceptical also of its readiness to hold to the proposed economies in government expenditure once they were worked out in detail: in the past ministers had hardly ever stood up to relatively minor cuts. He thought it unlikely, therefore, that the Chancellor's proposals would prove acceptable to the Cabinet or be welcomed by the Conservative Party.

As it happened, Hall was due to go on leave on 23 August but he came in for meetings with the Chancellor over the following week and did a preliminary draft of a paper for the Cabinet. Just before he finally got away he learned that the Prime Minister had received a letter from Roy Harrod suggesting that a powerful stimulus to the economy was needed and that it might take the form of abandoning purchase tax (which brought in about £460 million). Since the Prime Minister was said to be in sympathy with this idea, Hall doubted whether the Chancellor's proposals would get very far.

Over the next few weeks, according to Hall, the Chancellor took against all his officials (especially Hall himself), and summoned Lionel Robbins from holiday in Austria to advise him. The advice he received convinced him more than ever that the money supply was the root cause of inflation. Ministers then undertook the preparation of a statement issued on 19 September and officials were told that it was idle to protest since the policy had been settled. Hall was told by the Chancellor that everybody knew that it was the money supply that caused inflation. He continued, however, to argue that the immediate requirement was to stand up to wage claims over the winter and that it was a mistake to make a public commitment to engage in whatever measures of deflation were required to stop prices from rising without knowing how much additional unemployment would result.

Meanwhile the Chancellor was meeting with resistance from the banks, which would not accept the 5 per cent cut in advances, and from the Bank of England which refused to issue a directive requiring them to make the cut. The Chancellor was advised that under the 1946 Act he could neither oblige the Bank to issue a directive nor dismiss the Governor or the Court as he contemplated. There was a further disagreement over the increase in the bank rate, the Treasury arguing for a 6 per cent rate while the Governor wanted to go to 7 per cent. In the end the Treasury advised the Chancellor that if he contemplated sacking the Governor he could hardly afford to take what would seem a weaker line over the bank rate, and the increase to 7 per cent was agreed.

Before leaving for Washington for the Bank/Fund meeting the Chancellor set up a working party to study how the 1946 Act should be amended and how bank credit should be controlled. The Bank had to be more or less instructed to take part; Robbins was made a member; and Hall, instead of going to Washington, was also asked to join, while Downie acted as secretary. Hall and Robbins collaborated in framing recommendations, against strong opposition from the Deputy Governor, in favour of a prescribed liquidity ratio coupled with the introduction of something like Treasury Deposit Receipts (an illiquid alternative to bank-held Treasury bills). This recommendation took practical shape later in the scheme for Special Deposits first used in 1960. The remit to consider how the 1946 Act should be amended was left in abeyance.

These events put a great strain on Hall, who twice offered his resignation and looked round for another job but was persuaded to stay. The Chancellor tried to be conciliatory and took to consulting him on occasion while Hall, without querying the policy, tried to put the Chancellor's economic arguments in an intellectually defensible form. He was also reassured by indications that the Chancellor was now prepared to fight on the wage front and foresaw that the statement of 19 September might prove a useful psychological weapon in the struggle.

The year ended with what seemed at first the usual struggle by the Treasury to reduce the Estimates. Partly because of inflation and partly because of the entry into the national insurance scheme of a large block of pensioners, the total had risen by £175 million above the Estimates (including Supplementary Estimates) for 1957–8. To bring the Estimates within the limit of probable expenditure in 1957–8 – now regarded by the Chancellor as a matter of principle – required a cut of £150 million. Of this he reckoned that perhaps £40 million might be squeezed out in the course of Treasury scrutiny. But he insisted that the rest must be found, even if major changes in policy were required, and asked for economies of £100 million shared equally between welfare and defence services. When these proposals were rejected by the Cabinet, which found difficulty in putting together cuts of more than half of what he sought, the Chancellor resigned, along with the two junior Treasury ministers, Nigel Birch and Enoch Powell.[55]

After the September measures monetary policy fell back to the subordinate place it had previously occupied. Over the next two years the policy was relaxed and restrictions removed and it was not until 1960 that a fresh tightening began. So far as the Economic Section had a hand in the shaping of policy, it involved no major disputes.

55 In the event, the estimates for 1958–9 were only £42 million, or 1 per cent, above estimated expenditure in 1957–8, provided the £24 million raised through increased National Health Service contributions is treated as a reduction in expenditure.

# Chapter fifteen

# DEMAND MANAGEMENT: FISCAL POLICY TO 1951

The influence of the Economic Section on policy was nowhere greater or more visible than in relation to the annual budget. From 1947 onwards the Section supplied the Budget Committee with one or more economic assessments which provided a background to the final budget judgement. In addition, both Meade and Hall advised on the shape of the budget, the scale of the measures necessary, and the form that budgetary measures should take. While Meade's advice had only a limited influence on his Treasury colleagues (and still less on Dalton), in Robert Hall's period of office the Economic Section came to be regarded, in his words, as 'almost the responsible authority'; the budget judgement put to the Chancellor was his more than anyone's.

Because this was the most important (and perhaps also the most successful) of the Economic Section's activities, and because the internal debates on budgetary policy are more amply documented than almost any others on economic policy at the official level, it is worth reviewing the post-war record in some detail. In what follows, the proposals advanced by Meade in 1945–7 are first discussed and thereafter the contribution of the Section under Hall to successive budgets is examined one by one. This is done at considerable length since there is no published account of the official advice offered to the Chancellor on the most important single occasion in the financial year.

In wartime the Section had not been represented on the Budget Committee, nor was it privy to budget secrets. It had, however, a working relationship with Keynes and through Keynes with the Treasury. No doubt, too, Robbins was consulted on budgetary matters from time to time.[1] The work done by Meade and Stone on the White Paper on *National Income and Expenditure* in 1941 had helped to put a Keynesian stamp on the budget by setting it in the context of the national economy. The White Paper was followed by further collaboration with the CSO in improving the national income accounts and providing forecasts of national income after the war. These forecasts, as we saw in chapter 6, were helpful as a guide to the commitments on social service and other post-war expenditure that could reasonably be entered into while the war was still in progress.

Meade, from the time he became Director, and Hall, from shortly after his appointment as Director, were both members of the Budget Committee throughout their period of office. Both of them approached budgetary policy from a broadly Keynesian standpoint (although to judge from his advice to Dalton in 1946 Keynes himself might have taken quite a different line in the post-war years).[2]

In a succession of papers to the Budget Committee in 1946–7 Meade argued for a reduction in excess demand ('the inflationary gap') by means of a budget surplus and for substituting financial pressure for physical controls as soon as possible. The Budget Committee, however, in both 1946 and 1947, made no attempt to arrive at what would now be called a 'budget judgement' as to the extent to which the budget should seek to reduce excess demand. This does not mean that the Chancellor framed his budget without considering what change in the size of the budget surplus would be appropriate. It was rather that neither Dalton nor his Treasury advisers made the forecasts of excess demand in the Economic Survey their starting-point in making proposals as to the scale of budgetary action, and they did not relate their proposals to any estimate of the inflationary gap.

It became the practice after 1947 for the Economic Section to submit one or more economic assessments to the Budget Committee in advance of the budget, making an estimate of excess demand and recommending the scale of budgetary action required in order to keep inflation under control. A preliminary assessment of economic prospects came to be made in December and a more definite view to be taken in late January or February. These assessments usually

---

1 See chapter 8, p. 119. There is, however, no record of advice on taxation earlier than December 1944 when Robbins and Meade were consulted by Hopkins.
2 See, for example, the note of a meeting with Dalton and others on 20 February 1946 in PRO T 171/386 and Keynes's 'Post-budget reflections' in PRO T 171/389.

followed a forecasting exercise of some kind and were often lengthy documents ranging over the main issues of policy as seen by the Economic Section. They might also include detailed proposals for changes in taxation or expenditure in addition to the main recommendation as to the scale on which additional tax revenue should be raised or remitted.

In arriving at such a recommendation, the Section had to find some way of translating a forecast in terms of final demand into its equivalent in terms of budgetary action. The form of budgetary accounts did not, however, lend itself to this act of translation. The accounts made a rough separation of revenue and expenditure into current and capital items, the first going 'above the line' and the second 'below the line'. Unfortunately, so rough was the division that many items classed as 'current' had an impact on the economy more akin to capital transactions; and, apart from this, items properly treated as 'current' could have very different impacts on the economy although equal in amount. A surplus 'above the line' was thus a poor guide to the amount set aside or saved by the government and a still poorer guide to the effect of the budget on final demand and economic activity. An attempt was made shortly after the war to resolve the difficulty by devising an 'alternative classification' of items of revenue and expenditure. The White Paper on *National Income and Expenditure* also provided an estimate (on a calendar year basis) of the budget surplus 'on revenue (or current) account'. This could be used in conjunction with other data, to show the contribution to savings by public authorities (including the national insurance fund and local authorities).

Thus, at any one time in the early post-war years, there were quite a number of measurements of the budget surplus. The various measures differed quite widely and did not keep step with one another. For all except the surplus 'above the line', the figures for any single measure for any given year kept changing from one economic survey or white paper to the next. No explanation was provided but presumably the classification kept being revised. Expenditure on maintenance, previously excluded, would suddenly be included in capital expenditure. One year the figures would relate to the central government only, the next to all public authorities. Apart from one or two years, the figures (except again those for the 'surplus above the line') would relate to calendar, not financial, years. In these circumstances it is hardly surprising that discussion of the budget, in Parliament and press, was conducted in relation to the surplus or deficit 'above the line'. Economists might unite in dismissing it as highly misleading;

Professor Hicks might be coaxed (at the end of 1949) into writing a scholarly explanation of its failings; the form of accounts might continue to be argued over within the Treasury year after year. But for the average MP what mattered was the budget as presented, and for them the surplus or deficit as presented took precedence over all the reconstructed artefacts of professional economists. It was in terms of the wayward surplus they favoured that recommendations had to be presented.

Allied to the use of an inappropriate measure of the impact of the budget was the idea that there was something highly desirable about budgetary balance. Even in the mid-fifties, after many years of contact with the Economic Section, Treasury officials still regarded budget deficits with deep suspicion. Their antipathy was shared by Butler, Churchill, and probably most other members of the Cabinet. Their misgivings do not appear to have had anything to do with the monetary consequences of deficits (or of borrowing requirements, which are not the same thing). They arose largely out of fear of the effects of a deficit on confidence and the need to keep a tight grip on public expenditure. Acquiescence in a deficit might look like a surrender of control.[3]

Thus it was as if changes in the public sector borrowing requirement (PSBR) were the accepted touchstone of inflationary pressure and of the shifts in prospect in the level of economic activity. The budget surplus served as a proxy for the contribution to savings by the public sector and budget advice, although couched in principle in terms of a desired level of savings, was offered in practice in terms of the change that was called for in the excess of ordinary revenue over ordinary expenditure.

In the course of the 1950s this situation underwent important changes as demand management developed. The budget judgement ceased to be linked explicitly with forecasts of government revenue and expenditure and was made instead in direct relationship to the forecast of national income and expenditure, without specific regard to the effect on the prospective budget surplus or deficit. The action proposed was viewed, not in terms of the next twelve months, but with an eye on the situation expected at the end of the twelve months or even later. For this purpose quarterly, not annual, figures were required and became available from 1956 onwards. The tax changes – expenditure was separately discussed ahead of the budget – were

3 Tomlinson, J. (1987) *Employment Policy: the Crucial Years 1939–55*, Oxford: Clarendon Press, p. 148.

analysed so as to establish their incremental effect on demand, which differed from the effect on revenue in ways that varied widely between one tax and another. The monetary and balance of payments effects were likely also to be taken into consideration. But the fundamental change was that the inflationary gap approach disappeared along with excess demand after about 1951 and was gradually replaced by a demand management approach in which output was assumed to expand as the pressure of demand increased.

There was throughout a wide gulf between the Economic Section's conception of fiscal policy as an instrument of demand stabilization and that of Treasury officials and ministers. In the 1930s, fiscal policy was directed towards keeping the budget in balance and was little affected by any wider considerations of economic management. This did not prevent the acceptance of an enormous budget deficit in wartime and it was simply not feasible to get rid of the deficit at once when the war was over. The post-war period started with a large but declining deficit, which Dalton struggled to reduce and which, by the time he resigned after his fourth budget in November 1947, was heading for an all-time record surplus. Budgetary policy in 1945–7, however, remained separate from economic policy, the first coming under Dalton as Chancellor, the other under Morrison, as Lord President. None of the ministers saw the budget as the centre-piece of the economic planning to which they all paid lip-service; and none of them would have subscribed to James Meade's view that an early and sustained budget surplus was the most effective way of getting rid of excess demand and inflationary pressure. They assumed that economic planning in peacetime should rely on the same kind of controls as wartime planning, not on demand management through the budget; and were anyhow much more concerned to avoid the slump which they supposed was bound to arrive any day.

Thus, whereas James Meade from the beginning regarded the budget as the main instrument of planning, this was strange doctrine in the Treasury in 1946. Meade's efforts to link the Economic Survey, embodying the 'plan', with the financial year, and hence with the budget, by preparing a survey for 1946–7, won no support from Keynes, who distrusted systematic economic forecasts, nor from Dalton, who wanted to distance the budget from economic planning. The merging of the Treasury with the short-lived Ministry of Economic Affairs under Cripps in November 1947 created a more auspicious climate for uniting economic and financial policy, and the succession of crises in 1947 underlined the importance of such a policy by bringing home the dangers of growing inflationary pressure.

Cripps held on to the budget surplus that Dalton had initiated, in spite of a near-rebellion in the Labour Party in 1949 and much criticism from Cabinet colleagues. Ministers found difficulty in understanding why their proposals for additional expenditure should be rejected when the Treasury had ample funds. In March 1950, when Cripps invited members of the Cabinet to let him have written comments on his budget proposals, Viscount Addison, the Lord Privy Seal, attacked the budget surplus as discouraging work and saving. The government might save more but others would save less. The whole calculation that the surplus was disinflationary was 'exceedingly speculative'. The Prime Minister weighed in with a minute to Cripps suggesting that other ministers were equally foxed, and offering to arrange a meeting of the Cabinet to discuss the matter.

Robert Hall produced a paper for the occasion and sent a strong minute for the Prime Minister to be shown.[4] The economics profession as a whole, he maintained, would endorse his views as to the disinflationary effects of a budget surplus. To give up the policy of maintaining a surplus would be to abandon the principles of planning. 'It is the plain duty of the Government', he concluded, 'to support the policy.'

Cripps defended the policy in his last budget in April 1950. The budget, he said, was 'the most powerful instrument for influencing economic policy which is available to the government'.[5] But even he tended to hanker after a rule of policy such as that the budget should be in 'overall' balance, i.e. that all capital as well as current items should be covered by current revenue.

By the 1950s the Economic Section imagined that ministers (and officials) had been indoctrinated and that fluctuations between surplus and deficit were now accepted policy. It became clear in 1954–5 that this was not so. Conversion to budget surpluses did not carry with it conversion to budget deficits. As we shall see, prospective budget deficits had an effect on the thinking both of the Chancellor and of senior Treasury officials that showed how little they shared the perspective of the Economic Section.

The changes in 'ordinary' revenue and expenditure and in the balance between them are shown in table 15.1. Once demobilization was more or less complete in 1947 government expenditure was still at a level three times as high in nominal terms as before the war while

4 CP(50)35, 'Budget policy', memorandum by the Minister of State (Gaitskell), 15 March 1950, in PRO CAB 129/38. The other papers are in PRO T 171/400.
5 H. of C. Debates, 5th ser., vol. 474, col. 39, 18 April 1950.

Table 15.1 Central government revenue and expenditure 1945-60 (£m.)

| Year | 'Ordinary' revenue | 'Ordinary' expenditure | Surplus 'above the line' | Budgeted surplus^a | Public Sector borrowing requirement (in calendar year) | Net acquisition of financial assets by public sector (in calendar year) |
|---|---|---|---|---|---|---|
| 1944–5 | 3,238 | 6,023 | −2,825 | — | — | — |
| 1945–6 | 3,284 | 5,484 | −2,200 | −2,300 | — | — |
| 1946–7 | 3,341 | 3,910 | − 569 | − 726 | — | −646 |
| 1947–8 | 3,845 | 3,210 | + 635 | + 318 | — | −137 |
| 1948–9 | 4,007 | 3,176 | + 831 | + 789 | — | +270 |
| 1949–50 | 3,924 | 3,375 | + 549 | + 469 | — | +313 |
| 1950–1 | 3,977 | 3,257 | + 720 | + 443 | — | +352 |
| 1951–2 | 4,433 | 4,053 | + 380 | + 40 | — | −241 |
| 1952–3 | 4,438 | 4,350 | + 88 | + 431 (+80) | 771 | −552 |
| 1953–4 | 4,368 | 4,274 | + 94 | + 109 | 591 | −702 |
| 1954–5 | 4,737 | 4,304 | + 433 | + 10 | 367 | −435 |
| 1955–6 | 4,893 | 4,496 | + 397 | + 148 | 469 | −394 |
| 1956–7 | 5,158 | 4,868 | + 290 | + 460 | 564 | −547 |
| 1957–8 | 5,342 | 4,919 | + 423 | + 462 | 486 | −532 |
| 1958–9 | 5,479 | 5,102 | + 377 | + 364 | 491 | −448 |
| 1959–60 | 5,630 | 5,243 | + 387 | + 102 | 571 | −560 |

*Source: Financial Statements; Economic Trends Annual Supplement 1981.*

a This is the amount budgeted for at the beginning of the financial year and takes no account of supplementary expenditure or additional revenue after an autumn budget. The October 1945 budget was expected to add £283 million to revenue in 1945-6, the November 1947 budget £48 million, and the October 1955 budget £15 million.

GNP had barely doubled, again in nominal terms. The burden of financing this expenditure seemed crushing, especially as revenue had risen even more steeply than expenditure in order to leave room for a large budget surplus. The increase in nominal terms was more than fourfold and marginal rates of income tax ran as high as 97.5 per cent. After 1947 the climb in expenditure over the next eight years to 1955 was about 40 per cent and this outstripped the rise in prices by about 10 per cent. Thus the expenditure which had seemed unsustainably high in 1947 was appreciably higher ten years after the end of the war.

The story of revenue is similar. At the start of 1945, it was only 60 per cent of expenditure. By 1947, rising strongly, it was 20 per cent higher than expenditure. The climb in revenue from 1947 to 1955 was less steep than in expenditure and barely kept pace with the rise in prices so that, in relation to GNP, which grew steadily, revenue was somewhat less at the end of those eight years than it had been at the beginning.

Our main interest, however, is in the surplus. This emerged in 1947, peaked the following year, fell away under the strain of rearmament, and did not revive until 1954. If instead of looking at the budget surplus we focus on the savings of public authorities, the figures show a rapid improvement over the first two post-war years, a continuing rise for two more years, and a much less dramatic falling-off thereafter than in the budget surplus.

A better gauge of the pressure of the budget on the financial position of the private sector is provided by figures of the public sector's net acquisition of financial assets. This is shown in table 15.1 along with the surplus above the line and the public sector borrowing requirement. There were only three years in which the public sector had something left over from its savings and capital receipts after meeting the cost of public investment. These years were 1948–50, the years of Cripps's chancellorship; the figures testify to the effort made in those years to put the private sector in funds when personal savings were lacking.

We can now turn to the influence exerted by the Economic Section on successive budgets.

James Meade does not appear to have played a part of much importance in Dalton's first two budgets in October 1945 and April 1946. He was deeply engaged in the preparation of the 'Economic survey for 1946–47', which was in draft by 6 April 1946, and no doubt he regarded this as his contribution to the budget discussions.

## The 1947 budgets

Between January 1946 and April 1947 Meade submitted at least half a dozen papers to the Budget Committee, most of them lengthy documents.[6] Initially they tended to echo the draft economic surveys but they also contained specific proposals for budgetary action. Most of these had little influence on Dalton, who minuted that Meade's submission in early March 1947 'does not much change my mind though it may influence my presentation'.[7]

Meade's first paper on 25 April 1946 (i.e. after the budget) urged that an upper limit should be placed on food and housing subsidies and that a beginning should be made in allowing them to taper off.[8] Subsidies from which rich and poor alike could profit were less effective in redistributing income than family allowances, which chiefly benefited the poor, and should take up part of the savings that could be made in subsidies.[9] These views were rejected in 1946; but by November 1947, when Meade had gone, the Treasury was pressing the Chancellor to limit and reduce the subsidies (without making any offsetting increase in family allowances).

Meade also proposed an annual wealth tax if it were administratively practicable; this had the support of Hopkins and of Keynes.[10] Another proposal was for the taxation of inherited wealth by a progressive tax on legacies received. Yet another related to the repayment of post-war tax credits: repayment could be either in a lump sum or in variable annual amounts. If the first, it should be accompanied by a propaganda campaign in favour of savings; while, if the second, the flow of repayments could be regulated in the interests of stability of employment. Meade also suggested an examination of the balance of the budget in a 'normal' year once new financial commitments on social service expenditure had become fully operational.

Meade regarded control of investment as an important weapon in reducing inflationary pressure and backed the idea of reviewing all projects costing over £½ million with a view to delaying those not urgently needed. He shared the view of ministers that the balance had swung too strongly towards investment and that consumption should be allowed to increase in the interests of adequate incentives to effort.

6 The papers included: 'Note by Mr Meade', 25 April 1946: 'Control of inflation' (circulated on 17 June 1946): 'The inflationary pressure', 22 July 1946; BC(47)12, 'The economic survey for 1947 and the budget for 1947–48', January 1947; BC(47)13, 'Control of consumption expenditure in the interests of employment policy', February 1947; 'The economic crisis and the budget for 1947/8', early March 1947. All of these are in PRO T 171/384 or 389.

7 Minute by Chancellor, 14 March 1947, in PRO T 171/389.

8 'Papers leading up to 1947 budget, vol. I', PRO T 171/389.

9 ibid. The proposal was considered by the Budget Committee in July 1946.

10 Meade, diary, entry for 27 April 1946; note of meeting between Dalton, Keynes, Hopkins, Bridges, and Gilbert, 20 February 1946, in PRO T 171/386.

On the other hand, he was doubtful how long it would be possible to retain building controls, and for that matter other physical controls. It was his acute sense of the limitations of these controls that disposed him to advance constantly the alternative of using financial controls through the budget, monetary policy, and exchange rate adjustments.

A second paper, 'Control of inflation', followed shortly afterwards making use of the draft 'Economic survey of 1946–47'.[11] It discussed, along lines similar to the survey, the overhang of personal savings accumulated in wartime, the high rate of saving necessary to match the flow of consumer spending with expected supplies of consumer goods, and the simultaneous excess of investment demand over what was likely to be accomplished.

Against this inflationary pressure, direct controls had served as a bulwark. Among these, Meade laid particular stress on price control since even in the absence of rationing and licensing this effectively limited total expenditure: those who were unlucky in the queue had to take their money home and invest it in savings certificates. But there were serious drawbacks to price and other forms of direct control and these would multiply. Two particular difficulties were cited: the weakening of incentives when additional earnings could not be freely spent and the impossibility of making the labour market work under inflationary conditions. Rigid price control was incompatible with the use of the price mechanism to effect a redistribution of resources. To allow some rise in prices and wages in an 'undermanned' industry such as textiles or coal-mining would lead to sympathetic demands for similar increases in many other sectors, which, under conditions of universal excess demand, would be difficult to resist. Yet in the absence of labour direction, how else did ministers propose to plan the allocation of manpower? Only if there were insufficient demand at some points in the economy would labour move.

Meade then turned to discuss at some length the problem of cost inflation (see chapter 19) and renewed his attack on the various subsidies designed to stabilize the cost of living. These were expected to be running at £415 million a year by the end of 1946 and would automatically increase as food supplies improved or world prices rose. Meade proposed that all except the agricultural subsidies and subsidies to encourage the consumption of milk should be abolished. In compensation he suggested increasing national insurance and assistance benefits by £30 million to maintain their real value at the higher cost of

11 The paper is included in Meade, James E. (1988) *Collected Papers*, vol. 1, London: Unwin Hyman, pp. 275–96.

living that would result, and raising children's allowances by 50 per cent at a cost of £25 million. The net saving of £200 million a year would be appropriated to the Employment Stabilization Fund which he wanted to see established as a means of stabilizing the level of demand for labour.

If ministers were unwilling to cut food subsidies they could at least peg the cost of living at less cost. The subsidies stood to rise with every increase in rations and the rise would be inflated if the pegged index of the cost of living continued to give far more weight to food than accorded with current spending patterns. In working-class budgets of 1904, which formed the base of the index in use, food constitued 60 per cent of household expenditure whereas a survey of household budgets in 1937–8 showed that the proportion had fallen to 35 per cent. By introducing a new index, as the Section urged, expenditure on subsidies could be made less sensitive to sharp increases in international food prices and would rise less rapidly if, as expected, world prices of foodstuffs increased faster than other prices.[12]

Meade was anxious to avoid the kind of arguments with the Treasury over a budget deficit that had taken place in 1944 and put forward the idea of an Employment Stabilization Fund from which payments could be made in times of depression, leaving the ordinary budget in balance but allowing the same stimulus to demand as would be provided by a budget deficit. Payments into the fund should begin at once in 1947 and continue at £200 million a year for as long as a budget surplus was appropriate.

Meade went on to argue that, on White Paper principles, 'if it is really desired over the average of years to balance the Budget, there will never be a more appropriate occasion [than 1947] in which to contribute a Budget surplus'. There would come a time, however, when the manpower shortage would pass, especially if productivity rose appreciably, and provision should be made for such a time so as to make it possible to stimulate demand. One device would be to with-hold immediate repayment of post-war credits, amounting to £800 million, and release them as a regulator of consumers' expenditure.[13]

12 EC(S)(46)31, Nita Watts, 'The cost of living index', 25 June 1946, in PRO T 230/22; Nita Watts to Lord President, 'Proposal to reconstitute the Cost of Living Advisory Committee', 1 August 1946, in PRO CAB 21/2260; Rollings, N. (1988) 'British budgetary policy 1945–54: a "Keynesian revolution"?', *Economic History Review* May.

13 Meade's scheme would have permitted immediate repayment into a blocked savings account, with interest on the deposits and withdrawal at times when a stimulus to consumer spending was required.

There is no indication of how this paper was received by the Budget Committee and this is true also of the third paper by Meade in July 1946. This again stressed the limitations of physical controls and called for an early budget surplus.[14]

In January 1947 Meade was still insisting on the need to curtail demand. He made the novel proposal of a 20 per cent tax on investment, with subsidies to offset it in favour of such categories as housing and cotton-mills. The tax should be levied on all capital expenditure except on land and financial assets but including expenditure by nationalized industries and local authorities. A strong incentive to defer investment would be given by an undertaking to withdraw the tax once the need to restrain total investment had passed and by a promise to replace the tax by a subsidy of up to 20 per cent when a stimulus became necessary. The tax could be regarded as a substitute for raising the rate of interest and might be expected to bring in substantial revenue – probably over £150 million a year.

Another proposal with a similar aim was that distributed profits should be taxed more heavily than undistributed profits, again on the understanding that the discrimination would be reversed when there was a need to discourage rather than stimulate investment. Other proposals followed more orthodox lines: encourage savings, do not add to consumers' purchasing power by repaying tax credits or by reducing indirect taxation, do increase purchase tax where there is a particular need to discourage consumption (e.g. electric fires and other electrical apparatus). The earlier proposal on food subsidies also reappeared: a limit should be set £150 million below current levels with a 'rebate' of £50 million to increase children's allowances and national insurance benefits.

Just before the budget Meade tried again. He had some new and bold proposals. These included a 50 per cent increase in tobacco tax to bring in over £175 million;[15] and a tax on gas and electricity consumption that would raise £75–100 million from domestic consumers and £170–225 million if extended to all consumption. Another £150 million could be saved from food subsidies, making a total that could exceed £400 million. Against this, concessions might be made in favour of children, old age pensioners, and others at a cost

14 See Cairncross, Sir Alec (1985) *Years of Recovery*, London: Methuen, pp. 415–16.

15 Although Meade may not have been aware of it, the Treasury had earlier suggested an increase in tobacco duty by £100–120 million and Dalton had minuted 'Distinctly attractive, please pursue' (Gilbert to Chancellor, 18 January 1947, in PRO T 171/389). The additional revenue budgeted for in April was £77 million.

of, say, £50 million. Profits tax could also bring in a further £35–40 million, the rate being increased more on distributed than undistributed profits.

In view of what happened later in the year it is interesting to observe the immediate Treasury reaction. In a minute to Bridges, Gilbert, the Second Secretary responsible, dismissed the reduction of food subsidies by £150 million as 'quite impracticable' and certain to bring about another round of wage increases. Taxation of gas and electricity was regressive and 'would press very hardly on the poor'. Gilbert objected strongly to an increase of social security benefits by 10 per cent because it would wreck the contributory nature of social insurance and add permanent expenditure as an offset to a temporary increase of indirect taxation.[16]

Meade also touched on the misleading nature of the budget surplus from the economic point of view and the need to bring the form of government accounts more into line with economic thinking. There was a lot to be said for making revenue look bigger and expenditure smaller so as to minimize deficits in times of depression; and to do the reverse in times of inflationary pressures. 'This is not finance and it is not economics', Gilbert exploded, 'but a mixture of politics and psychology.'[17]

Yet the issues that Meade had raised met, after he had gone, a different reception. The form of national accounts occupied officials for many years – and perhaps still does. By the autumn the Treasury was in full cry in pursuit of a large budget surplus. It 'must deal openly and resolutely with the subsidies', which seemed to mean a cut of roughly £150 million. Investment, unchecked and largely uncontrolled, was to be cut substantially, but by administrative, not financial measures. By the end of 1947 the country was heading for the largest budget surplus (in 1948–9) in its history.

If Meade was not immediately successful in converting the Treasury, the Economic Section nevertheless had a powerful indirect effect on Dalton's first two budgets. This took the form of helping to accelerate the rundown in the armed forces and supply services, and hence to reduce government expenditure on defence. On this Dalton and the Economic Section saw eye to eye, especially as there was still a long way to go to balance the budget and the weight of continuing military expenditure abroad was playing havoc with the balance of payments. But, whereas Meade saw the need for a budget surplus as the key to the problem of inflation, Dalton took little stock initially of inflation in

16 Gilbert to Bridges, 14 March 1947, in PRO T 171/389.
17 ibid.

planning his budgets and only after long resistance succumbed to pressure from his officials and the media to aim deliberately at a surplus. It was the crisis of 1947 and the consequent collapse of the government's prestige, amid increasing clamour for measures to deal with inflation, that drove Dalton to impose new tax burdens in November 1947, not any persuasion by the Economic Section. Meade himself had left several months previously and Robert Hall was still very new to the affairs of the Budget Committee.

Robert Hall's first submission to the Budget Committee was made in advance of the November 1947 budget.[18] The convertibility crisis had forced Dalton to the conclusion that a supplementary budget was needed whose 'sole purpose would be to lessen inflationary pressure'.[19]

Hall's paper (probably drafted by Christopher Dow) began with the usual estimate of 'the inflationary gap', which he put at £490 million. But if the balance of payments deficit had to be removed there was an additional gap of £400 million. Against this could be set cuts in the investment programme ('say £120 million') and in the armed forces (£30 million) and an extra £100 million in exports, leaving £640 million to be found. It would be possible to get this down to £200–250 million if subsidies were cut in half, as Bridges was urging, and additional taxes yielding £170 million in revenue were imposed.

It was a complicated calculation that did not exactly convince the Chancellor in spite of powerful reinforcement by Bridges.[20] Dalton accepted the need for higher taxes (estimated to bring in £208 million in a full year) but declined to do more than put a ceiling on food subsidies and remove the subsidies on clothing and footwear.[21]

## The 1948 budget

Preparations for the 1948 budget began shortly after Cripps took office as Chancellor in November 1947. In alliance with Dalton he had already persuaded the Cabinet to make substantial cuts in the import programme and this had paved the way for Dalton's November

18 'The inflationary pressure', note by the Head of the Economic Section, '1947 supplementary budget', 1 September 1947, in PRO T 171/392.

19 Dalton first suggested such a budget on 11 August 1947 (PRO T 171/392).

20 Bridges to Dalton, 22 October 1947, in PRO T 171/392. The language of Bridges's minute (Cairncross, op. cit., p. 419) echoes the argument in Hall's memorandum.

21 Dow, J. C. R. (1964) *The Management of the British Economy 1945–60*, Cambridge: Cambridge University Press for National Institute of Economic and Social Research, p. 198, gives a slightly lower figure (£197 million) for the additional tax yield.

budget, since the cuts diminished the flow of goods and threatened an increase in inflationary pressure unless action was taken to reduce consumer demand. A large budget surplus was already in prospect, provided government expenditure could be held down.

Robert Hall's next paper to the Budget Committee, in January 1948, followed the same line of argument as his first.[22] It repeated, more concisely, Meade's analysis of suppressed inflation and his arguments for a budget surplus to reinforce, and later replace, the physical controls which had proved so inadequate in 1947. Inflationary pressure was unlikely to diminish in the year ahead if the external deficit were to be reduced as currently forecast, for this would make an additional demand on resources of £500 million.[23] On the other hand, the action taken to make drastic cuts in the investment programme was expected to produce a reduction by £150 million in 1948 and a corresponding fall in financial requirements. As for the level of saving, much of it in 1947 had not been voluntary but arose from inability to spend and was an undesired concomitant of inflationary pressure. To reduce the pressure, the budget should aim at an addition to revenue or a cut in expenditure of about £200–300 million.[24] This was essentially an intuitive judgement as to how much could be done in the year to damp down demand without sacrificing output. It was not closely related to the detailed calculations, which was just as well since nearly all the calculations looked different two months later when the *Economic Survey of 1948* and the white paper on *National Income and Expenditure* were published.

Cripps accepted that the surplus should be at least as large as the Economic Section proposed and confessed to some surprise that the inflationary gap should be put so low. But the tax changes in his 1948 budget probably added to the pressure on resources in demand terms rather than diminished it.[25] An increase in revenue of £118 million was almost entirely offset by tax concessions amounting to £108 million; and while the concessions (on income tax, purchase tax, and entertainment duty) took full effect on demand, the increases in tax, apart from higher duties on beer, tobacco, and betting, did not. Cripps

22 'Note on inflation', BC(48)3, January 1948, and BC(48)3, 2nd Revise, 17 January 1948, in PRO T 171/394.
23 On the most recent estimates the swing in the balance of payments between 1947 and 1948 was £405 million rather than £500 million.
24 On this occasion and for many years the Section's proposals related to the budget surplus, not to the desired change in final demand.
25 Dow, op. cit., p. 198. Cripps did, however, budget for a surplus 'above the line' higher by £155 million than the out-turn for 1947–8.

had decided in January 1948 that if he could not have a capital levy for lack of staff to operate it he would introduce 'some sort of non-recurrent anti-inflationary impost, for example doubling surtax or income tax for one year only'.[26] The Special Contribution, which was devised to meet this requirement, accounted for nearly half the additional revenue in 1948–9 (£50 million out of £118 million) and since it was likely to be paid out of capital could have little effect in checking spending.

Even before the 1948 budget had been introduced, Robert Hall suggested that the Budget Committee might apply itself to a study of longer-term issues over the summer months when it might be under rather less pressure. Pre-budget meetings never allowed enough time to discuss fundamental issues such as the impact of the tax structure on incentives or the consequences of overloading the economy through public expenditure. Perhaps there was something to be said for a Colwyn Committee to review such issues. Hall had the support of Plowden, who thought that policy was being framed with inadequate economic knowledge and reminded the Committee that the budget was now an integral part of general economic planning.[27]

It was agreed that Hall should prepare a paper on government expenditure over the next five years, with suggestions as to reductions in taxation that might provide stronger incentives. The paper was also to examine the general effects of taxation on the national economy. A draft prepared by Christopher Dow, 'Budgetary prospects and policy 1948–52', was circulated after the amendment by Hall on 17 July 1948 and discussed by the Budget Committee five days later.[28] The conclusion to which it pointed was that, at existing rates of tax and with existing policies on expenditure, revenue would increase somewhat faster than expenditure and that cuts might be made in taxation over the period of about £500 million. The Committee thought the estimates too optimistic: perhaps because they doubted whether existing policies on expenditure would be maintained. A highly condensed version of the paper was prepared by Gilbert and sent to the Chancellor on 10 September; but, when officials saw the Chancellor on 15 September, discussion turned on more immediate issues.[29]

26 Meeting of Chancellor and Budget Committee, 20 January 1948, PRO T 171/394.

27 Hall to Plowden, 12 March 1948: Plowden to Bridges, 23 March 1948; circulated to Budget Committee, 12 April 1948; in PRO T 171/397.

28 See chapter 12 for a fuller discussion.

29 The cut version was entitled 'Outline of the problems of a four-year budgetary policy' and retained the tables attached to the original draft as well as the conclusions (PRO T 171/397).

## The 1949 budget

By November 1948 there was evidence suggesting that expenditure in 1948–9 would be substantially in excess of estimates and the budget surplus correspondingly smaller. The scale of supplementary estimates had two consequences: it led Cripps to issue a Treasury circular insisting that there should be no supplementaries in 1949; and it also touched off a strong reaction against the expanding financial requirements of the National Health Service. Cripps had asked Plowden to enquire into the likely reaction on wage settlements of an addition of a shilling to weekly national insurance contributions levied specifically to help pay for the NHS. Plowden discussed the suggestion with Ince of the Ministry of Labour, who was confident that an addition of sixpence would have no effect but was not quite so sure about a rise of a shilling. There then ensued the first round in the battle that led eventually to the resignation of Aneurin Bevan two years later. Douglas Jay, the Economic Secretary, attacked the proposed charge as a regressive tax and argued that the sums involved were too small to be worth pursuing except in a crisis. The alternative of a higher rate of income tax at the lower tax bands was pursued and abandoned. All that survived was a decision by Cripps to include in his 1949 budget speech a 'strong statement' that the social services are not free.[30]

In his assessment of the situation in December 1948 Robert Hall pointed out that the 1948 budget had been successful in keeping down inflationary pressure in spite of a big increase in net exports and an unexpected increase in fixed investment. If the position was to be held in 1949 he would want to see an addition of £100 million to the prospective budget surplus.[31] By January this had gone up to a minimum of £150 million. The grounds for this proposal were that the central government's budget surplus on current account looked like being £150 million less in 1949–50 than in 1948–9. At that stage the 'revenue surplus' was expected to be only £130 million in 1949–50 compared with £295 million in 1948–9; and the ordinary 'above the line' surplus showed an even bigger drop.[32]

We need not pursue these figures, which in the event came out differently. For our purposes what matters is how the recommendation

30 PRO T 171/397. What he said (H. of C. Debates, vol. 465, col. 2077, 6 April 1949), was that it was not possible to get large increases of benefit through the budget and have decreases in taxation.
31 R. L. Hall, 'The problem of inflation in 1949', 6 December 1948, in PRO T 171/397.
32 BC(49)10 Revise, 'The problem of inflation in 1949', memorandum by the Economic Section, 20 January 1949, in PRO T 171/397.

of an addition of £150 million to the prospective budget surplus was arrived at. It was a judgement made in steps of £50 million and based on a view of what was required to keep savings and investment in balance. Fixed investment was planned to decline slightly in 1949 but any fall in volume would be offset by higher capital costs and by stock-building. Of course, there might, as in 1948, be a large unplanned increase in fixed investment, especially as direct control was not watertight or sufficiently supplemented by financial stringency (i.e. restriction of bank credit). On the basis of the forecast, however, and setting the elimination of the remaining external deficit (estimated then at £120 million) against an increase in depreciation allowances made both by the Inland Revnue and in companies' undistributed profits, the savings requirement in 1949 was not likely to be very different from 1948 and might be rather less. To reduce the inflationary pressure still evident in 1948 and to place less reliance on personal saving, the government should aim at a surplus no smaller and preferably a little greater than in 1948.

While some contribution might be made by cutting government expenditure the Economic Section obviously put little faith in this and insisted on a realistic forecast, not a target. It also accepted that little could be done to cut investment but assumed that everything would be done to prevent a further increase. Taxes, it concluded, would have to go up 'by several hundred £ million or else we will have to admit another round of inflation. As a rough quantitative judgement, a minimum of £150 million in extra tax revenue might be needed to prevent any increase in the inflationary pressure'.[33] The £150 million extra was said to correspond to a budget surplus 'on the conventional basis' of £400 million – a judgement very wide of the mark since the surplus above the line in 1949–50 turned out to be £549 million without any appreciable change in taxation.

Looking further ahead, the paper saw an increasingly difficult budgetary problem. Failure to raise taxes would only postpone the problem and submit the social stability of the country to the strain of renewed inflation – inflation that was a confession that the country had been unable to decide how to pay for the benefits it received from government expenditure. The rising trend in expenditure suggested an urgent need to re-examine the likely costs of, and methods of paying for, the social and other services.

In the 1949 budget Cripps aimed at a revenue surplus a little smaller

33 BC(49)10 Revise, para. 25, in PRO T 171/397.

than in 1948:[34] the external accounts were in balance and there was not the same urgent need to check domestic inflation. Nevertheless the budget was judged to be a tough one. There were to be no supplementaries and a ceiling of £465 million was imposed on food subsidies. The sentiments expressed by the Economic Section were echoed throughout the speech. It was necessary, Cripps told the House, to 'moderate the speed of our advance in the extended application of the existing Social Services to our progressive ability to pay for them'; and he added that in future 'we must rely rather upon the creation of more distributable wealth than upon the redistribution of the income that exists'.[35]

Even before the budget was introduced on 6 April, Hall had begun to question the existing parity of $4.86 to the £1. At the end of July, thanks largely to Jay and Gaitskell, a decision to devalue had virtually been taken but the fiscal implications had still to be accepted.[36] The struggle to get Cabinet agreement to the necessary accompanying cuts proved just as difficult as the struggle over devaluation.

The assessment of what was required was made by Hall in a paper circulated on 5 October to the Economic Policy Committee. He judged that cuts of £200 million were required merely to restore the pressure of demand to what had been assumed in the budget. This total could be reached either by adding the prospective shortfall of £160 million in the budget surplus (in consequence of supplementary estimates) to the £40 million fall in personal savings, or by taking as a guide the worsening of the visible balance of payments by £20 million per month at a time when unemployment was falling. A further £100 million would be needed in order to free resources for improving the balance of payments and changing the pattern of production. Hall advised the Chancellor on tactics in face of strong ministerial opposition, encouraging him to stick out for the full amount. Cuts amounting nominally to £280 million, half on public investment and half on consumption, were finally voted; but some were bogus and some rescinded later and many were not intended to take effect for some time, so that the impact on effective demand fell far short of £300 million.[37]

34  He aimed at what he called 'a true overall surplus' of about £300 million, i.e. it was on a current account basis, net of government capital expenditure. The comparable figure in 1948–9 was £319 million.

35  H. of C. Debates, vol. 465. col. 2084, 6 April 1949.

36  On the Economic Section's role in the devaluation of 1949, see pp. 296–7.

37  For a full account see Cairncross, op. cit., pp. 192–6, and Dow, op. cit., pp. 45–6.

## The 1950 budget

Preparations for the 1950 budget were complicated by the general election in February. Since in most respects the economic situation was relatively satisfactory there was tacit agreement to introduce what was virtually a standstill budget.

Over the winter there had been a great change in outlook. The balance of payments had moved into surplus and the gold and dollar reserves were rising with unexpected rapidity. The change in the exchange rate appeared to have brought nearer the ending of the persistent dollar problem. Prices, it is true, had been jacked up but wages held steady under an agreement with the TUC just after devaluation. The fresh crisis that was about to break in June 1950 with the start of the Korean War remained beyond the horizon.

In assessing the prospects for 1950 the Economic Section suggested that ideally the pressure of demand should be reduced by £250 million.[38] This was made up of £150 million to leave room for more exports, now that devaluation had improved their competitive attraction; and a nominal £100 million to lower the pressure in comparison with 1949 when it had still been too high. Not much help was to be expected from lower investment – perhaps £50–100 million: the cuts after devaluation had been slow to take effect and it would be 1951 before they amounted to much. On the other hand, private savings were not likely to rise much: larger sums put to reserve because of dividend limitation at the government's request and higher depreciation allowances might together yield an extra £50 million or so. The conclusion drawn by the Section was that, allowing for an easement of £100–150 million through changes in private saving and in investment, the central government's budget should contribute a similar easement of £100–150 million through an enlargement of·the expected surplus.

The estimates, although still provisional, were pointing to a fall, not a rise, in the current surplus of the budget. As usually measured, even with the 'alternative classification', the fall was about £200 million; but the revenue surplus used in the White Paper and the *Economic Survey* – a more appropriate measure – looked like being only £50 million lower.[39] The Section was content, therefore, to suggest an addition to

38 BC(50)3 Revise, 'The problem of inflation in 1950', note by the Economic Section, 9 February 1950, in PRO T 171/400.

39 The 'revenue surplus' definition included in current expenditure war damage payments and excess profits tax refunds, which the other definitions excluded as capital transfers.

the prospective budget surplus of £50–150 million.

Robert Hall was clearly in some doubt as to whether this was enough and his doubts were shared by the Budget Committee. They submitted a paper to the Chancellor putting the inflationary gap at £200 million. With estimates of government expenditure up by £155 million in 1950–1 in comparison with the original estimates for 1949–50, and government revenue expected to be down by £130 million, they were thoroughly alarmed by what they took to be a firm trend. What was particularly disquieting to them was the apparently inexorable growth in expenditure on the social services, particularly the National Health Service, and the acquiescence of ministers in continuing heavy expenditure on the food subsidies. 'We see no prospect whatever of any reduction of taxation in future years', they told the Chancellor, unless he accepted their recommendations to reduce government expenditure and exercise firm control over investment. A determined effort was needed 'to reduce government expenditure by at least £150 million this year and continue in the next two to three years'.[40]

Ministers seem to have felt that this left out of account the possibility of higher productivity. The Budget Committee, no doubt echoing Robert Hall, had shown that if production grew at 2½ per cent per annum for the next three years the addition of £800 million to national income that this would involve would be largely mortgaged in advance. Government expenditure would take over £200 million, higher investment at least £150 million, and the balance of payments would absorb £230 million if it was kept in surplus on the scale needed in the absence of Marshall Aid (this was put at £150 million a year). These items added up to £580 million before taking any account of what consumers would feel entitled to spend from their earnings.[41]

A supporting minute by Robert Hall pointed out that a higher rate of growth did not dispose of the inflationary danger since 'the national income goes in the first place to those who share in the productive process, i.e. in personal or corporate incomes'.[42] It was true that in 1949 production had risen by about 4 per cent and industrial production by 6 per cent but 40 per cent of the latter increase was accounted for by a quite exceptional expansion in the car industry.

40 BC(50)15, 'The 1950/51 budget', note by the Budget Committee, 22 February 1950, in PRO T 171/400.
41 'The budget position' (unsigned, but a summary of BC(50)15, 1 March 1950, in PRO T 171/400.
42 'Note on increases in the national income' by R. L. Hall, 2 March 1950, in PRO T 171/400.

Even if the experience of 1949 was repeated in 1950 it would add only £150 million to the revenue at current rates of taxation and would push up fixed investment and stock-building more than it added to company reserves.

Douglas Jay, the Financial Secretary, took a more optimistic view. A rise of one or two points a year in the cost of living was probably 'a necessary implication of full employment and does no serious harm'. Indeed, a general rise would relieve the dead weight of war debt and should not be regarded as proof of failure. At the same time he judged that productivity would rise as fast in 1950 as in 1949 and the additional output would ease the inflationary gap.[43]

The controversy over productivity continued until the summer and planning was conducted on the basis of alternative rates of increase of 2½ per cent (the Economic Section's view) and 4 per cent (the 1949 rate). The budget itself was designed to leave the surplus unaffected. A doubling of the duty on petrol and a higher tax on commercial vehicles were offset by reductions in the reduced rates of income tax. The effect on demand was probably, as in 1948 and 1949, to produce a small net expansion of around £50 million.[44]

## The 1951 budget

The Budget Committee had a busy time in 1950–1, meeting seventeen times between one budget and the next and considering eighty-two papers over the two years.

The Economic Section circulated a first assessment in July 1950, within a month of the outbreak of war in Korea.[45] This made two important points. First of all, the main impact of fiscal policy was on consumption while investment was regulated more by physical controls. Changes in inflationary pressure became apparent with less warning in the market for consumer goods than in that for capital goods. If market signals indicated approaching deflation fiscal policy should be softened so as to stimulate consumer demand, not investment. The second point, later to be repeated with more emphasis, was that the terms of trade were likely to deteriorate with rising import prices. If these took effect without interference they

43 Jay to Cripps, 2 March 1950, in PRO T 171/400.
44 Dow, op. cit., p. 199.
45 BC(50)17, 'The internal financial situation', note by the Economic Section, 17 July 1950, In PRO T 171/403.

would produce a deflation of demand automatically and might even stimulate additional exports. If on the other hand the government tried to hold down prices it would aggravate the balance of payments problem.

A few days later the Budget Committee minuted the Chancellor to warn him that, with the proposed increases in defence expenditure, 'drastic measures will be necessary'. Quite apart from defence, government expenditure was due to expand by £200 million in the next two years. This would include both higher food subsidies to match increased food consumption and more expenditure on the National Health Service 'unless indeed savings by the making of charges for the service are to be permissible'.[46]

In mid-October, when the Committee met again, ministers were reported to be concerned about the rising cost of living. The President of the Board of Trade (Harold Wilson) wanted subsidies on utility clothing and other goods, adding up to over £100 million, as well as an extension and tightening of price control.[47] This was precisely what Robert Hall had advised against in July. In the absence of the President's proposals he would have judged the appropriate reduction in demand to be nearer £100 million than £200 million; and, had there been no need to provide for additional defence expenditure, he would even have thought of recommending cuts in taxation. As things stood, he was anxious to see more stock-piling of imported materials, which he took to be preferable to adding to the foreign exchange reserves, especially as the Americans looked askance at the latter and might take it as a sign that Marshall Aid was no longer required – which is exactly what they did do a few weeks later. Stockpiling, since it was a suitable case for borrowing, would leave the surplus above the line unaffected, although, like all investment, it would add to inflationary pressure unless offset by disinvestment in the reserves.

The Budget Committee's own proposals consisted, as usual, of a cut in food subsidies, the imposition of NHS charges, and a reduction in the housing programme. Gaitskell, who took over as Chancellor from Cripps on 19 October, asked the Committee shortly afterwards for suggestions for additional taxation to bring in £100 million or so. The possibility of raising funds by selling council houses to sitting tenants was also raised.

The first full-scale assessment of the position by the Economic

46 'Budget prospects for 1951/52 and 1952/53', memorandum by the Budget Committee, 22 July 1950, in PRO T 171/403.
47 Budget Committee, 6th meeting, 17 October 1950, in PRO T 171/403.

Section was circulated on 27 November 1950.[48] Much uncertainty by now attached to the adequacy of the supply of raw materials, especially non-ferrous metals. Shortages would limit the rise in GNP; but if they held up investment or the defence programme they would make the budgetary problem easier. Another important uncertainty was the level of import prices. These were assumed to be 'more stable' in 1951, quite mistakenly; while the balance of payments was expected to deteriorate by £150 million and remain in surplus (latest estimates show a swing of £676 million from +£307 million in 1950 to −£369 million in 1951). The 'current surplus' of public authorities would fall by about £300 million but investment at home and abroad would show just as big a fall if measured at current prices.[49] On this showing 'the financial situation should be manageable. But there does not seem room for reductions in taxes'.

The Budget Committee found this much too optimistic in the circumstances. The paper was revised so as to canvas a less favourable outcome; with higher government expenditure, more stock-building, a bigger external deficit, and a more severe shortage of raw materials. An addition of 'at least £100 million' was therefore suggested to cover these contingencies, and possibly more once better information was available. Pressure on the government to offset the higher cost of living had also to be reckoned with. Since it would be hard to raise taxes when the cost of living was rising, 'we have a very difficult Budget in front of us'.

In the frequent meetings of the Budget Committee over the winter, the Economic Section stuck to the proposition that since higher import prices would deflate the economy there was no need for swingeing increases in taxation at the same time. This proposition, however, turned to some extent on what happened to wages and profits. If money wages had to be held down, profits (or at least dividends) would also have to be limited. Much time was spent discussing a scheme for dividend limitation devised by Nicholas Kaldor, but in the end a bill to introduce it was dropped. Money wages, which had held steady after devaluation until the middle of 1950, began to rise rapidly.

---

48 BC(50)25 Revise, 'The general economic outlook for the 1951 budget', note by the Economic Section, 27 November 1950. An earlier version had been circulated on 13 November and attacked as too optimistic.

49 This result was obtained on the assumption that stock appreciation, put at £200 million in 1950, would drop to zero in 1951, a highly optimistic assumption. The White Paper in 1953 (Cmd 8803) put stock appreciation at £700 million in 1950 and £900 million in 1951.

By the time the budget was opened in April the pace of inflation was quickening.

At the beginning of February, the Economic Section circulated its usual pre-budget assessment.[50] Revised versions followed at the end of the month and in mid-March[51] The forecasts now assumed a 4 per cent rise in productivity in 1951, a 7 per cent rise in money wages and other incomes, and a deterioration in the balance of payments of £205 million, of which £80 million was for additional strategic stockpiling of imported materials. The balance of payments forecast for 1951 and 1952 met the Chancellor's prescription that any deficit in 1952 (not just in 1951) should be limited to what resulted from building up strategic stocks; but it seriously underestimated the rise in the import bill in 1951 of over £1,100 million fob (nearly 50 per cent). Even so, the first of the three papers reached the conclusion that, with no change in fixed investment, higher profits and company savings, and a big drop in the balance of payments surplus, the central government's surplus on current account could be allowed to fall by as much as £330 million in 1951–2. This compared with a forecast that at current tax rates it would fall by £405 million. The budget surplus ought therefore to have been increased by £50–100 million. The more the balance of payments deteriorated, the less that figure would be. On the other hand, if it was decided to compensate the groups hardest hit by the rise in the cost of living (suggestions were made totalling £90 million) the required addition to the surplus would be raised *pro tanto*.

In a year when defence expenditure was expected to rise by nearly £500 million and civil expenditure by over £200 million, a proposal to limit budgetary action to £75 million seemed paradoxical. It was partly to be explained by the strong position built up in previous years and enabling a major contribution to be made by deferring any reduction in taxation and running a smaller external surplus.[52] But, in a year when the public had braced itself for renewed austerity and any forecasts were liable to underestimate the strain on the economy, £75 million seemed dangerously low. The Economic Section revised its calculations and suggested, first, £100–150 million and, later, £60

50 BC(51)16, 'The general budgetary problem in 1951', note by the Economic Section, 2 February 1951, in PRO T 171/403.

51 BC(51)37, 'The general budgetary problem in 1951', summary by the Economic Section, 27 February 1951, and BC(51)43 Revise, 'The general budgetary problem for 1951', note by the Director, Economic Section, 15 March 1951, in PRO T 171/403.

52 BC(51)37, paras 1 and 2.

million. The Budget Committee, in the middle of this reconsideration, put forward a figure of £150 million, and the Chancellor at a meeting with the Prime Minister on 6 March indicated a need for an extra £150–200 million in taxation. Robert Hall, reviewing the situation in a final submission on 15 March, told the Budget Committee that the most recent information had produced a revised estimate of £175 million but he saw no reason to justify a change in the recommendation already made by the Budget Committee for an addition of £150 million to prospective budget revenue.[53]

Gaitskell duly imposed an additional £150 million in taxation on consumers, putting sixpence on the income tax and adding £75 million to indirect taxation. In addition, he suspended initial depreciation allowances and raised the tax on distributed profits from 30 to 50 per cent, although neither change affected revenue in 1951–2. A surplus of £39 million 'above the line' was expected: instead there was a surplus of £379 million.

The budget of 1951 was one of great complexity, backed by careful reasoning and a much improved economic forecasting apparatus. It is doubtful if any budget has owed more to the work of the Economic Section and in retrospect the budget judgement that additional taxation should be limited to £150 million seems entirely defensible.

53 BC(51)43 Revise, para. 11, in PRO T 171/403.

# Chapter sixteen

# DEMAND MANAGEMENT: FISCAL POLICY AFTER 1951

It is not necessary to deal so fully with the Section's part in the budgets of the 1950s. The role of its members was already well established. It was they who prepared for the Budget Committee a succession of forecasts of economic prospects over the year ahead and it was to Robert Hall that the Committee looked for a judgement of the scale on which taxation should be added to or remitted. The forecasts became more elaborate and moved from year-on-year comparisons to predictions of the situation twelve months ahead based on quarterly data. The judgements continued to be based on Keynesian analysis, which neither the Treasury members of the Budget Committee nor the Chancellor, with their aversion to budget deficits, fully understood or accepted. Other instruments of policy than the budget continued to play an important part in the management of the economy. The last word inevitably rested with the Chancellor, who might (and did on occasion) reject the advice offered whether by the Economic Adviser or by the Budget Committee.

## The 1952 budget

The 1952 budget discussions came to be dominated by the controversy over Robot, the scheme discussed in chapter 17 for sterling convertibility combined with a floating pound and blocked sterling balances. In the run-up to the budget, which was first brought forward by a week to 4 March so as to permit of an early announcement of the scheme, and then put back to the date previously announced, 11 March, there was talk of stern measures with a view to lending support to sterling. In fact the 1952 budget turned out to be surprisingly mild. Income tax went back to nine shillings in the pound, the loss of revenue being largely offset by yet another increase in petrol duty and a cut of £250 million in food subsidies. The introduction of a levy on excess profits did not affect revenue in 1952–3. The net effect was expansionary; and this was fortunate since demand was unexpectedly depressed and output remained stagnant.

The major influence of the Economic Section was to insist that the economy needed no further disinflation. It was already undergoing moderate disinflation as a result of the rise in import prices and this would continue. A deficit in the balance of payments of £400 million in the second half of 1951 was expected to fall to zero in the second half of 1952, without further disinflationary action.[1] This assessment stunned the Budget Committee but carried the day despite pleas for a severe budget from Leslie Rowan of OF and Frank Lee of the Board of Trade. Robert Hall was also successful in limiting a move to reduce the budget surplus substantially, pointing to the effect of this on financial opinion abroad.[2]

To turn to the sequence of events leading up to the budget, it was already clear at the first meeting of the Budget Committee after the change of government, on 5 December 1951, that some further action was needed to supplement the import cuts announced on 7 November. Robert Hall suggested a tax on steel but this was not pursued. The Committee was more attracted by possible cuts in food subsidies but recognized that, while an immediate cut of £50 million might be made, no major attack on the subsidies was possible before the budget. By 18 January the Committee was thinking of a £200 million cut, offset to some extent by higher family allowances and pensions. They were also contemplating the postponement of initial (depreciation) allowances combined with reductions in income tax and profits tax. By this time the Commonwealth Finance Ministers, meeting in London, had agreed to aim at a surplus of £100 million in their trade with non-sterling countries in the second half of 1952 so as to reduce the strain on reserves.

1 BC(52)8, 'The economic outlook for 1952', note by the Director, Economic Section, 30 January 1952, in PRO T 171/408. These figures include military aid and are for the balance on current account.
2 Hall to Armstrong (for Chancellor), 5 March 1952, in PRO T 171/408. The Economic Section had pointed out that the proposed cut in food subsidies would add four points to the cost of living and probably even more to wage rates (BC(52)12, 6 February 1952). This had disturbed the Chancellor who, having been assured by Robert Hall that the rise in the cost of living could safely be offset by tax concessions and additional benefits, wanted to aim for a smaller budget surplus.

When the Budget Committee met again on 24 January after the conference, a second package of measures was in preparation, including further import cuts, for announcement at the end of January. The Chancellor felt that these measures were not enough and proposed to advance the budget to a date early in March (fixed later as 11 March). OF were by now considering more desperate measures: Rowan spoke of a scheme for dollar rationing but this was dismissed a fortnight later as impracticable.[3] Robert Hall's emphasis was on the need for drastic action by the Commonwealth countries. Meanwhile the proposals, later known as Robot, for combining immediate convertibility with a floating pound and blocking sterling balances were taking shape in OF and the Bank of England. An outline of the plan appeared on 25 January in a paper by R. W. B. Clarke.

The Economic Section's assessment of the prospects for 1952 was circulated at the end of January.[4] This showed a deficit of over £500 million in the balance of payments in 1951 compared with a forecast of £100 million in the *Economic Survey*. A major improvement was expected in 1952 to near balance both in the first half of the year and in the second half, counting in the military aid that was due to be paid.[5] On the other hand, domestic demand was not very buoyant and there was no point in depressing it further unless this would lead to an increase in exports. Consumer spending had been falling since the second quarter in 1951, fixed investment was unlikely to rise much, exports were falling (though not so fast as imports), and the only important addition to demand in 1952 would be from the rearmament programme. Taking account of a falling-off in the rate of stock accumulation (which turned out to be far larger than expected), the forecast showed a growth in output of £200–300 million (or 1–2 per cent), which was well within the limits of capacity.[6]

The Budget Committee considered whether the release of additional resources would benefit the balance of payments. The Economic Section thought not. What export markets were calling for was capital goods and these were not to spare. 'The beneficial effect on exports', it was argued, 'is inevitably problematical whereas the disorganisation

3 'Emergency action', 8 February 1952, in PRO T 236/3245.
4 BC(52)8, 'The economic outlook in 1952', note by the Director, Economic Section, 30 January 1952, in PRO T 171/408.
5 The current account deficit in 1951 is now put at £369 million and the surplus in 1952 at £163 million so that the swing was even larger than forecast.
6 Although in other respects the forecast was remarkably accurate, it was in serious error over stock-building and in consequence over GDP, which instead of increasing was unchanged between 1951 and 1952.

caused by serious disinflation at home would be tangible and immediate.'[7] An extra £250 million in taxation, the Section reckoned, would cause a fall of 1½ per cent in output and employment.

The Budget Committee, mesmerized by the arithmetic, agreed that a standstill budget was called for.[8] In briefing the Chancellor, Robert Hall admitted that there was 'a big margin of error' and that some reduction in home demand was needed in order to stimulate exports and free labour for the engineering industries. But the economy was already experiencing moderate disinflation. If food subsidies were to be cut by £200 million, he would be content to see compensating allowances of £60 million, leaving a balance of £140 million to be used to improve incentives to effort by appropriate tax cuts.[9] When the Chancellor suggested running a smaller budget surplus Hall told him that a cut of up to £50 million was bearable provided the other measures proposed (including a higher bank rate and credit restriction) were accepted. But £50 million was a maximum. 'We must think mainly', he said, 'of the impact of the Budget on external opinion.'[10]

The Committee's discussions were complicated by Inland Revenue proposals to exempt 8 million people from taxation by changes in the system of allowances and finance the scheme by putting a tax of £1 per ton on coal – a tax that Robert Hall supported but which was ultimately dropped.[11] The proposals soon brought other members of the Cabinet into the discussions (for example, Lord Leathers, who was strongly against a coal tax) and, on at least two occasions, the Prime Minister (who favoured the Inland Revenue scheme and had doubts about the size of the cut in food subsidies). Thus the new Chancellor had to prepare his budget with a larger dose of surveillance than is customary.

The Chancellor took credit for more than the £50 million off the budget surplus that Robert Hall recommended as a maximum. But he

7 BC(52)8, 'The economic outlook in 1952', note by the Director, Economic Section, 30 January 1952, in PRO T 171/408, para. 25.

8 Meeting of Budget Committee on 1 February 1952. This seems, however, to have left any cut in food subsidies on one side.

9 Hall to Chancellor ('The budget prospects'), 4 February 1952, in PRO T 171/408.

10 Hall to Armstrong, 5 March 1952, in PRO T 171/408. Hall's reaction foreshadowed the line he took on the 1955 budget.

11 Cockfield at meeting of Budget Committee with Chancellor on 7 February. Since the demand for coal could not be met at the current price, a tax would help to bring supply and demand into balance.

could claim later in the year that he had been too restrictive: stock-building had fallen off to an extent not foreseen.[12] The Chancellor was inclined to put this down later to the reactivation of monetary policy (the bank rate was increased to 4 per cent); and with this Robert Hall might have agreed. The tighter credit associated with a rise in the bank rate, he told the Chancellor, 'has a more direct influence than the rate itself'.[13]

For the first time since the war, production in 1952 ran almost flat and a margin of spare capacity appeared. The balance of payments remained a problem and the question how it could be influenced by the budget when the economy was underemployed preoccupied Robert Hall. Additional exports did not require the release of more capacity, and if made to countries other than the United States and Canada would soon lead to the imposition of import restrictions rather than bring in gold and dollars. OF wanted to aim at a current surplus of £300 million. But in order to achieve such a surplus it might well be necessary to lend the money, for example to Commonwealth countries, many of which had now 'uncomfortably low sterling balances'.[14]

## The 1953 and 1954 budgets

Discussion of the 1953 budget turned on rather different issues. Butler shared Cripps's liking for an overall balance. In 1952–3 he budgeted for an overall surplus of £4 million. But by October there was expected to be an overall deficit of about £250 million.[15] This turned out to be an underestimate: the budgeted surplus of £4 million finally ended up as a deficit of £436 million. On the other hand, the Economic Section reckoned that the economy had the capacity to increase output by £1,000 million, but would at most add £400 million to output in 1953 and might add nothing at all. Unemployment might even increase, although probably not by very much. There was a strong case,

12 See chapter 13, p. 204.
13 Hall to Armstrong, 5 March 1952, in PRO T 171/408.
14 Hall to Bridges, January 1953, in PRO T 171/413.
15 Bridges to Chancellor, 3 October 1952, in PRO T 171/413. This alarmed the Chancellor, who consulted the Prime Minister and was assured that he would have plenty in hand if he allowed no increase in civil expenditure in 1953. He 'should obviously not pay the American loan service of £60 million' and on no account should he increase taxation (Prime Minister to Chancellor, 13 October 1952, in PRO T 171/413).

therefore, for reducing taxation both on business and on consumers, whatever the budget deficit.[16]

For the first time, the Budget Committee was given estimates of the impact on final demand of reductions in tax: it was estimated that if taxation was cut by £100 million the net reduction in revenue would be substantially less: initially about £85 million and in later financial years £65 million.

The above-the-line surplus with existing taxes was forecast at about £200 million and this once again formed the basis of Robert Hall's budget recommendation. He accepted the likelihood that 'the psychological effect of moving to an above-the-line deficit this year would be very damaging' and suggested that tax cuts be limited to £150 million. Implicitly, this meant an overall deficit and Hall had some difficulty in convincing the Chancellor (and senior officials) that this was justifiable in the circumstances. Butler was torn between his desire to get taxes down and qualms over what he felt to be the rashness and impropriety of an overall deficit, but was happy to yield to Hall's advice.

What should go to make up the £150 million Hall did not prescribe; but he pointed out that tax reliefs to help business, such as the restoration of initial allowances, reductions in profits tax, and increased incentives to higher management would have little effect either on revenue or on spending in 1953–4. More could therefore be done by way of such reliefs without infringing 'strict principles' in 1953.[17]

The 1953 budget duly followed this advice: taxation was reduced more substantially than in any post-war budget; but since the biggest reductions were in business taxation it was not until 1954 and 1955 that their full effects were felt. In spite of the tax cuts the budget surplus above the line remained, as in 1952–3, just under £100 million.

By the end of 1953 the Economic Section, instead of being impressed by the rapid growth in output, was contemplating some further stimulus to demand, not perhaps in the budget but in the second half of the year, when there was 'an even chance' of a fall in production because of a lower level of exports or of investment in stocks. It looked as if there was 'a long run problem of keeping the economy moving upwards'.[18] Productive investment in particular was lagging badly: a Treasury committee had reported that investment in

16 BC(53)15, 'The economic and budgetary problem in 1953', note by the Director of the Economic Section, 9 February 1953, in PRO T 171/413.

17 ibid.

18 BC(54)25, 'The budgetary problem in 1954', note by the Director of the Economic Section, 22 February 1954, in PRO T 171/437.

manufacturing industry was more likely to fall than rise. Any stimulus, however, would have to be moderate or home demand would get in the way of exports. 'We seem to be in a cleft stick', Robert Hall told the Budget Committee. 'If we depress home demand too much, industry stagnates; if we carry expansion beyond a moderate limit, the balance of payments suffers.'[19]

Hesitations over budget deficits persisted. Not only was an above-the-line deficit of £53 million expected in 1954–5 but the Inland Revenue, a few weeks before the budget, revised their estimate for 1955–6 downwards by about £150 million, suggesting a much larger deficit, perhaps one of £300 million, in that financial year. The Prime Minister was reported to take 'a very serious view' of this prospect. The Budget Committee, meeting on 1 March 1954, recorded that

> the psychological effect of any departure from the policy of a balanced Budget might well be disastrous; it would be taken by spending Departments as a sign that the Treasury was prepared to relax; and through its effect on overseas opinion it might well react on the balance of payments'.[20]

The possibility that the recession in progress in the United States might deepen had also to be taken into account and alternative forecasts had been prepared to allow for this. But in the end Robert Hall was inclined to take an optimistic view, which was soon borne out by events.

His judgement at the beginning of February was that the existing stance of policy was 'about right'. He based his judgement, not on the budget figures which preoccupied the Chancellor and the Budget Committee, making them think that the country was on the verge of ruin, but on the general state of the economy.[21] That this was a better point of departure was shown by the wide margin at the end of the financial year between the budget estimate of a surplus of £10 million 'above the line' and the realized surplus of £433 million.

When Hall went on to talk of concessions to consumers to counteract a possible slackening in activity, the Budget Committee

---

19 BC(53)26, 'The budgetary problem in 1954', note by the Director of the Economic Section, 7 December 1953, in PRO T 171/437.

20 Budget Committee meeting on 1 March 1954 in PRO T 171/449. It later transpired that the Inland Revenue's revised estimate was based on the NIF Working Party's forecast of GNP in the event of a US recession – a forecast suggesting the need for some easing in the budget.

21 Meeting of Budget Committee with the Chancellor, 5 February 1954, in PRO T 171/437.

expressed strong dissent: they wanted disinflation and no concessions and even talked of higher taxes.[22] Robert Hall explained that he was not recommending any immediate stimulus but putting the Chancellor on warning that concessions might have to made in an autumn budget (especially if the US recession became more severe). This made it necessary to be circumspect in reacting to public pressure for reductions in tax in April. At the end of the discussion Bridges summed up in favour of a standstill budget.[23]

This was not entirely the end of the matter. Troubled by the failure of industrial investment to respond, Robert Hall brought forward the idea proposed by John Jukes, of an investment allowance (a tax credit for investment outlays) in place of the initial allowance for depreciation. There was a battle between the Economic Section and the Inland Revenue, which heartily disliked the idea of using taxes to serve economic ends and was never reconciled to the principle of investment allowances. At what must have been the most crowded meeting in the history of the Budget Committee on 18 March 1954, the Chancellor decided to go ahead. Introduced in 1954, investment allowances were withdrawn in 1956, reinstated after a renewed battle between the Economic Section and the Inland Revenue in 1959, and replaced by investment grants in 1966 until they, too, were withdrawn.[24]

## The April 1955 budget

Within a month or two of the 1954 budget it was clear that the American depression had had remarkably little effect on activity elsewhere in world. There was no contraction of international trade or fall in primary commodity prices. British exports continued on an upward trend and reserves of gold and dollars were higher than in the previous year. Production was growing fast and the pressure in the labour market mounting steadily. The shortage of labour had not yet reached the intensity of mid-1951 but by June there was already a large excess of vacancies over unemployment, even larger on a non-seasonally adjusted basis.

22 Budget Committee meeting, 25 February 1954, in PRO T 171/437.
23 ibid.
24 The controversy begins with BC(54)12, 'Investment from 1953/54 to 1956/57', report by the Treasury Investment Committee, 1 February 1954, and continues with BC(54)19, 'Incentives for investment', note by the Director of the Economic Section, 11 February 1954; BC(54)24, 'Increased annual allowances for depreciation', note by Board of Inland Revenue, 18 February 1954; and other papers in PRO T 171/442.

When the Chancellor first discussed the shape of the 1955 budget with senior Treasury officials, as early as the end of July 1954, however, there was no talk of labour shortage. The discussion turned almost entirely on alternative forms of tax relief, on the assumption that there was some scope for reductions in tax. The Chancellor appears to have taken a more optimistic view than his advisers, who thought it unlikely that there would be more than £30 million available while he raised a number of more expensive possibilities ranging from a cut in the standard rate to earned income relief, improved child allowances, and twopence a pint off beer.[25]

Robert Hall was not present at these meetings. But there is no reason to think that he would have dissented from the views of his official colleagues. In May 1954 the Economic Section told the Budget Committee that, even if the American economy began to recover soon, there was not likely to be much of an expansion in activity in the United Kingdom.[26] It took a pessimistic view of the prospects for private investment even after the introduction of the investment allowance and the withdrawal of building licensing in October; as late as February 1955, in admitting that 'investment is everywhere said to be increasing', it added that 'so far there is little statistical evidence of this'.[27] In July 1954 Robert Hall's emphasis had been on the need to use the budget to help expansion in the absence of any source of expanding demand; and in October he repeated that over the next few years the situation was 'far more likely to call for tax reductions than for tax increases'.[28]

It is clear in retrospect that the Economic Section misjudged investment prospects in 1954. In manufacturing industry, it is true, fixed investment was not perceptibly greater in 1954 than in 1952; the boom that added nearly one-third to the 1952 total by 1957 had hardly begun until late in 1954, when the difficulty of detecting changes in trends was aggravated by the removal of building controls (a matter on which the Economic Section was not consulted). But in other parts of the private sector there was already evidence of rapid expansion. Private house building in 1954 had nearly doubled since 1952 and increased still further in the next two years by 18 per cent. Other

25 Budget Committee meetings on 20 and 29 July 1954 and meeting with the Chancellor on 28 July 1954, in PRO T 171/459.
26 BC(54)45, 'The post-budget prospects for 1954', 19 May 1954, in PRO T 171/459.
27 BC(55)17, 'The budgetary problem in 1955 – 2nd assessment', 19 February 1955, in PRO T 171/459.
28 Note by Sir Robert Hall, 14 October 1954, in PRO T 171/459.

private sector investment (excluding manufacturing investment, which was much the largest component) was also increasing rapidly after 1952. For private fixed investment as a whole, the increase between 1952 and 1956 was roughly two-thirds, half of it in the first two years, half in the last two.[29]

But, if private investment proved unexpectedly resilient, public investment, against which the Bank of England inveighed throughout the summer, was equally unexpectedly moving in the opposite direction in 1955–6. This was entirely due to a large fall in council house building, the rest of public investment edging up a little above the 1954 level. These errors roughly cancelled one another out. When the forecasters made their predictions for 1955 in February, their total for fixed investment turned out to be too high, not too low. It was not because of a mistaken view of the prospects for fixed investment that the Economic Section underestimated demand in 1955. As so often happened, the biggest single source of error was stock-building. Instead of falling as expected, stocks increased dramatically.[30]

The Economic Section's initial assessment, in their submission to the Budget Committee in December, was that there was no appreciable piling up of orders or widespread shortages and that, while the economy was fully employed, labour shortages were not on a par with those experienced in 1951. An increase in taxation was not required but there was not much scope for any reduction either. On a close view of the figures, this was a rather optimistic view. Unemployment in October and November 1954 had been lower than in those months in any year since the war and continued to be lower up to the budget. Vacancies, although not so high as in the early post-war years, were at roughly the same level as in 1950 and higher at the end of the year than in December 1951. This was not a reassuring basis on which to build tax reductions.

It was expected that employment would rise more slowly in 1955 because of the low level to which unemployment had fallen. Yet the forecast in December allowed for only a negligible rise in imports of £10 million and a growth in GDP of £440 million, or nearly 3 per cent.[31]

At what proved to be a critical meeting of officials under Edward

---

29 *National Income and Expenditure 1963*, table 51. All increases relate to investment at fixed prices.
30 See chapter 13, p. 207.
31 'The budgetary problem in 1955 – first assessment', 13 December 1955, in PRO T 171/459.

Bridges on 16 December 1954, this forecast was taken in conjunction with one by Home Finance of budget prospects. It emerged that a substantial surplus at existing rates of tax was now expected. Robert Hall's reaction was that, whatever the surplus, the economic outlook did not justify a reduction in tax. Bridges, however, took a different view. The surplus, he maintained, afforded 'a rare opportunity . . . to reduce the standard rate of tax by sixpence'. If this were done as he proposed, the cost would be £140 million but less if a smaller reduction were made in the lower rates of tax. Much of the tax remitted would be saved and the reduction in tax would strengthen production incentives. It was a tempting prospectus, with which there was said to be 'general agreement'.[32]

By February the picture had changed for the worse. The Programmes Committee, which framed balance of payments forecasts, came forward in February with a prospective deficit on current account in 1955 of £70 million, instead of a surplus of £155 million as expected in December. This was a change of which the Chancellor did not learn, much to his annoyance, until just after the first rise in the bank rate, by only ½ per cent, at the end of January.[33] The change in the forecast reflected a rise in import prices and additional payments to Iran on account as part of the settlement of the Abadan dispute: instead of an extra £10 million, imports (including invisibles) were now expected to increase by £185 million.

It was at this stage that the decision was taken, against Economic Section advice, to allow the Bank of England to support the transferable rate.[34] Throughout the year debate continued within the government over further moves towards convertibility and modification of the exchange regime. It was the uncertainty generated by this debate, uncertainty heightened by the struggle to contain inflation, that brought on an exchange crisis in the autumn and made necessary the introduction of a second budget in October. The threat of inflation and the weakness of the balance of payments were alike aggravated by the expansionary influence of the April budget.

32 Meeting of officials, 16 December 1955, in PRO T 171/459. By March the prospective surplus had grown to £260 million and it was agreed 'not to give away more than half' of this in tax concessions (meeting between Chancellor and officials, 18 March 1955, in PRO T 171/459).

33 The Bank of England had argued against a bigger increase, preferring to see market rates rise gradually.

34 See p. 312. On this occasion, OF under Rowan was on the same side as the Economic Section but Bridges and Gilbert supported the Bank of England – the same line-up as in the early stages of the 1949 controversy over devaluation.

The new balance of payments forecast called for action and a list of measures was promptly put forward by Robert Hall. These included a further rise in the bank rate and a tightening of credit (he had been urging a more restrictive monetary policy for some time); hire-purchase restrictions; a reduction in council house building, which the Cabinet had already decided on but which was not being implemented by the minister concerned; economies in agricultural subsidies; and allowing prices to reflect costs (e.g. in the coal industry). All of these measures were approved and the first two formed part of the package that accompanied the decision to support the transferable rate on 24–5 February. The bank rate was raised to 4½ per cent, an order in council was made restoring the power to introduce hire-purchase restrictions, and the restrictions were reimposed. The Cabinet, however, refused to allow the Minister of Fuel and Power to put up the price of coal and the agricultural price settlement let the farmers off with more, not less, money.

At the beginning of 1955 Robert Hall's view was that there was quite enough employment, if not too much, without any tax concessions.[35] He was aware, however, that the buoyancy of the revenue in 1954–5 was likely to yield an unexpectedly large budget surplus, which would continue into 1955–6.[36] Even in January, Hall, recognizing that it was an election year and reflecting on the pressures the Chancellor was under, was in little doubt that some of the surplus would be 'spent' and that his colleagues in the Treasury, who thought it sufficient to aim at balance 'above the line', would approve of this. Hall was inclined to shrug his shoulders and comfort himself with the reflection that the economy was now much stronger than in earlier years and could stand some strain. The shape of the budget could not be settled, in any event, until it was known whether Churchill would resign on 6 April as planned.

The atmosphere in the Treasury by March was one of acceptance

35 He had advanced this view in December and warned the Budget Committee in February that 'if nothing else is done . . . any budgetary changes should be towards stiffening rather than easing the economy' (BC(55)17, 'The budgetary problem in 1955 – second assessment', 19 February 1955, in PRO T 171/459). The measures announced five days later are unlikely to have been sufficient to change that judgement.

36 The 1954 budget envisaged a surplus above the line of £10 million, the surplus in 1953–4 having been £94 million. In fact the recovery from 1952 onwards pushed up the revenue in 1954–5 by £200 million above budget, and expenditure fell short by an even larger amount, so that in the end the surplus came to £433 million.

that a standstill budget was out of the question politically. At a meeting of officials on 9 March it was argued that to do nothing 'would have a strongly disincentive effect' and that a reduction in the standard rate of income tax 'would be beneficial if it could be managed'.[37] It would, however, be useful to discuss soon with the Bank of England 'a further tightening of credit policy' and Bridges and Gilbert were asked to pursue this with the Deputy Governor. As for the balance of payments, it would be a mistake to impair confidence in a sustained high level of economic activity when the gold and dollar reserves were there to be drawn upon. The meeting also thought it desirable for the impending election to be out of the way as soon as possible. If it were held in late April or early May, it would be necessary to introduce a short Finance Bill continuing existing taxes.

In the end the budget was put back to 19 April and fell between the announcement of the Prime Minister's resignation on 5 April and the general election on 26 May.[38] The question was then how to make tax concessions in the budget in a way that was appropriate to a short Finance Bill, avoided taking undue risks with the economy, and looked as little like trying to bribe the electors as possible. The answer that officials (including Robert Hall) found acceptable in the circumstances was a reduction in the income tax by sixpence.

Robert Hall had more than usual trouble in helping to draft the budget speech because of the inherent contradictions in the policy it expressed. The tax concessions were not really warranted by the state of the economy, with overfull employment and a weak balance of payments. At the same time, the emphasis that this made it necessary to lay on monetary policy was not easily reconciled with the stress on more investment. Apart from that, Hall had reservations about the co-operation to be expected from the Bank of England, which had always resisted taking a tough line with the commercial banks, and, in spite of the Governor's assurances, was reported to be no more tough in 1955. The budget speech did, however, include the well-known commitment to continue reliance on the 'resources of a flexible monetary policy'.

The subsequent failure of monetary policy to cope with the boom is discussed in chapter 14 and the development of an exchange crisis in the autumn in chapter 18. Before the end of July the Chancellor's colleagues had begun bombarding him with memorandum after

37 Those present included Bridges, Gilbert, Rowan, and Hall. The minutes are in PRO T 171/464.
38 According to Robert Hall, the date of the election was not finally decided until 15 April, i.e. only a few days before the budget.

memorandum on the economic situation and the Treasury was advising him that an autumn budget was desirable.[39] A second budget was introduced on 26 October and put up indirect and profits taxes by nearly as much as income taxation had been reduced (for a different set of taxpayers) in April.

Looking back on the tax reductions of April 1955 in the light of later events, it is natural to ask why the Chancellor took such risks. Was it for electoral reasons? Or out of over-confidence in what credit restriction could do? Or because he thought it right to use the unexpected bonus of a large budget surplus? Or was he misled by his slogan 'invest in success' and anxious not to let die the still faint flame of industrial investment? He had awakened the public and the business community to the possibilities of sustained economic growth if only industry had the confidence to back that prospect with investment: a doubling of the standard of living within twenty-five years, he had told the party conference, was within the nation's grasp. It was not for him as Chancellor to throw doubt by restrictive measures on that prospect.

But, then, neither did industrial investment in fact need further encouragement. If income tax did not have to be reduced in 1954 why should it be necessary in 1955? Just as the boom of 1963–5 could only be sustained by running through the reserves, which was not likely to sustain confidence, so any concern for confidence in 1955 was self-defeating if the measures taken preserved domestic expansion at the expense of external imbalance.

There can be little doubt that electoral considerations played a part even if the date of the election was not settled until after the budget had taken shape. It was in everybody's mind that it was an election year and that ministers would be predisposed to make concessions if possible. If officials felt able to recommend a reduction in income tax, however, it was perhaps because they were emboldened by the size of the budget surplus. The insistence on a more restrictive monetary policy would seem to have come from Robert Hall, who was prepared to acquiesce but was a good deal more guarded. The indications are that he underestimated both the expansionary forces at work and the risks to the balance of payments. He may also have put more faith in

39 Memoranda entitled 'The economic situation' were circulated to the Cabinet by the Chancellor of the Duchy of Lancaster (CP(55)98, 27 July 1955); the Lord President (CP(55)106, 23 August 1955), the Foreign Secretary (CP(55)111, 30 August 1955) and the President of the Board of Trade (CP(55)118, 3 September 1952). These are all in PRO CAB 129/76.

monetary measures than was warranted, especially when he expected only half-hearted support from the Bank of England. But he held throughout and repeated in April that 'a cautious policy would be to leave the general level of taxation unchanged'.[40]

## The autumn budget 1955

At the end of May, when the Economic Section reviewed the situation there was little sign that the monetary and other restrictive measures adopted in February were taking effect. On the contrary, all the evidence pointed to further expansion.[41] As June wore on the Treasury became increasingly concerned at the continuing rise in bank advances. The Governor was equally concerned at the absence of supporting measures of economy in government expenditure.

On 5 July, a day on which the Economic Secretary was exhorting the bank chairmen to be more restrictive, the Governor submitted a memorandum arguing that the over-strain on the economy could not be overcome without the help of some cuts in the public sector.[42] Next day Brittain (a Third Secretary) prepared a list of possible deflationary measures. Among these he included an autumn budget. Proposals based on Brittain's list were put by the Chancellor to the Cabinet on 12 July and received support in respect of more resolute credit restriction and hire-purchase controls. Cuts in public investment and in the subsidies on bread and milk were, however, opposed, notably by the Prime Minister (Eden).[43]

The banks in the meantime were agitating for cuts in public investment and the Chancellor concluded that he could not count on their full co-operation in the credit squeeze if it seemed that the nationalized industries were exempt from it. The Chancellor received little co-operation from his colleagues and, when he made a statement to the House on 26 July on the economies he proposed, he was unable to quote an itemized list of reductions to be made nor had they been agreed a month later. Similarly the cuts in local authority spending were more of psychological than of practical significance.

At this point attention switched to the external situation. At a meeting of senior officials on 28 July, Sir Edward Bridges was in some

40 'The economic situation and prospects', 5 April 1955, in PRO T 171/459.
41 'The economic situation', note by Sir Robert Hall, 26 May 1955, in PRO T 171/456.
42 Memorandum by the Governor, 5 July 1955, in PRO T 171/456.
43 CM(55)22, 12 July 1955, in PRO CAB 128/29.

doubt whether the measures announced by the Chancellor would do all that was necessary, 'particularly as so much depends on opinion abroad', and invited the meeting to consider what might be done, including tax increases, to 'root out' inflation and restore foreign confidence.[44] He had minuted the Chancellor in similar terms the day before, raising the possibility that Parliament might have to be recalled if action could not be held over until after the IMF meeting in Istanbul in September.[45]

The Chancellor, who had foreseen the possibility of an autumn budget even before his statement on 25 July, concluded by the end of August that further deflationary action was necessary but saw no need to recall Parliament.[46] Robert Hall, in a minute to the Budget Committee, called for 'a decisive measure of deflation', adding that 'it would be unwise to rely any longer on credit policy alone'.[47] He had earlier suggested to Bridges a general increase in purchase tax as likely to be the most effective instrument. Hall's recommendation rested on an assessment of the domestic economic situation as increasingly inflationary, not on fears for the balance of payments. He drew attention particularly to the buoyancy of stock-building and the highly liquid position of the company sector, which made it unlikely that there would be a quick response to the credit squeeze.[48]

The Budget Committee recommended an increase in purchase tax and an extension in its coverage, together with an increase in the tax on distributed profits, and rejected as impracticable a mid-year increase in income tax and the introduction of a capital gains tax (which the Prime Minister strongly supported). The Chancellor, in presenting his proposals to Cabinet, now wanted Parliament to be recalled at the end of September, before the party conference in October.[49] Corrective measures were needed 'to restore confidence and to avoid a further run on the reserves'.[50] The Chancellor's speech at the IMF meeting however had checked the run and this threw doubt on the need to recall Parliament. The Chancellor continued to urge it but was overruled and Parliament assembled on the day originally arranged.

44 PRO T 171/456, 3(i).
45 ibid., 5(iv).
46 CM(55)29, 26 August 1955, in PRO CAB 128/29.
47 BC(55)35, 'The economic situation', 2 September 1955, in PRO T 171/469.
48 ibid.
49 He minuted the Prime Minister to this effect on 2 September, a week after advising the Cabinet that an early recall of Parliament was not necessary.
50 CM(55)30, 5 September 1955, in PRO CAB 128/29.

He was overruled, too – again by the Prime Minister – in his proposal to abolish the bread subsidy, a measure which had the strong support of the Governor of the Bank of England. The tax proposals recommended by officials were adopted and cuts were also made in building programmes. Local authorities were no longer allowed to borrow freely from the Public Works Loan Board and had to look to the capital market for finance. Subsidies to local authorities on houses built for 'general needs' were to be reduced and later abolished.

The autumn budget, introduced on 26 October, may have been superfluous from the point of view of restoring confidence in sterling but it was certainly not superfluous as a check to the strong inflationary forces released by the investment boom. In November the Economic Section could see little prospect of much easing in the pressure of demand or of a swing back into surplus in the balance of payments.[51] Unemployment continued to fall and investment plans were still expanding. At the beginning of January 1956 Hall came to the conclusion, on the basis of the latest figures for trade and unemployment, that there was still no sign of deflation. On Bridges's advice he minuted the new Chancellor, Harold Macmillan, and was instructed to draft a paper for the Economic Policy Committee setting out the need for further action and proposing a list of appropriate measures to follow.[52]

These, when put together with some enthusiasm in the Treasury, included the abolition of bread and milk subsidies, substantial cuts in investment, and some economies on defence spending and the civil service.[53] It was also proposed to increase minimum deposits on goods bought on hire-purchase. All of these measures were approved by the Cabinet except the first. This met with strong resistance from the Prime Minister, who kept making speeches calling for a reduction in prices and taxes while Robert Hall was writing papers saying precisely the opposite. After Macmillan had threatened to resign, agreement was finally reached that the subsidies should be reduced in stages and that as an offset to this, investment allowances should be suspended.[54] The

51 BC(55)40, 'Economic prospects for the next budget', 22 November 1955, in PRO T 171/469.
52 EA(56)4, 6 January 1956, in PRO CAB 134/1236.
53 The investment cuts were based largely on a report by the Treasury Investment Committee, TIC(55)12 (Final), 'Investment, proposed and forecast', 9 January 1956, in PRO T 171/469.
54 This proposal was not made by Robert Hall but he approved of it.

measures were announced on 17 February. The bank rate was raised from 4½ per cent to 5½ per cent on the previous day, explicitly as an anti-inflationary measure.

## The 1956 budget

Shortly after this, Robert Hall submitted his usual pre-budget assessment.[55] A slowing down in the expansion of demand was now expected. What had to be judged, as Hall pointed out, was what the pressure would be a year later if the slowing down continued, not how the average pressure in 1956 would compare with that in 1955. In order to make a forecast for a period twelve months later, seasonally adjusted quarterly figures for all the main components of final demand were required but did not exist. It was in fact the 1956 budget, with Macmillan's famous reference to 'last year's Bradshaw', that set on foot the preparation of quarterly national accounts. It was not, however, until 1958 that it was possible to make quarterly rather that annual economic forecasts.

The Economic Section was uncertain how quickly demand would fall off once the peak of the boom, which it judged to be near, had been reached. They suspected that it might be abrupt as the expectations of business men and consumers switched from optimism to pessimism – a suspicion that was to prove mistaken – but saw some advantage in an easing of demand from the point of view of wages and prices on the one hand and the balance of payments on the other. Robert Hall's recommendation was that the budget should make no concessions likely to add to the pressure of demand and this recommendation was accepted by the Chancellor.

The Economic Secretary, Edward Boyle, urged the Chancellor to go further, pointing out that the government could not risk having to introduce yet another set of restrictive measures if excess demand persisted after the budget. He suggested an increase in income tax by sixpence, and, although the Chancellor thought this retrograde and politically embarrassing, alternative plans were prepared for the budget and the budget speech, leaving the choice open between an increase in income tax and an increase in profits tax. When news of this reached Butler he threatened resignation and the plan to raise income tax was dropped. Instead, the Chancellor included in his budget speech a

55 BC(56)13, 'The economic situation and prospects', 28 February 1956, in PRO
   T 171/469.

proposal to cut public expenditure by £100 million: from what total and in what ways was left vague.[56]

As 1956 progressed it became clear that the pressure of demand was beginning to fall gently and that the balance of payments had swung back into surplus. In October the Economic Section was expecting some rise in consumer spending in 1957 as the deflationary impact of hire-purchase restrictions wore off. Against this, private investment seemed likely to flatten out or might even decline. The net increase in final demand was expected to be small. Whatever easing resulted was to be welcomed and existing policies persisted in; 'we ought not to run any risks', it argued, 'of getting back to the over-employment of 1954 and 1955'.[57] Stress was laid on the danger to the balance of payments of renewed expansion; the Overseas Finance Division argued strongly for a target surplus of £350 million in the balance of payments on current account (compared with a recorded surplus in 1956 for which the latest estimate is £210 million). This emphasis on the balance of payments contrasted strikingly with the comparative *insouciance* over the previous three years when much smaller surpluses were forecast.

The Suez crisis transformed the outlook for the balance of payments, converting an October forecast of a surplus of £165 million in the first half of 1957 into a November forecast of a deficit of £35 million (equivalent to a reduction of £400 million per annum). The Budget Committee recommended an increase in income tax by sixpence on the standard rate, and an extra shilling a gallon on petrol duty, to bring in an additional £200 million in revenue in a full year and provide 'a dramatic way of increasing our deflationary posture'. The increase in income tax would have been announced as coming into effect at the next budget had the Chancellor accepted the recommendation, which he did not. The only tax change included in the Chancellor's statement on 4 December was the rise in petrol duty, presented as a temporary impost to conserve supplies of oil and so avoid encouraging wage claims based on the rise in the cost of living.

## The 1957 budget

The effects of the crisis were unexpectedly mild. By February 1957 the forecast of a deficit in the first half of the year had given way to one of

56 Unspecified cuts of £100 million were a recurrent ploy of Chancellors and Prime Ministers. Usually in the 1950s cuts in public expenditure were from an authorized or programmed total, not from the actual level already reached.

57 'The economic outlook – October 1956', note by the Economic Section, 19 October 1956, in PRO T 171/478.

a surplus of £135 million, and this proved close to the actual. None the less the crisis had a profound effect on opinion. The weakness and vulnerability to pressure of the British economy in the absence of adequate reserves and the drawing back from a military operation only half-complete created a widespread uneasiness and a clamour for what the Governor of the Bank of England called 'a radical attack on the fundamentals'. He called for 'dramatic, far-reaching and convincing measures' to be initiated at once in the first three months of 1957. What he was asking for was a larger budget surplus, which, since he was no enthusiast for higher taxation, was likely to reduce in practice to the familiar prescription of lower government expenditure. The Chancellor took much the same view. The day before he became Prime Minister, Harold Macmillan was calling for a cut of £200 million in defence expenditure and £80–100 million from the social services, especially the National Health Service. The new Chancellor, Thorneycroft, held similar views.

Underlying this concern for a 'stronger' budget was the financial problem of meeting the public sector borrowing requirement. Macmillan thought it to be 'the orthodox financial opinion' that the budget should be in overall balance (inclusive of capital spending). The Governor was concerned at the failure of the nationalized industries to find a market for their bonds and the increasing quantity of them that had to be taken up by the Issue Department. Nothing less than overall balance, he maintained, would dispose of the problem.

These were views with which Robert Hall had had to contend before. In January 1957 he attached an appendix to his submission to the Budget Committee discussing the significance of budget surpluses. This pointed out that a current surplus (above the line) was a way of supplementing private savings so as to balance total savings and investment, irrespective of what surplus or deficit there was 'below the line'. An overall surplus or deficit might affect confidence but its main effect was on the size of the floating debt and hence on monetary policy.

Within the Treasury there was also some difference of emphasis between the Economic Section and Overseas Finance on the degree of deflation required in the 1957 budget. The repeated crises in the balance of payments and the need to repay the IMF drawing disposed OF to insist on a target surplus of £350–400 million on current account compared with a forecast surplus of about half that amount.[58] In

58 BC(57)3, 'Economic assessment', 11 January 1957, in PRO T 171/478.

pursuit of that surplus they were prepared to urge further deflation so as to limit the demand for imports and strengthen the competitive position of exports. The Economic Section was more conscious of the emergence of considerable unused capacity and doubted whether exports would benefit appreciably from further deflation but accepted the need to refrain from expansionary measures.[59]

This was a cautious judgement when output had risen in 1956 by less than 2 per cent and was expected to increase in 1957 by no more than 1 per cent. It paid regard to current anxieties, which became more acute as the year progressed, over inflation on the one hand and balance of payments prospects on the other. These anxieties, however, were curiously at odds with the changes observable in the behaviour of prices and the balance of payments, since retail prices had risen by only 3.2 per cent in the year to June 1957 compared with 5 per cent in the previous year while the balance of payments on current account was showing a larger surplus in 1957 than in any post-war year except 1950. Public opinion was thought to be increasingly restive over the continued rise in prices and the inflationary wage settlements that aggravated it; and at the same time Suez had driven home the vulnerability of a country with inadequate reserves of foreign exchange.

The Chancellor, while not dissenting from his officials' diagnosis, gave priority to a reduction in taxation, amounting in all to nearly £150 million in a full year, on the grounds that high taxation discouraged effort and risk-taking.[60] On the other hand, public expenditure on goods and services, in real terms, dipped in 1957 and the net effect of the budget on the flow of expenditure was negative.[61]

As the year progressed the Chancellor became increasingly alarmed and adopted the monetarist views described in the last chapter. 'We have been near to the edge of economic disaster', he told the Cabinet in October.[62] But, as we have seen, he failed to obtain Cabinet backing for the cuts he proposed and resigned in January 1958.

59  BC(57)15, 'Economic assessment', note by the Director of the Economic Section, 1 March 1957, in PRO T 171/478.
60  In addition the temporary increase in the duty on petrol was repealed.
61  Dow, J. C. R. (1964) *The Management of the British Economy 1945–60*, Cambridge: Cambridge University Press for National Institute of Economic and Social Research, p. 199, reaches this conclusion on the basis of tax changes only.
62  C(57)230, 'The economic situation', note by the Chancellor of the Exchequer, 14 October 1957, in PRO CAB 129/89.

## The 1958 budget

By the end of 1957 the Economic Section was well aware that the economy was slowing down and running below capacity. In mid-December Robert Hall thought that production was rising gently and that employment was stable but expected some slight decline, probably in the second half of 1958. Had full employment remained the overriding objective, he would have been recommending some stimulus in the 1958 budget 'by tax relief or relaxation of monetary policy or investment limits'.[63] But the policy objectives had changed and price stability took precedence over full employment. 'Economic policy is therefore directed towards minimising the annual wage round.'[64]

The Chancellor's determination to prevent any increase in the quantity of money had no effect on the way in which the Economic Section addressed the problem of short-term forecasting. This was still couched in terms of national income analysis, not of wage movement or the money supply. In September 1957 they concluded that no rise in output was to be expected in 1958, with fixed investment unchanged or falling, government current expenditure on goods and services also lower, and stock-building less than in 1957. Three months later, although fears of an American recession had grown, they took a more optimistic view and forecast a year-on-year rise of £300–400 million in output; but since output had been expanding during 1957 this pointed to only a small increase between the end of 1957 and the end of 1958. As the American recession deepened, the outlook for British exports deteriorated and there was more reason to expect a fall in stocks. A much smaller increase in output, year on year, was predicted in the pre-budget forecast; industrial production was now expected to remain flat throughout 1958; and unemployment was likely, therefore, to increase at a moderate rate. The margin of unused capacity in the economy, which had been growing over the past two years, would become steadily larger.

This forecast was near enough to the mark although the rise in unemployment was faster and more alarming than was implied. What may have had more effect on the budget was the forecast for the balance of payments. This was not because of the expected drop in exports, for the import bill seemed likely to fall even more, thanks

63 BC(57)26, 'Economic outlook – preliminary appraisal', note by the Director of the Economic Section, 13 December 1957, in PRO T 171/487.
64 ibid.

mainly to a large reduction in import prices. Indeed, the balance of payments on current account was expected to reach nearly £500 million – well above the best out-turn in any earlier post-war year. What registered more strongly was that the reserves were expected to fall in the second half of the year because sterling balances would be withdrawn by the primary producing countries affected by the American recession. This was interpreted by OF as pointing to a possible balance of payments crisis later in the year and moved Sir Leslie Rowan to support the view of the Governor that there should be no relaxation of existing policies and that, instead, the nearer the budget got to overall balance the better.

In any event a relaxation of policy was judged to be out of the question so soon after the September measures and the reaffirmation of policy by the new Chancellor in January. Robert Hall was also against relaxation in the budget so long as major wage claims were still under negotiation. While these negotiations were in progress, the government could not be thought to weaken. If the current wage round came out at a highish figure, such as 5 per cent, it would be necessary to take further deflationary action and the outcome was unlikely to be known until after the budget.

The Prime Minister wanted a reduction in income tax to give people encouragement: the view that high taxation was anti-inflationary had been 'pretty well exploded'. But he was persuaded by the Chancellor (Amory) to wait until 'the inflationary battle' had been won.

The 1958 budget was therefore designed as a holding operation until the main wage settlements were concluded, probably by June. Only minor changes in taxation were made, amounting in all to a reduction of £50 million in 1958–9 and twice that amount in a full year. Even before the budget was introduced, however, Robert Hall had outlined a strategy of reflation. His advice was that the recession in progress was likely to be short-lived, since it was largely the product of a fall in stock-building. Reflationary measures should therefore be quick-acting. This implied concentration on the stimulation of consumption by such means as repayment of post-war credits, relaxation of hire-purchase restrictions, and reductions in purchase tax.[65]

Reflation began with an amendment to the Finance Bill in June, raising initial allowances. The Chancellor intended to defer further action until after the engineering wage settlement. But the dispute dragged on and was not settled until October. In the meantime the

65 BC(58)21, 'Preparations for reflation', note by Sir Robert Hall, 31 March 1958, in PRO T 171/487.

forecasters were predicting a rise in unemployment, first in early June to 500,000 by August or September, and then to 700,000 by the end of the year. Under pressure from his colleagues the Chancellor agreed to relax hire-purchase restrictions and this took effect in mid-September. The Cabinet in July also sanctioned a small increase in public investment and further increases were approved in November 1958 and February 1959. Six weeks later the Cabinet authorized the complete withdrawal of hire-purchase restrictions provided the power to reintroduce them was retained. Meanwhile four successive cuts in the bank rate, beginning in May, reduced the rate from 7 per cent to 4 per cent. In addition, the ceilings on bank advances were removed in July.

As we have seen, Robert Hall had already sketched a strategy for reflation. In May he suggested 'taking the first cautious steps towards expansion' and in July he proposed that a stimulus of perhaps £100 million should be given to consumption over the next twelve months through relaxation of hire-purchase restrictions and greater freedom to spend on house maintenance. These measures, both of which were adopted, accorded with his suggested strategy. The approval of additional fixed investment did not: he warned against it in July as 'slow to start and hard to stop'. In May he also emphasized the need to accompany any reflationary measures by a more positive policy on wages. This might take the form of a 'guiding light', i.e. an announcement from time to time of the increase in wages that would be consistent with price stability. A committee of officials had already suggested such a policy in January and it had been rejected. Hall's proposal in May had no greater success.

At the end of 1958 the Chancellor thought that 'enough had been done for the time being'. The Economic Section, however, was already convinced that further measures were necessary. It expected the stimulus to consumption to peter out early in 1959 and unemployment to go on rising, although perhaps less than in 1958, leaving production at the end of the year at least 5 per cent below economic potential. The Economic Section, and Robert Hall too, seem to have concluded that the rise in unemployment reflected what was later called a 'shake-out' of labour and that there was a correspondingly larger margin of capacity to be drawn upon.

Although the Section recognized that the stimulus already given to the economy had been more powerful than expected, it seems to have misjudged the strength of the upswing in progress. Tax concessions of some £250–300 million were recommended; and in course of time grew to £300–350 million in a full year. In the April 1959 budget the tax concessions amounted to £360 million in a full year, to which must be added £71 million in post-war credits. Higher public expenditure reinforced the impact on economic activity. No post-war budget had approached such a total or given such a stimulus to the economy. Yet it might have been even larger, with a cut in income tax of a shilling rather than ninepence, had the Chancellor not become worried by the size of the projected overall budget deficit, at one time estimated at £800 million but limited to £730 million in the budget.

The 1959 budget provides a good illustration of a familiar sequence in demand management in which delay in adopting expansionary measures leads to overstimulation later. With a secular boom in progress all over the world, the underlying expansionary pressures were enough to arrest local depressions without more than the assurance of a governmental safety net. Tax concessions on the scale of the 1959 budget proved to be excessive and produced a violent upswing instead of a steady and prolonged expansion such as might have resulted had they been far more modest. By 1960 the economy was already nearing full employment, imports had expanded strongly, and the balance of payments was moving into deficit. A fresh balance of payments crisis was already on the horizon.

## Conclusion

We need not – indeed cannot – pursue the course of events further than the 1959 budget. Instead, we may review a few of the lessons to be drawn from post-war budget experience.

It was the great achievement of the Economic Section under Hall to build into the Treasury machine an annual process of economic assessment as a background to budget-making – a process which still continues. They adopted a Keynesian approach and established themselves as experts on the budget judgement. Indeed they could claim to have invented it since the Treasury made no such judgement in the early post-war years and had been strongly opposed in 1944 to any suggestion that the government should commit itself in the White Paper on *Employment Policy* to the use of taxation as a stabilizer. Cripps's three budgets accustomed the Treasury to accepting the Economic Section's advice on the scale of adjustment required, and thereafter there was no real competition from an established source, although individual members of the Budget Committee felt free to offer different advice.

The Economic Section's views did not always prevail and other members of the Budget Committee applied different criteria, attaching an overriding significance to the avoidance of a deficit. But economic expertise conferred an advantage that showed itself in superior judgement. The non-economists were in general far more erratic and arbitrary in what they selected for emphasis and the scale of action they proposed. This was partly because the budget accounts gave only a confused picture of the economic impact of the budget while at the same time the forecasts of revenue and expenditure were highly unreliable. The improvement in forecasting technique and in the statistical data assembled by the forecasters made judgement somewhat easier and more confident; but, as Robert Hall kept stressing, the central recommendation was a judgement, not a simple corollary of the forecasting process.

Judgement is not just a matter of expertise but of character and temperament as well. Robert Hall was able to establish an almost unquestioned authority in the Budget Committee because of cool and sustained common sense and an impressive track record. That does not mean that he made no mistakes: he was probably too slow, for example, in grasping the full momentum behind economic expansion in 1954. He was also fortunate in his early years in having Cripps as Chancellor and Plowden as a kind of interpreter. But the trust he won came from being right more often than others and providing an intelligible diagnosis of situations that others found baffling.

When one looks in more detail at the budgets on which he advised, the first thing that stands out is how little room for manoeuvre there seemed to be. The Treasury felt it virtually impossible to recommend an increase in taxation and, except in 1951 and October 1955, the increases added up to very little. Only once was income tax increased after 1947. Profits tax was a more common target. Even increases in indirect taxes tended to be confined to petrol and tobacco.

Much the same applies to the recommendations made by Robert Hall. The maximum, up or down, that he ever pressed on the Budget Committee, except in 1948, was £150 million. It follows that demand management over this period relied on rather gentle nudges rather than on body blows. There were, of course, other instruments than taxation available. Government expenditure, investment (public and private), monetary policy, hire-purchase restrictions, import and other controls, and foreign exchange reserves could all be brought into use. But taxation was probably the single most powerful influence on demand; and, if the fluctuations in the economy were no more that about 1½ per cent up or down (i.e. £150–175 million), changes in taxation of the same order of magnitude, if correctly timed, were all that was needed.

In the practice of demand management there was a clear antithesis, more or less throughout the period, between the view taken of the budget by the Economic Section and that taken by ministers and senior Treasury officials. The latter judged the macroeconomic impact of the budget by the expected surplus 'above the line' while the Economic Section sought to establish the change it would make to final demand and the level of economic activity. In both cases judgements were based on forecasts that were necessarily unreliable; but, whereas in the first case little attention was paid to the unreliability of revenue forecasts or to their neglect of the changes in progress in income flow, in the second the uncertainties could be carefully weighed and checked against straws in the wind that offered clues to impending changes in trend. The 'above the line' approach could lead to judgements that were wildly wrong, as in 1953 and 1955, and had no basis in economic logic. The Keynesian approach of the Economic Section could also lead to misjudgements since no one fully understood how the economy worked, the information available was late, inconsistent, and incomplete, and unforeseen changes were always occurring. But at least it fastened on meaningful variables.

Ministers hesitated between using the surplus 'above the line' as a guide and the surplus counting in items 'below the line'. Cripps, Butler, Macmillan, and probably other Chancellors as well hankered after a budget that balanced when all items of revenue and expenditure were included, rather as modern Chancellors seem now to aim at a PSBR of zero or at most 1 per cent of GNP. This is, of course, a far more rigorous requirement than balance 'above the line' and correspondingly more deflationary. But earlier Chancellors, many of them monetarist at heart, might have envied a Chancellor whose budgeting freed him from any need to borrow and left enough over to meet the needs of nationalized industries and local authorities as well: so little did they appreciate what was involved in planning for full employment.

Labour ministers, who turned a friendly eye on public expenditure, especially transfer expenditure, were more willing than their Conservative successors to accept the need for high rates of tax and less willing to accept high rates of interest. Conservative ministers, on the other hand, sought constantly to reduce government expenditure, or check its steady increase, with a view to getting taxes down. For this reason, they looked with more favour on monetary policy as a means of controlling inflation and disliked the idea of raising taxes for this purpose. They were particularly anxious to reduce income tax. The standard rate had been 10s. in the £ at the end of the war and was still 9s.6d. in 1951 when they took office. Ten years later, in 1961 it had fallen to 7s.9d. On the other hand, short-term interest rates, which had remained at 2 per cent until 1951 were never less than 4 per cent after 1955 and reached a peak of 7 per cent in 1957; while long-term rates, apart from a dip in 1946 and a more extended one in 1952–3, rose fairly steadily from the war onwards, whatever the complexion of the government in office.

The three budgets that can be singled out as of special importance were those of 1952, 1955, and 1959. The first of these astonished commentators by its mildness but from the point of view of employment policy was not mild enough. The budget of 1955 is generally agreed to have been a blunder, although it is hard to say whether a 'no change' budget would have done much to avoid the exchange crisis in the autumn. The Economic Section was not the architect of that budget; nor was it to blame for the failure to restrict credit in the months that followed it. The budget of 1959 was also a mistake by going too far to encourage expansion when the economy was already beginning to recover.

# Chapter seventeen

# EXTERNAL ECONOMIC POLICY TO 1951

In wartime, as we have seen, the Economic Section's involvement in external economic policy was a limited one. Other departments – the Treasury, the Foreign Office, the Ministry of Economic Warfare, the Board of Trade, and the still privately owned Bank of England, for example – concerned themselves with the regulation of exports and imports, commercial negotiations with other countries, bulk purchase agreements, exchange control, restriction of enemy access to supplies, and so on. With these matters the Section had little to do. It was actively involved early in the war in debates on import policy and export surpluses, and took part in discussions towards the end of 1942 on reparations and policy towards Germany after the war, Robbins, Meade, and Fleming all submitting papers to an interdepartmental committee on the subject.[1] Issues of commercial policy, forecasts of the post-war balance of payments, and preparations for what became the American Loan negotiations in 1945 also occupied the Section. In general, however, its main interests during the war in external economic policy was in the proposals discussed in chapter 7 for the establishment of new international institutions such as the IMF, IBRD, and ITO.

In the years after the war the main interest of the Section continued to be in domestic economic policy. But domestic economic policy was linked to, if not dominated by, the balance of payments and it was impossible for the Section to overlook the interconnections between the two. It was inevitably drawn into many aspects of international economic policy and had always to keep track of international

1 Cairncross, Sir Alec (1986) *The Price of War*, Oxford: Blackwell, pp. 19–26.

developments. In advising on the co-ordination of economic policy it could not stop short at any frontier. But whereas on employment policy, for example, the views of the Economic Section were likely to be given more weight than those of any other department, and no other department would have claimed precedence in offering advice on such matters, on issues of external policy there were other departments that were charged specifically with the duty of advising.

Partly for this reason it is more difficult to trace the influence of the Section on external than on domestic policy. On fiscal, monetary, and incomes policy the Section's advice is easy to isolate and the reactions to it are plain to see. There are occasions on which that is true also of external policy and these figure prominently in what follows. But there were many more occasions on which the Section put a view that is lost in the minutes of committees or appears in some anonymous document to which others contributed.

Since the duties of the Section included the briefing of ministers, they had to familiarize themselves with issues likely to involve the Lord President (until 1947) or Chancellor (after 1947) or that might appear on the agenda of Cabinet committees attended by them. For example, the Section continued to provide briefs on reparations for Morrison and Cripps without necessarily pursuing the subject beyond the documents on which they were asked to comment. As a rule, however, the need to keep up-to-date on issues of policy led to representation on whatever interdepartmental committee was dealing with those issues. Since there were many such committees, this took up a good deal of the time of the members of the Section specializing in external relations.

A further activity was that of providing economic intelligence. This took various forms. Immediately after the war, A. J. Brown prepared a massive one-man 'Overseas economic survey', outlining the economic situation and prospects in different parts of the world.[2] On his departure in mid-1947 there seems to have been something of a gap. In 1952 a whole series of papers were produced on the 'World economic situation', with virtually every member of the Section contributing.[3] Then in 1953 the Committee on World Economic

2 EC(S) (45)41, draft outline of 'Overseas economic survey', 23 November 1945, in PRO T 230/19; there are twenty-three further instalments, ending in July 1947, in PRO T 230/20–4.

3 These began with EC(S)(52)21, Miss Kelley, 'World economic situation: Latin America', 19 June 1952, and continued with EC(S)(52)22, 24, 25, 26, 27, 28, and 30.

Problems was created and began issuing regular reports. This was an interdepartmental committee but the Section usually provided a secretary and guided the discussions, which were intended to help in the preparation of balance of payments forecasts.

Another kind of economic intelligence work consisted of reports on practice in other countries. For example in 1950 Abramson prepared a paper on 'The control of commercial bank credit', discussing the techniques of credit control used elsewhere; Mrs Stamler in 1956 reported on 'Wage policy abroad'; and Christopher Dow in 1954 reported on how economists were used in government in the Netherlands and Scandinavia.[4]

In addition to briefing and attendance at committees, the Section was represented at various international gatherings. These included meetings of the International Bank and the IMF, which Hall sometimes attended; meetings of Commonwealth Finance Ministers and officials; and meetings of the Economic and Social Council of the United Nations, the Economic Commission for Europe, and OEEC. Marcus Fleming was given the job of expounding full employment policy in ECOSOC in New York[5] and he and Nita Watts also took part in the annual meetings of ECE in Geneva. After Fleming left, the Section continued to be represented at meetings in both places. Close links were maintained with the OEEC, many of the briefs and memoranda for Paris meetings being prepared by the Section, and it took part from time to time in discussions there (e.g. on internal financial stability in the early 1950s).

Members of the Section were also posted abroad. As we saw in chapter 9, members of the Section were serving in 1953 in OEEC, Nato, ECE, and Washington. Postings of this kind began in 1947 when first Nita Watts and later Richard Sayers were sent to Paris to assist Sir David Waley (who claimed to be in no need of assistance) in discussions on possible future financing arrangements for intra-OEEC trade. In 1949 when the Section was asked to contribute to the staffing

4 'The Control of Commercial Bank Credit', 11 January 1950, EC(S)(50)3; 'Wage Policy Abroad', 25 October 1956, EC(S)(56)13, and 'Government Economists in the Netherlands and Scandinavia', 22 December 1954, EC(S)(54)18.

5 The Labour governments of 1945–51 were particularly anxious to obtain international agreement on policies of full employment and advocated the public announcement by all members of the United Nations of a target for the normal level of unemployment (fixed by Gaitskell in 1951 at 3 per cent for the United Kingdom). For the Section's involvement, see Tomlinson, J. (1987) *Employment Policy: the Crucial Years 1939–55*, Oxford: Clarendon Press, pp. 126–30.

of the permanent delegation to the OEEC under Sir Edmund Hall-Patch, Nita Watts returned for a further twelve months. In the same year Butt was lent to the Australian government in return for their earlier loan of Swan; but these exchanges came to an end when the Australians declined to borrow Nita Watts, on the grounds of her sex, in exchange for Peter Lawler. In the later 1950s postings abroad became more infrequent and by 1961 only the Washington post remained.

This post went back to 1949 when Robert Hall decided that a member of the Section should be attached to the British embassy in view of the importance of forming an up-to-date view of economic prospects in America, which at that time accounted for half the world's industrial production. The post, which was held in turn by John Jukes, Fred Atkinson, John Grieve-Smith, and Kit MacMahon, carried the double duty of reporting on developments to London and advising the Economic Minister in Washington. The arrangement was highly successful. The Economic Section's representative was in such intimate contact with US departments that it was sometimes said that he helped to co-ordinate their activities. The post had the added advantage of familiarizing successive members of the Section in the course of their two-year stint with the American economy and with problems of international economic relations. The lack of such familiarity was a considerable handicap, not always appreciated in Whitehall; the Section would have gained from a more extensive investment in service abroad.

## The role of the Director

It was usually the Director who came into contact with the policy-makers of other countries and who attended the more important discussions of policy abroad. Lionel Robbins in wartime attended the Hot Springs conference in 1943 and took part with Keynes in the loan negotiations in 1945. James Meade spent his last months as Director taking part in the negotiations in Geneva in 1947 for an international trade organization (ITO), followed by Marcus Fleming and Nita Watts. Both Meade and Robbins took part in the Washington discussions in the autumn of 1943 (see chapter 7). Robert Hall made frequent visits to France and the United States.

In his first few years Hall was deeply involved in the affairs of the OEEC and in British policy towards Europe. He went first to Paris in July 1948 to join Robert Marjolin and Dåg Hammarskjöld in drawing up a questionnaire for participating countries to complete as the first stage in preparing a long-term recovery plan looking ahead to 1952. He was back in Paris in October to discuss what was to be done with the long-term programmes submitted in response to this questionnaire. In the spring of 1949 he and Plowden had conversations with Monnet on Anglo-French collaboration when Monnet still hoped to involve the United Kingdom in his plans for European integration. He continued to make frequent visits to Paris throughout the 1950s. In 1954 he was invited to act as chairman of a small international group of economic experts, including the Dutch economist, Jan Tinbergen, Otmar Emminger of the Bundesbank, and Gabriel Hauge, Eisenhower's economic adviser. The group, which met in Paris under the auspices of the OEEC, was essentially a forerunner of Working Party No. 3 and engaged in regular discussion of international economic developments: an exchange of views found helpful both by the participants and by OEEC. When the Development Advisory Group was set up in Paris in 1959, the OECD (as it had become) turned to Hall to act as chairman.

About twice a year Hall made visits to the United States, where he had many friends in top official positions and in the Federal Reserve Board and could sound out journalists like the Alsops and Walter Lippmann. In the course of a visit in January 1953, when the Eisenhower administration was just about to be inaugurated, he struck up a friendship with Gabriel Hauge, which proved particularly useful in the OEEC informal expert group mentioned above. Visits to Commonwealth countries were rarer but Hall kept in touch with both Canadian and Australian affairs. For example, he attended the meeting of Commonwealth Finance Ministers in Sydney in 1954 and meetings of the Anglo-Canadian Continuing Committee from its inception in 1955.

## The work of the Section

After the loan negotiations the Section's involvement in external economic policy was initially rather limited. Part arose from the preparation of economic surveys and the effort to produce a long-term plan, in which Tress participated: both surveys and plans had to present a view of how the balance of payments was likely to develop and what policies were appropriate in the circumstances. This led in turn to a consideration of related problems: the need to limit the release of sterling balances; the ways in which exports might be encouraged and outgoings reduced; the dollar problem, the redirection of exports from soft to hard currency markets, and the danger of unrequited exports if redirection proved impossible. Advice on these and allied questions, which were mainly the job of OF in the Treasury, was provided by Marcus Fleming and Nita Watts.

The Section took part, along with other departments, in the discussions in Whitehall throughout the post-war period on relations with Europe. Before the Marshall Plan their interest was more international than regional, but they were occupied with matters affecting particular countries such as the Monnet Plan, German reparations, and the various bilateral agreements. They took part also in the examination of Bevin's proposal early in 1947 for a Customs Union with other European countries – a proposal that elicited virtually every argument and reaction aroused by the debates in the 1950s leading up to the Treaty of Rome.[6] Then came the various discussions in 1947 with the United States over the Marshall Plan and with other European countries in Paris over plans for economic recovery. The Economic Section saw no prospect that Britain could take the lead in the economic integration of Europe, as the US would have wished, and pressed instead for closer co-operation through the planning of joint projects and co-ordination of investment programmes.

Issues raised by the Marshall Plan were considered by the London Committee, chaired by Otto Clarke, on which Robert Hall represented the Economic Section – as he did also on the Overseas Negotiations Committee, chaired by Rowan, which dealt with bilateral agreements. Other members of the Section took part in the usual way through briefs and memoranda; helped in the preparation of programmes, either short-term or long, for submission to the new 'continuing organization', OEEC; and analysed the submissions by other countries to show how far they were mutually consistent and what issues of policy they raised. The Section also took the initiative in pressing for freer importation from member countries through liberalization of quotas. They saw this as a way of mitigating inflationary pressure when the United Kingdom was in surplus with its European neighbours; and it had the added advantage of exposing British industry to greater competition and obliging it to look at its capacity to meet such competition. The Section, in the person of Fleming, also played an important part in the formation of the European Payments Union, as described on pp. 298–301.

Robert Hall's involvement in external economic policy began in 1947 well before he took over the directorship on a full-time basis in

---

6 The history of the proposal is discussed at length in Walford, Ian, 'On the verge of the promised land: Britain and the customs union proposal, 1947–48', M.Litt. thesis, 1987, Leeds University.

September. He was brought into the preparation of a long-term plan which had been in progress since the beginning of 1946 and was ultimately completed as 'The long-term survey 1948–52' by Austin Robinson. The balance of payments side of the work went forward intermittently in a committee under Otto Clarke in the Treasury, with Tress representing the Economic Section in consultation with Fleming, Arthur Brown, and Nita Watts. The Survey, when completed, fastened attention on long-run prospects for exports and on the level of imports that the country could afford if it had to balance its accounts.

Before long, however, more immediate balance of payments difficulties demanded attention. At the end of July 1947, in the middle of the convertibility crisis, Dalton asked Hall for his views on the measures to be put to the Cabinet. Hall suggested making as large and early a drawing on the IMF as possible, being less generous in the release of sterling balances, and taking action in the budget to counter the additional inflationary pressure that an improvement in the current account would create.[7] He then worked with Tress on a long memorandum on the balance of payments from mid-1947 to mid-1948, laying particular stress on capital exports, mainly to the sterling area, as a factor in the deficit. The memorandum was revised by Fleming and Nita Watts and circulated in mid-September.[8] In preparing the memorandum, Hall had approached the Treasury for their estimates and been refused. He had therefore set the Section to make their own forecast, much to the fury of Treasury officials when it reached them.

The Section was highly critical of what it regarded as much too generous a release by the Treasury of blocked balances.[9] Hall, in his minute to Dalton, cited the Egyptian settlement, while Sayers minuted the Lord President on releases to India and Fleming attacked the total scale of release as a factor in the convertibility crisis. The Treasury, on

7 Hall to Dalton, 'Balance of payments general policy', 31 July 1947, in PRO T 230/277. The first two of these points had already been made by Fleming and the third by Tress (Fleming to Clarke, 30 June 1947, and Tress to Hall, 17 July 1947, in PRO T 230/276).

8 EC(S)(47)31, 'United Kingdom balance of payments, mid-1947 to end-1948', 12 September 1947, in PRO T 230/25.

9 Sayers to Lord President, 6 August 1947, in PRO T 230/277; EC(S)(47)30, Fleming, 'Some aspects of the balance of payments crisis', 8 September 1947, in PRO T 230/25. For earlier views of the Section on sterling balances see EC(S)(46)56, Nita Watts, 'The settlement of the sterling balances', 9 December 1946, in PRO T 230/23.

the other hand, thought the Section, and Fleming in particular, much too optimistic in assuming that exports denied a market in countries drawing on their sterling balances would be diverted with success to the more difficult dollar markets if the balances were not released.

The main contribution of the Economic Section was its insistence on the importance of the capital account. But releases of blocked sterling were only part of the problem since capital transfers to the sterling area could be made freely and were on a larger scale than was currently recognized.[10] No one, however, seems to have proposed introducing control over these capital movements. The most the Economic Section could suggest, apart from less generous releases, was that other sterling area countries should be induced to borrow from the IMF.[11] Fleming had a more unorthodox idea: why not revalue the pound upward by 10 per cent and levy taxes on exports?[12] This received short shrift from Rowe-Dutton in the Treasury, who thought it a sufficient objection that it was a long time till the budget, and taxes could not be raised earlier.

In mid-October ministers took measures to improve the balance of payments, and the November budget – Dalton's last act as Chancellor – provided for a large budget surplus. The Economic Section's part in these measures was a modest one but they had been consulted by Cripps on the balance of payments and their views on the need for a deflationary budget had been studied by Dalton.[13] They supported the general strategy of the government in aiming to moderate the dollar drain without taking such drastic action as would have been necessary had all hope of Marshall Aid been abandoned. Hall also felt, in the spring of 1948, when the government jibbed at some of the provisions of the treaty with the United States under which aid would be forthcoming, that this was to ignore that rations and employment had already been staked on acceptance.

10 Fleming and Watts forecast capital exports to the sterling area in the last four months of 1947 at £130 million and in the year from mid-1947 at £235 million (Fleming to Hall, 11 September 1947, and Fleming to Watts, 'United Kingdom balance of payments mid-1947 to end-1948', 12 September 1947, in PRO T 230/277). For the calendar year 1947 the net rundown in sterling balances is now put at £130 million while other capital transfers to the sterling area seem to have been substantially in excess of £300 million: see Cairncross, Sir Alec (1985) *Years of Recovery*, London: Methuen, p. 155.
11 Watts to Hall, 27 September 1947, in PRO T 230/277.
12 EC(S)(47)33, Fleming, 'Devaluation plus export taxes', 14 October 1947, in PRO T 230/26.
13 See chapter 15, p. 244.

Many of the same points were raised again in 1948 as had been put in 1947. Hall returned in March to the need to set limits to capital exports to the sterling area but without indicating how it was to be done.[14] There was also much discussion of the problem of unrequited exports, that is of exports to soft currency markets in excess of what could be supplied in return – a problem which implied the export of capital or credit and was linked with the reluctance of exporters to tackle hard currency markets so long as soft currency markets were open to them. The completion of 'The long-term economic survey 1948–52' also threw into prominence the uncertainties of reaching external balance at a reasonable level of imports. If the best that could be hoped for was a 45 per cent increase in exports above the pre-war level, as the Board of Trade maintained, imports would have to be held to a volume lower than before the war. The conclusion drawn by Austin Robinson and the Planning Staff was that it would be wise to embark on a large expansion of agricultural production as the only way of engaging in import substitution at limited cost. This was a conclusion endorsed by Hall who thought it rash to assume, as the survey did, that the terms of trade would remain unchanged: if they changed for the worse it would be all the more necessary to push on with agricultural expansion.[15]

This view was elaborated by Swan, who had earlier taken a rather different line and queried whether it was right to make large irreversible investments in agriculture to meet a temporary emergency.[16] He now argued that there had been a change in the structure of world production with a rise of 30–40 per cent in industrial production and a lag in the production of food and materials. The shift in the pattern of trade and prices appeared for the time being as a dollar problem. If the problem was to be solved it required an adverse shift in the terms of trade: all the greater as the expanding American market absorbed more food and materials. There was no escape for a country like the United Kingdom that was in competition for these except by reducing its standard of living to correspond with the reduced productivity of British industry in terms of food and materials.

The government gave its blessing to agricultural expansion. But

14  Hall and R. G. D. Allen, 'Export of capital', 11 March 1948; Hall to Trend, 23 April 1948; in PRO T 230/278.
15  Hall to Hitchman and Plowden, 13 July 1948, in PRO T 230/278.
16  EC(S)(47)32, Swan, 'Replacement of imports by home production', 7 October 1947, and EC(S)(48)37, 'The balance of payments problems of Western Europe', 1 November 1948, in PRO T 230/26 and 28.

perhaps Swan's first thoughts were the more prescient. World trade expanded far beyond what had been assumed and with it supplies of food and materials from soft currency sources. The terms of trade, after a further adverse shift in 1950–1, improved steadily thereafter and with the improvement the dollar problem, too, disappeared. The Economic Section was not long in concluding that agricultural expansion had been overdone and seeking some abatement in the level of guaranteed prices for home-grown foodstuffs.

Much of 1948 was spent in giving shape to the European Recovery Plan, preparing programmes for submission to the new 'continuing organization' of Marshall Plan countries, OEEC, and debating what substance there was in the idea of European integration. In Hall's view the export forecasts submitted were too pessimistic, if not dishonest, and the bids for aid correspondingly suspect. He argued, too, that Whitehall was taking too narrow a view of relations with Europe, ignoring British obligations to assist the recovery plan, the dangers of Britain's trying to go her own way, and the importance of collaboration with European neighbours from the political and probably also the economic point of view.

1948 was a relatively calm year, in which things were moving in the right direction. 1949 was more turbulent. From March onwards, policy was dominated by the drift towards devaluation in the wake of a mild depression in America and by the debate over the measures to be taken after devaluation to limit government expenditure. Hall was too preoccupied with these events to see much of the Section, making two long visits to the US in May and June, a third, even longer, visit in August–September and visits to Paris in April and November.

At the beginning of the year he was again in conflict with the Bank of England over monetary policy although not as deeply as he was later over devaluation and the monetary and exchange rate policies to go with it. He was also occupied with the survey and the budget, arguing for cuts in the food subsidies and increased children's allowances as Meade had done two years before. In Paris he had talks with Monnet, who urged that a way must be found of catching the imagination of Europe by some scheme for closer economic relations between Britain and France; but the talks led nowhere although somewhat similar ideas took shape a year later as the Schuman Plan.

In all this, other members of the Section took little part, except in working out the likely effect of devaluation on the cost of living and the scale of depreciation to be aimed at. Bretherton, who had joined the Section as joint Deputy Director, took charge of a party on wage and price policy after devaluation.[17] Dow and Bretherton also contributed to a discussion of economic policy in a recession and Fleming did a number of theoretical papers on international commercial and financial policy.[18] Of more immediate importance, Fleming made various proposals during the year (and in early 1950) on schemes for intra-European payments agreements and was an important influence in British thinking on what came to fruition in July 1950 as the European Payments Union.[19]

Exchange rate policy had always been recognized by the Economic Section to be of central importance in the management of the economy. There had been discussions in wartime in the Section on the likely response of the balance of payments to changes in the rate, and Meade and Fleming had both engaged in controversy with Keynes early in 1944 on the relative merits of using import quotas or depreciation to remedy a persistent external deficit.[20] Meade and Fleming both favoured the use of exchange rate variations during the transition period after the war; but, given the continuation of import controls and the denomination of overseas income in sterling, there was obviously no great advantage in letting the rate fall.[21] This was also the Treasury view, although in June 1945 Otto Clarke argued for an early and modest devaluation of sterling without convincing Keynes or his colleagues in OF.[22]

In the next two years nothing much was heard of devaluation except in financial circles, where it was expected to occur sooner or later.[23] What precipitated renewed discussion was the problem of hard and soft currencies and the difficulty of inducing exporters to direct their efforts towards expanding sales in hard currency (dollar) markets. This

17 'Draft report of working party on Wages Policy and Devaluation', 6 August 1949, in PRO T 229/213.
18 All of these are in PRO T 230/143.
19 See pp. 298–301.
20 Keynes, Lord (1980) *Collected Writings*, vol. 26, Cambridge: Cambridge Unversity Press, pp. 283–304. Fleming was able to convict Keynes of an arithmetical blunder.
21 'UK post-war balance of payments 1940–2' and '1942–4' in PRO T 230/4 and 5.
22 Clarke, Sir Richard (1982) *Anglo-American Colloboration in War and Peace,* Oxford: Oxford University Press, pp. 108–9, 122–5.
23 In November 1947 Austin Robinson raised the subject at a meeting of the Overseas Negotiations Committee but the Treasury subsequently asked for the reference to be deleted from the record (see PRO T 236/641). We owe this reference to Professor Pressnell.

problem became acute in 1948 as trade with soft currency markets showed growing surpluses of 'unrequited' exports. Inconvertibility of currencies seemed in danger of dividing the world economy in two, with the soft currency countries sheltering their high cost production behind protective barriers.

Devaluation was again proposed by Clarke in February 1948 without effect and in September a group including Robert Hall considered the case for letting the pound float but decided against. Talk of devaluation was renewed in the spring of 1949 when the current account, which had been in rough balance in 1948, moved back into deficit as industrial production in the United States dipped and the market there for sterling area products weakened.[24]

At the end of March Robert Hall persuaded Bridges to set on foot an enquiry into the case for devaluation and embarked on a campaign to convert official opinion, beginning with Plowden, the Chief Planning Officer. This was a lengthy business; in mid-June Bridges told the Chancellor that 'most of us, with different degrees of emphasis, are opposed to devaluation *now*' although he did not exclude the possibility later on. But in the course of his visit to Washington in June with Wilson Smith, a Treasury Second Secretary, Robert Hall had been able to bring him to a more favourable view of devaluation; and, once he came round, other Treasury officials began to change, too, so that by early July there was fair agreement within the Treasury. The Chancellor, however, who had not been convinced when approached by Hall in March, remained strongly opposed to devaluation.

The final decision to devalue was largely due to Hugh Gaitskell, who was one of three ministers left in charge of economic policy when Cripps went off to a Swiss sanatorium in mid-July. Gaitskell's influence on the Prime Minister, who had taken over Cripps's duties, would have been much less had not the Treasury, persuaded by Hall, supported him. A minute to the Prime Minister on 26 July, signed by the three top officials in the Treasury and by Hall and Plowden, set out the case for a substantial readjustment of the sterling–dollar rate just before the critical meeting of the Cabinet on 29 July and was echoed in the letter sent to Cripps after the meeting. 'All of us are now agreed,' Cripps was told, 'including the responsible officials, that [devaluation] is a necessary step'.[25]

The Economic Section's influence was also felt in the choice of a rate. Marcus Fleming, in a paper in June, had examined the

24 Cairncross (1985), op. cit., p. 168.
25 For a full account, see Cairncross (1985), op. cit., chapter 7.

consequences of a devaluation by one-quarter and Hall had subsequently thought of a devalution by one-third. The rate suggested in Section papers in August was first \$2.75, then \$2.80.[26] But the Section (presumably Fleming) also suggested that a régime of variable exchange rates might be adopted 'for an experimental period', and Robert Hall later claimed to have advocated a floating rate until the Bank of England declared that it was 'totally impracticable'.[27] In the end, Bevin and Cripps fixed the rate on the basis of recommendations by officials who in turn had accepted the view put to them by Hall.[28] Sterling was devalued from \$4.03 to \$2.80 on 19 September.

The Section had also advised on the likely effect of devaluation on the cost of living. Early in May Dow made some elaborate calculations suggesting that a 25 per cent devaluation would raise import prices by 19 per cent and the cost of living initially by 2.7 per cent and eventually by 3.5 per cent, allowing for a 2 per cent rise in wages. Later he revised his estimate upwards to 5 per cent if food subsidies were not increased.[29] This estimate, which proved to be excessive, was accepted by Cripps but was regarded by the financial press when he made it public as much too optimistic.

Hall was one of the key figures in the subsequent battle over expenditure cuts. Officials had been insistent all along that cuts of some kind would have to accompany devaluation; indeed, those who were opposed to devaluation relied primarily on large cuts in expenditure in order to restore external balance – a view which the Prime Minister found peculiarly puzzling and perverse. Officials had also attacked 'the present policy of very cheap money' but were unsuccessful even in getting agreement to make the bank rate effective at its current rate of 2 per cent. On public expenditure they did succeed, a month or so after devaluation, in persuading ministers to make substantial cuts.[30]

What happened in 1949 was more a revaluation of the dollar than a devaluation of sterling, since most other currencies took their cue from sterling and devalued simultaneously. It was a more or less indispensable ingredient in the ending of the dollar problem; and from

26 ibid., p. 186n.; Downie to Hall, 'Choice of a new exchange rate', 6 August 1949, in PRO T 230/388, 'External economic policy 1949–1952'.
27 Cairncross (1985), op. cit., p. 187.
28 ibid., pp. 186–7.
29 Dow, 'Internal effects of a rise in import prices', 3 May 1949, in PRO T 230/388. The revised estimate is dated 10 June 1949. No later calculation for a 30 per cent devaluation appears to have been made.
30 See p. 249.

that point of view it might have been better at a somewhat earlier date. Its main effect in 1949–50 was to put an end to a speculative run on the reserves and convert it into a speculative inflow. By the winter of 1950–1 this had reached such proportions that it became necessary to consider revaluation of the pound. Prices were rising as rearmament gathered speed and revaluation offered a way of checking the rise.

On this occasion there was no difference of view between the Treasury and the Economic Section. Both were against revaluation. The Treasury argued that if the pound was likely to remain strong the right course would be to admit imports costing dollars more freely especially as the pound was expected to weaken appreciably in the second half of the year. Nita Watts calculated that a 25 per cent revaluation would reduce prices by 2 per cent and improve the balance of payments by £140 million. But these gains did not justify revaluation, which ought to occur only in conditions of 'fundamental disequilibrium'. She ended with the usual Section recommendation to let the rate float for a time before settling on a new fixed rate. The Treasury and Bank of England, however, were adamantly opposed in principle to a floating rate. Minutes by Otto Clarke and George Bolton declared that it was incompatible with exchange control, with the sterling area, and with the newly created European Payments Union and the International Monetary Fund.[31] No action was taken.

## The European Payments Union

Meanwhile the Economic Section had played a critical role in shaping British views on a European Payments Union. As early as September 1947 the Committee on European Economic Co-operation (preparing the setting up of the OEEC) had pledged its members to abolish restrictions on their mutual trade 'as soon as possible', to study the possibility of forming a customs union, and immediately to try to work out a scheme for complete transferability of European currencies within the group, combined with gold or dollar settlement of balances exceeding credit swings under bilateral payments agreements. Various modifications of the initial network of bilateral trade and payments agreements followed, but it was not until 1948–9 that a real drive began for European trade liberalization supported by a genuinely multilateral payments scheme covering the OEEC area. By late 1949 it seemed to the Section that devaluation had opened the way to a new and simpler scheme for payments arrangements which would parallel

31 Cairncross (1985), op. cit., pp. 236–7.

the steps taken to liberalize trade in Europe. Fleming set out the options in a series of papers towards the end of 1949 and an interdepartmental committee reported on them in November.[32] Fleming favoured a clearing union or fund on the model of the IMF, but with greater automaticity of borrowing rights and fractional settlements in a mixture of gold and credit designed to make currencies scarce gradually rather than suddenly. Trade rules would also be required to limit the freedom of members to restrict imports from other members. The majority of the committee supported the idea of such a scheme for the settlement of surpluses and deficits but the Bank of England had doubts and these doubts prevailed with ministers.[33]

The Bank pointed out that the United Kingdom had already put up £570 million since the war to finance international payments and that sterling, of which European countries held £400 million, was the only European currency enjoying administrative transferability within Europe. They feared a breakup of the sterling area and were anxious to maintain the use of sterling as an international currency. They were opposed to any new inter-governmental organization and wanted instead to build on existing bilateral agreements by providing additional credit from a pool of currencies when a member country's resources and credit margins proved insufficient.[34] The Chancellor supported the idea that the Union should be a lender of last resort and that 'any new scheme should leave undisturbed the existing monetary agreements entered into by the United Kingdom'. It was 'a cardinal principle' that the multilateral facilities offered by sterling must be not only maintained but increased. The alternative scheme for a full-blown clearing union would make it necessary to freeze sterling held by other member countries and would risk the use of sterling held or earned outside the system in settlement of a bilateral deficit with the United Kingdom while the United Kingdom itself had to settle its bilateral deficits by overdrawing its account with the Union.[35]

32 EC(S)(49)29, 'Intra-European trade and payments', 2 November 1949; EC(S)(49)36, 'Some alternative payments schemes', 2 December 1949; EC(S)(49)42, 'European credit pool', 20 December 1949; all by Fleming and in PRO T 230/143. The Report of the Subcommittee on ED(49)21, 'The future of intra-European payments', 24 November 1949, is in PRO CAB 134/192.

33 EPC(49)159, 'A new scheme for intra-European payments', note by the Chairman, 10 December 1949, in PRO CAB 134/223.

34 Note, unsigned but probably by the Bank, 29 November 1949, in PRO T 273/310.

35 C(50)30, 'European Payments Union', Memorandum by the Chancellor of the Exchequer, 27 January 1950; annex to EPC(50)28, 10 February 1950, in PRO CAB 134/225.

The scheme submitted to the OEEC on 14 December 1949 was thus a very different one from what Fleming had proposed. But ministers were dead against full participation in a clearing union. Jay argued that if there had to be a scheme it should 'do the minimum' and Gaitskell not only feared a loss of control but would have liked to ban the use of gold in settlements with other members of OEEC.[36] American officials visiting London, and Hoffman and Harriman in Paris, did their best to represent the dangers of the British attitude and the advantages that full membership would bring.[37] To other delegations in Paris, they said, it looked like a case of the United Kingdom versus the rest. By mid-February it was clear that the British scheme stood no chance of acceptance and Hoffman was threatening to establish a clearing union without British participation. As the Chancellor pointed out, this would probably preclude British membership at a later date.[38]

A new scheme, which also proved unacceptable, was prepared in February envisaging British participation on terms different from other countries.[39] The Treasury and Bank of England wanted special rules for British membership, and in return were willing to forego access to the credit facilities of the Union.[40] The Economic Section dissented, arguing that the United Kingdom should join on the same basis as other members. In March Gaitskell took over responsibility from Cripps and after a visit to Paris at the end of the month began to modify his views, influenced by talks with American officials and with Marjolin, the Secretary-General of OEEC.[41] At the beginning of May, however, officials were still unwilling to see proposals tabled on the

---

36 Jay to Bridges, 28 November 1949, in 'Economic planning 1949–50', in PRO T 273/310. For Gaitskell's views see 'Fundamentals: gold and European payments', memorandum by the Minister for Economic Affairs, 17 April 1950, in '1950 fundamental discussions with the United States', PRO T 232/199, and Williams, P. M. (ed.) (1983) *The Diary of Hugh Gaitskell*, London: Jonathan Cape, pp. 178–82.

37 For Hebbard's visit to London see TP(L)(50)20, 1 February 1950, in PRO CAB 134/721; for Hoffman and Harriman, see EPC(50)28, 'Proceedings at the meeting of OEEC ministers in Paris', report by the Chancellor of the Exchequer, 10 February 1950, in PRO CAB 134/225.

38 EPC(50)28, 'Proceedings at the meeting of OEEC ministers in Paris', report by the Chancellor of the Exchequer, 10 February 1950, in PRO CAB 134/225.

39 EPC(50)31, 'European Payments Union', memorandum by the Chancellor of the Exchequer, 3 March 1950, in PRO CAB 134/225.

40 H. Wilson Smith to Armstrong (for Chancellor), 18 February 1950, in PRO T 273/310; for Fleming's draft see ER(L)(50)41 in PRO T 230/157.

41 Williams, op. cit., pp. 178–82.

lines suggested by Fleming, who again dissented and was allowed to minute the Chancellor.[42]

This seems to have been the turning-point. A few days later, Playfair, the chairman of the Subcommittee on Intra-European Trade and Payments, submitted a memorandum to ministers indicating that there was now agreement to join 'as full ordinary members of the scheme if it makes adequate provision for the maintenance of bilateral monetary and credit arrangements' and 'to renounce the right to discriminate between member countries in the application or suspension of liberalisation of trade'.[43] This was followed on 13 May by a paper from Fleming showing that, had the scheme been in operation over the eighteen months to 31 March 1950, the United Kingdom, France, Germany, and other countries would have been able to finance deficits and surpluses at every stage quarter by quarter, without paying or receiving gold.[44]

What part this played in reassuring ministers is not clear. Their chronic fears for British gold and dollar reserves had already been allayed by a dramatic rise over the winter and spring. Gaitskell seems also to have been influenced by Fleming's demonstration that the credit limits offered to the United Kingdom if it was ever in deficit with Europe were far wider than the credit it could enjoy from the monetary and payments agreements it was so anxious to keep. The discussion with Katz and other ECA officials in London on 12 and 13 May also helped to clarify ideas.[45] By the middle of May ministers were agreed that negotiations should proceed for full membership on the same terms as other members, subject to assurances on specific points.[46] The Economic Section, having argued strongly and persistently for the kind of scheme which ministers now finally accepted as in the national interest, could take credit for an important contribution to the change of view. The scheme adopted, however, was fundamentally of American, not British, origin.[47]

42 TP(L)(50)16M, 4 May 1950, in PRO CAB 134/720, and TP(L)(50)59 (Fleming's memo) in PRO CAB 134/721. It may be significant that Fleming was awarded a CMG in the June 1950 honours list.

43 Memorandum by E. W. Playfair to the Economic Policy Committee, 10 May 1950, in PRO T 273/310.

44 TP(L)(50)63, 'European Payments Union', note by the Economic Section, 13 May 1950, in PRO CAB 134/721. The paper may have been drawn to Gaitskell's attention earlier.

45 The minutes are in TP(L)(50)64, 17 May 1950, in PRO CAB 134/721.

46 CAB(50)30M, 12 May 1950, in PRO CAB 128/17.

47 Most of the credit goes to Robert Triffin, who was the main author of the ECA scheme submitted to OEEC on 24 November 1949.

# Chapter eighteen

# EXTERNAL ECONOMIC POLICY AFTER 1951

## Robot

We come next to the balance of payments crisis in the winter of 1951–2, when the Economic Section played a critical role. Soaring import prices associated with world rearmament had turned the terms of trade steeply against the United Kingdom, while the primary producing countries in the rest of the sterling area were spending heavily out of their extra earnings in 1950–1 on higher imports from dollar countries. The reserves, which had increased in the wake of devaluation, reached a peak in the first half of 1951 and then fell in the second half of the year by $1,500 million with a prospective further loss of $700 million in the first quarter of 1952. This would leave a balance of only $1,500 million in the reserves – a figure that might well produce an exchange crisis when made public. The government took steps to cut imports in November 1951; again in January, after a Commonwealth Finance Ministers meeting in London at which other sterling area countries agreed to take parallel action; and yet again in March when the reserves were still draining away.

A new Conservative government was in office and ministers were talking of 'freeing the pound'. The outlook seemed to many to call for drastic measures. In February, when the outlook was particularly black, the Bank of England and the Overseas Finance Division of the Treasury came forward with a scheme for blocking sterling balances, letting the pound float, and introducing convertibility for non-residents of the sterling area.[1] The scheme, christened Robot, was first considered over dinner on 18 February by the Prime Minister, the Chancellor, the Leader of the House, and the Governor of the Bank, and it was agreed that the Chancellor should announce it, if accepted by the Cabinet, in his budget a fortnight later on 4 March. Robert Hall, dumbfounded that a scheme of such importance and complexity should be adopted with so little time for further examination, protested to Bridges and the Chancellor and was successful in securing agreement to a postponement of the budget for a week. He also expressed his misgivings to the Chancellor but without shaking him. Hall helped to brief Lord Cherwell, the leading opponent of the plan, and Sir Arthur Salter, the Minister of State for Economic Affairs, another strong opponent.

Curiously enough, the scheme's main authors, Bolton and Clarke (Rowan – Head of OF – being the third), were now as insistent on floating as they had been a year previously on its unacceptability; while the Economic Section, which usually championed the idea of floating, was now firmly against it. The internal controversy that ensued was protracted and bitter and soured the Economic Section's relations with OF for a long time.

The advocates of the scheme did not disguise its disadvantages. It would mean abrogating the United Kingdom's monetary and payments agreements with other countries, might lead to withdrawals from the sterling area, could torpedo the EPU, and would be received with 'mixed feelings' by the US government. Against this, it was claimed that it would automatically put an end to the dollar drain as the exchange rate 'took the strain'. Dealings in cheap sterling, which the Bank abominated, would virtually cease. Sterling balances would no longer threaten the stability of the exchange rate. Above all the plan was a major step on the road to convertibility.

Robert Hall's reaction was one of alarm at the domestic and

---

1 For a detailed account of the scheme see Cairncross, Sir Alec (1985) *Years of Recovery*, London: Methuen, chapter 9; MacDougall, Sir Donald (1987) *Don and Mandarin*, London: John Murray, chapter 5; and Plowden, Lord (Sir Edwin) (1989) *An Industrialist in the Treasury*, London: André Deutsch, chapter 14. Earlier accounts appear in Birkenhead, Lord (1961) *The Prof in Two Worlds*, London: Collins: and Salter, Lord (Sir Arthur) (1967) *Slave of the Lamp*, London: Weidenfeld & Nicolson. None of the three promoters of Robot subsequently published their mature reflections on the episode but it is not on record that they ever changed their minds. Butler admitted to Bridges that he was wrong but said the opposite in Butler, Lord (R. A. Butler) (1971) *The Art of the Possible*, London: Hamish Hamilton.

international repercussions of so drastic a step. If the fundamental problem was to close the gap between exports and imports, the Robot proposals would have the opposite effect. They would cause the rate to slide and turn the terms of trade against the United Kingdom, make a still bigger export effort necessary, and raise import prices when there was already a danger of serious inflation. He foresaw a large depreciation of sterling and a weakening or destruction of the machinery built up since the war to cope with the dollar shortage. He and Plowden wanted a cut in the defence programme consisting of £150 million in the load on the engineering industries and £50 million in the load on building; a cut in the housing programme by 25 per cent; the withdrawal of depreciation allowances; and other specific measures. What was approved by the Cabinet on 29 February, when it put aside the Robot scheme for the time being, were measures akin to those proposed by Hall and Plowden.

The exchange crisis so confidently predicted by OF and the Bank never took place. Shortly after the budget on 11 March was found not to include the Robot proposals, the drain on the reserves virtually ceased and in April a slow improvement began. Not that the proposals were withdrawn. They continued to simmer in the Treasury and to be the subject of dispute between OF and the Economic Section. The Chancellor made a fresh attempt at the end of June to enlist support but failed and did not even put the matter before Cabinet.

The Robot plan provides us with a good illustration of the Economic Section in action as a team. Between the first discussion of the plan in the Treasury on 19 February and its considerations by the Cabinet on 28–9 February, paper after paper was prepared by members of the Section for internal circulation, faster than Robert Hall could read them, and a Section view gradually took shape. Nita Watts had already produced a critique of the plan on 20 February and she and other members of the Section contributed to some of Hall's papers on it.[2] On 25 February she elaborated an alternative scheme which would have blocked sterling balances held by non-residents only, and left sterling area countries free to draw on their sterling balances but not on the central reserves of gold and dollars, which would be divided up between the various members of the area. Each country would then have to balance its accounts with non-sterling countries bilaterally or using barter, although it might be possible to form an enlarged

2 N. Watts, 'What happens when the reserves run out?', 19 February 1952; 'The Bank's plan for overseas sterling', 20 February 1952, in PRO T 236/3245; 'Alternative exchange policies', 25 February 1952, in PRO T 230/389.

payments union in which settlements were made multilaterally in sterling. A scheme for a sterling payments union was prepared by Neild.[3] These papers assumed that rates of exchange would be fixed. Jukes, however, thought a floating exchange rate 'the least objectionable feature of the Bank plan' and proposed 'a course of action which most of the Section clearly regarded as lunacy'.[4] This combined inconvertibilty with a floating pound and was bolstered by further cuts in imports, cuts in consumption and investment, some borrowing from the IMF, threats to cut the defence programme and develop trade with eastern Europe if the US offered no help, and an intensified dollar-saving drive.

Downie also favoured an inconvertible, floating pound but on different grounds. In his view, convertibility would remove the incentive all over the world to discriminate against hard currency imports and this would create unemployment in the industries no longer benefiting from discrimination. Exchange rates would drop, prices would rise, and the world would revert to beggar-my-neighbour policies. Once government realized that full employment and convertibility were incompatible, they would abandon convertibility and would already have been forced off fixed rates of exchange. If this was what was in store, why not short-circuit the process and float at once, retaining incovertibility?[5] Neild, however, pointed out that Downie had provided no arguments as to why floating should make things any better than sticking to a fixed rate or indeed why it should not make things worse.[6] Peggy Hemming and Butt also circulated papers attacking the plan for external sterling and offering their own prescriptions. Dow, who put the Section point of view to the Budget Committee, was only prevented from joining in because he was busy assessing the budgetary consequences of adoption of the plan.[7]

The argument continued after the Cabinet decision on 29 February

3 R. R. Neild, 'The mechanics of sterling union', n.d., in PRO T 230/389.

4 J. Jukes, 'What we should do', 27 February 1952, in PRO T 230/389.

5 Downie to Hall, 27 February 1952; Downie to Hall, 'A course of action', n.d., in PRO T 230/389.

6 Neild to Downie, 28 February 1952, in PRO T 230/389.

7 Peggy Hemming circulated two papers, one commenting on 26 February on an OF exposition of the plan and one on alternatives to it. Butt circulated five papers in all between 26 and 29 February, attacking 'Jukes' folly' and 'Downie's desperation' and outlining 'Butt's abortion'. On 27 February he suggested boosting exports by putting whopping taxes on whisky and reviving raw material allocations that favoured exporters. Dow's paper on 'Budgetary propects in the light of external decisions' is discussed in chapter 14. All of these are in PRO T 230/389.

not to proceed with the plan. At first there was a lull with some looking back to previous experience of fluctuating exchange rates (Nita Watts) and suggestions for tightening commercial credit by requiring heavy down payments on imports and earlier surrender of export earnings (Robert Neild). Then Butt reported to Hall after a meeting of seven members of the Section that 'we are all very near agreement'. On 14 March he assigned to each of the seven a share in an elaborate work programme, the first fruits of which began to appear in a series of papers a week or so later. Nita Watts was to write on 'What has gone wrong?', Jukes on 'Alternative policies', Dow and Downie on 'Present policy and targets', Butt on 'Pros and cons of the external sterling plan', and Peggy Hemming and Robert Neild on four other topics.

There was some support for Neild's proposal for a sterling union. This was based on the existence of a persistent dollar shortage, convertibility only within the union, each member forswearing the earning of dollars from other members and accepting payment in sterling, and fixed exchange rates in order to avoid the danger of letting rates fall below the optimum and so aggravating the dollar shortage. Limits to creditor and debtor positions would be set by using interest rates and import restrictions, with discrimination against extreme creditors.[8] Hall was uncertain about this proposal and repeated to Butt the worries of MacDougall that the United States could not be expected to take kindly to a trading world pledged openly to discrimination against it, while some possible member countries would be placed in great difficulties if they were denied all possibility of earning dollars in trade with other members.[9]

Drawing on the various proposals advanced by members of the Section, Robert Hall put round a paper on 25 March on 'The future of sterling'.[10] This attacked Robot as a move in the wrong direction, putting excessive faith in price adjustment as a means of recovering trade imbalance. Hall's alternative proposals combined those of Nita Watts and Robert Neild. It thus assumed that some radical change was necessary and it also recognized the risks of letting the exchange rate 'take the strain' under conditions of extreme international imbalance. Automatic gold payments between non-dollar countries would cease,

8 Neild(?) to Hall, 'Sterling union: an alternative to Robot', 20 March 1952; 'Proposals for sterling union', 21 March 1952, in PRO T 230/339.

9 Hall to Butt, 21 March 1952, in PRO T 230/389. Hall had little use for MacDougall's own plan for an Atlantic payments union, which he thought almost as objectionable as Robot and unwise tactically.

10 Hall, 'The future of sterling', 25 March 1952, in PRO T 236/3242.

the EPU would be transformed into an extension of the sterling area, and the non-dollar world would try to insulate itself from the dollar world. Eventually, the two worlds would be reunited with the help of some adjustment in exchange rates. But for the time being, when there was a danger that all the strain of adjustment would be borne by the weaker party, the countries outside the dollar bloc should go their own way together, forswearing the use of dollars in dealing with one another, and offering wider credit margins within a revised and enlarged payments union.

These were not very realistic proposals since the United Kingdom's continental neighbours did not share her acute exchange difficulties and would have been most unlikely to show any enthusiasm for a sterling payments union. They were also based on a false premise: that the reserves would continue to drain away. The Treasury continued to expect the worst and were still expecting the sterling area as a whole to be in deficit in 1952 as late as the end of October. By that time the reserves had been rising slowly for six months and OF had completely revised their Robot plan.

There was no longer to be any blocking of sterling balances and a whole series of conditions and safeguards were now attached to the proposal. A large support fund to supplement the reserves was thought necessary before sterling could be made convertible and the United States would be asked to provide it. It was proposed to move in conjunction with the main European countries (France, Belgium, and Holland in the first instance) and discussions would be necessary with those countries too. Some modification of IMF and GATT arrangements would also be required, involving still more discussions. Other features of the revised plan were that there should be a joint effort to reduce and then remove quantitative restrictions on imports by as many countries as possible, subject to continuing discrimination against persistent creditors; and that 'good creditor' policies on the part of the United States should be a precondition of convertibility.[11]

These proposals, labelled the 'Collective Approach', were tried out on a preparatory Commonwealth Economic Conference (of officials) in October 1952. They had rather a lukewarm reception, some countries attacking the limitation of convertibility to non-residents of the sterling area and others the use of a floating exchange rate. The Economic Section still thought the plan misconceived. It was not true,

11 CEC(O)(HD)(52)1 Final, in Annex II to C(52)373, Report on Finance and Trade of Commonwealth Economic Conference, 15 October 1952, in PRO CAB 129/56.

Robert Hall argued, that existing policies could not continue: the proposal was based on 'an exaggerated view of the necessity for a decisive advance' towards convertibility.[12] Its adoption would allow other countries to earn dollars at Britain's expense by limiting their purchase of British exports and converting the sterling saved into dollars. Sterling area countries would buy more dollar goods and speed up the removal of all quota restrictions. There would be pressure, once a start was made, to move more quickly to full convertibility. But did ministers appreciate how severe would be the measures needed to balance the international accounts in a world of convertible currencies once import restrictions and discrimination faded away?[13]

OF and Bridges, without seeing the point of the question, maintained that tougher internal measures were needed, whatever was done. For Bridges it was 'now or never' in a move towards a freer economy while Rowan was confident that sterling would strengthen, claiming that, according to expert opinion, 'had we gone convertible in March, the pound would now be *above* par'.[14]

The other members of the Section shared Hall's view of the Collective Approach. Some hankered after an Atlantic Payments Union which had been proposed by MacDougall.[15] Neild and Lawler thought that the new plan would break up the sterling area.[16] Of its three main features, non-resident convertibility did not commend itself to the rest of the sterling area, nor continuing discrimination to the United States, nor a floating pound to continental Europe.

After the new proposals had been put in December to a conference of Commonwealth Prime Ministers, Eden and Butler visited the United States to seek support including a large US loan and an IMF stand-by. The American response was that there was simply no possibility that Congress would approve help of this kind and that in their view the move to convertibility was premature. The Europeans disliked being kept in the dark while all these discussions were in progress – all the more when they came to nothing and there was so little to reveal. When at last consulted, they showed no more enthusiasm than the Americans. They welcomed neither the idea of a floating pound nor that of winding up the EPU nor that of giving up

12 Hall to Armstrong (for Chancellor), 'Collective Approach to freer trade and currency systems: misc. papers', 23 October 1952, in PRO T 273/377.
13 ibid.
14 Bridges to Chancellor, 24 October 1952; Rowan to Bridges, 1 November 1952; in PRO T 273/377.
15 Hemming to Hall, 'General objectives of the Commonwealth Economic Conference 1952', 29 August 1952, in PRO T 230/263.
16 Neild and Lawler to Hall, 3 September 1952, in PRO T 230/263.

discrimination against dollar imports. It was to be six more years before full convertibility was established in December 1958 for all the leading European currencies, in a move initiated not by the United Kingdom but by Germany.[17]

The Economic Section was out of sympathy with the manoeuvres of 1952–3 and felt that convertibility was a plunge not to be taken before testing the water. The Bank of England was over-anxious to make the pound convertible and kept preaching the need to 'maintain the momentum' as if that were an object in its own right. The Economic Section, on the other hand, thought it better to begin by removing discriminatory trade restrictions first. This would be more to the liking of Europe, the Commonwealth, and probably also the United States. The restrictions could be removed gradually, as was already happening, while non-resident convertibility was a single act that might incite the sterling area to call for resident convertibility, spend dollars more freely, and put an end to discrimination before the risks involved could be faced with confidence.[18]

The controversy over Robot and the Collective Approach left its mark in later years. The idea of a floating pound had a particular appeal for Conservative ministers, some of whom (including Butler) still favoured it long after Robert Hall had come to oppose it. As late as March 1958 Hall was amused to be called upon by Rowan to do a paper for the Prime Minister (by that time Macmillan) setting out the case against it. Months later, shortly before the pound was made fully convertible, Butler still came down in favour of a float.[19]

The next two years following 1952 were comparatively uneventful. The balance of payments showed a small surplus on current account, the gold and dollar reserves continued to rise slowly until the middle of 1954, and the dollar exchange rate remained consistently above par. The Economic Section debated exchange rate policy without much wish to see an early introduction of convertibility. In June 1953 Ross quoted with approval the view of the Minister of Materials that 'the dollar gap will for a long time be unbridgeable by any measures now adopted or contemplated'.[20] There was little concrete evidence,

17 For the later history of the move to full convertibility see J. J. Kaplan and G. Schleiminger *The European Payments Union* (forthcoming) and J. S. Fforde *The Bank of England 1945–58* (forthcoming).

18 R. R. Neild, 'External economic policy, 1954', in PRO T 230/393.

19 Information from Lord Roberthall.

20 Ross to Hall (?), 'The general economic situation', 23 June 1953, in PRO T 230/402. Less than a year later, Neild expressed a very different judgement: 'within a few years the dollar problem may have vanished' (EC(S)(54)8, 'Supply and demand for US dollars', 20 April 1954, in PRO T 230/342).

however, on how far there was to go to reach convertibility on the side either of trade or of payments.

The Section attempted in 1954 to measure the first part of the gap by estimating the cost in additional imports of removing discrimination against dollar imports. A first estimate by Scott yielded a total of £600 million for the United Kingdom, £100 million for the rest of the sterling area, and a further £700 million for continental Europe. Another estimate by Miss Maton of the Board of Trade gave a lower total of only £280 million for the United Kingdom and £245 million and £525 million under the other headings. These estimates were a great deal higher than one made by Robert Triffin, who suggested an aggregate of £650 million, less than half that of Maurice Scott.[21] A year later Day and Sadler produced a more elaborate calculation, drawing on the work of no less than four committees which had been considering the matter since the summer of 1954. Their estimate, which related exclusively to British trade, showed a total of just over £300 million, consisting of an extra £165 million in imports and a fall of £138 million in exports.[22] This was close to Miss Maton's figure but less than half that given by Scott. Even at £300 million (for British trade alone and without taking account of repercussions), this seemed quite a high price to pay for convertibility, if, as the continentals argued, it spelt an end to discrimination against dollar goods.

By 1954 the Bank of England had concluded that the Collective Approach was stalled and that if progress was to be made it should be through a series of less dramatic moves. They began by seeking agreement in November 1953 to the unification of all non-dollar, non-resident sterling within a single transferable account area, with a view to allowing a regular market to develop in overseas countries in transferable sterling, without the restrictions previously imposed in order to discourage operations in cheap sterling. It was envisaged that the rate at which transferable sterling could be exchanged for dollars would fluctuate below the official rate and that 'occasional intervention' might take place in order to narrow the spread between the two rates. Shortly afterwards this proposal was expanded so as to envisage a 'bridge' period of official intervention to keep the rates closer together,

---

21 EC(S)(54)9, Scott, 'The effect of removing discrimination against dollar countries exports', 21 April 1954, in PRO T 230/342; Dow, 'Cost of removing discrimination against dollar goods', 31 May 1954, in PRO T 230/393.

22 EC(S)(55)6, Day and Sadler, 'Estimates of the effect of removing dollar discrimination', 5 March 1955, in PRO T 230/281. The removal of quantitative restrictions was estimated to add a further £47 million to British imports.

followed by an approach to the IMF and the USA to seek their blessing for an unofficial and informal widening of the spread in the the official rate to $2.75–2.85 instead of $2.78–2.80. This in turn would be succeeded by a coalescence of the official and transferable rates involving *de facto* convertibility (even if it were not so described officially).

Of these proposals the first – unification of the rates for transferable sterling – was accepted in March 1954.[23] A year later, this brought in its train the second – official intervention – when the two rates began to diverge after a period in 1954 when they remained fairly close. But the Treasury was unwilling to accept the rest of the Bank's plan of action when the preconditions of the Collective Approach were still unfulfilled. As a result, the government adopted half the plan and then found itself obliged, by speculative pressure on the one hand and the need to placate European opinion on the other, to repudiate any intention of widening the spread or letting the pound float. The Economic Section woke up in July 1955 to the fact that there was no chance of combining convertibility with a floating rate.

The Section does not appear to have been aware of the Bank's proposal for a wider spread until April 1954 when George Bolton put it forward, declaring himself at the same time against a floating rate, which, he argued, was irrevocable and ruled out the reintroduction of a fixed rate later. This mystified Dow who could see nothing irreversible in a float and suggested that the right course might be to float first and go convertible later.[24] Hall pointed out that Bolton's proposal abandoned the conditions prescribed for the Collective Approach and must be regarded as an alternative to it.[25]

Meanwhile Neild and Little were contemplating some form of European credit union to succeed EPU, which was likely to disappear with convertibility. Neild wanted to clear the way to convertibility by removing controls and relaxing discrimination but was prepared to contemplate action in the first quarter of 1955.[26] When the EPU came

23 The sequence of events in 1954 can be traced in the minutes of a Treasury Committee under Sir B. Gilbert, in PRO T 230/261. In March the American Treasury expected 'a convertibility operation before long'. Talk of convertibility continued in the autumn but died away by December. According to George Bolton, financial markets expected convertibility in September 1954 (meeting under T. L. Rowan, 27 June 1955, in PRO T 236/3942).

24 Dow to Hall, 4 May 1954, in PRO T 230/264.

25 Hall to Gilbert, 5 May 1954, in PRO T 230/264.

26 Neild, 'The problem of reaching convertibility', 26 May 1954, in PRO T 230/393.

up for renewal, the United States would be recovering from the 1954 recession and the pound would be seasonally strong. Little, who, with Dow, had doubts about floating, had even greater doubts about convertibility and suggested letting the pound float down in the near future so as to forestall a move to convertibility from weakness. But he had no expectation that his advice would be taken unless the balance of payments was much weaker: to float without convertibility or non-discrimination would be 'too much of a smack in the eye for IMF'.[27]

Pressure was building up in 1954 to an extent not appreciated. The balance of payments, as was later apparent, had begun to deteriorate. In November 1954 the forecast for 1955 was of a current account surplus of £155 million compared with an expected £210 million in 1954. But by February 1955 the forecast for the year showed a deficit of £70 million, a change of view which contributed to the measures announced by the Chancellor on 24 February 1955 to tighten credit, raise the bank-rate, and reimpose hire-purchase restrictions.

The deterioration had another and more important consequence. On 20 January the Governor pressed once again to be allowed to intervene in the market for transferable sterling. He wanted to hold both the official rate and the rate for transferable sterling within a spread of $2.70 to $2.90 without any formal commitment as to long-term policy.[28] The move was to be represented as 'an instalment of the Collective Approach'; but of course it was nothing of the kind since it neither fulfilled the prior conditions laid down for a move to convertibility nor could it be represented as tentative and reversible and therefore not committing the government. As Heathcoat Amory told the House of Commons in January 1959 when the decision to make sterling convertible *de jure* was under debate:

> Some have argued, I know, that . . . we had freedom to allow the discount to widen in times of strain . . . but, in practice, that freedom has simply not been there. . . . Falls in the transferable rate . . . would have advertised a weakness in sterling.[29]

This was also the view taken at the time in OF. The Governor's proposals, they argued, amounted to convertibility on external account in practice even if there was no legal obligation to merge dollar and

27 Little to Hall, 26 November 1954, in PRO T 230/393.
28 'Sterling exchange rate policy and convertibility 1955', memorandum by the Governor, 20 January 1955, in PRO T 236/3941A.
29 H. of C. Debates, vol. 598, col. 1083, 28 January 1959.

non-dollar accounts. The world would interpret the move as one implying convertibility and there would in consequence be such pressure that the formal distinction would soon vanish.[30] Nevertheless the question whether the Governor's proposals were tantamount to convertibility *de facto* continued to be debated within the Treasury and the Bank well into the summer.[31] The Governor's view at the time of the move was that it was from 70 per cent convertibility to 80 per cent convertibility.[32] The Treasury thought of it very differently.

What had moved the Governor to put forward his proposals? He recognized that the Collective Approach provided no basis for action in the next twelve months. But he was concerned that the payments system was lagging behind in comparison with the freedom enjoyed in trade, commodity, and other markets and he wanted action that would allow sterling to hold its own in competition with other currencies. The root trouble was the re-emergence of cheap sterling and commodity shunting. The scale of operations in transferable sterling at rates well below the official rate was difficult to estimate but it was thought to be between £1½ and £3 million per day. Transactions financed in cheap sterling, he maintained, not only gave foreign traders a competitive advantage but reduced the flow of hard currency into the reserves.[33]

The initial Treasury reaction was unfavourable. A meeting between the Economic Secretary (Edward Boyle), Bridges, Gilbert, and Rowan concluded that 'there were strong grounds, economic and political, against proceeding with the programme of action' suggested by the Governor.[34]

For OF it was largely a matter of timing. They wanted internal measures to strengthen the balance of payments before any action was taken on the exchanges. But, after the election that lay ahead or, alternatively, towards the end of the year, the Governor's proposals might provide a suitable transition to convertibility. In the mean time the Bank should be allowed to intervene in the transferable sterling

30 'Exchange rate policy', memorandum on the Governor's proposals by T. L. Rowan, 10 February 1955, in PRO T 273/379.
31 'Sterling exchange rate policy and convertibility 1955', meeting between Chancellor, Governor, and others, 24 June 1955, in PRO T 236/3942.
32 Governor to Chancellor, 24 February 1955, in PRO T 236/3941A.
33 'Sterling exchange rate policy and convertibility 1955', memorandum by the Governor, 20 January 1955, in PRO T 236/3941A.
34 Annex A to Rowan's memorandum of 10 February: minutes of meeting on 27 January 1955, in PRO T 273/379.

market without seeking to maintain any fixed relationship with the official rate.[35]

OF were in no doubt that intervention in the transferable exchange market would create a presumption in favour of fixed rates but did not 'attach any decisive importance to this point'.[36] They recognized also that Europe would offer more support if the United Kingdom pressed for fixed rather than flexible rates of exchange.[37] But at this stage there was no suggestion that the rate would remain fixed after convertibility. Nor was it proposed to block sterling balances or revert to the use of import controls.

Robert Hall's reaction to the Governor's proposals is expressed in a minute to Bridges on 10 February 1955:

> I always find it difficult to see how the damage, whatever it is, from the operations in transferable sterling can be alleviated by measures tending to make such sterling more convertible. . . . If people think dollars are better at $2.72 surely they will think so even more if dollars become cheaper.

To support the transferable rate without being strong enough to sustain it, he went on, 'would be like living extravagantly in order to reassure the tradesmen about their unpaid bills'. How was it possible to reconcile the proposals with the Governor's view that sterling was undervalued?[38]

This was very different from the language used by OF, with whom, in other respects, Hall now saw eye to eye. He wanted full convertibility, not some half-way house; and he wanted to move from strength, not weakness. He was in agreement, therefore, that internal measures were required in order to correct the balance of payments position before action was taken on the exchanges. He did not, however, see any need for drastic measures such as the Chancellor appeared to envisage, and was doubtful of the government's ability to select them. The world of international finance would be more impressed by evidence of a steady and continuing determination on the

---

35 Memorandum by T. L. Rowan, 10 February 1955, in PRO T 273/379.

36 Rowan, memorandum of 10 February 1955, in PRO T 273/379.

37 'External economic policy', memorandum by Rowan submitted by Bridges to Chancellor, 27 May 1955, in PRO T 236/3941A.

38 Hall to Bridges, 10 February 1955, in PRO T 273/379. Ian Little, advising Hall to resist intervention tooth and nail, dismissed the Governor's proposals as 'frightening the patient with threats of a heart attack in order to get him to agree to take a drug that will give him one' (Little to Hall, 11 February 1955, in PRO T 230/394).

part of the monetary authorities than by measures implying the need for violent corrective action. Relatively mild measures on a number of fronts would suffice and would both make concessions in the budget more defensible and give them less the appearance of a political manoeuvre. The measures he proposed were partly monetary: the bank rate should be raised and the higher rate made effective; long-term borrowing from abroad on the London market should be reduced; some active collaboration in credit control from the Bank of England was necessary and there should be 'regular and full consultation' between the Bank and the Treasury on credit and exchange rate policy. Other measures were more direct: a cut in agricultural and housing subsidies; an increase in coal prices; the reintroduction of hire-purchase restrictions. If all this were done, 'there might still be room for some budgetary relaxation'.[39]

His support for early convertibility rested, however, on acceptance of 'some form of floating rate'. He was concerned that the instruments of economic management were gradually narrowing down to the exchange rate, the budget, and credit policy. None of these could be abandoned. As Butler put it to George Humphrey in December 1953, how could the freedom of the economy be sustained 'without some of the old-fashioned methods and in particular without the advantage of a flexible rate'?[40]

At a meeting on 7 February with the Chancellor, the Governor reiterated a request he had made in his memorandum to be allowed to consult close friends in the market and his fellow Governors at the BIS meeting in Basle on 12 February. It was objected that such discussions would prejudice the government's freedom of action as against a régime in which there were no announced limits to the movement in exchange rates. The Bank doubted whether there could be complete freedom when 'the whole movement of thought and opinion had been towards greater stability' of exchange rates. A 6 per cent spread would give adequate market latitude and would be unlikely, in the Bank's view, to carry sterling below $2.75. They would like to indicate to the Managing Board of the EPU the size of the spread as a working hypothesis, not binding on any future government, so as to allow the EPU to take it into account in their consideration of the problems that

---

39 'Miscellaneous economic papers 1955', Hall to Bridges, 10 February 1955, and Hall to Bridges, 18 February 1955, in PRO T 273/317.

40 'Miscellaneous economic papers 1953–54', meeting between Chancellor and George Humphrey at 11 Downing Street, 16 December 1953, in PRO T 273/316.

would arise once two or three currencies became convertible.[41]

The issues raised at this meeting proved to be more troublesome than those who attended it foresaw. The proposal for a 6 per cent spread soon became widely known; the Governor himself told the Chancellor on 24 June that 'the idea was current in Paris that we were thinking of 6 per cent'.[42] A leading article in the *Financial Times* on 11 July contrasted the progressive attitude of the Bank of England with the obscurantism of the Treasury on exchange policy in terms that left little doubt as to its inspiration and the source of its information.[43] The Treasury became convinced that the Bank was deliberately leaking information in order to put pressure on the government. Meanwhile speculation against the pound reached dangerous proportions. If the pound was to be allowed to fluctuate within wider limits and remained weak, it could only go down and reward bear speculators.

A second development was equally important. The discussions in OEEC as to what was to follow the EPU put pressure on the government to keep the permitted spread within narrow limits. In the process, the idea of a freely floating exchange rate gradually disappeared from sight. The government, caught in the tangles of a 6 per cent spread and the speculation it provoked, ended up with *de facto* convertibility at a fixed rate – something it had never planned to adopt.

But this is to anticipate. After authorizing discussion of the Governor's proposal in Basle, the Chancellor remained undecided. The Governor informed him on 17 February that a bear position in sterling was building up and that he might have to act quickly. A few days later he estimated the drain from the reserves in February at $65–100 million.[44] This seems to have satisfied Butler of the need to act. It was now a month since he had received the Governor's memorandum. On 22 February he told the Cabinet that he would be submitting proposals 'at an early date' to deal with 'trafficking in transferable sterling through commodity operations which affect the strength of the pound'.[45]

---

41 Minutes of meeting in Chancellor's room on 7 February 1955, in PRO T 273/379. The meeting was attended by the Economic Secretary and officials from the Bank and Treasury (including Robert Hall).

42 Meeting at the Treasury of Chancellor, Governor, and others on 24 June 1955, in PRO T 236/3942.

43 *Financial Times*, 11 July 1955. Later in the month, on 19 July, Sir Roy Harrod weighed in with a letter to the editor of the *Financial Times* arguing against a wider spread.

44 Minute of meeting between Chancellor, Governor, and others on 21 February 1955, in PRO T 273/379.

45 CM(55)16M, 22 February 1955, in PRO CAB 128/28.

A day later he put to the Cabinet orally a number of proposals of which only one, for an increase in the price of coal, gave rise to much debate. The proposal to make use of the Exchange Equalization Account to support the rate for transferable sterling was hardly discussed. This step, Butler explained,

> was not designed as a further step towards convertibility of sterling. The Cabinet should understand, however, that it would have the effect of bringing the transferable rate more nearly into line with the official rate and, to that extent, would make it easier, when the time came, to take the next step forward towards full convertibility.[46]

There is no indication that this highly disingenuous defence of a very dubious move was accompanied by any explanation of the importance of the matter, or by any reason why it should be decided at a moment's notice, or by any reference to the doubts expressed by some of his Treasury advisers.

Although intervention in support of the transferable rate had been sanctioned, no mention was made of a wider spread. Neither the Bank nor OF felt that matters could be left where they were. OF prepared a long memorandum submitted by Bridges to the Chancellor just after the election in May arguing that the best course would be to adopt 'strong internal policies' and use the time before their effects became visible to enter into negotiations for convertibility, which could be introduced after the period of seasonal weakness in the autumn.[47]

The Bank still held to the proposals they had made in January. On 24 June the Governor pressed for a widening of the spread and the unification of official and transferable rates before the EPU came up for renewal.[48] The Chancellor asked whether such action was not tantamount to convertibility, whether it did not constitute devaluation, and whether it was necessary in the interests of multilateral settlements. He was assured by the Governor that the answer in each case was 'no'. Technically Cobbold may have been right but in a broad sense the answer is more doubtful.

Acceptance of the Governor's proposal, as Rowan pointed out, would have meant the end of EPU and the abandonment of the Collective Approach. It would also have exposed the government to

---

46 CM(55)17M, 23 February 1955, in PRO CAB 128/28.
47 'External economic policy', memorandum with annexes by T. L. Rowan, 27 May 1955, in PRO T 273/317.
48 Meeting of Chancellor, Governor, and officials, 24 June 1955, in PRO T 236/3942.

the charge of bad faith since the Chancellor, in addressing the OEEC, 'had clearly pointed to no early action on convertibility'. The negotiations in progress in the OEEC over the credit arrangements that would apply on the termination of the EPU might have to start all over again. If all the work already done was thus upset by unilateral action on the part of the United Kingdom, European governments would be greatly disconcerted and the Chancellor's position as chairman of the OEEC would be seriously shaken.[49]

Central to the whole argument was the future of the European Payments Union. It was agreed in OEEC at the end of June 1955, with the Chancellor in the chair, that it should continue for another year if necessary but terminate at once if countries accounting for 50 per cent of total quotas made their currencies convertible. In anticipation of this, a scheme for multilateral settlements in the absence of EPU was being worked out and a statement would have to be made in Paris on the limits within which sterling would be free to vary. The Bank of England wanted to see an end to the EPU and 'patched up solutions' that kept it in being. If the Governor's proposal were adopted, that would settle the matter. If not, the continental countries would not be prepared to work a scheme unless the spread in rates were narrow.[50]

The Chancellor deferred a decision for a week, pointing out that it would be necessary to put the matter to the Cabinet, the Commonwealth, and the IMF. So far as Paris was concerned, it would be sufficient to promise to consider the needs of an acceptable scheme in deciding on the spread.[51] A memorandum on exchange rate policy was prepared by Rowan in consultation with Gilbert, Brittain, and Hall and submitted on 29 June. It opposed the immediate adoption of the Governor's proposal for reasons given on pp. 312–13, recommended consultation with the Commonwealth in September at the annual meeting of the IMF, and called for 'strict internal measures to improve the balance of payments . . . so that we can move to convertibility and

---

49 'Exchange rate policy', memorandum by OF, 29 June 1955, in PRO T 236/3942. It was also pointed out that the proposed moves might be construed as a device to allow discrimination against the dollar to continue after convertibility and might encourage discrimination by other countries against sterling. If the exchange rate opened under $2.78, suspicion of an impending devaluation would revive.

50 Discussion on exchange rate policy between Chancellor, Governor, and others, 24 June 1955, in PRO T 236/3242.

51 ibid.

a flexible rate'. In view of developments in July the last three words are of some importance.[52]

The Governor's proposals were not adopted. The Chancellor was convinced by Hugh Ellis Rees, who was brought over from Paris, that there was no possibility of getting international agreement to a scheme on the lines of the Governor's proposals. Butler thought it wiser to stick to the Collective Approach, to move forward by degrees, and to tighten up the domestic economy before making any change in exchange rate policy. The Governor, with considerable prescience, foresaw a danger 'of our getting into the position of being convertible on a fixed rate, which was not a position which really suited us'. We might drift along with existing arrangements and then 'have to make a statement that we were not contemplating any change . . . for a considerable time'.[53] Speculation, he predicted, would continue until the government's final policy was announced. Internal measures would not by themselves restore stability until plans for a wider spread were 'clarified'.[54]

Meanwhile the rate for transferable sterling had been held for several months within about 1 per cent or less of the rate for official sterling. As the summer advanced the official rate became the subject of speculative pressure. At the beginning of July there were rumours of impending devaluation.[55] The impression gained ground in banking circles that the government had agreed to let the Bank of England do what it had long wanted to do and make the pound convertible. The United Kingdom had expressly sought the right to withdraw from the EPU if sterling became convertible in the next twelve months. More important had been the argument over the size of the spread and suggestions at OEEC that the pound might be allowed to float, presumably downwards. As the rumours grew, the Chancellor had at first refused to deny this possibility. But on 26 July he made a statement repudiating it:

> There is no doubt about the policy of the Government in relation to the exchange value of sterling. . . . It has been and will continue to

52 'Exchange rate policy', memorandum by OF (and agreed without reservation by Gilbert, Brittain, Hall, and Rowan), 29 June 1955, in PRO T 236/3242.

53 Minute of meeting between Chancellor, Governor, and others on 7 July 1955, in PRO T 236/3942.

54 Minute of discussion between Governor and Bridges, 30 June 1955, in PRO T 236/3242.

55 E. C. Kahn to France, 7 July 1955, in PRO T 236/3242.

be the maintenance of the exchange parity of 2.80 dollars to the £, either in existing circumstances or when sterling is convertible.[56]

The statement followed a series of Treasury drafts, all of which took for granted the need for a wider, publicly announced, spread in rates: at first, $2.70–2.90, then 3 or perhaps 2 per cent either side of $2.80, and finally 3 per cent. A note on exchange rate policy by Rowan on 21 July called for a public statement by the Chancellor that the rate would be held within limits of 3 per cent on either side of parity.[57] No such statement was made. The Chancellor refrained from making any reference to wider spreads.

It was not until 26 July that Robert Hall became aware of Rowan's note of 21 July and exploded. There could be no reason for confidence that the rate could be held within so small a distance of $2.80 after convertibility. Officials had reported that the ending of non-discrimination, a concomitant of convertibility, would put up dollar expenditure by the sterling area by £200–300 million. So the rate would be subject to a heavy strain, unrelieved by American policy since the United States was unlikely to go on pumping out dollars in military aid. 'In effect,' he argued, 'we have decided to adopt free trade and the international value of sterling as objectives instead of the maintenance of the level of economic activity.' With import controls abandoned and discrimination on the way out, to give up exchange adjustment would leave everything to be done by internal deflation.[58]

Two days later he returned to the charge. It was OF that had always insisted on the need to preserve flexibilty of exchange rates if the pound were made convertible. The Bank and OF had felt the need for some guarantee against deflation with convertibility and had found it in floating. In November 1952 the original exposition of the Collective Approach had stated that 'there would be no intention of establishing a range of a fixed amount above or below the present parity within which the rate would be held in all circumstances'. The move seemed to him 'to have taken away the one thing that makes convertibility in the near future desirable, namely exchange freedom'. 'If my fears are realised,' he went on, 'we shall more and more be faced with

56 For the rumours and press comment on them see Dow, J. C. R. (1964), *The Management of the British Economy 1945–60*, Cambridge: Cambridge University Press for National Institute of Economic and Social Research, pp. 87–90.

57 'Sterling exchange rate: policy and convertibility', Rowan to Bridges *et al.*, 21 July 1955, in PRO T 236/3942.

58 Hall to Bridges, 26 July 1955, in PRO T 236/3942.

something that is a devaluation, with all the unpleasant circumstances attending it, instead of a movement of a rate to which we were not pledged.'[59] It was a note that he struck repeatedly in the months that followed. In September, for example, he was asking 'are we prepared to face convertibility with no mechanism left to deal with balance of payments crises?'[60]

By the end of July the Chancellor was beginning to feel that he and Bridges must 'have it out with Mr Governor'.[61] He was doubly irritated with Cobbold, both as the suspected source of damaging rumours about sterling and as the purveyor in the past of bad advice. Reflecting on the arguments put to him, he found them troublingly circular. In order to maintain confidence, we must keep moving forward. The only possible move on the exchange front, his Treasury advisers insisted, was convertibility from strength and the move should be made only from strength. But 'strength' implied internal economic measures so strict that the Cabinet would never approve them. Hence no further move forward was possible for an indefinite period.[62]

In August, with rumours of devaluation persisting, the Chancellor had a long discussion with the Governor at Knebworth. The Governor maintained that there would have to be 'either a convertibility operation within the next six months or a devaluation'.[63] But no further action was taken. The Chancellor took pains in Istanbul to convince Finance Ministers one by one that no change in policy was in prospect and made a statement in terms even more emphatic than that of 26 July.[64] No further attempt to introduce *de jure* convertibility was made until 1958; and it was accepted that when it came it would be at a fixed rate.

The convertibility debate did not, however, end in 1955. The rate for transferable sterling was held at a discount of about 1 per cent below parity, sometimes by intervention to sell sterling on the market

---

59 Hall to Bridges, 29 July 1955, in PRO T 236/3942.
60 Note by R. L. Hall, 5 September 1955, in PRO T 273/379.
61 Bancroft to Bridges, 30 July 1955, in PRO T 273/317.
62 Petch to Bridges, 29 July 1955, in PRO T 273/317.
63 Minute of Chancellor's discussions with Governor, 11 August 1955, in PRO T 273/379.
64 He told the IMF, 'My Government has taken no decision upon the timing of the convertibility of sterling nor upon the nature of the exchange arrangements after that date. . . . All discussion and rumours about impending changes of the parity, or margins for sterling, are both unrealistic and irrelevant.' (Speech to IMF.)

for transferable sterling and so keep the two rates apart, sometimes by selling dollars to reduce the margin between them.[65] The Governor, arguing that 'the present arrangement . . . is something of a nonsense', called for action to bring the two rates together in April 1956, and again in 1957 and 1958; but nothing was done.[66] There were also recurrent proposals in favour of wider spreads or floating.[67] But the time for both had passed. Hall, asked what he thought of floating in July 1957, wanted 'resolute action' to avoid it. The government should fight as hard as possible to hold the rate since to do otherwise would be taken as an admission that it had given up the struggle against inflation.[68]

In the discussions before the final move to convertibility in December 1958 there was no disagreement at the official level. When Rowan suggested in August a move before the end of the year neither the Bank nor the Economic Section showed any enthusiasm. Hall was opposed to convertibility so long as an American depression was in the offing, even if it offered little protection, while the Bank would have preferred to wait until the spring. Later, however, the Economic Section, the Bank, and OF all wanted action before Parliament rose for Christmas. It was ministers who remained hesitant until France and Germany both pressed for an early move for their own reasons.

In the years after 1955 external economic policy was increasingly concerned with relations with Europe. Before the signature of the Treaty of Rome in March 1957 efforts were made to establish a free trade area that would include the six members of the European Economic Community but would be confined to manufactured products and would exclude agriculture. Members of the Economic Section took an active part in the formulation of the proposal but were not its authors. To trace in any detail the contribution of the Section to this and other moves towards closer economic unity in Europe would be a difficult task. We must leave for later research the role of the Section in such matters, recognizing that the economic element in the issues involved was often subordinate to political considerations.

65 WM(56)9, 11 September 1956, in PRO T 236/4363; Boyle to Bridges, 13 August 1956, in PRO T 273/312.
66 Governor to Chancellor, 12 April 1956 and 30 May 1957, in PRO T 236/3940.
67 In July 1956, for example, Erhard suggested a spread of 5 per cent on either side of parity (Erhard to Chancellor, 3 July 1956, in PRO T 273/312). In August 1957 he wanted a period of floating rates as a preliminary to a realignment of currencies (*Financial Times*, 21 August 1957).
68 Hall to Rowan, 9 July 1957, in PRO T 236/4364.

# Chapter nineteen

# INCOMES POLICY

The danger of inflation had been a principal concern of the Stamp Survey in 1939–40 and it continued to preoccupy the Economic Section. From the beginning they recognized that there were two ways in which inflation might arise according as it originated on the side of demand as excess demand or on the side of supply in the form of rising costs of labour and materials. Once prices began to rise, both kinds of inflationary pressure were likely to come into play, a rising cost of living provoking wage claims, and higher wages in turn adding to costs and the pressure of demand. Price control might hold in check the pressure on the cost of living exerted by excess demand, and subsidies might offset higher costs attributable to rising import prices. But what of wages in a world of full employment? How were they to be prevented from rising steadily once organized labour awoke to its much enhanced bargaining power? And, if wages rose faster than productivity, would not price control become futile or subsidies impossibly high?

In wartime it was also necessary to find a way of reducing the claims of wage-earners on resources needed for the war effort without provoking the wage claims to which higher prices would normally lead and without weakening the incentive to produce. These results were obtained by a combination of taxation, post-war credits, and rationing, and by a diversion of consumer spending towards goods with a high tax content. Of these devices, the Economic Section attached special importance to an extension of rationing. Patriotism, persuasion, and the threat of direction were sufficient to resolve the further problem of attracting more manpower to the munitions industries from unemployment, household duties, and work of lower priority.

The first papers on wages policy by members of the Economic Section appeared early in 1941 at a time when issues of post-war reconstruction were just beginning to emerge. Both Dennison and Robbins circulated papers entitled 'Wage policy' early in March 1941 and in April Meade introduced the subject into the final version of his paper on 'The prevention of general unemployment'.[1]

Robbins argued that it was futile to think either of reducing wages or of imposing a wage stop. It was impossible to prevent wages from following the cost of living upwards. In any event, it was positively desirable to raise wages in industries short of manpower since cuts in other industries were ruled out and without changes in wage relationships labour mobility would suffer. In his view, what was wanted was a cost of living stop. Labour had not 'behaved badly' since the outbreak of war (although he quoted no figures); and, if cost of living increases could be eliminated, this would wipe out 'most of the influences which make for a vicious spiral'. Subsidies alone would not accomplish this – 'a policy of *unlimited* subsidy is clearly absurd'. Retail prices should be stabilized by limiting consumption; and, since there were limits to what taxation could do, 'a very considerable extension of rationing' was indispensable.

For adjustments in relative wages Robbins thought that there was a strong case for 'a general wages tribunal'. But of course all adjustments in wages are in fact relative, so that the scope of such a tribunal could be very wide and elastic. What Robbins had in mind, however, was 'a number of *ad hoc* revisions, here and now, where the differences are obviously wrong', leaving the rest to the existing machinery of negotiation and arbitration. With this reservation, Robbins had no wish to change the policies of the Ministry of Labour and looked instead to other initiatives via taxation and rationing.

Dennison's papers were more concerned with analysis of trends than with policy. He emphasized the divergence between rates and earnings that we have since learned to call 'drift', and insisted that policy had to be in terms of rates, not earnings. There were strong tendencies for earnings to increase because of overtime and simplification of

---

1 EC(S)(41)15, and EC(S)(41)18, 'Wage policy', memorandum by Professor Dennison, 17 February 1941 and 7 March 1941; EC(S)(41)19, memorandum by Professor Robbins, 3 March 1941; EC(S)(41)23, 'The interrelation of wages, prices and consumption', memorandum by Professor Dennison and Professor Robbins, 26 March 1941; and EC(S)(41)22, 2nd Revise, 'The prevention of general unemployment', memorandum by Professor Meade, 30 April 1941; all in PRO T 230/13.

processes, while rates were simultaneously inflated by sliding scales or by wage claims justified by the movement in the cost of living. Neither rates nor earnings were such as to promote the transfer of labour (or at least of female labour) to war work that was urgently needed. Like Robbins, Dennison wanted stabilization of the cost of living, reinforced by financial measures, and supplemented by 'controlled [wage] increases where necessary' in the interests of labour mobility.

When Robbins and Dennison put round a joint, revised paper its conclusions were not greatly altered, but rather milder. The wages tribunal had disappeared in favour of 'a special review of relative wages'. Appropriate increases would then be made through 'the ordinary mechanism of industrial negotiation'. As for wages in non-essential industries, perhaps after all a 'stop' might be considered or, preferably, a tax might be imposed on employment.

Meade's treatment of the subject, which was brief, was in terms not of labour mobility but of employment policy. The question for him, looking ahead to the post-war world, was whether wage policy could play a significant part in reducing unemployment. He admitted that there could be circumstances in which wage cuts in a particular area or industry would add to employment. There was also a danger that, if money wage rates were increased as unemployment fell, 'a vicious spiral of inflation might result' and cause the effort to reduce unemployment to be abandoned. But he gave no indication that measures might be taken to check or prevent the increase in wages.

Over the next three years discussion in the Economic Section on wages policy arose mainly in the context in which Meade had treated it; the threat of excessive wage increases under conditions of full employment. Informal talks took place between Robbins and Sir Frank Tribe of the Ministry of Labour in 1942 on the basis of a draft for submission by the Ministry to an interdepartmental committee on post-war problems. The first draft came down firmly in favour of free collective bargaining after the war but did not discuss wage policy in relation to the avoidance of post-war unemployment. However, a new section dealing with this aspect of the matter and based on a note by Robbins was added in the draft circulated in June 1942. This concluded that 'a moderate wage policy is a *sine qua non* of a successful anti-depression policy'.[2] It drew attention to the value of compulsory arbitration, if acceptable to both sides, in securing greater stability, and

2 Quoted by Jones, Russell (1987) *Wages and Employment Policy*, London: Allen & Unwin, p. 21.

the need to avoid indexation of wages. Unusually in a Ministry of Labour document, it accepted that if wages rose too fast, state control of wages might have to be imposed.[3]

This document elicited a response from Meade and Dennison along the lines of their 1941 papers, Meade repeating his fears and Dennison his faith in educating opinion. Marcus Fleming took a more radical line. Guidelines on wage settlements should be 'avoided like the plague'. Instead he argued for a voluntary or, if necessary, a statutory upper limit on wage increases of, say, 5 per cent per annum, combined with dividend limitation and anti-monopoly legislation. This proposal found some support from Meade who saw it as a way of stopping 'monopolistic wage-earners [from] preventing the proper development of employment'. He also suggested job evaluation as a possible way of overcoming wage control in detail. The Treasury at this stage was more inclined to look for a remedy in straight deflation.[4]

In 1943 the Section prepared a paper for the Cabinet Committee on Reconstruction Priorities, dealing mainly with employment policy, but touching on the danger of wage inflation. This emphasized the need for linking the rate of wage increases to the growth of productivity in order to keep prices stable, but raised the possibility of an imposed limit such as Fleming had suggested, with the threat of abandonment of full employment if wages rose too fast.[5]

The Section's paper, when the matter was considered in the Cabinet, led to the setting up of a Steering Committee under Sir Richard Hopkins to report on post-war employment and its report in turn was the basis of the White Paper on *Employment Policy*.[6] The report drew on a memorandum by Robbins submitted in December 1943 based on the earlier work of the Economic Section.[7] It highlighted the choice between price stability and full employment if wages rose too fast, but rejected central control of wages or a ceiling to wage increases in arbitration awards on account of the political and administrative difficulties involved. Free collective bargaining should first be given a trial.

The White Paper, issued in the middle of the biggest strikes in the war, took an optimistic line. It invited workers to 'examine their trade practices and customs to ensure that . . . they do not defeat the object

3 ibid.
4 ibid., p. 22.
5 ibid., p. 23; PR(43)26, 'The maintenance of employment', 18 May 1943, in PRO CAB 87/13. On this and what follows see chapter 6 above.
6 *Employment Policy*, Cmd 6527, 1944.
7 Jones, op. cit., p. 25.

of a full employment policy'. Employers and workers must 'exercise moderation in wage matters' and allow increased expenditure to swell employment rather than prices, especially if unemployment was rising and an expansionary policy was being followed. Changes in relative wages should be such as to promote the movement of labour to places and industries where labour was scarce but should not set off a general inflation of wages. The government for its part would try to hold the cost of living as steady as possible and continue to use subsidies for this purpose but without commitment to complete stability. It was up to employers and employed to play their part and 'consider together all possible means' of keeping internal costs from rising. The commitment to 'a high and stable level of employment' was explicitly conditional on such a response. Although this was not inconsistent with the views of Meade and Robbins, it may reflect more strongly the intervention of Sir Hubert Henderson, who was concerned with the threat that full employment might pose to the balance of payments and the exchange rate, and foresaw a danger that devaluation might provoke a wage–price spiral.[8]

Thus the commitment to full employment in the White Paper was doubly limited: by its reluctance to contemplate a continuing budget deficit and by its insistence on 'moderation in wage matters' as a precondition. On the precondition the Economic Section would not have dissented. Robbins hoped that in the end the unions would learn habits of responsibility and believed that detailed wage controls by government would do more harm than good. Meade was less optimistic and feared for a breakdown of the full employment policy. Fleming continued to look to the 'imposition of centrally defined maximum wage norms' as the only solution.

During the post-war years nearly all the ideas that have since emerged in the efforts of successive governments to find a workable incomes policy were advanced by members of the Economic Section or by others in Whitehall. There were those who took the white paper line that all should 'work together to keep the level of internal costs down' while the government 'supported by the co-operation of all sections of the public' did its best to prevent 'temporary and considerable rises in the cost of living' by providing subsidies.[9] This implied a policy of education and persuasion but with no active intervention in wage disputes or direct measures to stabilize wages. Such a policy might (and did) lead to the issue of white papers setting

8 ibid., pp. 26–7.
9 *Employment Policy*, Cmd 6527, 1944; para. 16(b).

out for the guidance of both sides of industry the principles that should be followed in the interests of price stability: for example that wages should rise no faster than productivity. Later, this line of thought was to lead to the propounding of a 'guiding light' for wage increases.

Policies of this kind had no sanctions behind them. But the government might convey to the trade unions a threat of inaction in the face of growing unemployment if wages rose too fast. Conceivably, it might announce a target for the growth of money GDP and leave the unions to choose whether this would support full employment at a sustainable rate of increase in wages or force down the level of employment if wages rose faster and cut into the growth of real GDP. Such a policy would have required more flexibility in government expenditure than proved possible under post-war conditions. It also attributed to the unions a novel power (and inclination) to take united action on behalf of the unemployed.

Another line of thought was to make use of advisory bodies (such as the National Joint Advisory Council or the Council for Prices, Productivity and Incomes or the National Incomes Commission) to make pronouncements on how wages should behave and perhaps also enforce their pronouncements under statutory powers. Such proposals usually assumed that the trade unions would be represented on the advisory body and would bow to its authority.

The question of sanctions was not at first much discussed nor was the idea of taking statutory powers. The devices more commonly suggested were to disallow excessive wage increases where there was price control or to penalize firms granting such increases in the placing of government contracts or to impose a tax on employment in the industry concerned.

The discussion usually focused on long-term issues of principle while action was invariably a response *ad hoc* to some immediate problem. The main debates, except in 1945, took place during or in the wake of a crisis such as that of 1947 or 1949 and the action taken was explicitly temporary in character – usually a wage-freeze of some kind.

The post-war discussion opens with a 'very short' memorandum on 'Wages policy and unemployment', drafted by James Meade in May 1945 at the request of Sir Alan Barlow for circulation by the Ministry of Labour to its local branches.[10] The danger of wage inflation under full employment was, in his view, 'a very real one' and might threaten the whole policy of maintaining demand. The rule that Meade suggested for wage-fixing was that, where there was unemployment in

10 Meade, diary, 13 May 1945.

an industry, claims for wage increases should be discouraged and in industries that were short of labour they should be permitted (within reason). Ideally, wages would rise at a rate that matched the growth of productivity so that prices and employment would remain stable.[11]

A few months later, after the Labour government took office, an interdepartmental working party was set up by Bridges to report on wages policy.[12] A paper was prepared by Richard Sayers (then Deputy Director) after discussion within the Section and submitted to the working party in February 1946.[13] This concentrated on the role that education and persuasion could play in wage policy. 'Experience in war-time', Sayers wrote, 'encourages the belief that much can be done by general education and persuasion of the trade union movement.' General statements should be issued outlining the limits for non-inflationary wage claims and factual briefs should be released as background for those engaged in wage negotiations of special importance. It was for consideration whether wage-induced increases in costs should be accommodated by matching increases in food subsidies.

When the working party was preparing its report, Meade helped to persuade it to include a reference to a 'national industrial conference' as a means of improving general understanding by workers and employers of the implications of a full employment policy.[14] When the report was considered by ministers the only concrete results were the reconstitution of the wartime National Joint Advisory Council to fulfil this role and the issue of a rather tame White Paper. Morrison, however, echoing a brief from Meade, summed up by recording as 'the general view' that there was likely to be a need as time went on 'for the Government to take a more positive part in shaping wages policy'.[15]

Food subsidies, as we have seen, were viewed differently by ministers and their advisers. By 1947 they had risen to £1 million per day and they accounted for half the budget deficit in 1946–7.[16] The

11 Meade, 'Wages policy and employment', 1 March 1945, in PRO T 230/111.
12 Meade, diary, 13 January 1946; Official Working Party on Wages Policy, PRO CAB 124/783.
13 EC(S)(41)14, and W(46)3, R. S. Sayers, 'Wages policy', 26 February 1946, in PRO T 230/20.
14 Meade, diary, 23 June 1946.
15 Meade to Lord President, 27 March 1946, in CAB 124/783. See also Max Nicholson, 'A national industrial conference', 20 July 1946, in PRO T 230/111 and LP(46)11, 29 March 1946, in PRO CAB 132/1.
16 Pliatzky, Sir Leo (1982) Getting and Spending, Oxford: Blackwell, p. 2.

Economic Section had come to attach more significance to their budgetary cost, their distorting impact on the price structure, and their sapping of employers' resistance to wage claims, than to any compensating effect they might have on the claims themselves. The redistribution effect of the subsidies, to which ministers attached such importance, could be better obtained through family allowances and cuts in indirect taxation.[17]

The Section was also convinced that the cost of living index, which it was the purpose of the subsidies to hold steady, was not only quite out-of-date but would be under increasing attack as a misleading measure of the rise in prices. If a new index was introduced, as the Section urged, it would then be necessary to step up the subsidies if the aim of price stability was to be fulfilled.[18] In the early summer of 1947 a new index was introduced and the Chancellor announced a modification of policy under which the aim of the subsidies would be, not to hold the index steady, but to exert 'a stabilising influence on prices'.

Ministers continued to discuss wages policy throughout 1946 with Shinwell and Bevan arguing for state participation in wage agreements and the majority of the Cabinet reluctant to abandon free collective bargaining. The Steering Committee presented a lengthy report in December 1946 to the group of ministers under Morrison in charge of economic planning.[19] Two months later, in February 1947, they submitted an abbreviated version putting more emphasis on long-term objectives and in particular on the need for a flexible wage structure.[20]

Meade, as a member of the Steering Committee, took part in the preparation of these reports. The line that he took is evident from his brief to the Lord President in December 1946 when the first of the two reports from the Steering Committee was about to be considered. 'The peculiar difficulties of wage policy', he told Morrison, were 'due in large measure to . . . general inflationary pressure'. It was essential 'to do everything that was feasible to move towards a condition of greater

17 Meade to Lord President, 'Wages policy and the cost of living', 31 October 1946, in PRO CAB 124/785; Meade to Lord President, 24 December 1946, in PRO CAB 124/898.

18 Nita Watts to Lord President, 'Proposal to reconstitute the Cost of Living Advisory Committee', 1 August 1946, in PRO CAB 21/2260.

19 MEP(46)17, 'Wages and prices policy and means of carrying out planning decisions', report by the Steering Committee, 21 December 1946, in PRO CAB 134/503.

20 MEP(47)4, 'Wages policy', report by the Steering Committee, 21 February 1947, in PRO CAB 134/503.

balance between supply and demand', for example by reducing food subsidies.[21] Meade's emphasis on the incompatibility of a wages policy with excessive pressure of demand was one that his successors would have endorsed from later experience.

Meanwhile the government had issued in January a rather timid *Statement on the economic considerations affecting relations between workers and employers*.[22] After the convertibility crisis in the autumn they contemplated a further statement and set up a new working party on the stabilization of wages.[23] This reported in September 1947 but it was five more months before a White Paper on *Personal Incomes, Costs and Prices* was issued in February 1948.[24] In the meantime various radical proposals for checking wage inflation were advanced. These included making the National Joint Advisory Council express a published view on major claims, setting up a Central Appeal Tribunal to which claims thought to be against the national interest could be referred, imposing a wage-freeze in the public sector or alternatively a universal and statutory freeze across the whole economy, and assigning a government representative to all major wage negotiations. While the Economic Section took part in discussion of these proposals, it would not appear that they were protagonists of any of them. Robert Hall, who had taken over from Meade as Director, was broadly satisfied with the 1948 white paper as a first exploratory step in the search for a wages policy.

When the White Paper appeared, it followed the conservative approach of the Ministry of Labour and would have nothing to do with direct government intervention in wage negotiations. Instead it called for a voluntary freeze both on wages and on 'incomes from profit, rent or other like sources'.[25] An exception was made for undermanned industries that could attract labour in no other way; but in general there could be no justification for an increase in money incomes 'without at least a corresponding increase in the volume of production'.[26]

The policies adopted, thanks to disinflation and the limited

21 Meade to Lord President, 24 December 1946, in PRO CAB 124/898.
22 Cmd 7018, January 1947.
23 'Report of Working Party on the Stabilisation of Wages', 22 September 1947, in PRO T 238/65; for the minutes and memoranda of the Working Party, see PRO T 229/85.
24 Cmd 7321, February 1948.
25 ibid., para. 8.
26 Cmd 7321, para. 6.

co-operation of the TUC and FBI, seemed to be fairly successful.[27] In Britain as in the rest of Western Europe, 1948 was a year of marked recovery and much steadier prices. In April the Chancellor drew attention to the moderation in wage inflation over the previous year and Attlee in the following month reaffirmed the policy in answer to a Parliamentary question.[28]

It was at this point that a fresh internal debate began in the Economic Section on wages, prices, and full employment. The longest and most pessimistic paper, by Jack Downie, began by doubting whether 'under existing conditions of free collective bargaining, wage-earners, or even trade union leaders, [could] in the long-term be educated into a "sense of responsibility" . . . for more than a very limited period'. He went on to attack 'special appeals', such as the 1948 white paper, which in his view served merely to 'approve implicitly the normal practices of trade unions and therefore make more difficult an eventual change in the methods of wage fixing'. Downie wanted a long-term wages policy but was at a loss to see how any such policy could meet what he saw as the basic conditions for its success (administrative practicability and acceptability to the vast majority of wage-earners) without involving the government in too many decisions favouring one section of the community at the expense of another. By implication, the only sure means to avoiding excessive wage increases were deflation and unemployment.[29]

A second paper, by Marcus Fleming, recalled the conclusions reached in the earlier debate in 1945 and listed what he took to be the options for future policy: higher unemployment, state control over wages, or a floating rate of exchange.[30] There was also a third paper, by Peggy Hemming, which developed the theme that wages should not rise faster than productivity.[31] Within the scope that this provided for wage increases in particular industries, there was need for more information on unemployment and unfilled vacancies industry by industry so that workers could see how wage increases were graduated in relation to the degree of imbalance. It was the need to maintain price stability that should be paramount, not distributive justice; and what

27 CM(49)15, 28 February 1949, in PRO 128/15.
28 H. of C. Debates, 5th series, vol. 464, cols 645–6, 2 May 1949.
29 EC(S)(49)11, J. Downie, 'Wage policy', 26 April 1949, in PRO T 230/143.
30 EC(S)(49)13, J. M. Fleming, 'Wages policy', 27 April 1949, in PRO T 230/143.
31 EC(S)(49)15, M. F. W. Hemming, 'Wage policy', 29 April 1949, in PRO T 230/143.

success wages policy had in achieving stability under conditions of full employment rested on the will of the general public.

It was not long, however, before this exchange on the long-term issues of wages policy was overtaken, as in 1947, by the need to devise measures attuned to an immediate crisis. At the end of June, as the prospect of devaluation loomed, Cripps warned his colleagues on the Economic Policy Committee of 'the absolute need for a standstill in personal incomes'.[32] No action was taken, however, to give effect to this until two months later when the decision to devalue had already been taken. An official working party was asked to consider how the relative cost advantages that devaluation would bring could be preserved by an appropriate wages and prices policy.

The working party considered a paper by Russell Bretherton, who had succeeded Sayers as joint Deputy Director of the Economic Section. This harked back to the earlier debate in April, arguing that 'We have not yet learned how to reconcile our wage policy in a state of full employment with even the most general requirements of internal price stability and our balance of payments.'[33] Without a successful long-term wages policy, successive devaluations were likely to be the order of the day. For the immediate future, which the working party had been asked to consider, other parts of the paper led to the recommendation of a further voluntary wage-freeze for at least six months. This should be as wide as possible and include the million and a half workers on cost of living sliding scales. A proposal by the Ministry of Labour for a tax on employers granting excessive wage increases was rejected on administrative and political grounds. So, too, was Cripps's suggestion of a statutory freeze for six months of wages, prices, and profits. The working party agreed, however, to recommend more stringent price control and an extension of voluntary dividend limitation.[34]

In considering the report, the Cabinet agreed to exempt low-paid workers and to an increase in profits tax by 20 per cent. An approach to the TUC by Cripps and Bevin procured a recommendation from them to their members on 23 November 1949 of a one-year freeze of

32 EPC(49)72, 'The dollar situation', memorandum by the Chancellor of the Exchequer, 28 June 1949, in PRO CAB 134/222.
33 'Wages and devaluation', memorandum by R. F. Bretherton, 19 August 1949, in PRO T 229/213.
34 'Draft Report of Working Party on Wages Policy and Devaluation', 6 September 1949 in PRO T 229/213; see also PRO PREM 8/1568, the Prime Minister's personal file on wages policy 1946–51.

wage rates and a suspension of cost of living adjustments provided retail prices did not rise by more than 5 per cent. In January 1950 the recommendation was approved by a narrow majority at a special executive conference called by the TUC, with a general election about to take place in February. With the future of the policy in doubt, Cripps contemplated concessions in his budget in April but accepted the advice of Vincent Tewson, the TUC General Secretary, that the unions would not respond to the notion of a 'social wage', and contented himself with a tribute to the restraint shown by the unions and an appeal for their continued forbearance.[35]

The wage-freeze broke down at the end of June 1950, just as the war in Korea was beginning. Officials began again to look at the problem in long-run terms, increasingly convinced that inflation rather than unemployment would remain the main economic problem in future. As an Economic Section memorandum put it in September 1950, 'the trade unions are being asked to exercise special restraint because of special and temporary circumstances' when in fact it was a new and abiding trend that needed treatment.[36]

Meanwhile the Economic Section was still debating wage policy without coming to agreed conclusions. In March, Downie pointed out that domestic factor costs had risen significantly faster on the average since the war than during the war itself. One of the forces making for higher wage claims was the growing claim of investment and exports on industrial output and the consequent pressure in the consumer goods market. It would have to be made possible for trade unions and employers to take into account wider interests than their own; and for those wider interests only the government could be the spokesman. It would not be enough, he added in May, for the goverment to compute and announce the net permissible average increase in wages: that is, a 'guiding light'. That was no solution. What industry needed was information that it could put to use in specific wage negotiations. Returning to the subject once again in June, he examined two proposals and reviewed the objections to them: calling on the TUC to undertake a preview of wage claims and pass judgement on them; and setting up a tribunal to review all wage claims and make awards. He accepted that intervention in the process of collective bargaining, to be acceptable to the trade unions, would need to be accompanied by intervention in prices and profits, and that might prove difficult and

35 Jones, op. cit., p. 38.
36 'The reason for a wages policy', memorandum by the Economic Section, 15 September 1950, in PRO T 172/2033.

ineffectual.[37] Atkinson, wrestling with much the same problem, saw no escape from modifying the full employment guarantee and, like Meade, recommending the government to aim at sustaining a level of monetary demand sufficient to take up output at constant prices but insufficient if prices increased. In order to secure such a result, it might be useful to revive statutory limits to the size of the note issue.[38] The use of monetary targets to stem inflation is not a new idea, nor is targeting money GNP.

When Gaitskell took over as Chancellor in October 1950 he was anxious to produce a new white paper on employment policy. Such a White Paper could also be used to expound the line the government proposed to take on wages policy. A draft synopsis was prepared by the Economic Section and the CEPS in October.[39] This proposed the creation of an 'advisory council on wage and salary problems'. This was to be a large and formally independent body to 'provide advice on all collective negotiations on rates of remuneration', taking into account a periodically announced assessment by the government of what increase in average wages would be consistent with the national interest. The council would have power to obtain what statistical information it required from the negotiating parties and would form and publish an opinion on whether any claim merited more or less than the published average. No resort to compulsion was envisaged: 'voluntary collective negotiation' was still to be 'an essential part of our democratic way of life'.[40]

The Economic Policy Committee gave its formal backing to the drafting of a White Paper early in November but it was accepted that the synopsis would need considerable elaboration to do justice to experience with full employment and the techniques to maintain it. Ministers also noted that 'the problem of wage restraint would need very careful treatment'. Gaitskell and his advisers (Plowden and Hall) were well aware of the deficiencies of the synopsis and had every intention of revamping it before issuing a White Paper. They accepted the need to give more thought to profit and dividend control, as had

37 EC(S)(50)14, 'Full employment and cost inflation', 8 March 1950; EC(S)(50)24, 'The problem of wage pressure', 9 May 1950, in PRO T 230/338; EC(S)(50)30, 'Action against wage pressure', 19 June 1950, in PRO T 230/338.
38 EC(S)(50)22, 'The wages problem', 2 May 1950, in PRO T 230/338.
39 'Synopsis of a White Paper on full employment, incomes and prices', in PRO T 229/323. For the history of 'the White Paper that never was', see Tomlinson, J. (1987) *Employment Policy: the Crucial Years 1939–55*, Oxford: Clarendon Press, pp. 130–7.
40 ibid., PRO T 229/323.

been argued in the September memorandum on 'The reason for a wages policy', and they thought that the existing synopsis underplayed the idea of making the proposed council 'educative'. An interdepartmental committee under Robert Hall was given the job of drafting a new document with assistance from the CEPS and the Economic Section.[41]

Just before Christmas Gaitskell circulated an updated draft of the synopsis, which was intended to provide both the basis of the wages policy section of the White Paper and the groundwork for discussions with the TUC. A new point in the draft was that the 'advisory council' should be tripartite and include an independent member as well as representatives of both employers and unions. In presenting the draft to the Economic Policy Committee, Gaitskell argued that the government could not 'go on devising a series of *ad hoc* methods to prevent excessive wage increases'. It had to choose between 'a policy of laissez-faire and an attempt to set up permanent machinery'. He also emphasized the educative role of the council, and made it clear that his staff were looking further into ways of limiting profit and dividend distributions.[42]

Issacs, the Minister of Labour, although 'to a great extent in agreement with the Chancellor's views', suggested that the National Joint Advisory Council 'be adapted to perform the advisory functions suggested'. In the general debate which followed, Aneurin Bevan took a leading role. Echoing many insiders' thoughts, he argued forcefully that it would be unwise to rely on such an 'unwieldy and conservative body' as the National Joint Advisory Council to operate such a 'revolutionary idea'. The Committee agreed and approved the suggestion of a new 'wages advisory service', calling at the same time for immediate discussions between the government and trade union leaders, and within the Labour Party, on the subject.

Gaitskell, together with Bevan, who had recently become Minister of Labour, met representatives of the trade unions at the beginning of February 1951. Prior to the meeting, despite the fact that in September the TUC Conference had voted against any formal wage policy, Bevan was sure that, as he was on good terms with all the trade union leaders, he would be able to talk them round. As it turned out, Bevan was far too optimistic. The Chancellor reported afterwards that he and Bevan:

41 ES(50) 8th meeting, 7 December 1950; ES(50)20, 'White Paper on full employment', both in PRO CAB 134/263.
42 'Economic policy', memorandum by the Chancellor of the Exchequer, 22 June 1951, in PRO CAB 134/230.

had given an explanation of the need . . . for bringing to bear upon wage negotiations the general national interest as opposed to that of the employers or work people in the industry concerned, and hinted at the possibility of an advisory service for the purpose.

The TUC, however, while they did not show a wholly irresponsible attitude, could not agree to an advisory committee, and did not think there was any chance that formal wage restraint could be accepted without rigid price control. Gaitskell had to abandon the wages advisory council or try to set it up without union backing. He chose the former course, at the same time asking his advisers to look into ways of linking wages directly to prices.[43]

Over the following weeks the White Paper on full employment was dropped, along with the 'full employment bill'. In the absence of an agreement with the trade unions, a major theme of the white paper had lost its point. The government's attempt to institute a more active long-term wages policy and to modify the nature of voluntary collective bargaining had failed.

While Gaitskell continued to support a wages policy for the remainder of Attlee's second term, he was forced to set his sights rather lower.

In effect he returned to the *ad hoc* solutions which he had rejected the previous year. It remained his intention to introduce an incomes policy; but, before he could do so, the Labour government fell from office.

The Economic Section became increasingly worried about wage inflation throughout this period, and played an important part in the development of wages policy through their membership of various committees and working parties, their ability to come up with ideas to meet individual situations, and the influence that Robert Hall in particular exerted on Sir Stafford Cripps and Hugh Gaitskell. They were articulate critics of both the industrial appeasement policies of the Ministry of Labour, and the over-ambitious interventionist wage policies suggested by certain ministers and officials. The Section stood in the middle ground, believing that free and unfettered collective bargaining and full employment would prove incompatible and likely to lead to a series of exchange crises and devaluations. They sought sensible demand-management policies that did not overstimulate the economy, and urged that no effort should be spared to find a long-

43 'Report by the Chancellor on his discussions with TUC representatives on 6 February 1951', in PRO T 172/2033.

term method to modify the collective bargaining process and mobilize public support behind moderate settlements and flexibility in wage relationships. The record shows that the Section was not very successful in achieving either aim. In the exceptional circumstances of the transition to peace, excess demand was never completely eliminated under the Labour government; and, while *ad hoc* appeals for wage restraint in the aftermath of economic crises did achieve considerable short-term success, the one real attempt to change the face of the collective bargaining process, put to the unions at a most unfortunate time, came to nothing.

The tendency for wage increases to outstrip productivity growth under conditions of full employment remained a central problem of economic policy, and the issue with which it faced the Economic Section in these years changed little over the next three decades. The solutions, too, that were suggested by the Section were to reappear in Whitehall with stunning regularity.

For the next decade, 1951–61, incomes policy was in eclipse. The Conservative government had no wish to tangle with the unions or to enunciate general principles of wage determination that it had no power to enforce. Its approach to inflation was much more through the employers, for example in an effort to achieve a price plateau in 1956, or through monetary policy as a restraining influence on demand.

By good luck, the economic environment in the early years of Conservative government made intervention in the labour market far less necessary. A continuing improvement in the terms of trade not only was helpful in improving living standards and real wages at an unchanged level of money wages but also strengthened the balance of payments against the rise in money wages that did occur. On top of this, resources could be diverted from 1952 onwards to meet consumer needs, the painful adjustment in favour of exports, investment, and rearmament having been completed under the Labour government. A consumer boom dampened the wage claims that less prosperity might have bred.

Even so, the Economic Section remained convinced that a long-term wages policy would still have to be worked out. As Robert Hall told Edward Bridges: 'experience suggests that very high levels of unemployment indeed are necessary to put a really effective stop on wage increases . . . no government in the UK would be likely to push unemployment as far as this'.[44] It followed that workers would always be in a sufficiently strong bargaining position to pose a threat of

44 Hall to Bridges, 28 November 1951, in PRO T 229/402.

excessive wage increases and a rising price level. Workers must be educated to recognize the choice facing them of accepting an indefinite obligation to be moderate in their claims for higher wages or forfeiting the prospect of full employment. He was optimistic enough to believe that, faced with such a choice, people would choose moderation in preference to inflation on the one hand or deflation and unemployment on the other. Hall's recommendation was that the choice should be expounded in a White Paper, such as had been contemplated under Gaitskell, that outlined the consequences of full employment for the price level, the balance of payments, the mobility of labour, and so on.

Butler was at first drawn to this idea and informed the Cabinet in December 1951 that a White Paper 'in simple language' was under preparation and would appear in January.[45] No White Paper, however, ever appeared, presumably because of pressure from other ministers or from the Prime Minister. Butler continued to ask for wage restraint from the TUC but received only qualified acceptance: the TUC would go no further than recommending 'responsible' collective bargaining.[46]

In the course of 1952 inflationary pressure died away and by the spring of 1954 the rise in wages was not appreciably greater than in productivity: prices were at least more or less stable. The moment seemed to the Ministry of Labour propitious for the issue of a White Paper on the lines suggested earlier by Robert Hall. While prices were stable the annual wage round had taken firm root and the danger remained of a recrudescence of excessive wage claims. The Ministry of Labour prepared a draft which the Treasury thought too diffuse and unconvincing. An alternative version was then drafted by Clem Leslie, head of the Treasury Economic Information Division, with the assistance of Robert Hall.

The draft encountered strong criticism from the Financial Secretary, Reginald Maudling, who advised the Chancellor that it would do more harm than good. It was too full of exhortation, too detailed, too much like a learned treatise. At the Chancellor's request, he produced his own version, but in the meantime the Chancellor had concluded that the public would interpret the appearance of a White Paper as an indication of impending crisis and shelved it. Instead, the Minister of Labour made a full statement in the National Joint Advisory Council (NJAC) outlining the government's thinking on wages and the press was encouraged to give it wide publicity.

45 'Inflation and the wage price spiral', memorandum by the Chancellor of the Exchequer, 10 December 1951, in PRO CAB 134/886.
46 Jones, op. cit., p. 50.

At last, in March 1956, the White Paper which Robert Hall had urged on successive Chancellors appeared under the title *The Economic Implications of Full Employment*. The occasion for its publication was a renewed danger of rapid wage inflation, with wage earnings rising in 1955 at 9 per cent per annum and unemployment at a record low. Another round of wage increases like the last, Robert Hall warned ministers, would bring devaluation in sight and people might come to have doubts about the future value of money.

It had always been his view, more or less since he joined the Section, that full employment and price stability were incompatible unless labour exercised self-restraint. There was no determinate relationship between the state of the labour market and the movement of money wages: the rise in wages could be speeded up by militancy or slowed down by restraint. The Section had drafted repeated White Papers to explain what was at stake, but ministers of both the main parties had in the end decided against publishing them. Now the government suddenly decided to issue the current version shortly before the 1956 budget. Macmillan, the new Chancellor, was looking for a way of moderating inflation without a substantial rise in unemployment.

The new version was the work of Dick Ross of the Economic Section and Burke Trend, then attached to the Lord Privy Seal (Butler). It covered much the same ground as the Treasury draft of 1954, explaining the danger of exploitation by employees of the strong demand for labour under full employment and the consequent need for self-restraint.

The White Paper was followed in May 1956 by an appeal to the business community for a temporary 'price plateau' while prices were frozen in the public sector. An effort was made by the Prime Minister to induce the TUC to accept a corresponding freeze in wages. This came to nothing. The TUC contented itself with a renewed warning against irresponsibility in wage-bargaining. Later in the year, at its annual conference, a resolution was passed against 'proposals to recover control by wage restraint' and upholding 'the right of labour . . . to use its bargaining strength to protect the workers from the dislocations of an unplanned economy'.

It was all done, in Hall's view, in quite the wrong way. In the first place, the timing was unfortunate: to call for restraint at the top of a boom, before there was any evidence that deflation was working, was to ask too much of the unions. George Woodcock, at that time Assistant Secretary General of the TUC, never disguised his belief that union leaders could not hold back workers' demands for very long when employers were desperate to find labour. It would have been wiser to make sure first that demand was declining. In addition, the White Paper jumped the gun on price policy. The government wanted to raise prices in the nationalized industries as a preliminary to cutting subsidies to them; this would help to remove the threat of further increases after the White Paper policy was in force. To launch a campaign for wage and price stability leaving to the future price increases that would throw doubt on the government's good faith was a mistake. One nationalized industry – coal – got its prices up while another – the railways – was too late.

The initiative had been taken by the Prime Minister, who was well to the left of his party and had some very woolly ideas about reducing prices and taxes when Hall was writing paper after paper urging the reverse. Eden set up meetings with the TUC, FBI, and BEC (the British Employers' Confederation), and the nationalized industries; but, as he had no policy to put to them, they accomplished little.

Robert Hall then drafted a paper for the Chancellor to put to the Cabinet. This set out his proposed strategy: price increases within the government's control to be made first and got out of the way; then a campaign to persuade employers and workers to keep prices and wages steady; only then, with a reasonable prospect of price stability would it be right to seek agreement to a long-term wage policy. The Cabinet approved the strategy but did not agree to the publication of a statement after the next round of talks with the TUC as Hall had suggested. Ministerial statements at the meeting and afterwards to the press made little impact. They had made no real effort, in Hall's view, to make a major occasion of the appearance of the White Paper. Instead they looked to him to move *The Times* to publish a strong leader without explaining how this was to be done in the absence of an effective policy.

In 1957, when Thorneycroft had succeeded Macmillan as Chancellor, Hall continued to urge the importance of action to procure wage restraint. His proposal of a 'guiding light' for wage settlements was put by the Chancellor to the Cabinet but rejected. Ministers feared that the norm might become the minimum and were in any event averse to intervention. Later in the year, however, they accepted the proposal for a Council on Prices, Productivity, and Incomes to report on what could be done to secure 'reasonable stability in prices and the level of incomes'.

This was to be the first of a succession of advisory bodies, made up wholly or in part of independent members, that post-war governments have asked to offer impartial guidance to the general public on issues of wage policy. The Council was intended to create a further appreciation of the facts, not to pronounce on specific wage claims. The experiment, however, met with little success and it was not until 1961 that a fresh effort to introduce an effective incomes policy was attempted.

Looking back on the 1950s after his retirement from the Treasury, Robert Hall wrote that

> with the passage of time the number of adherents of extreme positions has diminished and a large body of opinion now thinks that some form of wage policy other than leaving wages to free collective bargaining is necessary if full employment and stable prices are to be combined.[47]

He cited as evidence of the trend in professional opinion the OEEC report on 'The problem of rising prices' and he might also have pointed to the Fourth Report of the Council on Prices, Productivity, and Incomes which argued in July 1961 that 'removing excess demand was not of itself enough. . . . Inflation had another cause, an upward push [on] rates of pay'.[48]

But, if opinion was changing, it had got no further than the conclusions reached twenty years earlier by the Economic Section: there was an element of indeterminancy in the movement of wages not explicable in terms of market forces and open to influence by public opinion. Equally, if the form that wage policy should take was still obscure, so it had been in the 1940s and so it remained in the 1980s.

47 *The Economist*, 16 September 1961.
48 This was the last publication of the Council, which at that time consisted of Sir Geoffrey Heyworth (chairman), Sir Harold Emmerson, and Professor Henry Phelps Brown.

# Chapter twenty

# CONCLUSION: ECONOMIC ADVISING THEN AND NOW

This has been a book about economic advising in its infancy. It covers a small group of advisers concentrated in a single department over a span of about twenty years. The record of their experience raises a number of questions and suggests some conclusions.

*First of all, why was the group so small?*

It may seem strange that no professional economist was employed in any of the central economic departments at the outbreak of the Second World War; and stranger still that in 1961 the employment of economists in Whitehall (Agriculture and Defence apart) remained almost entirely confined to the group in the Treasury calling themselves the 'Economic Section'. So much has changed since 1939 that it is easy to forget how different everything was then.

To begin with, there were comparatively few professional economists to employ and there was very little economic research going on. The National Institute of Economic and Social Research had just been founded, only one or two universities had a full-time academic economic research unit, and the number of British economists with a Ph.D. was negligible. Most of the economists who joined the Economic Section during the war were in their twenties or thirties and nearly all of them are still alive in 1989. Economists older than 50 were rare birds at the outbreak of war.

There were also very few statistical series for economists to work on. Apart from the *Trade Accounts*, official statistics were mainly on an annual basis. There was no *Monthly Digest*, no *Economic Trends* or *Financial Statistics*. There were no official estimates of the national income or of its components, no detailed estimates of the balance of payments, no annual figures for employment or monthly figures of industrial production, and few reliable indices of price movements. Most current statistical information used by economic advisers 'goes back no further than the revolution in statistics that was set on foot in 1940–1 by the Economic Section and its twin the Central Statistical Office.

Much more space is now given over in the daily press to economic affairs, and major changes have taken place in financial journalism. What once were esoteric expressions such as 'the terms of trade', 'the current account deficit', and 'seasonally adjusted unemployment' now appear on the front page, and initials once unknown like GNP and PSBR are in everyday use. Many new publications, including the bank reviews, cater for a public educated in elementary economics that was far smaller or non-existent in 1939.

The biggest change of all has been in government. Its role has expanded enormously; and, however much it may try to pull back from intervention in the market, its activities impinge on economic organization and behaviour in all directions. The needs of government for economic advice have grown correspondingly and so has the consciousness that the advice should be professionally based. It is this that has led to a remarkable enlargement of the Government Economic Service, involving the recruitment of economists to virtually every department in Whitehall. Where in 1961 the Economic Section numbered about a dozen, now the Government Economic Service employs nearly 400 economists. The Treasury alone employs about five times as many as a generation ago.

*Next, what of the organization of economic advice? Did it work satisfactorily or would some other arrangement have been better?*

There is no doubt that senior administrators valued the services of the Economic Section and were glad to see it continue after the war. In 1943 Bridges told Robbins: 'you gravely overestimate the difficulty of continuing in peace the work so admirably begun in war . . . there is an essential need for some apparatus specifically designed to survey the problem as a whole'.[1] His relations with Robbins's successors were equally warm. Norman Brook, too, was a strong supporter of the Section and valued their advice: he encouraged Hall to bring in more economists from the universities and it was as the result of his pressure

1 Bridges to Robbins, 21 January 1943, in PRO T 230/283.

that the practice of employing academic economists on secondment for a two-year spell was introduced.

The favourable judgement of Bridges and Brook related to the Section's advice on high policy and on matters normally dealt with by the Treasury. Other departments, however, were left for nearly the whole period with no economic advisers of their own; although in principle they could seek advice from the Section, at least while it was still in the Cabinet Office, they rarely did so. It is probable that the Foreign Office and the Board of Trade, to mention only two departments, would have welcomed the appointment of an economic adviser, the Foreign Office after the departure of Lionel Robbins (of whom they had made use in wartime) and the Board of Trade to succeed Austin Robinson and Cairncross after 1949. But when Hall was so hard put to it to find staff for his own purposes, including service abroad, there was little hope of his sparing (or finding) staff for other departments in Whitehall. Moreover, he (and his successor) took the view that it might be better to have no economist at all than have one whose abilities were in doubt; and the supply of economists of unquestioned ability who were willing to serve in Whitehall was very limited, particularly if they had also to be non-partisan and able to fit comfortably into the government machine. Whether for these reasons or because no adequate effort to recruit to other departments was made, professional economic advice was almost entirely confined to the Treasury. From that point of view the system could hardly be said to have been satisfactory and the absence of adequate economic advice on microeconomic problems was particularly damaging, as members of the Section reported.[2]

The services of the Economic Section were nevertheless of value to other departments than the Treasury. Through their membership of virtually all interdepartmental committees, they were in a position to educate other officials in the economist's way of thinking, provided the Section representative was reasonably articulate and received some encouragement from the chairman in expounding the Section view. The Section also took a hand in the instruction in practical economics of young graduates in other departments who were new to the government machine.

What of the Treasury itself? Was it satisfactory that the economists were grouped together in a specialized Section rather than planted out

2 See, for example, Henderson, P. D. (David) (1961), 'The use of economists in British administration', *Oxford Economic Papers* January, and Little, I. M. D. (1957) 'The economist in Whitehall', *Lloyds Bank Review* April.

in the various Treasury Divisions as most Treasury economists are nowadays? The task of economic co-ordination is always best conducted by a small group in intimate daily contact with one another, so that each knows the other's mind and can be kept abreast of emerging issues. The group has to retain its independence and coherence, share a recognizable philosophy and approach, and be easily mobilized when major issues are at stake. But it cannot afford to distance itself from the operative divisions to which information flows and in which action is recommended or authorized. From this point of view there were important advantages in the small size of the Section. Against this, it was not big enough to do justice to the whole range of issues on which the Treasury had to pronounce, and it had to leave large areas of policy (e.g. the work of the expenditure divisions) almost entirely on one side.

There were those who thought that the Section should have stayed in the Cabinet Office so that it could have maintained its wartime stance of complete independence and enjoyed the trust of other departments when in conflict with the Treasury. It may be that this would have made some difference but Hall for one did not think that the move to the Treasury changed matters. The Section's influence had to be exerted through some minister or it would become ineffective, as in the autumn of 1940 when the minister charged with economic co-ordination was himself ineffective. But who, other than the Chancellor, could that minister be? Experience of leaving one minister to co-ordinate financial policy and another economic policy has not been a happy one. If it was the Chancellor who was to be advised, was it not in the end preferable to have all his advisers in one department? This did not prevent the Section from taking a line of its own: members of the Section continued to claim 'independence' of the official Treasury. It also gave them a chance to raise the level of economic expertise among their Treasury colleagues.

Christopher Dow, after some years in the Section, saw the possibilities of organizing economists in other ways than through membership of the Section. They could, as they now do, play a role that was not simply advisory but carried administrative duties as well. But there had to be some degree of centralization. In the Netherlands, economists were grouped in a large, comparatively isolated, unit in the Planbureau. This meant going to one extreme and seemed to work only because of the outlook, personality, and political influence of its Director, Jan Tinbergen. The important thing was that economists should be close to the action, as they were in the Treasury. In this way they avoided the risk that they might come forward with good ideas but at the wrong time, or fail to be aware of problems that others regarded as urgent. They could inject their ideas at that stage when policy was still in flux instead of annoying everybody by advancing them in a brief just when a decision was about to be made.[3]

It was characteristic of the Section from the very beginning that its members concerned themselves with what policy should be and not just with setting out the pros and cons or advising on how policies should be carried out. This was particularly true in wartime when there was a single overriding aim that was not in dispute. Of course, if the government had already taken a firm decision on some clear and attainable policy objective, then it was the business of any government servant to accept it and suggest the best way of reaching the goal. But government aims are seldom so clear-cut and mutually consistent. Economic advisers have to consider ends as well as means, if only because there are trade-offs between ends on which their advice may be indispensable. In an uncertain world the business of an adviser is rarely to assist a minister in achieving some clearly stated objective and more commonly to advise him on how to run his risks when information is limited, the outlook is obscure, and policy objectives conflict.

The Section had views on economic policy and urged them on ministers when occasion offered, without waiting for inspiration to come from ministers themselves. They shared a strong belief that government influence on the working of a market economy was inevitable and had better be exercised rationally; a preference for reliance on financial instruments to influence market forces rather than on administrative controls to supersede them; a belief in an external economic policy based essentially on free trade and combined with a 'lubricating' international monetary mechanism. They had no hesitation in suggesting policies in keeping with these beliefs but at no time did they seek to thwart the declared policy of the government.

*Next, was the advice taken?*

The most important influence of the Economic Section on policy after the war was on the budget. Here it came to be accepted that it was for the Section to advise on the 'budget judgement'. But neither the Chancellor nor senior Treasury officials accepted the judgement without reservation. Meade in 1945–7 had little success while still Director; it was only after he had gone that budget policy was in

3 Dow, talk to Manchester Statistical Society, 1953, manuscript in PRO T 230/283.

accord with at least some of his ideas. Hall, on the other hand, was the key figure in budget discussions after 1947 and his advice was rarely contested except when it ran foul of the Inland Revenue (as on the investment allowance) or of the obsession with the need to avoid an 'above the line' budget deficit and the strong urge to get taxes down. Chancellors made up their own minds about the shape of their budgets but so far as they were guided by officials on the 'budget judgement' it was to the Economic Section that they turned.

On monetary policy the Section was inclined to stress the limitations of monetary weapons and to look to credit control rather than higher interest rates as the most useful of them in checking inflation. Both Meade and Hall, however, wanted to see use made of monetary policy and believed that it had a role to play of some importance in the management of the economy. Meade exercised no influence on Dalton's monetary policy and Hall, until late in the day, was in frequent collision with the Bank of England. What influence he had was mainly on the direction of policy rather than on specific measures. This applied particularly to bank rate changes: on credit squeezes and hire-purchase restrictions he was in a more influential position.

On external economic policy his interventions were often decisive. The outstanding example is the devaluation of 1949. In the argument over Robot and convertibility he also played a major and, on the whole, successful part. He helped to counter the urge to press on with convertibility and 'maintain the momentum' from 1952 to 1955 when the pound was still relatively weak. But he failed to secure the retention of a floating rate as a precondition for convertibility; and it must be doubtful whether such a move would have proved acceptable in the 1950s to other countries in the Commonwealth and in Europe.

On no aspect of policy did the Section try harder and to less effect than incomes policy. They wrote papers and minutes by the score suggesting this device and that. But in the 1940s they made little progress towards the adoption of a long-term policy and in the 1950s, after Gaitskell lost office, they prevailed no further than the White Paper of 1956 and the appointment of the Council for Prices, Productivity, and Incomes. The disproportion between the effort expended and the minuteness of the results rankled with Robert Hall more than anything else in his directorship.

It would be a mistake to measure the Section's success in terms of a few key decisions on matters of high policy. They were there to make their contribution day by day to economic problems as they arose, advising their colleagues as much as ministers, providing a view of the economic situation as it developed, and conveying a philosophy of approach that would lend consistency to decisions. What they did to develop economic forecasting, for example, and to improve the statistics from which forecasts were prepared, was just as important as their advice in specific areas of policy. Equally, the host of little decisions to which they contributed could be more important in the aggregate than the occasional big decisions.

*Was the advice good and did it work?*

In retrospect the Economic Section comes well out of a study of its policy recommendations. Half the game in economic advising is in spotting a problem before others are alive to it and spotting it before it becomes acute. The machinery of economic intelligence and forecasting built up within the Section was central to this function. It was relatively primitive in 1945 under the new circumstances of peace, as it had been in 1940 with the change to wartime conditions. But it improved steadily and by the late 1950s compared favourably with the machinery in most other industrial countries. But it did not prevent mistaken assessments. The most conspicuous example was in 1953–4 when industrial investment was beginning to gather speed just when the Section despaired of finding new expansionary influences and pressed for the introduction of investment allowances. On other occasions, too, the Section underrated the recuperative power of the economy from a cyclical depression, though it was not always their fault if governments overdid expansionary measures.

Whether the Section's advice on fiscal policy was well conceived is not altogether easy to establish and would require elaborate analysis. Changes in the level of taxation of the order of £150 million (which were all that Hall proposed in most years) seem extraordinarily small alongside the destabilizing forces in a national income of, say, £10,000–20,000 million. Stock-building alone could rise by £800 million in a single year (as in 1951) and might move back again by over £500 million in the following year (as in 1952). When the tax changes were reinforced by other action, such as import cuts or hire-purchase restrictions, they could become a good deal more powerful; and so long as the underlying rising trend remained undisturbed they seem to have been adequate as correctives. Given the stresses and strains on the economy, particularly in the early years, it is remarkable that expansion was so continuous, the worst that happened being a brief halt to growth in 1952 and 1958. But one can understand Robert Hall's fears in the mid-fifties as he saw the removal of one control after another, the economy exposed to increasing pressures from without, and no weapons to counter them except outright deflation.

On monetary policy Robert Hall was surely in the right to insist that what was wanted was a limitation of credit and that it was the job of the Bank of England to propose ways of accomplishing this. But the Bank had a better case than he allowed for insisting that the fundamental difficulty was the government's financing requirements. So long as the government could not find a market for its bonds, it had to pour out liquid assets, which put the banks in an unassailable position to continue lending. In these circumstances the only effective restraint was a ceiling on bank lending and this could not go on indefinitely.

We can leave aside incomes policy since so little action was taken and the Section's advice was not put to the test except in a half-hearted and ill-conceived way in 1956. Hall's advice on external economic policy would stir controversy even now. The devaluation of 1949, seen as a means to ease the dollar shortage (even although that was not in the minds of those who made the decision), was undoubtedly a wise move and almost certainly contributed to that end. On Robot and convertibility Hall would also seem to have been in the right. The delay of three years to near-convertibility and six years to *de jure* convertibility was sufficient to convert the dollar shortage into a dollar surplus and make convertibility a far less hazardous affair. If Hall's advice on external policy was not always taken (as in February 1955), some of the major decisions of the post-war years were in accord with it and for one at least, devaluation, he had as much responsibility as anyone.

### Why then has the Economic Section ceased to exist?

In 1964 the Economic Section was still the small compact body it had always been. But with the creation of the Government Economic Service in that year it ceased to enjoy a virtual monopoly of professional advice in Whitehall as one department after another formed a staff of their own. The sharp line of division within the Treasury between economists and administrators had already begun to be blurred as economists were posted to Treasury divisions (a practice going back to the 1950s). Economists were later seconded to those divisions or allowed to transfer to the administrative grade, until today the work of the Treasury is carried on by a blend of economists and administrators in most divisions. The economists may still, in a sense, be under the direction of the Chief Economic Adviser. But there is no longer the unity and coherence of a group calling itself the Economic

Section and entertaining a common Section view of economic issues. It would perhaps be right to conclude, therefore, that the Economic Section was no more than an episode – although one of great interest and importance – in the evolutionary process by which the government machine becomes adapted to new problems and new responsibilities.

# Appendix

# MEMBERS OF THE ECONOMIC SECTION
## (including all who served, however briefly, before 1960)

| | | |
|---|---|---|
| Abramson, S.[a] | 1948–50 | (later Under-Secretary, Department of Trade) |
| Atkinson, F. J.[a] | 1949–69, 1977–9 | (later Sir Fred: Head of Government Economic Service, 1977–9) |
| Baster, A. S. J. | 1941–2 | (later Professor of Economics, University of Exeter; deceased) |
| Bensusan-Butt, D. M. | 1946–54 | (Professorial Research Fellow, Australian National University, 1962–76) |
| Bretherton, R. F.[ac] | 1949–51 | (joint Deputy Director, 1949–51; Under-Secretary, Board of Trade 1954–61, Treasury 1961–8) |
| Brown, A. J.[ab] | 1945–7 | (Professor of Economics, Leeds University, 1947–79) |
| Brown, Miss M. P.[a] | 1959–85 | (Under-Secretary, Treasury, 1972–85) |
| Brunner, J.[a] | 1958–61 | (later Sir John) |
| Cairncross, A. K.[ab] | 1940–1 | (later Sir Alec; Director of Economic Section, 1961–9; Head of Government Economic Service, 1964–9) |

a Included in *Who's Who*.
b Fellow of the British Academy.
c Administrative officer on loan.
d On loan from PM's Department, Commonwealth of Australia.

| | | |
|---|---|---|
| Campion, H.[a] | 1939–40 | (later Sir Harry; Director of Central Statistical Office, 1941–67) |
| Chantler, P.[a] | 1941–7 | (Economic Adviser to Ministry of Fuel and Power, 1947–60; Under-Secretary 1960–5; Chairman, NW Planning Board, 1965–9; died 1987) |
| Chester, D. N.[a] | 1940–5 | (later Sir Norman; Warden of Nuffield College, Oxford, 1954–78; died 1986) |
| Chilver, Mrs E. M.[a] | 1940 | (Principal, Lady Margaret Hall, Oxford, 1971–9) |
| Day, A. C. L.[a] | 1954–6 | (Professor of Economics, LSE, 1964– and Pro-Director, 1979–83) |
| Dennison, S. R.[a] | 1940–6 | (Principal, University of Hull, 1972–9) |
| Devons, E.[a] | 1940–1 | (Professor of Commerce, LSE, 1959–65; died 1967) |
| Dow, J. C. R.[ab] | 1945–54, 1962–3 | (Assistant Secretary-General, OECD, 1963–73; Executive Director, Bank of England, 1973–81; Adviser to Governor, 1981–4) |
| Downie, J. | 1948–61 | (Assistant Secretary-General, OECD, 1961–3; died 1963) |
| Durbin, E. F. M.[a] | 1940–2 | (Parliamentary Secretary, Ministry of Works, 1947; drowned 1947) |
| Fearn, J. M.[ac] | 1947–8 | (Secretary, Scottish Education Department, 1973–6) |
| Figgures, Frank[ac] | 1955–7 | (later Sir Frank; Deputy Director, joined Treasury after military service in 1946; Director of Trade and Finance, OECD 1948–51, Under-Secretary, Treasury, 1955–60) |
| Fleming, J. Marcus[a] | 1942–51 | (Deputy Director, 1946–51; Deputy Director, Research Department, IMF, 1964–76; died 1976) |
| Fleming J. Miles | 1952–4 | (Professor of Economics, University of Bristol, 1970–8) |
| Forsyth, Miss J. M.[a] | 1947–9 | (Under-Secretary, Treasury/ Department of Transport, 1975–84) |

| | | |
|---|---|---|
| Fowler, R. F. | 1940 | (Director of Statistics, Ministry of Labour, 1950–68) |
| Franklin, M. D. M.[ac] | 1952–5 | (later Sir Michael; Permanent Secretary, Ministry of Agriculture, Food, and Fisheries, 1983–7) |
| Godley, W. A. H.[a] | 1956–70 | (Director, Department of Applied Economics, Cambridge, 1970–) |
| Grieve-Smith, J. | 1949–57 | (Senior Bursar, Robinson College, Cambridge, 1982–) |
| Hall, R. L.[a] | 1947–61 | (later Lord Roberthall; Director, 1947–61; Economic Adviser to HMG 1953–61; died 1988) |
| Hemming, A. F.[a] | 1940 | (Administrative Head, CEIS, 1939–40; Director of CSO, 1941; Under-Secretary, Ministry of Fuel and Power, 1946–53) |
| Henderson, P. D.[a] | 1957–8 | (Professor of Economics, UCL, 1975–83; Head of Economics and Statistics Division, OECD, 1984–; Reith Lecturer, 1985) |
| Hopkin, W. A. B.[a] | 1948–50, 1958–72, 1974–7 | (later Sir Bryan; Deputy Director, 1958–65; Head of Government Economic Service, 1974–7; Professor of Economics, University of Wales, Cardiff, 1972–82) |
| Howell, D. A. R.[a] | 1959–60 | (Secretary of State for Energy, 1979–81; for Transport, 1981–3) |
| Howell, Miss K. (Mrs Jones) | 1945–60 | (Secretary, National Institute of Economic and Social Research, 1968–) |
| Jefferies, G. P. | 1946–9 | (later Assistant Secretary, Department of Trade and Industry) |
| Jewkes, J.[a] | 1939–41 | (Director, 1939–41; Professor of Economic Organization, Oxford, 1948–69; died 1988) |
| Jones, D. J. C.[a] | 1950–3 | (Minister for Hong Kong relations with EEC, 1982–) |
| Joseph, Miss M.W.B. (Mrs Hemming) | 1940–3, 1947–55 | (Senior Research Officer, NIESR, 1956–70) |
| Jukes, J. A.[a] | 1948–54 | (Deputy Director-General, DEA, 1964–7; member, CEGB, 1977–80) |

| | | |
|---|---|---|
| Keane, J. W. P. | 1947–53 | (Director, International Affairs, British Steel Corporation, 1973–83) |
| Kelley, Miss. J.[a] | 1949–54 | (Under-Secretary, Treasury, 1979–87) |
| Kennedy, M. C. | 1956–65 | (later Senior Lecturer, University of Manchester) |
| Lawler, P.[ad] | 1952–3 | (later Sir Peter; Australian Ambassador to Ireland and the Holy See, 1983–7) |
| Le Cheminant, P.[ac] | 1950–2 | (Second Permanent Secretary, Cabinet Office, 1983–4) |
| Licence, J. W. V. | 1948–52 | (Managing Director; Economic Planning, British Gas, 1972–82) |
| Little, I. M. D.[ab] | 1953–5 | Deputy Director, Professor of Economics of Underdeveloped Countries, Oxford, 1971–6) |
| MacDougall, G. D. A.[ab] | 1945, 1969–73 | (later Sir Donald; Head of Government Economic Service, 1969–73; Chief Economic Adviser, CBI, 1973–84) |
| Mackintosh, A. S. | 1957–61 | (deceased) |
| McMahon, C. W.[a] | 1954–60 | (later Sir Kit; Deputy Governor of Bank of England, 1980–5; Chairman, Midland Bank, 1987–) |
| Marley, Miss J. | 1940 | (later Central Statistical Office) |
| Meade, J. E.[ab] | 1940–7 | (Director, 1946–7; Professor of Commerce, LSE, 1947–57; Professor of Economics, Cambridge 1957–68; Nobel Laureate, 1977) |
| Neild, R. R.[a] | 1951–6 | (Professor of Economics, Cambridge, 1971–84) |
| Nove, A.[ab] | 1956–8 | (Professor of International Economics, University of Glasgow, 1963–82) |
| Opie, R. G.[a] | 1958–60 | (Fellow of New College, Oxford, Oxford, since 1961) |
| Parkinson, J. R. | 1945, 1963 | (Professor of Economics, University of Nottingham, 1969–) |
| Richenberg, L. | 1955–7 | (later in merchant banking and insurance) |

| | | |
|---|---|---|
| Robbins, L. C.[ab] | 1940–5 | (later Lord Robbins; Director, 1940–5; Professor of Economics, LSE, 1929–61; President, British Academy, 1962–7; died 1984) |
| Roberthall, Lord | | see Hall, R. L. |
| Robinson, E. A. G.[ab] | 1939–42 | (later Sir Austin; Professor of Economics, Cambridge, 1950–65; Secretary, Royal Economic Society, 1945–70) |
| Ross, C. R.[a] | 1952–5 | (Deputy Secretary, CPRS, 1971–8; Vice-President, European Investment Bank, 1978–) |
| Sadler, J. S.[a] | 1954–6 | (Deputy Chairman, John Lewis Partnership, 1984–) |
| Sayers, R. S.[ab] | 1945–7 | (joint Deputy Director, 1945–7; Cassel Professor of Economics, LSE, 1947–68; Vice-President, British Academy, 1966–7) |
| Scammell, W. S. | 1956–8 | (Professor of Economics, McMaster University, Ontario, 1970–87) |
| Scott, M. F. | 1953–4 | (Fellow in Economics, Nuffield College, 1968–) |
| Shackle, G. L. S.[a] | 1945–9 | (Professor of Economic Science, University of Liverpool, 1951–69) |
| Soutar, Miss M. S. (Mrs Muray) | 1940–5 | (later Deputy-Head of St Christopher's School, Letchworth) |
| Stamler, Mrs H. | 1954–6 | (Senior Economic Adviser, Treasury, 1974–) |
| Stewart, M. J.[a] | 1957–62 | (Reader in Political Economy, UCL, 1969–) |
| Stone, J. R. N.[ab] | 1940 | (later Sir Richard; Professor of Finance and Accounting, Cambridge, 1955–80; Nobel Laureate, 1984) |
| Swan, T.[d] | 1947–9 | (later Professor of Economics, Australian National University) |
| Tress, R. C.[a] | 1941–7 | (Master of Birkbeck College, London, 1968–77) |
| Troup, G. W. | 1957 | |
| Wannan, Miss G.[c] | 1956–8 | |
| Watts, Miss N. G. M. | 1941–55, | (Deputy Director, Research Division, |

|                         |          | UN Economic Commission for Europe, 1959–64; Vice-Principal, St Hilda's College, Oxford, 1968–81) |
| Watts, P. E.            | 1954–9   | (Commercial Controller, Central Electricity Generating Board, 1960–) |
| Wilson, J. H.[a]        | 1940–1   | (later Lord Wilson; Prime Minister, 1964–70; 1974–6) |
| Wilson, P.              | 1941     |          |
| Wilson, T.[ab]          | 1945–6   | (Adam Smith Professor of Political Economy, University of Glasgow, 1958–82) |
| Wood, J. B.             | 1944–6   | (Deputy Director, Institute of Economic Affairs, 1968–) |

# SELECT BIBLIOGRAPHY

**Public records**

*Cabinet*

CAB 21   Cabinet briefs and miscellaneous
CAB 23   Cabinet minutes to 1939
CAB 24   Cabinet memoranda to 1939
CAB 66   War Cabinet minutes, 1939–45
CAB 67   War Cabinet memoranda, 1939–45
CAB 72   Committees on Economic Policy, 1939–45
CAB 87   Committees on Post-war Reconstruction
CAB 89   Survey of Economic and Financial Plans Committee
CAB 123  Lord President of the Council Secretariat, 1940–5
CAB 124  Lord President of the Council Secretariat, post-1945
CAB 128  Cabinet minutes from 1945
CAB 129  Cabinet memoranda from 1945
CAB 130  *Ad hoc* Cabinet committees
CAB 132  Lord President's Committee, post-1945
CAB 134  Cabinet committees, post-1945

*Treasury*

T 161   Treasury supply files
T 171   Budget and Finance Bill papers
T 172   Chancellor of the Exchequer's Office: miscellaneous papers
T 227   Social Services Division
T 229   Central Economic Planning Division
T 230   Economic Advisory Section

T 232   European Economic Co-operation Committee (OEEC)
T 233   Home Finance Division
T 234   Home and Overseas Planning Division
T 236   Overseas Finance Division
T 237   (Marshall Aid Division)
T 238   Overseas Negotiations Committee
T 247   Keynes papers
T 267   Treasury historical memoranda
T 269   Devaluation and consequential measures, 1949
T 273   Bridges papers

## Offical reports and papers

*CSO*

*Annual Abstract of Statistics*
*The Economic Implications of Full Employment* (1956, Cmd 9725)
*Economic Trends Annual Supplement*
*Monthly Digest of Statistics*
*National Income and Expenditure* (annual, from 1952)
*National Income Statistics: Sources and Methods* (1956)

*Foreign Office*

*European Co-operation: Memoranda Submitted to the OEEC Relating to
    Economic Affairs in the Period 1949 to 1953 (including The Long-Term
    Programme)* (1948, Cmd 7572)
*Proposals for Consideration by an International Conference on Trade and
    Employment*, Miscellaneous No. 15 (1945, Cmd 6709)

*Ministry of Reconstruction*

*Employment Policy* (1944, Cmd 6527)

*Prime Minister*

*Statement on the Economic Considerations affecting Relations between
    Employers and Employed* (1947, Cmd 7018)
*Statement on Personal Incomes, Costs and Prices* (1948, Cmd 7321)

*Treasury*

*An Analysis of the Sources of War Finance and an Estimate of the National
    Income and Expenditure in 1938 to 1940* (1941, Cmd 6261)

*National Income and Expenditure of the United Kingdom* (annual, 1946–51)

*Preliminary Estimates of National Income and Expenditure* (annual, from 1952)

*United Kingdom Balance of Payments* (annual or twice yearly, from 1948)

*Economic Survey* (annual, 1947–62)

*Financial Agreement between the Governments of the United Kingdom and the United States, dated 6th December 1945* (1945, Cmd 6708)

*Committee on the Working of the Monetary System: Report* (1959, Cmd 827)

*Committee on the Working of the Monetary System: Minutes of Evidence and Memoranda* (1960)

*Others*

(Beveridge) *Report on Social Insurance and Allied Services* (1942, Cmd 6404)

*Reports of Council on Prices, Productivity, and Incomes* (1958–61)

## Published works

*Books*

Beveridge, Lord (Sir William) (1948) *Full Employment in a Free Society*, London: Allen & Unwin.

Birkenhead, Lord (1961) *The Prof in Two Worlds: the Official Life of Professor F. A. Lindemann, Viscount Cherwell*, London: Collins.

Brittan, Sam (1971) *Steering the Economy*, Harmondsworth: Penguin Books.

Butler, Lord (R. A. Butler) (1971) *The Art of the Possible*, London: Hamish Hamilton.

Cairncross, Sir Alec (1971) *Essays in Economic Management*, London: Allen & Unwin.

(1985) *Years of Recovery*, London: Methuen.

(1986) *The Price of War*, Oxford: Blackwell.

Chester, Sir Norman (ed.) (1951) *Lessons of the British War Economy*, Cambridge: Cambridge University Press.

Churchill, W. S. (1949) *The Second World War*, vol. 2 *Their Finest Hour*, London: Cassell.

Clarke, Sir Richard (R. W. B.) (1982) *Anglo-American Collaboration in War and Peace 1942–49*, Oxford: Oxford University Press.

Coats, A. W. (ed.) (1981) *Economists in Government*, Durham, N. Carolina: Duke University Press.

Dow, J. C. R. (1964) *The Management of the British Economy 1945–60*, Cambridge: Cambridge University Press for National Institute of Economic and Social Research.

Feinstein, C. H. (1972) *National Income, Expenditure and Output of the United Kingdom 1865–1965*, Cambridge: Cambridge University Press.

Gardner, R. N. (1956; new and expanded edition, 1980) *Sterling–Dollar Diplomacy*, Oxford: Oxford University Press.

Hicks, Sir John (1950) *The Problem of Budgetary Reform*, Oxford: Oxford University Press.

Howson, Susan and Winch, Donald (1977) *The Economic Advisory Council*, Cambridge: Cambridge University Press.

Hutchison, T. W. (1968) *Economics and Economic Policy in Britain*, London: Allen & Unwin.

Henderson, Sir Hubert (1955) *The Inter-war Years and Other Papers*, (ed.) H. Clay, Oxford: Clarendon Press.

Jones, Russell (1987) *Wages and Employment Policy*, London: Allen & Unwin.

Keynes, John Maynard (1940) *How to Pay for the War*, Macmillan: London; *Collected Writings*, vols 25, 26 and 27, Cambridge: Cambridge University Press.

Leith-Ross, Sir F. W. (1968) *Money Talks*, London: Hutchinson.

MacDougall, Sir Donald (1987) *Don and Mandarin*, London: John Murray.

Macmillan, Harold (1969) *Tides of Fortune 1945–55*, London: Macmillan. (1971) *Riding the Storm 1956–59*, London: Macmillan.

Meade, James (1988) *Collected Papers*, vol. 2, 'Value, distribution and growth', (ed.) S. Howson, and vol. 4, *Diary*, (ed.) S Howson, London: Unwin Hyman.

Pechman, J. (ed.) (1989) *The Role of the Economist in Government: an International Perspective*, Washington D.C.: Brookings Institution.

Pimlott, Ben (1985) *Hugh Dalton*, London: Jonathan Cape.

Pliatzky, Sir Leo (1982) *Getting and Spending*, Oxford: Blackwell.

Plowden, Lord (Sir Edwin) (1989) *An Industrialist in the Treasury*, London: André Deutsch).

Pressnell, L. S. (1986) *External Economic Policy since the War*, vol. 1 *The Post-War Settlement*, London: HMSO.

Robbins, Lord (1971) *Autobiography of an Economist*, London: Macmillan.

Salter, Lord (Sir Arthur) (1967) *Slave of the Lamp*, London: Weidenfeld & Nicolson.

Sayers, R. S. (1956) *Financial Policy, 1939–45*, London: HMSO.

Seldon, Anthony (1981) *Churchill's Indian Summer: the Conservative Government 1951–55*, London: Hodder & Stoughton.

Shonfield, Sir Andrew (1959) *British Economic Policy since the War*, Harmondsworth: Penguin Books.

Tomlinson, J. (1987) *Employment Policy: the Crucial Years 1939–55*, Oxford: Clarendon Press.

Ward, T. S. and Neild, R. R. (1976) *The Measurement and Reform of Budgetary Policy*, London: Heinemann for Institute of Fiscal Studies.

Williams, P. M. (ed.) (1983) *The Diary of Hugh Gaitskell 1945–56*, London: Jonathan Cape.

Worswick, G. D. N. and Ady, P. (1952) *The British Economy 1945–50*, Oxford: Clarendon Press and (1962) *The British Economy in the Nineteen-Fifties*, Oxford: Clarendon Press.

(1962) *The British Economy in the Nineteen-Fifties*, Oxford: Clarendon Press.

## Articles, etc.

Booth, Alan (1932) 'The "Keynesian revolution" in economic policy-making', *Economic History Review* 36 (spring).

(1985) 'Economists and points rationing in the Second World War', *Journal of European History* 14(2).

(1986) 'Economic advice at the centre of British government 1939–41', *Historical Journal* 29(3).

Boyle, Lord (Sir Edward) (1979) 'The economist in government', in J. K. Bowers (ed.), *Inflation, Development and Integration*, Leeds: Leeds University Press.

Cairncross, Sir Alec (1962) 'On being an economic adviser', in *Factors in Economic Development*, London: Allen & Unwin.

(1984) 'An early think-tank: the origins of the Economic Section', *Three Banks Review* December.

(1987) 'Prelude to Radcliffe', *Rivista di Storia Economiche* December.

Chester, Sir Norman (1981) 'The role of economic advisers in government', in A. P. Thirlwall (ed.), *Keynes as an Economic Adviser*, London: Macmillan.

Hall, Robert (Lord) (1955) 'The place of the economist in government', *Oxford Economic Papers* June.

(1959) 'Reflections on the practical applications of economics', *Economic Journal* December.

(1969) Introduction to 50th issue, *National Institute Economic Review* November.

Henderson, P. D. (David) (1961) 'The use of economists in British administration', *Oxford Economic Papers* February.

Howson, Susan (1987) 'The origins of cheaper money, 1945–47', *Economic History Review* August.

(1989) 'The problem of monetary control in Britain 1948–51' (forthcoming).

Kennedy, M. C. (1969) 'How well does the National Institute forecast?', *National Institute Economic Review* November.

Little, I. M. D. (1952) 'Fiscal policy' in G. D. N. Worswick and P. Ady *The British Economy 1945–50*, Oxford: Clarendon Press.

(1957) 'The economist in Whitehall', *Lloyds Bank Review* April.

(1962) 'Fiscal Policy', in G. D N. Worswick and P. Ady (eds) *The British Economy in the Nineteen-Fifties*, Oxford: Clarendon Press.

Marris, Robin (1954) 'The position of economics and economists in the government machine', *Economic Journal* December.

Neild, R. R. and Shirley, E. A. (1961) 'An assessment of forecasts, 1959–60', *National Institute Economic Review* May.

Rollings, Neil (1988) 'British budgetary policy, 1945–54: a "Keynesian revolution"?', *Economic History Review* May.

## Unpublished works

Campion, Sir Harry (1987) 'The origins of the CSO', talk given at the CSO, 29 October.

Chester papers, Nuffield College Library.

Dalton, Lord, Post-war *Diary* in British Library of Political and Economic Science.

Fforde, J. S. *The Bank of England 1945–58* (forthcoming).

Holmans, Alan, *Demand Management in the United Kingdom, 1952–58* (forthcoming).

Kaplan, J. J. and Schleiminger, G. *The European Payments Union* (forthcoming).

Robinson, E. A. G. (1946) 'The long-term demand for British exports', Board of Trade memorandum, July.

Robinson papers, Churchill College Library.

# INDEX